RETHINKING
the ATONEMENT

"Rarely does a new body of scholarship come along that compels us to rethink what we thought we knew about the New Testament. Moffitt's work on the Letter to the Hebrews is exactly that sort of game-changing intervention. This new collection of deeply researched essays builds upon and persuasively amplifies his earlier interpretations of resurrection and atonement in Hebrews, while also illuminating the theology of other New Testament documents. For those whose faculties have been trained by practice to recognize serious and illuminating exegesis, this book is not milk but solid food."

—**Richard B. Hays**, Duke University (emeritus)

"A new publication by David Moffitt is always a treat. This book brings together a number of seminal essays in which Moffitt applies his precise and illuminating analysis of the biblical logic of sacrifice to Hebrews and other NT texts. Using a combination of exegetical rigor and theological insight, Moffitt makes a compelling and urgent case for re-examining the saving significance of Jesus's resurrection and ascension (as well as his death) within the biblical understanding of atonement. This volume will be indispensable for the study of Hebrews, and it should be foundational for the development of atonement theology."

—**Loveday Alexander**, University of Sheffield (emerita)

"From the author who has revolutionized Hebrews' studies, *Rethinking the Atonement* presents in one place many of David Moffitt's exegetical arguments. Readers are challenged to recover a holistic affirmation of God's work in Christ: incarnation, death, resurrection, ascension, and session. Moffitt has changed not only how I read Hebrews but how I conceive of my faith. I'm eager to put this volume into the hands of my students and parishioners."

—**Amy Peeler**, Wheaton College

"Moffitt argues compellingly that while Jesus's death on a cross completes the earthly work of salvation, his priestly work in heaven continues, and this too is part of his saving, and atoning, work. This collection of essays is not simply a rethinking but a Copernican Revolution in atonement theology, both because it concerns the movement of a celestial body (the risen and ascended Jesus Christ) and because it calls for a reversal of some traditional soteriological polarities."

—**Kevin J. Vanhoozer**, Trinity Evangelical Divinity School

"*Rethinking the Atonement* represents rigorous, in-depth biblical scholarship of the highest order. It is not merely original; it promises to be no less than field changing. That is because it will no longer be possible to write on the atonement, let alone Christology, without engaging in detail with the exegetical arguments that Moffitt presents. What is most exciting, however, is not simply the lucid way in which he demonstrates that widely held assumptions about the atonement are deeply flawed but that he does this in a way that brings the gospel alive. This is one of those rare books in biblical scholarship that should be compulsory reading not only for biblical scholars but also for academic theologians, students, and pastors alike. I cannot recommend this remarkable volume highly enough!"

—**Alan J. Torrance**, University of St. Andrews (emeritus)

"This is a spectacular set of essays from one of the greatest living New Testament scholars—David Moffitt. This collection provides a convenient and affordable anthology of some of his most influential work. For those who are unfamiliar with Moffitt, this is your chance to remedy that, and for those who are familiar, this is your chance to have some of his most influential work readily available."

—**Madison N. Pierce**, Western Theological Seminary

RETHINKING
the ATONEMENT

New Perspectives on Jesus's
Death, Resurrection, and Ascension

DAVID M. MOFFITT

Foreword by N. T. Wright

Baker Academic
a division of Baker Publishing Group
Grand Rapids, Michigan

Published by Baker Academic
a division of Baker Publishing Group
PO Box 6287, Grand Rapids, MI 49516-6287
www.bakeracademic.com

Printed in the United States of America

Library of Congress Cataloging-in-Publication Data
Names: Moffitt, David M., author.
Title: Rethinking the atonement : new perspectives on Jesus's death, resurrection, and ascension / David M. Moffitt ; foreword by N. T. Wright.
Description: Grand Rapids, Michigan : Baker Academic, a division of Baker Publishing Group, [2022] | Includes bibliographical references and index.
Identifiers: LCCN 2022018532 | ISBN 9781540966230 (paperback) | ISBN 9781540966452 (casebound) | ISBN 9781493440955 (ebook) | ISBN 9781493440962 (pdf)
Subjects: LCSH: Atonement. | Jesus Christ—Crucifixion. | Jesus Christ—Resurrection. | Jesus Christ—Ascension. | Bible—Theology.
Classification: LCC BT265.3 .M64 2022 | DDC 232/.3—dc23/eng/20220808
LC record available at https://lccn.loc.gov/2022018532

Chapter 2 was originally published in a similar form as "Modelled on Moses: Jesus' Death, Passover, and the Defeat of the Devil in the Epistle to the Hebrews." In *Mosebilder: Gedanken zur Rezeption einer literarischen Figur im Frühjudentum, frühen Christentum und der römisch-hellenistischen Literatur*, ed. Michael Sommer et al., 279–97. WUNT 1/390. Tübingen: Mohr Siebeck, 2017. Used by permission.

Chapter 3 was originally published in a similar form as "Wilderness Identity and Pentateuchal Narrative: Distinguishing between Jesus' Inauguration and Maintenance of the New Covenant in Hebrews." In *Muted Voices of the New Testament: Readings in the Catholic Epistles and Hebrews*, ed. Katherine M. Hockey, Madison N. Pierce, and Francis Watson, 153–71. LNTS 565. London: Bloomsbury T&T Clark, 2017. Used by permission.

Chapter 5 was originally published in a similar form as "'If Another Priest Arises': Jesus' Resurrection and the High Priestly Christology of Hebrews." In *A Cloud of Witnesses: The Theology of Hebrews in Its Ancient Contexts*, ed. Richard Bauckham et al., 68–79. LNTS 387. London: T&T Clark, 2008. Used by permission.

Chapter 6 was originally published in a similar form as "Blood, Life, and Atonement: Reassessing Hebrews' Christological Appropriation of Yom Kippur." In *The Day of Atonement: Its Interpretations in Early Jewish and Christian Traditions*, ed. Thomas Hieke and Tobias Nicklas, 211–24. Themes in Biblical Narrative Series 15. Leiden: Brill, 2012. Used by permission.

Chapter 7 was originally published in a similar form as "Weak and Useless? Purity, the Mosaic Law, and Perfection in Hebrews." In *Law and Lawlessness in Early Judaism and Early Christianity*, ed. David Lincicum, Ruth Sheridan, and Charles M. Stang, 87–101. WUNT 1/420. Tübingen: Mohr Siebeck, 2019. Used by permission.

Chapter 8 was originally published in a similar form as "Serving in the Tabernacle in Heaven: Sacred Space, Jesus's High-Priestly Sacrifice, and Hebrews' Analogical Theology." In *Hebrews in Contexts*, ed. Gabriella Gelardini and Harold W. Attridge, 259–79. Ancient Judaism and Early Christianity 91. Leiden: Brill, 2016. Used by permission.

Chapter 9 was originally published in a similar form as "It Is Not Finished: Jesus' Perpetual Atoning Work as the Heavenly High Priest in Hebrews." In *So Great a Salvation: A Dialogue on the Atonement in Hebrews*, ed. Jon Laansma, George H. Guthrie, and Cynthia Long Westfall, 157–75. LNTS 516. London: Bloomsbury T&T Clark, 2019. Used by permission.

Chapter 11 was originally published in a similar form as "Jesus' Heavenly Sacrifice in Early Christian Reception of Hebrews: A Survey." *JTS* 68 (2017): 46–71. Used by permission.

Chapter 12 was originally published in a similar form as "Righteous Bloodshed, Matthew's Passion Narrative and the Temple's Destruction: Lamentations as a Matthean Intertext." *Journal of Biblical Literature* 125 (2006): 299–320. Used by permission.

Chapter 13 was originally published in a similar form as "The Sign of Jonah and the Prophet Motif in the Gospel of Matthew: Moving toward the Gentile Mission." In *How Jonah Is Interpreted in Judaism, Christianity, and Islam: Essays on the Authenticity and Influence of the Biblical Prophet*, ed. Mishael Caspi and John T. Greene, 233–45. Lewiston, NY: Mellen, 2011. Used by permission.

Chapter 14 was originally published in a similar form as "Atonement at the Right Hand: Exploring the Sacrificial Significance of Jesus' Exaltation in Acts." *NTS* 62 (2016): 549–68. Used by permission.

Chapter 15 was originally published in a similar form as "Affirming the 'Creed': The Extent of Paul's Citation of an Early Christian Formula in 1 Cor 15,3b–7." *ZNW* 99 (2008): 49–73. Used by permission.

22   23   24   25   26   27   28   7   6   5   4   3   2   1

*To my parents, who showed me the way and,
by their example, taught me to walk in it*

Contents

Abbreviations

General

BCE	before the Common Era	MS(S)	manuscript(s)
CE	Common Era	n.	note
chap(s).	chapter(s)	v(v).	verse(s)
esp.	especially		

Old Testament

Gen.	Genesis	Ps(s).	Psalm(s)
Exod.	Exodus	Prov.	Proverbs
Lev.	Leviticus	Isa.	Isaiah
Num.	Numbers	Jer.	Jeremiah
Deut.	Deuteronomy	Lam.	Lamentations
Judg.	Judges	Ezek.	Ezekiel
Ruth	Ruth	Obad.	Obadiah
1–4 Kgdms.	1–4 Kingdoms (LXX)	Jon.	Jonah
1–2 Sam.	1–2 Samuel	Mic.	Micah
1–2 Kings	1–2 Kings	Hab.	Habakkuk
1–2 Chron.	1–2 Chronicles	Zech.	Zechariah
Neh.	Nehemiah		

New Testament

Matt.	Matthew	Col.	Colossians
Rom.	Romans	Heb.	Hebrews
1 Cor.	1 Corinthians	1 Pet.	1 Peter
2 Cor.	2 Corinthians	2 Pet.	2 Peter
Gal.	Galatians	Rev.	Revelation

Bible Versions

LXX	Septuagint
MT	Masoretic Text
NA[27]	*Novum Testamentum Graece*. Edited by [E. and E. Nestle,] B. Aland et al., 27th rev. ed. Stuttgart: Deutsche Bibelgesellschaft, 1993
NA[28]	*Novum Testamentum Graece*. Edited by [E. and E. Nestle,] B. Aland et al., 28th rev. ed. Stuttgart: Deutsche Bibelgesellschaft, 2012
NETS	A New English Translation of the Septuagint
NRSV	New Revised Standard Version
RSV	Revised Standard Version

Old Testament Apocrypha / Deuterocanonical Books

1–4 Macc.	1–4 Maccabees
Sir.	Sirach
Wis.	Wisdom (of Solomon)

Old Testament Pseudepigrapha

Apoc. Ezra	Apocalypse of Ezra
Apocr. Ezek.	Apocryphon of Ezekiel
Apoc. Sedr.	Apocalypse of Sedrach
3 Bar.	3 Baruch (Greek Apocalypse)
1 En.	1 Enoch (Ethiopic Apocalypse)
2 En.	2 Enoch (Slavonic Apocalypse)
Jub.	Jubilees
Pss. Sol.	Psalms of Solomon
T. Ab.	Testament of Abraham
T. Levi	Testament of Levi
T. 12 Patr.	Testaments of the Twelve Patriarchs

Targums

Tg. Isa.	Targum Isaiah
Tg. Lam.	Targum Lamentations
Tg. Neof.	Targum Neofiti
Tg. Zech.	Targum Zechariah

Other Rabbinic Works

Lam. Rab.	Lamentations Rabbah
Mek. Amalek	Mekilta Amalek
Mek. Pisha	Mekilta Pisha
m. Zebaḥ.	mishnah Zebaḥim
Pesiq. Rab.	Pesiqta Rabbati
Pirqe R. El.	Pirqe Rabbi Eliezer

New Testament Apocrypha and Pseudepigrapha
Apos. Con.   Apostolic Constitutions and Canons

Greek and Latin Works
Irenaeus
Haer.   Against Heresies

Josephus
Ant.   Jewish Antiquities

Origen
Hom. Lev.   Homiliae in Leviticum

Philo
Congr.   De congressu eruditionis gratia
Legat.   Legatio ad Gaium
Mos.   De vita Mosis
QE   Quaestiones et solutiones in Exodum
Somn.   De somniis
Spec.   De specialibus legibus

Modern Works
AB   Anchor Bible
ANF   Ante-Nicene Fathers. Edited by Alexander Roberts and James Donaldson. 10 vols. Reprint, Peabody, MA: Hendrickson, 1994.
BECNT   Baker Exegetical Commentary on the New Testament
BETL   Bibliotheca Ephemeridum Theologicarum Lovaniensium
BNTC   Black's New Testament Commentaries
BZNW   Beihefte zur Zeitschrift für die neutestamentliche Wissenschaft
CBQ   Catholic Biblical Quarterly
CCL   Classic Commentary Library
CPG   Clavis Patrum Graecorum. Edited by Maurice Geerard. 5 vols. Turnhout: Brepols, 1974–87.
CSCO   Corpus Scriptorum Christianorum Orientalium. Edited by Jean Baptiste Chabot et al. Paris, 1903.
CSEL   Corpus Scriptorum Ecclesiasticorum Latinorum
DDD   Dictionary of Deities and Demons in the Bible. Edited by Karel van der Toorn, Bob Becking, and Pieter W. van der Horst. Leiden: Brill, 1995. 2nd rev. ed. Grand Rapids: Eerdmans, 1999.
EDSS   Encyclopedia of the Dead Sea Scrolls. Edited by Lawrence H. Shiffman and James C. VanderKam. 2 vols. New York: Oxford University Press, 2000.

EKKNT	Evangelisch-katholischer Kommentar zum Neuen Testament
EvT	*Evangelische Theologie*
FC	Fathers of the Church
FRLANT	Forschungen zur Religion und Literatur des Alten und Neuen Testaments
GCS	Die griechischen christlichen Schriftsteller der ersten drei Jahrhunderte
Greg	*Gregorianum*
HBM	Hebrew Bible Monographs
HTR	*Harvard Theological Review*
ICC	International Critical Commentary
JAJS	Journal of Ancient Judaism Supplements
JSJSup	Journal for the Study of Judaism Supplements
JSNT	*Journal for the Study of the New Testament*
JSNTSup	Journal for the Study of the New Testament: Supplement Series
JSOTSup	Journal for the Study of the Old Testament: Supplement Series
JTS	*Journal of Theological Studies*
KEK	Kritisch-exegetischer Kommentar über das Neue Testament (Meyer-Kommentar)
LHB/OTS	The Library of Hebrew Bible / Old Testament Studies
LNTS	Library of New Testament Studies
NICNT	New International Commentary on the New Testament
NIGTC	New International Greek Testament Commentary
NovT	*Novum Testamentum*
NovTSup	Supplements to Novum Testamentum
NTAbh	Neutestamentliche Abhandlungen
NTL	New Testament Library
NTS	*New Testament Studies*
PG	Patrologia graeca [= *Patrologiae cursus completus*: Series graeca]. Edited by J.-P. Migne. 162 vols. Paris, 1857–86.
PO	Patrologia Orientalis. Translated by F. G. McLeod.
SBLDS	Society of Biblical Literature Dissertation Series
SBLMS	Society of Biblical Literature Monograph Series
SBLRBS	Society of Biblical Literature Resources for Biblical Study
SC	Sources chrétiennes
SNTSMS	Society for New Testament Studies Monograph Series
STDJ	Studies on the Texts of the Desert of Judah
TCLA	Texts from Christian Late Antiquity. Translated by Thomas Kollamparampil.
TJ	*Trinity Journal*
TSAJ	Texts and Studies in Ancient Judaism
TWNT	*Theologische Wörterbuch zum Neuen Testament*. Edited by Gerhard Kittel and Gerhard Friedrich. Stuttgart: Kohlhammer, 1932–79.
WBC	Word Biblical Commentary
WMANT	Wissenschaftliche Monographien zum Alten und Neuen Testament
WS	Woodbrooke Studies. Edited by A. Mingana.
WUNT	Wissenschaftliche Untersuchungen zum Neuen Testament
ZNW	*Zeitschrift für die neutestamentliche Wissenschaft und die Kunde der älteren Kirche*

Foreword

The question of atonement has continued to challenge preachers, teachers, theologians, and exegetes, as well as "ordinary" Christians who want to understand what it means to speak of God rescuing humans from sin through the work of Jesus. In the Nicene Creed, the mysterious phrase "for us and for our salvation" refers to the full story of Jesus, including not only his death but also his incarnation, resurrection, ascension, and return. But theological inquiry and popular preaching regularly assume that salvation and atonement have to do mainly with Jesus's crucifixion. Thus the word "atonement" itself now suggests to most Christians the idea, however interpreted, that it was specifically Jesus's death that dealt with the problem of human sin, that achieved reconciliation between God and humans, and that ultimately accomplishes full salvation. Particular "theories of atonement" have then been advanced, particularly in the Protestant churches, as to how that death "works." Some such interpretations have attained the status of official church dogma.

In such discussions, the notion of sacrifice has often been central. When Jesus's Jewish contemporaries (it is assumed) brought animals for sacrifice, they supposed that they were transferring their sins to an animal, so that the animal's death took the place of their own, thus freeing them from God's displeasure or judgment. Since the early Christians frequently invoked sacrificial imagery when writing about Jesus's saving work, this assumption about the significance of Jewish sacrifices has sustained the interpretation of atonement in which Jesus himself dies the death that sinners had deserved. Here we need to be careful, because the New Testament does indeed invoke the idea of substitution at various points in interpreting Jesus's death, albeit not always in the way popular theology has imagined.[1] It has thus been all too easy to suppose that when the early Christians bring in references to the sacrificial system in connection with Jesus's salvific accomplishment, this is what they mean. When we then turn to discuss Jewish sacrifices and early Christian belief, we quickly arrive at the Letter to the Hebrews. Not surprisingly, people have regularly assumed that Hebrews teaches this now-standard view of atonement.

But does it? And how—to press the question again—does all this work in terms of Israel's Scriptures, Jewish beliefs in the first century, and, particularly, early Christian beliefs about God, Jesus, and salvation? We are not helped here by the fact that the seismic shifts that have taken place in other areas of New Testament studies—I think most obviously of the "New Perspective" on Paul—have not seen a corresponding shift in the interpretation of Hebrews. The "New Perspective" was driven primarily by the historical question of what first-century Jews actually believed and how we should read Paul in the light of that.[2] But, though Paul himself does use sacrificial ideas to interpret Jesus's accomplishment, one can provide a fairly full account of his view of Jesus's death without probing too far into the details of how he and his contemporaries would have understood the Levitical system. With Hebrews, the question cannot be avoided. And, though Hebrews has of course remained officially in the church's canon, it has received considerably less attention than Paul or the Gospels in the scholarship of the last generation. It is clearly time for a reappraisal.

The present volume answers this need and does so abundantly. It builds on David Moffitt's groundbreaking earlier work *Atonement and the Logic of Resurrection in the Epistle to the Hebrews*. Here Moffitt brings together several substantial, probing chapters covering a wide range of issues, mostly in Hebrews but with important extra material on Matthew, Luke-Acts, and the early "creed" in 1 Corinthians 15. Backed up by a wealth of detailed exegetical and theological argument, he engages with scholarly debate not only to answer critics of his earlier proposals (though he does that trenchantly, not least by a detailed study of patristic sources) but to extend his proposals into several areas where the modern reappraisal of the ancient Jewish world,

1. On substitution and the way it works within the early Christian view of Jesus's death as victory over evil, see my *The Day the Revolution Began: Reconsidering the Meaning of Jesus's Crucifixion* (San Francisco: HarperOne, 2016). I did not in that work discuss the Letter to the Hebrews. Obvious examples of substitution would include Rom. 8:1–4 (there is "no condemnation" because on the cross God "condemned sin"; NRSV) and the Gospel accounts of Jesus taking the place of Barabbas (e.g., John 18:40).
2. On the "New Perspective," see particularly my *Paul and His Recent Interpreters* (Minneapolis: Fortress, 2015), chaps. 3, 4, and 5.

so vital for today's studies of Jesus and Paul, needs to be worked through in terms of what Hebrews is actually saying—which is somewhat different from what many have assumed. The result is an eye-opening series of arguments, each of which now needs to be pondered and integrated into our overall assessment of Hebrews and its contribution to early Christian thought as a whole. Moffitt clearly relishes both the fine-grained detail of biblical exegesis and the large theological picture that emerges from it, and all who share these passions will richly enjoy his writing.

It might even turn out that, having too long been the poor relation, Hebrews might now itself suggest new lines of inquiry, not least in Pauline interpretation. After all, though nobody today thinks that Paul wrote Hebrews, that old assumption, reflected in the book's title in the King James Version, was not quite so foolish as sometimes imagined. Paul and Hebrews work with similar biblical themes (from Pss. 8 and 110, for instance); they both highlight the role of Abraham; they both pick up Habakkuk's line about the righteous living by faith; and so on. Of course, it isn't difficult to show that they seem to treat these themes in rather different ways. But it is also possible that some apparent differences emerge more from the modern assumptions we have brought to the texts than from the texts themselves. Thus the present volume might not simply contribute to further fresh study of Hebrews (and, in the final four chapters, of Matthew, Luke-Acts, and the early Christian confession of faith in 1 Corinthians 15) but open up questions we had not previously thought of asking.

The chapters speak for themselves, but it is worth highlighting here some of the major issues that will cause this book to be cited when scholars and teachers think of atonement in general and Hebrews in particular.

One has to do with the word "atonement" itself. Moffitt points out that this English term has come to stand, in both popular and scholarly minds, for the salvific achievement of Jesus's death and, behind that, for the salvific effects (such as they were) of the Jewish sacrificial system as set out in Leviticus and elsewhere. But the popular assumptions, at least since Anselm's day, both about the problem for which this was the divinely provided solution and about the way that solution functioned, are by no means as clear-cut as has usually been imagined. We should beware of our own shorthand—and recognize, indeed, that it is shorthand. When we meet the word "atonement" in Bible translations, we need to probe deeper and see what is going on. In a sense, this entire book is offering a series of such probes, and we would do well to avoid quick and easy answers. We need to learn to think like first-century Jews (and then like first-century Jews who believed that Jesus of Nazareth was God's promised Messiah), not like medieval or Renaissance theorists who used ancient texts to address questions quite foreign to their original intention. The word "atonement" thus constitutes a question to which Hebrews gives particular kinds of answers rather than an assumed fixed quantity.

The question comes into stark focus when we consider what actually happened in the ancient Jewish sacrificial system. Several of Moffitt's chapters take as their starting point the fact that in Leviticus, and (so far as we can reconstruct it) in the sacrificial worship of Jesus's day, the killing of the sacrificial animals was not the central event—however much the word "sacrifice," like indeed the word "atonement" itself, has shrunk in the popular mind to refer to that killing. When animals were brought to the temple (or, in Leviticus, to the tabernacle), they were slaughtered not on an altar but elsewhere in the precincts. (Pagan sacrifices could often involve animals being killed on altars, but this is a highly significant difference.) Sacrifices within the Levitical system, which included things like grain offerings (i.e., offerings involving neither animals nor blood), served a variety of purposes, at the heart of which was the desire to give a gift to God as a symbol of one's devotion. Within that, when purification was required, this was accomplished not by the act of killing itself but by making available the animal's life-blood, which then functioned as the purifying agent to cleanse the holy place and its furniture—and in some cases the worshipers themselves—from the ongoing pollution either of sin or of impurity. This in turn was necessary because the tabernacle, and then the temple, was the place where Israel's God had promised to dwell in the midst of his people—which could not happen if the shrine was polluted. The underlying narrative is quite different from the one assumed in Western theology for many centuries. Hebrews is not asking how sinners can find their way to a holy God but how the holy God can dwell in the midst of his people. The answer is that the sacrificial life-blood removes the taint of death that is produced both by sin and by impurity. The point has often been made, but it is worth repeating: the only animal in Leviticus that has sins confessed over its head is the only animal that is not then killed. The "scapegoat," now polluted by bearing the people's sins, cannot be offered to God in sacrifice. It is driven away into the wilderness.

Therefore, when we use the word "sacrifice" in reference to the elaborate procedures set out in Leviticus and invoked in the New Testament in relation to the achievement of Jesus, we need to make a conscious effort—which these chapters in various ways help us to do—to think of the longer sequence of actions involved. The death, whether of the animals or of Jesus himself, is only one part of it. The aim, the goal, is for the purifying blood to be presented before God, enabling fellowship between God and the worshipers. This relationship is then sustained by the continuing work of Jesus as the one who is now alive, in his risen and ascended humanity, making intercession for his people.[3] This is where Moffitt's earlier seminal work on the significance in Hebrews of Jesus's bodily resurrection and ascension comes into its own, being applied in these chapters to a wide range of consequent issues.

This means, controversially, that the work of Jesus on behalf of his people is not "finished" on the cross, as in the famous Protestant slogan "the finished work of Christ." Of course, Jesus died once and only once. He does not need to die again; he has done so once for all time (Heb. 9:26). Something really was "finished" with his death, as John makes clear in Jesus's dying words (John 19:30). That is the point emphasized by traditional Protestant polemic, warding off any suggestion that Jesus might be crucified again and again with every Mass. But if the "sacrifice" to which Hebrews refers is the larger sequence of events, not just Jesus's death, then his ongoing work of covenant maintenance continues to the present time and beyond to the ultimate future in, as Moffitt puts it, his "perpetual atoning work." Stressing the "finished work" for reasons to do with much later church polemic will often disguise this vital biblical emphasis—so much so that many modern Christians are genuinely unsure what they should be celebrating on Ascension Day. I suspect that this point has many homiletic applications (for instance, to strengthen the resolve of weary Christians as the long haul of mission and holiness takes its toll). These chapters, in this and other respects, point not only to scholarly outcomes but to questions of preaching and pastoral ministry.

All this highlights a major problem in reading and appropriating Hebrews: What is the relationship between the tabernacle (or temple) on earth and the heavenly tent into which Jesus went at his ascension? How can we today envisage the different levels or layers of created reality that the author of Hebrews seems to take for granted? Moffitt insists on two vital points.

First, Hebrews belongs in the world not of Platonic idealism but of Jewish apocalyptic. The heavenly world is not the nonmaterial, atemporal sphere imagined by the philosophers but the biblical "heaven." This heaven was always designed to come together with earth so that Jesus's bodily ascension into heaven—which makes no sense for a Platonist—is the sure indication that God's intended eventual new creation, already a reality laid up in store, will finally come to pass. This is the kingdom that cannot be shaken (Heb. 12:28).

Second, as a result, the present Jerusalem and the earthly work of Jesus function for Hebrews not as a metaphor for his heavenly ministry in the heavenly temple but as an analogy. The earthly cult, itself originally modeled on

---

3. Heb. 7:25; this suggests another Pauline parallel, as in Rom. 8:34.

the heavenly shrine that Moses was shown on the mountain, points to that same shrine in the highest heaven, which is not a Platonic abstraction or a metaphor for the interior illumination or existential well-being of the believer but the reality that God the creator has always intended to be brought into existence on earth as in heaven. Both heaven and earth need to be shaken (Heb. 12:26, quoting Hag. 2:6, 21), and from this alarming prospect, God's new world will emerge.

This warning about apparently fixed entities being shaken applies to the arguments of this book as a whole. Moffitt's careful and detailed exposition of Hebrews within its wider cultural—and, especially, scriptural—context will challenge its readers to rethink not only words like "atonement" and "sacrifice" but also the assumed narratives, biblical and hermeneutical, within which those words have commonly been understood. This rethinking is not easy. As with the New Perspective on Paul, habits of thought, not least theological thought, are not easily changed. For change to take place, it isn't enough to sketch alternative viewpoints in quick generalizations. What it takes is relentless attention to exegetical and historical detail. That is what we have in this book.

With that focus on first-century history and meaning, we find a point of great importance in today's wider discussions. Our contemporary identity politics have given fresh impetus to the older questions about possible anti-Jewish views in the New Testament. Some have then accused this or that early Christian writer of supersessionism, the belief that a largely gentile community of Jesus-believers had now "superseded" the (still largely unbelieving) Jewish people in the purposes of the creator God. This charge has sometimes been leveled at Hebrews itself. If that seems odd—because the book so obviously breathes the air of the Jewish world of the time—we must remember that, particularly when the letter has been read with Platonic resonance, people have easily slipped into the mistake of supposing that the author of Hebrews was doing "comparative religion," contrasting two different "systems" to the advantage of something called "Christianity" over against something called "Judaism." But that very modern way of posing the question—and those all-too-easy anachronistic labels—is light-years away from Hebrews. Hebrews is thinking in terms of biblical narrative, explaining how Israel's Scriptures repeatedly pointed beyond themselves to a coming reality, and about how the unexpected and shocking arrival of Jesus as Messiah—crucified, raised, ascended, and interceding—seems clearly to be the focal point and the active agent of that promised future. Comparative religion is a modern fad, at best a parody of the question the early Jesus-followers were addressing. They were concerned with messianic eschatology.

After all, the question of how the ancient promises were to be fulfilled, and what would happen if and when they were, was one of the major issues in the Jewish world of the first century. There were many messianic or quasi-messianic movements, of very different types, within a hundred years or so either side of Jesus. Members of the Herod family were busily rebuilding the temple, as David's true successor was supposed to do; Bar Kochba had the yet-to-be-rebuilt temple displayed on his coins. All such claims were, in that sense, supersessionist. So (in its way) was the Qumran sect. So (in its very different way) was the compilation of the Mishnah. Each was claiming that this (and not, therefore, that) was how the ancient promises were being fulfilled. In particular, everybody knew that if the true Messiah really did show up, this would be God's way of fulfilling his promises and transforming his people once and for all. Any who refused to get on board would be writing themselves out of their scriptural heritage—just as the Qumran sect issued dire warnings against other groups, such as the Pharisees, and just as the Mishnah anathematized the Sadducees. To suggest that such beliefs might be "anti-Jewish," or that to quote Israel's Scriptures in support of a messianic claim was to cut off the branch one was sitting on, would be nonsense.

To look more widely, John the Baptist was not being anti-Jewish when he spoke of the axe being laid to the roots of the tree or of God raising up children for Abraham from the riverside stones. Something similar is happening when Hebrews reads Israel's Scriptures—as many other Jews at the time read them—as constituting a story in search of a God-given ending, and then claims to know what the ending is. The long list of the faithful in chapter 11 reaches its climax in 12:1–2 with Jesus himself. That constitutes a particular kind of claim, no more and no less controversial (but no less obviously Jewish) than when Ben Sira ends his own list of famous men with Simon son of Onias (Sir. 44–50). And here Moffitt's earlier argument about the significance (for Hebrews) of Jesus's resurrection and ascension comes back once more. What makes Jesus the ultimate "pioneer and perfecter" of faith is precisely his postmortem elevation to God's right hand (12:2 NRSV).

The debates that will continue in this whole area, sharpened by our present cultural and political contexts and sensibilities, must constantly return to the task of actual historical exegesis, of comparing like with like in the Jewish writings of antiquity, and of weighing our all-too-easy contemporary assumptions about difficult ancient texts in the balance of linguistic, contextual, and historical investigation. But this will never remain merely a matter of scholarly argument and definition. When it comes to "atonement," especially with the larger vision of this word that Hebrews offers, the preacher or pastor is just as much involved. Moffitt's work not only provides a great deal of material for such fresh, multilayered investigation and application; it exemplifies the kind of patient historical and theological scholarship that is required if our questions about this vital text are to receive wise answers, and if those answers are to bear fruit.

N. T. Wright
former Bishop of Durham; professor emeritus
of New Testament and Early Christianity,
University of St. Andrews;
senior research fellow, Wycliffe Hall, Oxford

1

Rethinking the Atonement

An Introduction

When the English Reformer William Tyndale translated the Greek New Testament into English in 1525, he used the language of "atonement" to render some of the Greek terms used by Paul to describe the reconciling effects of Jesus's saving work (see Rom. 5:11; 2 Cor. 5:18–20). In Tyndale's New Testament, the gospel proclaimed by Paul was the good news of "the atonement," or reconciliation between God and humanity brought about by Jesus. Later, when Tyndale turned his attention to translating the Hebrew Bible into English, he drew again on the language of "atonement" and "reconciliation." This time he employed these terms in the context of certain Levitical sacrifices, even though the underlying Hebrew terms did not have the same meaning as the Greek terms for reconciliation used by Paul.[1]

By applying language that was originally used to express reconciliation in the Greek New Testament to features of sacrifice in the Hebrew Old Testament,

---

1. Tyndale first used atonement terminology to translate instances of reconciliation language in Paul (καταλλαγή in Rom. 5:11 and 2 Cor. 5:20; καταλλάσσω in 2 Cor. 5:18–19). In Tyndale's New Testament, Paul speaks of Jesus's saving work in terms of the atonement—an act that reconciled God and humanity. Tyndale clearly viewed the language of "reconciliation" and "atonement" as synonymous. In 2 Cor. 5:18–20 he uses these terms interchangeably for words from the same Greek root: to reconcile two parties is to bring them together so they are "at one." Later, however, he again used atonement language when he began translating the Hebrew Bible into English. Here he made a more questionable decision, choosing to translate several instances of the Hebrew verb כפר in the piel stem in sacrificial contexts with the language of "reconciliation" and "atonement."

1

Tyndale fostered a degree of conceptual confusion in English theological discourse. Specifically, his translation identified the *mechanism* in the act of applying blood to the Levitical altars—a mechanism that resolved certain problems between God and his covenant people—with the *result* that this mechanism aimed to achieve: atonement/reconciliation. The translators of the King James Version expanded the use of atonement language with respect to the Old Testament sacrifices. This solidified the use of atonement language in the English translation tradition and therefore in theological reflection on Jesus's death.

Tyndale's choice to use atonement language in relation to certain sacrificial rituals suggests that he grasped a significant point about Levitical sacrifice: Old Testament sacrifice is deeply relational. Indeed, sacrifice is at the heart of the worship of Israel's God by his people. Sacrifice *is* a constitutive element of worship. Tyndale rightly perceived that the offering of particular Levitical sacrifices (especially the so-called sin and guilt offerings as well as certain burnt offerings) resulted in a restored relationship between God and his people when particular problems introduced impediments in that relationship (especially the problems of sin and impurity). These sacrifices helped remove the barriers to the relationship and by so doing allowed God and his people to be reconciled to one another.

The problem, however, is that the Hebrew verb Tyndale translated as "to atone" (sometimes as "to reconcile") does not itself express the relational result of these sacrifices. Rather, the verb refers to a mechanism (a cleaning, purification, or removal of some hindrance) that *contributes* to the resulting restoration in the relationship. If atonement were itself the mechanism in play, there would be a kind of tautology at the core of sacrifice: making atonement by sacrificing on the altar makes atonement. But reconciliation between God and his people (especially in terms of forgiveness of sins) is *not* itself the means or mechanism for achieving that reconciliation. Rather, because these sacrifices do what they do, they allow for the possibility of reconciliation. This is really another way of saying that the sacrifices described in the Old Testament did not work merely by way of performing the proper ritual. Reconciliation rests with God, not with completing the right rituals.[2] The rituals, however, are given by God as a means for creating the conditions within which he will be reconciled to his people.

In Leviticus 17:11 God identifies the application of blood upon the altar as the most significant and effectual element of sacrifice. Blood upon the altar

---

2. As many Hebrew Bible scholars note, God is never either the subject or the object of the verb כפר in the piel stem. He is, however, the subject of the verb "to forgive" (סלח). Sacrifices help remove a barrier in the relationship, but reconciliation is ultimately always God's prerogative.

is central to the mechanism whereby certain problems are resolved so that God can be reconciled with his people. Because blood on the altar does what it does, reconciliation between God and his people can then follow. God has sanctioned this activity and given his people the right to use blood for this very reason. Tyndale's choice to translate the verb used to describe that mechanism with atonement language led to the eclipse of the mechanism by the desired result. In other words, Tyndale's use of atonement language for Old Testament sacrifice has the effect of obscuring the means by which sacrifices, and in particular the priests' application of blood to the altar, make reconciliation possible, precisely because it substitutes this result for the mechanism itself.

Yet another element of confusion results from Tyndale's decision. The use of this language with respect to the message about Jesus's saving work in the New Testament and the use of it in the context of certain Old Testament sacrifices can leave English Bible readers with the impression that both Jesus's work and Old Testament sacrifice aim to accomplish the very same thing in the very same way.[3] Jesus's death can therefore be self-evidently viewed as the sacrifice that replaces and supersedes all Jewish sacrifice—a notion that has had no small influence on modern interpretation of the Epistle to the Hebrews.

Since Tyndale's time, confusion has grown as the term "atonement" has greatly expanded in meaning and scope, especially in the context of Christian theological reflection on the death of Jesus. The idea of reconciliation has not been lost, but a number of other meanings have been added. Today, the language of "the atonement" frequently functions as a shorthand for soteriology in general. All the ways that Jesus is thought to save humanity are often lumped together under the rubric of the atonement. Moreover, these factors, together with the association of atonement with Paul's discussion of reconciliation, have contributed to a reductive idea about the crucifixion. All the saving work of Jesus is often thought today to consist self-evidently in the work he did when he died on the cross. The atonement and the death of Jesus tend to be viewed as coextensive. This has further opened the door to conceptual confusion when thinking about Old Testament sacrifice and the death of Jesus.

Christians believe, as Matthew 1:21 states, that Jesus saves his people from their sins. But how does Jesus do this? This question stands at the heart of theological reflection on the atonement. Any historically interested study of Christian theology reveals that Christians in various times and places have held a number of different understandings of how atonement works. In modern

---

3. Those reading the biblical texts in Greek and Hebrew would not see the connections so directly (it is worth noting that LXX never translates the relevant כפר verbs with forms of καταλλάσσω).

times, there has been a pronounced tendency to assume that how Jesus atones for his people is primarily (often exclusively) bound up with the event of his death. Jesus's death becomes the central (for some the *only*) mechanism of atonement. The atonement, no matter how one imagines this mechanism to work (e.g., penal substitution, *Christus Victor*, ransom theory), is usually seen as a function of the crucifixion. Often, this assumption correlates with at least two others: (1) Jesus's death is the extent or sum total of his atoning sacrifice when, as the great high priest, he offered up his life to God by dying on the altar of the cross; and (2) as concerns atonement, the resurrection and exaltation of Jesus serve primarily to prove that his death was effective, for in raising Jesus from the dead, God showed that he accepted the suffering and death of Jesus as an atoning sacrifice.

The title of this volume—*Rethinking the Atonement: New Perspectives on Jesus's Death, Resurrection, and Ascension*—signals a different approach to understanding Jesus's atoning/salvific work than that assumed by many today. The book can broadly be understood to engage the ambiguity and confusion surrounding the language of atonement in two ways. On the one hand, if one uses the language of "atonement" as a synonym for all of Jesus's salvific work, then many of the chapters can be seen as arguing that Jesus's death, resurrection, and ascension all contribute to the work Jesus does to accomplish salvation. The atonement in this sense can be reframed as encompassing far more than simply Jesus's death. On the other hand, if one narrows the meaning of the term "atonement" to the realm of Levitical sacrifice (in keeping with the long-standing tradition of using this language to describe aspects of priestly ministry and Old Testament sacrifices), there is evidence to suggest that at least some of the books in the New Testament focus far more sustained attention on Jesus's resurrection, ascension, and ongoing intercession before the Father than on his death. Jesus's high-priestly and sacrificial work—and in this sense his atoning work—are in these texts connected to his heavenly session and ongoing intercession in God's presence. For the balance of this chapter, I unpack how the studies in this volume rethink both these broader and more narrow perspectives on the atonement.

The essays collected in this book all address the topics of Jesus's death, resurrection, and ascension to one degree or another. Most of them have been previously published, but in addition to this introduction, two have not appeared in print before (chaps. 4 and 10). Most deal with the Epistle to the Hebrews (chaps. 2–11). Some deal with one of the topics noted above more than others. Chapters 2–4 focus primarily on Jesus's death. They explore ways that Hebrews identifies the death of Jesus as the means for defeating the Devil and for inaugurating the new covenant. Chapters 5–7 largely focus on ways in which Hebrews draws upon the confession of Jesus's resurrection to explain his high priesthood and his high-priestly ministry and to identify his life as the sacrifice he offers. Chapters 8–11 emphasize aspects of Jesus's ascension and ongoing heavenly ministry in Hebrews, while chapter 14 argues that the book of Acts works with some of the same ideas. Not all of the chapters explicitly deal with the topic of atonement. In particular, chapters 12, 13, and 15 explore more general aspects of Jesus's death and resurrection that are sometimes overlooked in the arguments about particular parts of the New Testament (specifically in Matthew and 1 Cor. 15).

Since these essays were first presented or published individually in different journals, volumes, and academic conferences over the past twenty years, no one overriding thesis binds them all together. However, most of them aim to offer new perspectives on the saving work of Jesus by examining some of the ways the New Testament reflects on the saving benefits of Jesus's death, resurrection, and ascension. Due to this wider focus on Jesus's saving work, these essays generally fall within the purview of contemporary discussion of the atonement. Yet they also challenge the commonly held assumption that the atonement is entirely bound up with the event of the crucifixion. Not only do these essays aim to show that there is a good deal more significant reflection on Jesus's resurrection and ascension in parts of the New Testament (especially in Hebrews) than is sometimes recognized; most of them also aim to show that this reflection attributes saving work to Jesus's death, resurrection, and ascension. I argue at points that not all this saving work can or should be described in terms of Levitical sacrifice. Many of these essays, however, seek to demonstrate that there are times when Levitical sacrificial categories and concepts of sacrificial atonement are most closely linked in the New Testament (especially in Hebrews and Acts) not with Jesus's death but with his ascension and exaltation to God's right hand.

Most of these essays therefore suggest that Jesus's death, resurrection, and ascension are all essential (in distinct ways) for the salvation of his people. In the broadest sense of the word "atonement," these are all important for salvation because all of them do important, saving work. Jesus's resurrection and ascension are not merely events interpreted in early Christian belief to show that Jesus's atoning death was really accepted by God and thus effective. The resurrection and ascension are not just important addenda to the main event of the crucifixion—or, as in some modern theologies, important expressions of the *meaning* of the main event. Rather, Jesus's resurrection and ascension are themselves fully and robustly salvific. If the atonement is broadly understood in terms of Jesus's salvific work, the goal of many of these essays is to show that Jesus's death, resurrection, and ascension are all atoning.

To paraphrase Paul, Jesus saves his people by dying, yes, but *even more* by rising, ascending, and now interceding for them at the right hand of the Father (cf. Rom. 8:34). Because the love of Jesus for his siblings extends beyond the cross to include his ongoing intercession, nothing can separate us from God (cf. 8:35–39). Not only did Jesus die *for us*; he also now intercedes *for us* before the Father. These aspects of his saving work are held together in his person. They are part of who he is. Jesus is the one who died, rose, ascended, and is seated at the right hand of the Father. These creedal affirmations, which help to identify who the Son of God is, are all part of how *he* saves his people from their sins. There is no one event in the life of the incarnate Son of God that does all the work of salvation. As essential as all of these several events are for salvation, they are held together in the person of the incarnate Son—*Jesus* saves his people from their sins, not the death of Jesus or even the so-called Christ event. These essays attempt to explore specific ways in which early Christians thought about Jesus's death as salvific but also ways in which his resurrection and ascension were thought to be salvific and, so, atoning.

If, however, one wishes to narrow the use of "atonement" to sacrificial contexts and to considerations of sacrifice in relation to Jesus, then within the dynamics of God's covenant relationship with his people, it seems clear that some of the texts in the New Testament—the Epistle to the Hebrews in particular but also, as I argue in chapter 14, in Acts—think consistently in terms of Jesus's sacrificially atoning work occurring in the place to which he ascended: the heavenly holy of holies. This is the place where Jesus now serves as the atoning high priest interceding for his people. This is the means whereby his people are assured of salvation, when he will one day finish his atoning work and return to his siblings (Heb. 9:28; 10:35–39), and they will all inherit the promised unshakable kingdom.

I have made a number of minor corrections, modifications, or edits in preparing these essays for inclusion in this volume (for example, while in the past I happily used the language of "the Christ event" to speak about a complex of events involved in salvation, I have removed that term in favor of incarnational language). Original language citations have been retained, but English translations have also been provided. Various stylistic changes have also been made across the essays to harmonize them in this volume. In a few places some further clarification has been offered and noted mistakes have been corrected. I am especially grateful to Melisa Blok for her very careful copy editing and helpful suggestions. I have not, however, attempted major revisions. For the most part, these essays are presented in the form in which they were originally published with very little updating. Thus, for example, I have not revised references to the NA[27] or UBS[4], even though these updated versions of the Greek New Testament have subsequently been published. This also means that there is from time to time a degree of repetition in some of these chapters. This is especially true when, in the context of an individual essay, I deemed it essential to the specific argument being advanced to lay out central assumptions about how Levitical sacrifice worked. Readers may wish to skim some of these sections—though I hope that where there is repetition, it will serve to highlight important places where, it seems to me, we must place emphasis to reorient much modern thinking about what Levitical sacrifice and atonement actually were and how they functioned.

2

Modeled on Moses

*Jesus's Death, Passover, and the Defeat of the Devil
in the Epistle to the Hebrews*

An evaluation of the figure of Moses in the Epistle to the Hebrews is fraught
with difficulties, not least because it raises the thorny question of the relationship between the community this epistle presupposes and other Jewish
communities at the time. While many today would rightly eschew simplistic
dichotomies between "Jews" and "Christians" in the first century CE, Hebrews' repeated claims that Jesus is superior to prior Jewish figures and institutions, together with the epistle's categorical critique of the ultimate efficacy of
animal sacrifice, are often interpreted as a nascent Christian supersessionism
or replacement theology.[1] From this perspective, Moses can appear to be little
more than either a foil or a cipher for the author's preformed Christology.

Some argue that the author has so shaped the idea of Moses in this ancient
text in light of his predetermined Christology that he has made Moses into

I am grateful to my colleague Elizabeth Shively for her critical engagement with an earlier version of this essay. I am also grateful to the Department of New Testament at the University of
Pretoria, where I am currently a research associate in the Mission and Ethics project.

1. For a few especially clear examples, see A. N. Chester, "Hebrews: The Final Sacrifice," in
Sacrifice and Redemption: Durham Essays in Theology, ed. S. W. Sykes (Cambridge: Cambridge
University Press, 1991), 57–72; S. Haber, "From Priestly Torah to Christ Cultus: The Re-Vision
of Covenant and Cult in Hebrews," *JSNT* 28 (2005): 105–24; A. J. M. Wedderburn, "Sawing
Off the Branches: Theologizing Dangerously *ad Hebraeos*," *JTS* 56 (2005): 393–414.

a "Christian."[2] In her important study of Moses in Hebrews, Mary Rose D'Angelo suggests that the author's retrospective approach to Moses means that he actively conforms Moses to Christ and not the other way around.[3] She states unequivocally, "For Hebrews, it is never the case that Jesus is like Moses."[4] Thus Hebrews, she continues, "is an ideal subject for an examination of the workings of Christology as a principle of interpretation of the scripture within the New Testament."[5] Moses, when seen in this light, becomes "the model of the Christian and the imitator of Christ" in that he chose to suffer with God's people.[6] His work for and among God's people does not inform that of Jesus but rather serves as an example of what it means to be faithful to Jesus. For D'Angelo, this conclusion follows from the fact that the author of Hebrews believes that when Moses saw the glory of God on Sinai, he was in fact seeing the glory of Christ, the eternal Son of God.[7]

Pamela Eisenbaum agrees that Hebrews turns Moses into a Christian.[8] She argues in addition, however, that the author intentionally diminishes Moses's role as a national liberator and leader of God's people. Eisenbaum thinks that Hebrews appeals to Moses in order to make him a witness to individual virtues (especially his faith). Thus she writes, "The emphasis on Moses' personality . . . deflates Moses' role as a savior of the people of Israel. Instead of being depicted as a man who leads the people of Israel out of bondage, he is a man who makes wise choices for himself."[9] Even in Hebrews 11:28, where Moses is portrayed as doing something on behalf of the people, "the symbolism of the Passover is not employed in the service of prefiguring the

2. Esp. M. R. D'Angelo, *Moses in the Letter to the Hebrews*, SBLDS 42 (Chico, CA: Scholars Press, 1979), e.g., 12; cf. J. Barclay, "Manipulating Moses: Exodus 2.10–15 in Egyptian Judaism and the New Testament," in *Text as Pretext: Essays in Honour of Robert Davidson*, ed. R. P. Carroll, JSOTSup 138 (Sheffield: JSOT Press, 1992), 28–46, here 44–45.

3. D'Angelo does not deny that the earliest Christology was shaped by the influence of Old Testament figures such as Moses. She claims, however, that by the time of the writing of most of the New Testament texts, the more fluid process of creating Christology has shifted into apologetics. With this transition, early Christians—and this is especially clear in Hebrews—begin to work actively to show that Scripture's authoritative figures and institutions actually conform to Jesus and not the other way around (*Moses*, 2–3). Importantly, D'Angelo is not arguing that the author of Hebrews imagines that this conformity diminishes Moses. Rather, as she states clearly, the author himself assumes a "high Mosesology" (257). It is just that this high view of Moses is itself subordinated to and dependent upon the author's even higher Christology. Thus, "the principle of [Hebrews'] exegesis is Christ" (260).

4. D'Angelo, *Moses*, 11.

5. D'Angelo, *Moses*, 11.

6. D'Angelo, *Moses*, 254.

7. D'Angelo, *Moses*, esp. 177.

8. P. M. Eisenbaum, *The Jewish Heroes of Christian History: Hebrews 11 in Literary Context*, SBLDS 156 (Atlanta: Scholars Press, 1997), 220.

9. Eisenbaum, *Jewish Heroes*, 170.

death of Jesus."[10] That is to say, even here there is no sense that Moses's actions are being celebrated as a salvific event. Like D'Angelo, Eisenbaum thinks that Moses functions solely as an ethical model for the present community of those who follow Jesus to imitate, not a model whose work and service informs how one should understand Jesus or what Jesus has done to bring salvation to his people.

John Dunnill argues somewhat differently that Hebrews portrays Moses as an intentionally ambivalent figure—one whose merits are seriously diminished by the author's attention to his failures. Thus, Moses is depicted as a faithful servant and as someone who had the privilege of meeting God and who showed appropriate reverence and trembling in his presence. Nevertheless, the author criticizes the covenant and the law that Moses gave as being provisional and insufficient to bring the people into the land God promised them. For Hebrews, then, Moses ultimately "failed in his task as leader. In his ambivalent status he is perhaps an emblem of Judaism as it appears from the point of view of the author."[11] Whatever his praiseworthy qualities, "Moses' reputation is diminished by association, as mediator of such a deficient covenant."[12] Moses serves primarily, then, as a negative foil for Jesus, not as a positive model.

I suggest that such assessments of Hebrews' engagement with Moses do not do full justice to the complexities of the epistle's argument. Moses plainly does serve as a model in Hebrews for the readers to emulate, especially in Hebrews 11. But it is worth noting that Jesus does as well.[13] Moreover, some of the roles that Moses holds in Hebrews indicate that the author respects Moses (and the larger pentateuchal narrative of the exodus) and uses him to inform his understanding of Jesus and his salvific work.[14] While the writer's conception of Jesus indubitably informs his interpretation of Moses and the exodus (he

10. Eisenbaum, *Jewish Heroes*, 171.

11. J. Dunnill, *Covenant and Sacrifice in the Letter to the Hebrews*, SNTSMS 75 (Cambridge: Cambridge University Press, 1992), esp. 168.

12. Dunnill, *Covenant and Sacrifice*, 169.

13. See esp. Heb. 12:1–10, where Jesus, like Moses and the rest of those celebrated in Heb. 11, looked beyond the discipline he endured to the eternal glory of God's promises. Jesus is the chief model of obedience to the Father in the midst of suffering in Hebrews (see, e.g., 5:7–10). In this way Jesus and Moses are likened to each other, even though the author of Hebrews clearly thinks of Jesus as the superior figure.

14. While discussing Heb. 3:1–6, D'Angelo states that in these verses, "like other treatments of Moses in the letter, [Hebrews' midrashic interpretation of Scripture] is guided by the author's Christology rather than by any inherited or contemporary picture of Moses" (*Moses*, 69). D'Angelo does not deny the influence of traditions about Moses on Hebrews. However, she largely limits this influence to determining the shape of the structure of the argument of Hebrews' initial chapters rather than to contributing substantively to the content of the comparison and contrast of Moses with Jesus. D'Angelo argues that the latter is strictly driven by the author's Christology insofar as the author thinks that Moses's heavenly vision on Sinai

clearly reads Jewish Scripture retrospectively in light of Jesus and identifies patterns that can be seen to prefigure Jesus only from the vantage point of the particularities of the incarnation), an equal and opposite interpretive force is also in play—elements from the biblical accounts and later traditions about Moses, especially regarding his role during the exodus, positively inform Hebrews' Christology.[15] The author of Hebrews allows the discrete witness of Scripture to construct and determine aspects of his Christology, particularly as these relate to Jesus's salvific work.[16] Moses is an important figure in this regard. Thus, while Hebrews clearly considers the person and work of Jesus to be superior to those of Moses, the writer does not thereby criticize Moses or force him into a typological straitjacket that sees his value only in terms of how he conforms to Jesus.[17] Rather, for Hebrews, Moses serves as a central model, one that informs the writer's understanding of some of the most significant soteriological roles that Jesus performs on behalf of his brothers and sisters.[18]

Rather than attempt a study of all the ways that Hebrews engages with Moses, in this chapter I explore only one of these roles: Moses as the one whose faithful performance of the first Passover protected God's people from the Destroyer.[19] I argue that the author links Moses and Jesus by way of a

---

(see Exod. 33–34), the source of his great insights and revelations, depends on the fact that his encounter with the glory of God was actually an encounter with the eternal Son of God, Jesus.

15. J. Lierman's extensive study on traditions about Moses in the Second Temple period and in early Judaism helpfully traces some key ways that the figure of Moses likely informed the development of early Christian thinking about Jesus (*The New Testament Moses: Christian Perceptions of Moses and Israel in the Setting of Jewish Religion*, WUNT 2/173 [Tübingen: Mohr Siebeck, 2003]).

16. A. T. Lincoln makes a similar point when he writes, "Interaction between the Jewish Scriptures and Christology does not take place for the first time when the writer brings his christological key to the reading of Scripture. Interaction has already been taking place in formulating the Christology that now provides the key. So there should be no room for thinking that a Christological interpretation merely involves a one-way movement from the new to the old" ("Hebrews and Biblical Theology," in *Out of Egypt: Biblical Theology and Biblical Interpretation*, ed. C. Bartholomew et al., Scripture and Hermeneutics Series [Grand Rapids: Zondervan, 2004], 313–38, here 320).

17. C. L. Westfall makes a case for a similar conclusion relative to Heb. 3:1–6 ("Moses and Hebrews 3:1–6: Approach or Avoidance?," in *Christian-Jewish Relations through the Centuries*, ed. S. E. Porter and B. W. R. Pearson, JSNTSup 192 [Sheffield: Sheffield Academic Press, 2000], 173–201). My view about the identification of the house in this passage differs (see my comments on the matter in n. 21 below), but I fully agree with Westfall that the force of the argument in Heb. 3:1–6 relies on a positive comparison of Jesus with Moses, not a pejorative one (cf. H. W. Attridge, *The Epistle to the Hebrews*, Hermeneia [Philadelphia: Fortress, 1989], 105).

18. The discussion in this chapter is in no way intended to reduce either the person or the work of Jesus, as these are described in Hebrews, merely to the points made herein.

19. A number of other important roles of Moses could arguably be considered. These include Moses as priest and possibly apostle (Heb. 3:1–3; see esp. Lierman, *New Testament*

larger, pentateuchally shaped pattern or narrative. His use of this pattern implies that more dialogical and intertextual relationships than are sometimes supposed are in play between biblical texts and Jewish traditions about Moses, on the one hand, and the author's Christology and soteriology, on the other. Specifically, I argue here that the author of Hebrews deduces aspects of the significance of Jesus's death—in particular that this event marks the defeat of the Devil and the liberation of God's people, who are then freed to journey through the wilderness toward their promised inheritance—largely on the basis of the story and actions of Moses at the first Passover. Moses is, therefore, a sine qua non for the Christology and soteriology developed in Hebrews, for Moses and his role in the first Passover explain the logic that underlies the author's claim that Jesus's death defeated the Devil and liberated God's people from the fear of death. To put the point differently, one key way that Jesus is like Moses concerns the role his death plays in defeating the malevolent angel bent on destroying God's firstborn people. Jesus's death, I argue, is compared in Hebrews with Moses's performance of the first Passover.

Allusion to Moses and the First Passover in Hebrews 2

Hebrews first mentions Moses explicitly in 3:2–6.[20] As part of an extended comparison with Jesus, the author describes Moses in positive terms through language drawn from Numbers 12:7.[21] Moses, he states, was faithful as a

---

Moses, 272–73), Moses as authoritative lawgiver (esp. 7:11–19; 10:28), Moses as covenant and cult inaugurator as well as covenant mediator (chaps. 8–9), Moses as faithful and virtuous leader (11:23–28), and Moses as shepherd of God's people (see the allusion in 13:20 to Isa. 63:11, which speaks of God bringing up Moses as the shepherd of the sheep—a point made in the brief discussion of this verse in P. R. Jones, "The Figure of Moses as a Heuristic Device for Understanding the Pastoral Intent of Hebrews," *Review and Expositor* 76 [1979]: 95–107, here 101–3).

20. Moses is explicitly mentioned in Heb. 3:2, 3, 5, 16; 7:14; 8:5; 9:19; 10:28; 11:23–24; 12:21.

21. D'Angelo states, "I would assert that the text cited in Heb. 3:2 is not Num. 12:7 (although the allusion is present and held in abeyance) but 1 Chron. 17:14, most probably according to the Septuagint" (*Moses*, 69). She makes a strong case for the influence of the Nathan oracle on this section of Hebrews. Nevertheless, her statement seems to get the identification of the citation and allusion backward. The author's use of Num. 12:7 comes close to citation in Heb. 3:2, and the verse is cited explicitly in 3:5, while his use of 1 Chron. 17:14, if present, is much more allusive (cf. Attridge, *Hebrews*, 109n53). When the relationship of these texts is seen thus, D'Angelo's conclusion that Jesus is presented as the builder of the house in Heb. 3:4–6 is significantly weakened. For D'Angelo, this conclusion follows from the Nathan oracle, where David's son is the one who will build God's house. Hebrews, however, identifies God as the builder of the house under discussion in 3:2–6, not Jesus. It may well be that, as in Heb. 1, the author plays on the identification of God and the Son in these verses. Of equal importance, however, is the distinction between God and the Son here, especially

servant in God's house. It is worth asking, however, why the author first turns explicit attention to Moses at just this point in his homily.

Moses's Ascension and the Logic of Hebrews 2

I have argued elsewhere that the writer's appeal to Psalm 8 in Hebrews 2:5–9 occurs in the context of a discussion about the ascension of an embodied human being into the heavens and the corresponding elevation of that person above the angels.[22] This use of Psalm 8 resonates well with the logic of some Second Temple and later rabbinic texts that attest to a tradition about Moses's ascension into the heavens and corresponding relationship to the angels when he went up Sinai to receive the law. The author of Hebrews is likely playing on this tradition when, with some rhetorical panache in Hebrews 2:9, he delays mentioning Jesus's name while identifying Jesus as the one who has ultimately fulfilled Psalm 8's implied claim that humanity (ἄνθρωπος) would one day be elevated above the angels in the created order. Therefore, some conception of Moses already informs, albeit allusively, the author's ongoing argument in Hebrews 2 for the elevation of Jesus above the angels.[23]

Once this is recognized, a remarkable aspect of the references in Hebrews 2:14–15 to Jesus's defeat of the Devil and to the release of those who were enslaved to the fear of death emerges. The author's discussion here, particularly when viewed in light of some Jewish traditions about the identity of the Destroyer and the first Passover (see pp. 16–19), continues to suggest that the influence of Moses lies just below the surface of the argument. While many commentators note the potential importance of exodus themes for the author's claims about Jesus's death in Hebrews 2:14–16,[24] fewer argue for a

---

as this distinction drives both the logic of the comparison between the Son and Moses and the identification of the audience as "his [i.e., God's] house" (3:6). As most commentators agree, only one house is in question in the passage—God's house. The author is comparing Moses and Jesus, not two different houses. His change from the first-person speech of God in Num. 12:7 (or, *mutatis mutandis*, 1 Chron. 17:14) to the third-person in Heb. 3:2 and 3:5— he alters the genitive pronoun modifying οἶκος from μου to αὐτοῦ—dictates the meaning of all the pronouns in 3:5–6. They all have God as their antecedent. God, who built all things, is the builder of this house (3:4). Jesus and Moses are, therefore, faithful in their respective positions *to the same house.* Moses was a faithful servant within God's house, but Jesus is the Son over God's house (cf. 10:21).

22. See D. M. Moffitt, "Unveiling Jesus' Body: A Fresh Assessment of the Relationship between the Veil and Jesus' Flesh in Hebrews 10:20," *PRS* 37 [2010]: 71–84.

23. Moffitt, "Unveiling Jesus' Body," esp. 80–81.

24. E.g., C. R. Koester, *Hebrews: A New Translation with Introduction and Commentary,* AB 36 (New York: Doubleday, 2001), 234, 240. While Attridge recognizes the influence of the exodus on the passage (*Hebrews*, 93), he does not think this is the dominant idea here (93n161). L. T. Johnson, based largely on the fact that the verb ἀπαλλάσσω is not used in the exodus

more particular allusion here to the first Passover.[25] Nevertheless, three points support this conclusion.

First, the Pentateuch's depiction of Moses as the one who, having been instructed by God, directed the Israelites regarding the first Passover is significant.[26] As a result of Moses's command to the Israelites to apply the blood of the Passover lambs to the lintels and doorposts of their houses, the Israelites were protected from experiencing the death of their firstborn. When viewed through the lens of at least some Second Temple reflection on Moses, Moses's role of faithfully performing the first Passover corresponds well to Hebrews' identification of Jesus as the one whose own death has defeated the malevolent angel who wields the power of death—the Devil.

Second, the fact that the first Passover enabled Moses to lead the people out of their bondage in Egypt nicely aligns with the link between Jesus's defeat of the Devil and his freeing his people from bondage. That is, if the author alludes to the Passover in Hebrews 2:14, it is unlikely to be a coincidence that his reference to Jesus's defeat of the Devil is immediately followed in 2:15 by the claim that Jesus has released his siblings from their perpetual enslavement to the fear of death. Hebrews does not just draw broadly on the exodus here but focuses specifically on the event that initiates the exodus—the first Passover.

Third, a further point of correspondence with the larger pattern of the Passover and exodus account is noteworthy. Once the people were freed from their enslavement to Pharaoh, Moses led them into the wilderness, where they met and worshiped God at Sinai. It is striking how well this aspect of the story aligns with the author's moves in Hebrews 3–4, in which he not only makes his first explicit comparisons between Jesus and Moses but also goes on to compare his audience with the exodus generation—the very generation

---

account, denies that the exodus plays any significant role in Heb. 2 (*Hebrews: A Commentary*, NTL [Louisville: Westminster John Knox, 2006], 100).

25. Attridge states that "Hebrews does not make explicit any symbolic or typological significance of [the Passover]" (*Hebrews*, 343; cf. Eisenbaum, *Jewish Heroes*, 171; Koester, *Hebrews*, 504). But see P. E. Hughes, who briefly asserts a link between Heb. 11:28 and 2:14–16 (*A Commentary on the Epistle to the Hebrews*, NICNT [Grand Rapids: Eerdmans, 1977], 500–501), and Johnson, who allows a connection between the complex of the Passover lamb's death and the people's liberation, on the one hand, and the salvific effect of Jesus's death, on the other (*Hebrews*, 303). By way of contrast, J. Dunnill sees Passover (which he argues joins together the motifs of blood, ritual death, expiation, and the founding of the covenant) as a substantial theme informing various parts of the argument of Hebrews (*Covenant and Sacrifice*, esp. 127–28, 154–55, and 159 [cf. 107]).

26. Given the context of Num. 12:7, where Moses's faithfulness is linked with his direct access to God and God's direct speech and instruction to Moses, the faithfulness of Moses in all of God's house likely includes his performance of the first Passover. This may be why it is precisely Moses's use of the Passover blood that the author highlights in Heb. 11:28 as an aspect of his acting in faith. He was simply doing what God told him to do.

that was liberated from Egypt and then journeyed into the wilderness.[27] It is also striking that, later in the homily, the author links his audience with the "congregation of the firstborn," who, like Moses and the exodus generation at Sinai, are gathered around Jesus at Zion.

Echoes of Passover in the Letter to the Hebrews

The author of Hebrews explicitly mentions Passover only once in his homily. In Hebrews 11:28 he states that by faith Moses "performed the Passover and the aspersion of blood" (πεποίηκεν τὸ πάσχα καὶ τὴν πρόσχυσιν τοῦ αἵματος) so that "the one who destroys the firstborn" (ὁ ὀλοθρεύων τὰ πρωτότοκα) would not touch the people and livestock of Israel.[28] This reference to "the one who destroys" (ὁ ὀλοθρεύων) recalls the curious statement in Exodus 12:23 LXX that, because of the blood on the doorposts and lintels, the LORD would "not permit the one who destroys" (οὐκ ἀφήσει τὸν ὀλεθρεύοντα) to enter the houses of the Israelites and strike their firstborn. This reference to the Passover in Hebrews 11:28, particularly when understood in light of some Jewish exegetical traditions concerning the Destroyer of Exodus 12:23, suggests that when the author mentions Jesus's defeat of the Devil and the liberation of his kin from the fear of death in Hebrews 2:14–15, he is alluding to Moses, who held the Destroyer at bay by performing the first Passover.

The Destroyer of Exodus 12:23

While throughout most of the Passover account the text of Exodus typically identifies the LORD himself as the agent who struck down Egypt's firstborn in the final plague (e.g., Exod. 12:13), the mention of the Destroyer in 12:23 being prevented by the blood from striking the people poses an exegetical curiosity for anyone paying close attention to the details of the text. Why does the text of Exodus refer here to the one who destroys? This odd statement allows the implication that some other figure, someone distinct from the LORD, did the smiting at the first Passover.[29] If this is so, who is this Destroyer? Significantly,

27. In addition to the allusions I argue underlie the larger argument of Heb. 2, it is worth noting that the author's apparent reference in 2:2 to a tradition about angels mediating the law on Sinai offers a further indication that he has the story of Moses, the exodus, and Sinai in mind in this portion of his homily.

28. In keeping with the account in Exodus, the neuter plural τὰ πρωτότοκα in Heb. 11:28 implies that God even spared the firstborn of Israel's livestock, not just the firstborn Israelite children.

29. Early Jewish interpretation indicates that just such an exegetical possibility was explored and developed. I focus on Jubilees below. In the Tannaitic period, however, some of the rabbis attest to this tradition by explicitly rejecting the view that an angel or agent other than God

some ancient Jewish interpreters concluded that 12:23 points to an agent other than God who carried out the actual work of smiting in the final plague—the malevolent angel of death.

A host of texts, including some in the New Testament, indicate that many Jews of the Second Temple period believed that demonic forces were at work ravaging the world and attacking God's people. Moreover, one particular figure, the angel of death—sometimes referred to as the Satan or the accuser and sometimes described with what appear to be proper names such as Belial and Mastemah—was thought to be the chief of all these demonic forces.[30] Evidence from Second Temple and rabbinic-era texts reveals that some Jewish interpreters not only concluded that the reference to the Destroyer of Exodus 12:23 indicated an agent distinct from the LORD but also identified this figure with the great Satan, the chief of the demons and the angel of death.[31]

In Jubilees, for example, the Destroyer of Exodus 12:23 is linked with the figure Mastemah, whom the text also refers to as Belial in a few places (Jub. 1:20; 15:31–33). Throughout Jubilees, Mastemah, the leader of all the destroying spirits, functions as the chief spiritual opponent of God's people.[32] Mastemah is identified as controlling a demonic horde whom he uses to influence people to fashion idols and to commit other heinous sins (e.g., Jub. 11:4–5; cf. 12:20). Like the malevolent accuser (the Satan) depicted in Job 1–2 and Zechariah 3, Mastemah can stand in the heavenly court and accuse God's people (Jub. 17:16; cf. 1:20; 10:8; 48:9). In Jubilees 48, Mastemah tries to kill Moses (48:2). He then motivates Pharaoh and the Egyptians to oppose

did the smiting (e.g., Mek. Pisha 7.28–30; 13.9–11, though see also 11.61–62; Mek. Amalek 1.128–29, where the activity of an angelic agent is simply assumed). Later rabbinic texts tend to distinguish between God and the Destroyer (e.g., Tg. Neof. Exod. 12:23; see also the evidence given in L. Ginzberg, *The Legends of the Jews*, 2nd ed. [Philadelphia: Jewish Publication Society, 2003], 1:537–38; M. Segal, *The Book of Jubilees: Rewritten Bible, Redaction, Ideology and Theology*, JSJSup 117 [Leiden: Brill, 2007], 210n20).

30. *Mastemah* is not always a name in the Qumran scrolls. Sometimes the term is used to describe Belial, an angel of hostility, or groups of hostile angels. It is likely, however, that in 1QS 3.13–4.26 this figure Belial/Mastemah is to be identified with the Angel of Darkness, who, together with his minions, rules the world and misleads humanity. These hostile figures oppose God, but they are nevertheless created by God and at times do his bidding. See M. Mach, "Demons," *EDSS* 1:189–92.

31. The name *Mastemah* derives from the Hebrew noun מַשְׂטֵמָה, meaning "hostility." The noun's Hebrew root is שׂטם, a variation of the root שׂטן, from which the term "Satan" derives (J. W. van Henten, "Mastemah," *DDD* 1033–35).

32. E.g., Jub. 17:19. The Ethiopic term *Mäśṭäm* (a transliteration of the Hebrew term מַשְׂטֵמָה) most likely functions as a proper name in Jubilees (so van Henten, "Mastemah," 1033). This particular demon is often equated with the Devil in Ethiopic traditions (see B. Burtea, "Demons," *Encyclopaedia Aethiopica*, ed. S. Uhlig et al., 5 vols. [Weisbaden: Harrassowitz, 2003–2014], 2:130–32).

Moses and the Israelites (e.g., 48:9, 12). Pharaoh finally relents and allows the people to go only when some of the good angels bind Mastemah for a time (48:15, 18). Once Mastemah is released, however, the Egyptians change their mind and, again under the evil one's direct influence, pursue the people in order to re-enslave them (48:12, 16–17).

Intriguingly for the purposes of this study, Jubilees 49:2 describes the final plague on Egypt as being carried out by "all the forces of Mastemah," who "were sent to kill every first-born in the land of Egypt—from the pharaoh's first-born to the first-born of the captive slave-girl at the millstone and to the cattle as well."[33] The sign of the blood of the Passover sacrifice on the doorposts and lintels of the Israelite houses prevented Mastemah's servants from entering and destroying their firstborn.

This evidence from Jubilees suggests the following two inferences: (1) the Destroyer mentioned in Exodus 12:23 is interpreted in Jubilees as the malicious angelic agent Mastemah, whose minions are sent to kill all the firstborn in Egypt;[34] and (2) the first Passover is understood to be both a liberation from enslavement to Pharaoh in Egypt and a release, even if only temporarily, from the dominion of Mastemah, who was at work in Pharaoh and the Egyptians.

These conclusions find some confirmation in other passages where Jubilees reflects on Israel's eschatological future. In Jubilees 50:5 the text envisions a future time when the land of promise will be ultimately purified and the conjoined problems of the people's sins and their ritual impurities will be finally resolved. When this happens, no satan or evil one who destroys will again be able to trouble God's people (cf. 23:29). As the Satan par excellence

---

33. Translation from J. C. VanderKam, *The Book of Jubilees*, CSCO 511, Scriptores Ae-thiopici 88 (Leuven: Peeters, 1989), 315. According to Jubilees, Mastemah was bound at the time and unable to do the smiting himself. Halpern-Amaru rightly suggests that attributing the smiting to Mastemah's forces and then explaining that these forces were following YHWH's orders is how Jubilees solves the exegetical issue of YHWH doing the smiting in some texts, while in Exod. 12:23 "the Destroyer" does it (see B. Halpern-Amaru, "The Festivals of Pesaḥ and Massot in the Book of Jubilees," in *Enoch and the Mosaic Torah: The Evidence of Jubilees*, ed. G. Boccaccini and G. Ibba [Grand Rapids: Eerdmans, 2009], 309–22, here 313).

34. Jubilees shares the ambiguity of Exodus here in that both God's forces and the forces of Mastemah are identified as executing the final plague (compare Jub. 48:5–8; 49:2; and 49:4; see also 48:12, 15–17). But Mastemah is not depicted as God's equal, and throughout Jubilees it is clear that God is fully in control of history. Nevertheless, the identification of the Destroyer with the Satan who accuses and threatens God's people is indicative of a significant interpretive move that links this hostile figure with the angelic accuser mentioned in other parts of Scripture and with several key events in which God's people faced various threats. M. Segal may be correct that this tension is one indication that Jub. 48 and 49 reflect different sources that have been redacted (*Book of Jubilees*, esp. 210–28), but this kind of theological tension is well attested in other Second Temple texts (see Mach, "Demons," 191). For an especially clear expression of such a dynamic, see the depiction of the Angel of Darkness in the "Treatise of the Two Spirits" in 1QS 3–4 (see n. 30 above).

in Jubilees (cf. 10:11), Mastemah is clearly the primary spiritual enemy and destroyer, who one day will never again be able to trouble God's people. There are, in other words, significant links in Jubilees between the first exodus, with the limited liberation from Mastemah and his forces that it achieved, and the future, new creation when God's people will ultimately be freed from sin, impurity, and every accusing satan.

The evidence in Jubilees 48–49 for the identification of the Destroyer in Exodus 12:23 with Mastemah and his forces potentially sheds light on Hebrews' reference to Moses's role in the first Passover vis-à-vis the one who destroys the firstborn mentioned in Hebrews 11:28. Specifically, the sort of exegetical reflection on the exodus narrative (and especially on Exod. 12:23) attested in Jubilees[35] is suggestive for Hebrews. The author of Hebrews could plausibly have assumed that the reference to a destroying figure in Exodus 12:23 identified some agent other than God as the one who killed the firstborn in the last plague—namely, the great Satan, the chief cosmic accuser and opponent of God's people.

I am not claiming that the author of Hebrews must know and be dependent upon Jubilees. Rather, I am arguing that the kind of interpretation of Exodus 12:23 that Jubilees attests provides a way to understand the identity of the Destroyer whom Moses faced in Hebrews 11:28. If the writer and his audience share with Jubilees a common tradition that identifies the Destroyer of Exodus 12:23 as the chief angelic opponent of God's people, then the author would likely identify the figure whom Jesus defeats in Hebrews 2:14—the Devil—with the Destroyer whom Moses faced in 11:28.[36]

The Devil in Hebrews as the Destroyer of Exodus 12:23

Three additional lines of evidence in Hebrews bear out the supposition that the author identifies the Devil with the Destroyer from whom Moses

35. A similar identification between a figure who brought death upon God's people in the wilderness and the Destroyer is found in some other Second Temple and rabbinic-era texts. See Wis. 18:25 and 1 Cor. 10:10, which both identify the figure who struck the wilderness generation with death as "the Destroyer." Notably, Wis. 18:25 does not identify this figure with the one who struck the Egyptians (18:13–19). See also the discussion in n. 29 above.

36. Dunnill argues that Hebrews embraces the ambiguity of Exod. 12 and views God as both the Destroyer and the one who protects his chosen people (Dunnill, *Covenant and Sacrifice*, esp. 107, 159). In my view, Dunnill does not take seriously enough the evidence of texts like Jubilees wherein the Destroyer is independent of God and hostile to God's people, even though he cannot act unilaterally and will one day be stripped of all power. This interpretive tradition takes seriously both (1) God's ultimate control of creation and (2) the presence of a hostile angelic accuser and his minions who are distinct from God but to whom God grants a significant role in creation for set periods of time. See also n. 34 above.

protected God's people at the first Passover. First, the imperfective aspect of the participle ὁ ὀλοθρεύων in Hebrews 11:28 allows the inference that this figure is characterized by destruction. That is to say, this agent is not merely identified as carrying out a particular/one-off task during the first Passover. He is not just "the one who *destroyed*" the firstborn in Egypt. The epithet "the one who *destroys*" suggests instead that destruction is what he continually does. Destroying is part of his identity. Turning again to Jubilees, not only does the Destroyer spur Pharaoh to pursue the Israelites after they leave Egypt, but he is depicted throughout Jubilees as the one who threatens God's special people. In fact, Jubilees portrays the Akedah as the result of Mastemah's agitation. In Jubilees 17:16, Mastemah comes before God in heaven and challenges Abraham's faith. According to Jubilees, it is Mastemah who proposes that Abraham be tested by having him offer up Isaac as a sacrifice.

Intriguingly, too, Jubilees makes a clear connection here between the Akedah and the first Passover when it both identifies the date of the Akedah with that of Passover and explicitly calls Isaac Abraham's "firstborn" (Jub. 18:11, 15).[37] Jubilees appears to take the fact that Scripture identifies Israel as God's firstborn and the notion of the Destroyer of the firstborn in Exodus 12:23 as one indication that Israel is a prime target for this figure. From this perspective, Hebrews 11:28's mention of the "one who destroys" can plausibly be identified as a reference to the cosmic enemy of God's people whose very inclination is to destroy them. This malevolent Destroyer was prevented from harming the firstborn of God's people in Egypt by Moses's application of the Passover blood to doorways of their houses.

Second, if for a moment the preceding observations about the identity of the Destroyer in some Second Temple exegesis of Exodus 12:23 are posited as informing Hebrews 11:28, the further identification in Hebrews 12:23 of the homily's intended audience as part of "the congregation of the firstborn" (ἐκκλησία πρωτοτόκων) can be seen to suggest that the author wants them to understand themselves as being caught up in the cosmic battle between "the one who destroys the firstborn" and the primary object of his hostility—God's people, "the congregation of the firstborn."[38] In other words, they are those whom, like the firstborn of Israel in the exodus, God has protected and liberated. This analogy allows the further inference that the Destroyer of Exodus 12:23, the figure mentioned in Hebrews 11:28, could plausibly be identified with the malevolent being who has always accused

---

37. So Segal, *Book of Jubilees*, 191–98.

38. It is worth noting that Exod. 4:22–23 explicitly connects the plague on the firstborn in Egypt with Pharaoh's refusal to release Israel, God's firstborn son.

God's people and who would therefore also be the enemy of those whom Hebrews addresses—the Devil.

The preceding two lines of reasoning give rise to a third point. The imagery the author uses to describe his readers in relation to the congregation of the firstborn gathered around Zion is redolent of the larger pentateuchal narrative of the exodus. The author's comparison and contrast in Hebrews 12:18–23 between Jesus and God's people at Zion, on the one hand, and Moses and the exodus generation who gathered at Sinai, on the other, makes the conceptual connection especially clear. Just as the people were liberated from Egypt and led by Moses in the wilderness to Sinai in order to worship God, so the audience can understand themselves as those who have been liberated from the Devil, have been led into their own wilderness time by Jesus, and have come to Zion, where they worship God.

The larger analogy between the audience and the exodus generation has already been made in Hebrews 3–4. The imagery of Hebrews 12 develops yet another aspect of it. But the recognition that the exodus narrative informs the argument here further substantiates the suggestion made above that those addressed in Hebrews 12:23 as the "congregation of the firstborn" are to liken themselves to the firstborn mentioned in 11:28. They are, that is, like those firstborn whom Moses protected from the Destroyer, liberated from their bondage in Egypt, led into the wilderness, brought to Sinai, and then guided toward their promised inheritance.

These three points suggest that the author of Hebrews has a keen interest in developing and extending the analogy he has already drawn in Hebrews 3–4 between the congregation to whom he writes and the exodus generation. Indeed, when viewed as a whole, this evidence indicates that the author's analogy between Jesus and his audience, on the one hand, and Moses and the exodus generation, on the other, is pervasive.[39] The contours of this analogy are as follows: On the one hand, Moses performed the Passover and was instrumental (1) in protecting God's people from the hostile Destroyer, (2) in liberating them from their slavery in Egypt, (3) in leading them in the wilderness to worship their God at Sinai (where some traditions even claim he ascended into the heavens), and (4) in bringing them to the edge of the promised

---

39. Interestingly, the sectarians at Qumran also interpreted their situation by way of a pervasive analogy between their situation and that of Moses and the exodus generation (see, e.g., the discussion in W. A. Meeks, *The Prophet-King: Moses Traditions and the Johannine Christology*, NovTSup 14 [Leiden: Brill, 1967], 172–73). In fact, the notion of God's people being in the wilderness was widespread in the Second Temple period and could be employed in a variety of ways, often in relation to the exile (see H. Najman, "Toward a Study of the Uses of the Concept of Wilderness in Ancient Judaism," *Dead Sea Discoveries* 13 [2006]: 99–113).

land. On the other hand, Jesus saves God's people in part by (1) defeating the Devil and (2) liberating them from the fear of death such that (3) they are now in the wilderness gathered around Zion (and their ascended leader) but also (4) standing at the edge of the ultimate promised inheritance.[40]

If these are the basic contours of this analogy, an obvious question naturally arises. Has Jesus done something like Moses's faithful aspersion of blood that results in the protection and liberation of his people from the Destroyer and issues in their being led into the wilderness? If so, what did Jesus do? The author of Hebrews does in fact think that Jesus has done something like Moses's performance of the first Passover—specifically, Jesus suffered, died, and was perfected so that he could lead many children to glory (Heb. 2:9–10, 14).[41]

Jesus's Death as a New Passover in Hebrews 2

In Hebrews 2:14 the author speaks of Jesus defeating "the one having the power of death" (τὸν τὸ κράτος ἔχοντα τοῦ θανάτου)—the Devil (τὸν διάβολον). Moreover, Hebrews claims in 2:15 that Jesus released (ἀπαλλάξῃ) his people from their fearful bondage (δουλείας) to the power of death that the Devil wields (cf. Heb. 2:10).[42] From the perspective of the analogy laid out above, especially in view of the exegetical tradition about Moses and the Destroyer evident in Jubilees, the language of Hebrews 2:14–15 is highly evocative of the first Passover and subsequent exodus. But recognizing the allusion allows one to pinpoint the conceptual location of Jesus's death in relation to the role of Moses in the account of the exodus. Jesus's death functions like Moses's aspersion of blood at the first Passover. Thus, it is "through his death" (διὰ τοῦ θανάτου) that Jesus defeated the Devil.

---

40. This analogy is complex and functions at different levels. My point here is neither to identify all the ways the author plays it out nor to reduce it to the level of a consistent chronology. Clearly, for example, the identification of the audience as both gathered around Zion and on the boundary of the inheritance shows how the author can explore multiple aspects of the larger analogy. My goal is only to highlight a few of the interrelated aspects that have tended to be overlooked, not to exhaust, reduce, or overly simplify the rich tapestry of metaphors the author develops or alludes to on the basis of his analogy between the audience and the exodus generation.

41. I have argued elsewhere that Jesus's perfection in Hebrews is largely, though not exclusively, a way of referring to his bodily resurrection (D. M. Moffitt, *Atonement and the Logic of Resurrection in the Epistle to the Hebrews*, NovTSup 141 [Leiden: Brill, 2011], esp. 198–200; see also chap. 7 in this volume).

42. While the verb "release" (ἀπαλλάσσω) is not attested in LXX accounts of the exodus, the language of "bondage" (δουλεία) is common with reference to Egypt and the exodus. Indeed, every use of the term in LXX Exodus and Deuteronomy refers to the people's bondage in Egypt (see Exod. 6:6; 13:3, 14; 20:2; Deut. 5:6; 6:12; 7:8; 8:14; 13:6, 11; cf. Lev. 26:45).

In the case of Moses, then, the important pivot in the exodus story—the event that Hebrews identifies in 11:28 as protecting the people from the Destroyer, leading to their release from bondage, and initiating the exodus into the wilderness—is Moses's obedient application of the Passover blood. In the case of Jesus, the pivotal event that liberates his followers from bondage to the Devil, frees them from their enslavement to the fear of death, and issues in their going into the wilderness is, as Hebrews 2:14 makes clear, his death.

The broad analogy the author constructs between the audience and the exodus generation in Hebrews 2–4 appears, therefore, to form an essential part of the conceptual framework of the homily such that its recurrence in Hebrews 11 and 12 can hardly be either accidental or incidental.[43] Hebrews, in other words, develops a robust analogy between the exodus generation and the epistle's intended audience, an analogy that recurs in various ways throughout the epistle. Within this analogy, Jesus's death can be seen to be the essential Passover-like event that, like Moses's aspersion of blood at the first Passover, brings protection and liberation from the great enemy of God's people and initiates their time of journeying in the wilderness.

Moses as Model

When taken together, the preceding arguments suggest the following inference: the author of Hebrews understands the Destroyer of the firstborn who threatened God's people during the initial Passover to be none other than the Devil, the malevolent angelic figure who holds the power of death. Jesus's death stands at the beginning of a new exodus narrative in Hebrews. In keeping with this, the audience are to envision themselves as in the wilderness and about to enter the inheritance God has promised for his people. In light of the larger analogy between the community and the exodus generation in Hebrews and the identification of the Devil with the Destroyer of the first Passover, the author's statement that Jesus's death defeated the Devil draws a comparison between the singular death of Jesus and the unique performance of the first Passover that initiated the original exodus. The discussion of Moses's performance of the initial Passover in order to protect God's people from the Destroyer implies that in Hebrews 2:14–15 Jesus's death functions as a Passover-like event that liberates humanity from the enslaving power of death and the great destroyer who wields that power—the Devil. Jesus's death initiates an exodus-like event wherein God's people are finally

---

43. I offer a more detailed discussion of the significant role and influence of Exodus and the exodus narrative in Hebrews in D. M. Moffitt, "Exodus in Hebrews," in *Exodus in the New Testament*, ed. S. M. Ehorn, LNTS 663 (London: T&T Clark, 2022), 146–63.

and fully freed from the dominion of the Devil. Hebrews does seem to work with a "new exodus" model but not one that is conceptually driven by the reality of ongoing exile.[44]

If this is more or less on target, then Jesus's liberating work in Hebrews 2:14–16 is modeled on Moses's key role in liberating God's people from slavery (cf. Heb. 3:16). The figure of Moses is, therefore, central to the claim that Jesus defeated the Devil, for it was Moses who defeated the Destroyer when, by faith, he manipulated blood at the first Passover. This conclusion not only sheds fresh light on the meaning and logic of the emancipation Jesus has effected in Hebrews 2:14–16 (his death is a Passover-like act that brings liberation from enslavement to the Devil) but also implies that the author respects the role of Moses in the Passover and the exodus. Moses's performance of the Passover and his role as liberator of the people are not being critiqued, downplayed, or made to conform to Jesus. Rather, the author draws upon Moses's act of blood manipulation at the first Passover and his leading the people into the wilderness to explain something about who Jesus is and how his death is salvific.

The analogy implies that Jesus's death is the Passover-like event that ultimately leads to the liberation of God's people from the power of the angel of death and allows them to enter into a wilderness-like period as they head toward the eternal inheritance God promises them. The author is not, then, forcing the liberating act of Jesus back into the exodus story as a hermeneutical key to show the true significance of that earlier event. Instead, he appeals to the pentateuchal account of Moses to draw an extended analogy that enables him to identify points of continuity between Jesus and Moses, points that help to inform the true nature of Jesus's salvific work.

---

44. M. Thiessen makes the intriguing argument that the author thinks Israel's exodus from Egypt has never come to an end ("Hebrews and the End of Exodus," *NovT* 49 [2007]: 353–69). The author does not think in terms of an ongoing exile. Rather, he relegates all of Israel's history after the exodus to an extended time of wandering in the wilderness. Thiessen therefore suggests that "new exodus" language is inappropriate for Hebrews (355n7). A full discussion of this interpretation lies beyond the scope of this chapter. Nevertheless, I suspect that Thiessen's thesis does not recognize just how far back the author locates God's people in redemptive history. The author of Hebrews seems to think that God's people had never really been liberated from slavery prior to Christ. Like Jubilees, Hebrews suggests that God's people were never fully freed from the real source of their true slavery—the Devil. In a sense, then, Jesus effects *the* exodus when he defeats this perennial foe. By the same token, the audience are now in *the* wilderness waiting to enter *the* inheritance. This does not mean, however, that the writer denies the reality of the exodus that Moses led or of Joshua's and the people's entrance into the promised inheritance. The scriptural narrative of these events provides essential categories for the author as he reflects on who Jesus is, what he has done, and how the homily's audience ought to think of themselves. When viewed this way, it seems completely appropriate to speak of Jesus leading a new exodus in Hebrews.

Yet another important point follows from the preceding argument. Both Jesus and Moses were faithful *when they faced the same opponent*—the malicious angelic agent who has always been intent on the destruction of God's people. Both were, in their own ways, victorious over that figure because they were faithful to God's instructions/will. Their victories differ in kind and degree. In Hebrews, Jesus's death is clearly depicted as the superior Passover-like event. While Moses earned a partial liberation from the enemy and brought God's people out of bondage in Egypt by performing the Passover, the problem of death and enslavement to death continued, and, as the author emphasizes by way of Psalm 95 in Hebrews 3–4, the wilderness generation did not ultimately enter the true promised rest toward which they were being led. Jesus, however, has finally defeated the Devil and ultimately liberated God's people from the fear of death. Because of his resurrection and ascension, Jesus has gone ahead of his people and opened a new and living way into the inheritance God has promised them.

If this interpretation is largely correct, there does not here appear to be any attempt to tarnish the importance of Moses at the first Passover or to force him to conform to Jesus. Indeed, the opposite impulse seems to be at work. The author finds in the first Passover a basis from which to draw out aspects of the significance of Jesus's own death. By analogy to the redemption of God's people from Egypt, Jesus's crucifixion and resurrection liberate God's people from the accusing angel and from his power to enslave them. Moses, Passover, and the exodus, far from being mere ciphers for the author's christological and soteriological views forced back into holy writ, offer the writer authoritative paradigms for thinking about Jesus as a liberating figure and about how his death brought God's people liberation from their enslavement to death and the Devil—Jesus's death is a Passover-like event that initiates an exodus-like liberation from the great Destroyer.

Conclusion

Within the claims and logic of Hebrews 2:14–16 concerning Jesus's defeat of the Devil and subsequent liberation of God's people, the allusive presence of Moses and his salvific work at the first Passover suggests that the witness of Scripture and other traditions regarding Moses's central role in the exodus narrative inform the author's understanding of what Jesus's death accomplished. Moses is not a wax nose for the author of Hebrews, nor is his role as liberator of God's people diminished by being made to conform to the enduring, atemporal work of Christ. True, as a faithful servant in God's house, Moses testifies to the good things that are to come (Heb. 3:5). This likely implies, in part, that the author envisions Moses's faithful performance of the Passover as foreshadowing or providing the pattern for the ultimate liberation that Jesus effected. But it follows from this that Moses's leadership of God's people in performing the Passover, helping to protect them from the Destroyer, and leading them out of Egypt and into the wilderness is not diminished or displaced by Jesus's "better" work. Rather, these elements of Moses's work provide a model for the author to use when reflecting on the salvific work of Christ.

Doubtless the larger connections between Jesus and Passover are not original to this author but are, as the Gospels attest, common stock in early Christianity. Hebrews nevertheless offers us insight into the dialogical reasoning of some of the earliest Christians as they thought through the complex relationships they assumed must be present between Jesus and the biblical texts, figures, and traditions they assumed to be divinely revealed and therefore authoritative. For the author of Hebrews, at least, the preceding arguments indicate that it was important to locate Jesus within the larger biblical pattern of God's liberating work through his faithful servant Moses. In particular, Moses's faithful service through his obedient aspersion of blood at the first Passover illuminates who Jesus is and what he accomplished in his death by providing a scriptural frame within which to think about these matters. Hebrews draws on Moses's role in the first Passover and the way this inaugurated the exodus to add depth and texture both to Jesus's identity and to how one understands what he has done to bring salvation to his brothers and sisters. Jesus is a Moses-like figure whose death is a new Passover that has defeated the Devil and freed God's people from enslavement. Hebrews, in other words, presents Jesus as the one who performed *the* Passover par excellence. The audience can now identify themselves as in a new wilderness period gathered around Zion, where they worship God as they wait for their covenant mediator to return from his ascended position in God's presence and lead them finally into the fullness of their inheritance.

All of this implies that Moses is for the author tightly linked with the special event of the first Passover and with the subsequent exodus. Specifically, Moses is viewed as an active agent who listened to God's instructions and faithfully performed them. As noted above, Moses, like Jesus, serves as a model for the audience to imitate. The views of D'Angelo and Eisenbaum are correct on this point. But Moses is not simply a role model for the audience because he, like Jesus, performed an essential saving act on behalf of God's people. Moses's use of blood at the Passover protected God's people and led to their liberation from Egypt. The temporal sequence of the history of God's people as narrated in the Pentateuch puts Moses in a unique position relative to the rest of God's people.

Jesus's death, as the event that initiates the new exodus of God's people, is also a unique and unrepeatable event. The first Passover, which Moses performed in order to protect God's people from the Destroyer, to liberate them from Egypt, and to initiate their journey toward their promised inheritance, is repeatedly remembered in the annual Passover feast but is never itself repeated. In a similar way, Jesus's Passover-like submission to death has defeated the Devil, liberated God's people from the tyranny of death's power, and initiated their journey into the wilderness of the last days, where they wait to enter fully into their promised inheritance. This event is remembered in the Eucharist, but it is never again to be repeated. Hebrews' comparison of Jesus's death with Moses's faithful performance of the first Passover therefore spotlights the cross as the event that set in motion the new and ultimate exodus of God's people from their enslavement to death and the Devil.

In sum, the preceding arguments demonstrate that the hermeneutical dynamic at the center of Hebrews' dialogical engagement with Scripture is not unidirectional. Rather than forcing Moses or the first Passover or the exodus to mean what they mean only in light of Jesus, the logic and sequence as well as the perceived meaning of these aspects of Scripture helps explain who Jesus is, what he has done, and how he has done it.[45] From this perspective, Moses provides a model for the author to explore some of the essential elements of the salvific work that he confesses Jesus to have accomplished.

---

45. The author's interpretation of Scripture clearly can take temporal sequence seriously. This is evident in his engagement with Ps. 95 in Heb. 3–4 (see esp. Heb. 4:1–11). For a useful discussion of the significance of temporal sequence in Hebrews' exegetical engagement with Ps. 95 see N. J. Moore, *Repetition in Hebrews: Plurality and Singularity in the Letter to the Hebrews, Its Ancient Context, and the Early Church*, WUNT 2/388 (Tübingen: Mohr Siebeck, 2015), 111–15.

3

Wilderness Identity and Pentateuchal Narrative

Distinguishing between Jesus's Inauguration and Maintenance of the New Covenant in Hebrews

Motifs that recall Israel's time in the wilderness after the exodus are found throughout the Epistle to the Hebrews.[1] The writer's use of these motifs to develop analogues to his readers' situation inculcates a wilderness identity among them. The analogies encourage them to see themselves as currently in their own time of wilderness. But what drives this identification with Israel's wilderness generation? Does Hebrews simply spiritualize Israel's story in order to draw out the moral point that perseverance in trial is necessary if one is to reach the ultimate inheritance?

While the author clearly educes moral lessons from Israel's history (e.g., Heb. 4:1–6), a more fundamental rationale for Hebrews' wilderness identity can be detected. Throughout his epistle the writer draws upon a pentateuchally shaped narrative to help form the identity of his intended recipients. Significantly, the structure of this narrative correlates with a distinction between

---

1. E.g., Israel's failure to obey God's command to enter the promised land is referred to in Heb. 3–4; the author reflects extensively on the tabernacle in chap. 9; he speaks in 9:15 of the promised inheritance (cf. 11:9); the Sinai event is discussed in chap. 12. For my more thorough discussion of Exodus and the exodus narrative in Hebrews see D. M. Moffitt, "Exodus in Hebrews," in *Exodus in the New Testament*, ed. S. M. Ehorn, LNTS 663 (London: T&T Clark, 2022), 146–63.

Jesus's liberating and covenant-inaugurating death, on the one hand, and Jesus's ongoing, high-priestly work of covenant maintenance in the heavens, on the other. Closely associated with this distinction between the effects of Jesus's death and those of his ascension is the fact that the epistle's intended readers have not yet entered their promised inheritance.

To put these points in pentateuchal terms, for the readers of Hebrews to be identified as God's sons (e.g., Heb. 2:10; 12:5) and even members of the congregation of the firstborn (12:23), to be freed from the power that enslaved them (2:14–15), to have entered into covenant relationship with God (e.g., 8:6; 9:15), to have a high priest interceding for them (7:25; 8:1–2) and to have come to Mount Zion (12:22) but at the same time to not yet have taken full possession of their inheritance (4:1–2; 6:12) and to be waiting for their Ἰησοῦς to return to them (9:28; cf. 10:35–39) puts them into a state analogous to that of Israel in the wilderness.[2] This underlying analogy between Jesus and his followers and the Pentateuch's account of Israel's exodus and journey into the wilderness under the leadership of Moses and then Joshua plays, I suggest, a determinative role in identity formation within Hebrews. To see this clearly, one must begin by addressing a misconception about Hebrews' use of certain covenantal categories.

Hebrews and the Conflation of Covenant Inauguration with Covenant Maintenance

Shortly before her untimely death, Susan Haber published a fascinating article on the use of the categories of covenant and sacrificial cult in Hebrews.[3] Haber suggests that the conception of the new covenant found in the epistle is rooted in an anti-Jewish perspective. She especially interrogates the way Hebrews relates Jesus's atoning sacrifice to the inauguration of the new covenant.[4] She concludes that the author conceives of atonement and covenant in ways that are inimical to the Mosaic covenant and the priestly and sacrificial system detailed in the Torah.

---

2. I have argued elsewhere that this conception of time and place correlates well with the author's eschatological identification in Heb. 1:2 of the current period as "these last days." See D. M. Moffitt, "Perseverance, Purity, and Identity: Exploring Hebrews' Eschatological World-view, Ethics, and In-Group Bias," in *Sensitivity to Outsiders: Exploring the Dynamic Relationship between Mission and Ethics in the New Testament and Early Christianity*, ed. J. Kok et al., WUNT 2/364 (Tübingen: Mohr Siebeck, 2014), 357–81.

3. S. Haber, "From Priestly Torah to Christ Cultus: The Re-Vision of Covenant and Cult in Hebrews," *JSNT* 28 (2005): 105–24.

4. I cannot here engage all Haber's arguments. My focus is limited to her central discussion of the relationship between the ritual of covenant inauguration and the maintenance sacrifices as these pertain to Hebrews.

According to Haber, the writer of Hebrews depicts the Mosaic law's "mechanism of atonement through the sacrificial cult" in ways that are "antithetical to the belief in salvation through Christ."[5] Because the author of Hebrews locates the law's essential flaw in its prescribed sacrifices and their limited atoning effects, his "negative portrayal of Judaism in Hebrews may be characterized as a polemic against a competing theology of atonement that threatens the Christological view of expiation from sin."[6]

The basic problem concerns Hebrews' conflation of the covenant ratification ceremony detailed in Exodus 24:1–8 with the account of the tabernacle's inauguration in Numbers 7:1–2 (cf. Exod. 40:9; Lev. 8:10).[7] By blending these events the author is able to collapse the purification of the tabernacle and the atoning sacrifices offered within it into the ritual act of ratifying the covenant depicted in Exodus 24. According to Haber, the rationale for this linkage lies in the writer's belief that Jesus's death is both the event that inaugurates the new covenant and at the same time the fully atoning sacrifice of that covenant. The Pentateuch, that is, presents the Mosaic covenant as first requiring an act of ratification (Exod. 24:1–8) that is then followed by the inauguration of the tabernacle (Num. 7:1–2) and the ongoing priestly ministry and atoning sacrifices. The centrality of Jesus's death in Hebrews, however, requires that the acts of covenant ratification and the sacrificial act that forever purifies and forgives those within that covenant be one and the same event. Jesus's death therefore inaugurates the new covenant and its cult and at the same time serves as the fully sufficient sacrifice that maintains this covenant. In short, covenant inauguration and covenant maintenance are collapsed in Hebrews into the

5. Haber, "Priestly Torah," 107.

6. Haber, "Priestly Torah," 121.

7. One of Haber's arguments emphasizes the distinction between the sprinkling and function of blood in Exod. 24:1–8 and those of oil in Exod. 40:9 and Lev. 8:10, which specify that the tabernacle was consecrated with oil ("Priestly Torah," 110–11). The Pentateuch itself does not explicitly mix blood and consecrating oil in these texts, and Haber is right that Exod. 24:1–8 does not speak of purification or consecration. Her claim that Hebrews conflates Exod. 24:1–8 with Num. 7:1–2 because Numbers does not specify what substance was used to consecrate the tabernacle is, however, not persuasive. That Hebrews has conflated these texts is plausible (though the use of the verb "to sprinkle" rather than "to anoint" in Heb. 9:19 may suggest Lev. 8:10 LXX). That Hebrews only mentions blood and not oil is also clear. That a Second Temple reader might nevertheless infer that Exod. 24:1–8 depicts an act of purification seems a reasonable conclusion, particularly given the role of blood in sacrificial purification. Moreover, in Josephus there is a hint of a notion that the purification both of the tabernacle with all its vessels and of the priests and their vestments required not only oil but also the sprinkled blood of bulls, rams, and goats (*Ant.* 3.204–6). While Exod. 24 is not in the mix here, Josephus's comments about the sprinkling not only of the priests and their vestments but also of the tabernacle and its vessels with blood may be a conflation of Lev. 8:30 (cf. Exod. 29:21) and Lev. 8:10. At the very least, Josephus's logic implies a close association of the sprinkling of blood for the consecration of both the tabernacle and the priests.

death of Jesus.[8] This conflation is then read back into Exodus 24. Hebrews therefore forces the logic of the Mosaic covenant to conform to that of the new covenant as this is revealed in the atoning death of Jesus.[9]

Haber's focus on the relationship between covenant and cult/sacrifice is shrewd and important. She has identified a potential flaw in Hebrews' logic that, if correct, has too often escaped the attention of modern commentators on Hebrews (to say nothing of larger biblical and systematic theological accounts of Jesus's once-for-all sacrifice). To put this concern slightly differently, Haber helpfully gestures toward a significant problem in the sacrificial logic of certain expressions of Christian atonement theology that go largely unnoticed by most Christian exegetes and theologians. Specifically, her argument suggests that as early as the penning of Hebrews some Christian accounts of Jesus's sacrifice deliberately confused and conflated the bloody, ritual act of ratifying the Mosaic covenant with the later acts of purification that inaugurated the covenant's tabernacle and priesthood, and with the bloody sacrificial acts of the Levitical cult that served to maintain the covenant relationship. Already in Hebrews, then, one can see that some forms of early Christian reflection on sacrifice and atonement were essentially anti-Jewish precisely to the extent that they willfully misconstrued the interrelated roles and logic of covenant and sacrifice within the Mosaic economy.

In sum, one key difference Haber identifies in Hebrews between the Mosaic covenant and the new covenant consists in the fact that the new covenant is not only inaugurated with Jesus's death but also perfectly and perpetually maintained by that singular event. The audience can now, therefore, view themselves as members of the new covenant perfectly forgiven and forever purified—in need of no further covenant maintenance because of the once-for-all sacrifice of Jesus's death. Thus, they need no longer look toward Jewish rituals of purification and sacrifices or toward the Jewish communities with whom they share so much for their core identity.

If the preceding analysis correctly identifies Haber's central concern—that Hebrews understands the role of Jesus's death in terms of the singular sacrifice that both inaugurates *and* eternally maintains the new covenant—then her larger point further implies that the early Christian identity that the author of

---

8. It should be noted that Haber does not use the language of covenant maintenance that I adopt here. However, insofar as she highlights Hebrews' correlation of purification by way of sacrificial blood with the act of covenant ratification, she puts her finger on the potential problem in Hebrews of conflating the inauguration of the new covenant with the atoning sacrifice that keeps its members forgiven, pure, and holy. To keep members of the covenant relationship in these states or to restore them to these states is central to the logic of sacrifice. A major rationale for sacrifice, then, is the maintenance of the covenant relationship.

9. Haber states, "In Hebrews the Mosaic covenant *is* a cultic order" ("Priestly Torah," 109).

Hebrews constructs has a radically supersessionist hermeneutic at its center. Hebrews does not abandon the Jewish Scriptures as Marcion later would, but the author has clearly muted and muffled the voice of those Scriptures. His appeal to Jewish Scripture is driven by a preformed Christology and soteriology that seek to apply language and imagery from the Mosaic covenant and its sacrificial system to the event of Jesus's death, but he cares little for the actual meaning or logic of that covenant and those sacrifices as presented in the very Scriptures to which he appeals. Instead, he uses the event of the crucifixion to impose a new pattern on the biblical texts in order to compel them to witness, albeit in an imperfect way, to the new reality effected by Jesus's death.

This brings me to the first major question explored in this chapter: Has Hebrews actually conflated covenant inauguration with covenant maintenance in the way just described? Does the author really reduce Jesus's sacrificial and atoning work to the singular event of the crucifixion, while also imagining that the cross is the event that inaugurates the new covenant? Haber is correct when she notes that Hebrews presents the events of Exodus 24:1–8 as both inaugurating the Mosaic cult and providing some kind of ritual purification (Heb. 9:19–22).[10] She is also right to point out that the author argues that the sacrifices performed according to the law were only effective in obtaining a limited ritual purification (9:13). It stands to reason that a great many Second Temple Jews would take extreme umbrage at the latter remark. Haber is right that Hebrews is polemical.

Does this polemic mean, however, that the author's conceptions of Jesus's covenant, sacrifice, and atonement are antithetical to the conceptions of these categories as they are found in the Pentateuch? Here I think Haber's argument goes awry but in a highly illuminating way. Her misstep is that of many modern interpreters of Hebrews—she assumes that the soteriology of this epistle pivots primarily around the death of Jesus. On this assumption, Haber's case is likely to be right. If Jesus's death works in Hebrews in the ways described above, then the author does appear to hold a reductive account of covenant and sacrifice that cares little for the actual interrelated logics of the Mosaic covenant and Levitical sacrifice as the Pentateuch presents them.

Such an assumption, however, misses the important roles that Jesus's bodily resurrection and ascension play in the author's argument.[11] If he does not reduce sacrifice to the event of slaughter/death but thinks instead in terms of a larger, hierarchically structured process consisting of several necessary

10. See my discussion in n. 7 above.

11. I lay out a detailed case for the presence and importance of Jesus's bodily resurrection and ascension in Hebrews in D. M. Moffitt, *Atonement and the Logic of Resurrection in the Epistle to the Hebrews*, NovTSup 141 (Leiden: Brill, 2011).

elements that culminate in the conveyance of the sacrifice into God's presence, then, particularly given his emphasis on Jesus's ascension, a very different interpretation of Jesus's sacrifice in his epistle becomes possible.

By way of contrast to Haber's claim that Hebrews reflects on the relationship between covenant and sacrifice in ways that are essentially antithetical to Jewish Scripture, practice, and belief, I suggest that the author conceives of the inauguration of the new covenant and Jesus's atoning sacrifice in ways that are in fact analogous to the relationship of the Mosaic covenant and Levitical sacrifices as depicted in the Pentateuch. Hebrews both understands and works with a logic of covenant and sacrifice that distinguishes between the inaugurating covenantal event and the cultic sacrifice and priestly ministry that maintain that covenant relationship. The author, I argue, links Jesus's death with the former and his ascension with the latter. In this way, he respects the larger narrative pattern of the Pentateuch—the exodus, followed by covenant inauguration, followed by the establishment of the tabernacle, priesthood, and sacrifices. His use of this narrative pattern, I argue further, is generative of the author's use of the wilderness generation to shape the identity of his readers. I lay out this argument in the three remaining sections of this chapter, beginning with a discussion of sacrifice.

Sacrifice and Hebrews

In this section I argue that Hebrews' logic of covenant and sacrifice works by way of analogy to the priestly ministry and sacrifices of the Mosaic covenant.[12] Thus, the author thinks of Jesus's sacrifice not as a momentary event that is reducible merely to the crucifixion but as a multistep process that culminates in his entry into God's presence in the heavenly holy of holies, where he presents himself to God and intercedes for his people. These last points are important, for they imply that Jesus's self-presentation and ongoing intercession should be understood as a central aspect of his covenant maintenance work. While Leviticus both speaks at length about what to do for particular sacrifices and offers assurance that these sacrifices are effective, the text provides little explicit reflection on how these sacrifices work. Nevertheless, enough description is given to conclude that Levitical sacrifice consists of an irreducible, hierarchically structured process.[13] In the Levitical system a

12. For a more detailed justification of this point, see chap. 8.
13. See R. E. Gane's excellent discussion and explanation of this larger point in *Cult and Character: Purification Offerings, Day of Atonement, and Theodicy* (Winona Lake, IN: Eisenbrauns, 2005), 3–24.

sacrifice entails a sequence of events that culminate in a priest drawing near to God and conveying the offering into his presence.[14]

When a sacrifice aims to effect atonement, certain elements in this process are more closely linked in the biblical texts with the obtainment of this goal than are others. Sacrificial atonement—forgiveness of sins and/or effecting ritual purification, depending on the sacrifice—occurs with the acts of applying blood to holy places and appurtenances (especially the altars) and with the act of burning part or all of the body of the victim and especially its fat (if required).[15] Thus, the culminating events in the larger process—the elements wherein the atoning goal of the process is achieved—consist in those activities performed by the priests as they draw near to the altars and bring the elements of the sacrifice into God's presence.

All of this implies that the priest's conveyance of the elements of the sacrifice—parts of the body and blood of the victim—to the altars is the effective center of blood sacrifice. The point of such sacrifice, in other words, is to bring the elements of the offering into God's presence. This is how a sacrifice is *offered* to God. It follows, then, that a reduction of blood sacrifice to the act of slaughtering the victim misapprehends what stands at the core of the ritual—drawing near to God and offering him gifts. Offering sacrifice is a central aspect of how one ministers to God. Moreover, in the performing of a sacrifice, benefits such as atonement are achieved both for the worshipers and the cultic spaces.

Leviticus does not, therefore, support the inference that the act of slaughter alone, "bloodshed" in the English sense of the term, either constituted a sacrifice or achieved by itself the atoning goals of atoning sacrifices—forgiveness of sins and/or purification. None of this implies that the slaughter is dispensable for blood sacrifice. Because the blood (i.e., the life) of the victim belongs to God, it is to be given back to God on the altar (cf. Lev. 17:11), and none of it can be withheld. Leviticus indicates, therefore, that when a blood sacrifice is offered, the act of slaughter is a necessary step in the process of transferring the sacrifice to God, but it is neither the sum total of nor the central atoning act in the larger process. This observation likely explains (1) why the slaughter never occurred on any of the Israelite or Jewish altars, (2) why in Leviticus the slaughter was not always performed by a priest, and (3) why killing the victim was never by itself

---

14. Gane succinctly defines "sacrifice" as "a religious ritual in which something of value is ritually transferred to the sacred realm for utilization by the deity" (*Cult and Character*, 16).

15. For more detailed discussion of this point see, e.g., C. A. Eberhart, *The Sacrifice of Jesus: Understanding Atonement Biblically*, Facets (Minneapolis: Fortress, 2011), 85; Gane, *Cult and Character*, esp. 67.

sufficient to procure the atoning benefits that the entire process aimed to obtain.[16]

In sum, the hierarchical structure of the sacrificial process indicates that the atoning benefits of sacrifice are connected with the priestly activities that occurred at the altars as the priests drew near to God and conveyed the material of the sacrifice into his presence.[17] When the process is so understood, one can see how a ritual death/slaughter can be rightly identified as sacrificial while not itself being equivalent to the sacrifice.[18]

If the author of Hebrews failed to grasp these points (as I suspect a great many of us moderns do) or if he intentionally misconstrued sacrifice so as to reduce the larger process merely to the act of slaughter, then, as noted above, an essential element of Haber's argument outlined above is basically proven. Hebrews cares little for what Leviticus actually says and how the sacrifices prescribed there seem to work. The author simply raids Leviticus for useful or evocative images from which he crafts metaphors to make concrete his abstract conception of Jesus's salvific work. The Jewish Scriptures are, to put it bluntly, little more than proof texts for his preformed Christology and soteriology.

However, once the role of Jesus's resurrection and ascension in Hebrews are properly noted, a striking shift of perspective occurs. The author's discussion of Jesus's sacrifice can be seen as emphasizing the very acts of conveyance and presentation that Leviticus places at the center of the ritual process of sacrifice. Just as the Levitical high priests offered the Yom Kippur sacrifices or obtained the atonement that those sacrifices had as their goal not merely by slaughtering a bull and a goat but rather by taking the sacrificial blood into the holy of holies and sprinkling the blood there before God (see esp. Lev. 16:15–16), so Hebrews links Jesus's high-priestly offering with his passing

---

16. The same logic holds for the other elements of the process as well. None of them can stand alone. To quote Gane again, "Like systems in general, rituals are structured hierarchically, with smaller systems constituting wholes embedded in larger systems. At each level, a 'whole possesses distinctive emergent properties—properties not possessed by the parts comprising the whole.' In the Israelite system of rituals the whole is indeed greater than the sum of its parts. A ritual or ritual complex achieves its goal only if it is performed in its entirety, with its activities in the proper order" (*Cult and Character*, 19–20).

17. See, e.g., Ezekiel's emphasis on the priests approaching God and offering him blood and fat in Ezek. 44:15–16.

18. One can speak, in other words, of a sacrificial death (a death that is part of a sacrifice) without confusing that death with the entirety of the sacrifice itself. One might even say that this logic implies that the key to identifying a given death as sacrificial or as part of a sacrifice lies not in the slaughter per se but in what follows—where the body and the blood go next (the altars) and who actually takes them there (the priests). If the elements are brought to an altar by a priest, then the slaughter is part of a sacrifice. If they are not, then the slaughter of an animal is just a slaughter—the kind of thing that happens periodically on the farm.

through the heavens in order to enter into the heavenly holy of holies (e.g., Heb. 8:1–5) and to appear in the presence of God. This is how and where he offered God the sacrifice of himself (9:24–26). For the author, Jesus is at one and the same time the human high priest of Melchizedek's order and the ultimate Yom Kippur offering, but the performance of his high-priestly service and the presentation of his sacrificial offering are not reduced to his death on the cross. In his humanity, the incarnate Son fulfills both the sacrificial and high-priestly Yom Kippur roles when he ascends into the heavenly tabernacle. Jesus's ascension is when and where the elements of his sacrifice—his resurrected body and blood—are presented to the Father.[19]

The author's belief in Jesus's bodily resurrection implies that his claims about Jesus offering the sacrifice of himself before God in the heavenly holy of holies are best understood by way of analogy to the entry of the Levitical high priest into the earthly holy of holies (see Heb. 9:7, 11–12, 24–26; cf. 13:11–12). When the author says that Jesus appeared before God in the heavenly holy of holies to offer his sacrifice (esp. 9:24–26), he means this literally. The proper analogy for understanding the process and meaning of this event is provided in the layout of and service performed in the earthly tabernacle.

If all this is correct, it lends further support to the assumption that Hebrews understands Jesus's atoning sacrifice along the lines of the hierarchically structured process discussed above in Leviticus. From this perspective Jesus's death can rightly be called sacrificial, but it is neither the effective center nor the sum total of his sacrifice (any more than the slaughter of the victim is the effective center or sum total of sacrifice in Leviticus). By analogy to the Levitical Yom Kippur sacrifices, the center of Jesus's sacrifice consists of his bodily entry into the heavenly sanctuary as the high priest who conveys and presents the material of the atoning sacrifice—namely, himself—to God.

I stress these points not only to restate and clarify my position on sacrifice in Leviticus and Hebrews but also to highlight the significance of Jesus's heavenly sacrifice. Here I intend, however, to draw out some further conclusions that depend upon but also move beyond the points just made. The idea that Jesus offers himself to God as a sacrifice in heaven indicates that the author of Hebrews reflects on Jesus in ways that cohere with the logic of Levitical sacrifice. Together with these points, however, it should be noted that his comment in Hebrews 7:25 that Jesus always intercedes for his people as their high priest implies that a concept of covenant maintenance by way of Jesus's high-priestly intercession in the holy of holies is also in play. God's people, as

---

19. My arguments for this claim are set out in Moffitt, *Atonement and the Logic of Resurrection*, esp. 220–85.

the writer says in 2:11, "are being sanctified" (οἱ ἁγιαζόμενοι[20]) and as such remain in need of continual intercession even though they are members of the new covenant community.

Covenant maintenance is among the primary roles of the Levitical sacrificial system.[21] When forgiveness and purification were needed to rectify everyday sins and impurities that could threaten the covenant relationship—that is to say, when atonement needed to be made—Levitical sacrifices were a central element in the attainment of that atonement. This was partly effected by offering sacrifice. Insofar as Yom Kippur served as the major day of forgiveness and purification for the tabernacle and all the people, these goals were partially achieved by presenting the blood of the sacrifices in the holy of holies and, at least in the late Second Temple period, by the high priest's intercession there on behalf of the people.[22] In the case of Jesus, then, the fact that his intercession is ongoing, as he now serves as the great high priest and sacrifice in the heavenly holy of holies, strongly implies that it is precisely by his presence with the Father, where he always intercedes for his people, that he mediates and maintains the new covenant.[23]

20. The English translation tradition's tendency to translate the present participle in terms of a completed state is odd (see, e.g., ESV, KJV, NIV, NRSV, RSV). One typically expects the present tense to depict an action as if it were ongoing.

21. E. P. Sanders makes this point when he writes, "The law provides for means of atonement, and atonement results in . . . maintenance or re-establishment of the covenant relationship" (*Paul and Palestinian Judaism: A Comparison of Patterns of Religion* [Minneapolis: Fortress, 1977], 422). Sacrifice is one of the conditional elements of the covenant. It is given by God partly as a means to deal with sin and impurity, both of which threaten the well-being of the ongoing relationship between God and his people. Maintenance answers one of the central "whys" of Jewish sacrifice. See also the brief discussion in n. 8 above.

22. According to Philo (cf. Josephus, *Ant.* 3.189, 191), the offerings of sacrifice and prayers for the people are among the primary roles of the priests and the high priest in particular (see esp. the evidence and discussion in J. Leonhardt, *Jewish Worship in Philo of Alexandria*, TSAJ 84 [Tübingen: Mohr Siebeck, 2001], 228–33). These roles, it should be noted, cohere well with the concept of covenant maintenance. Josephus is particularly clear that before God's presence would indwell the tabernacle, it was essential to have a high priest who could offer sacrifices and prayers on the people's behalf (esp. *Ant.* 3.189). It is unsurprising, therefore, that the high priest is supposed by Philo to offer incense and prayers when he enters the holy of holies once a year on Yom Kippur (*Legat.* 306; see discussion in Leonhardt, *Jewish Worship*, 128–29). High-priestly intercession in the holy of holies is a given. For further discussion and justification of this claim see D. M. Moffitt, "Jesus as Interceding High Priest and Sacrifice in Hebrews: A Response to Nicholas Moore," *JSNT* 42 (2020): 542–52.

23. It may be objected that one must distinguish between the offering of Jesus's high-priestly sacrifice and his high-priestly intercession. Yet the only time the Jewish high priest could intercede for God's people in the holy of holies would be on Yom Kippur when he was presenting the incense and the sacrificial blood of the bull and the goat. Simply put, there is no high-priestly intercession in the holy of holies apart from the presentation of the Yom Kippur sacrifice. See also the discussion above in n. 22.

One more angle of approach may help clarify this larger relationship between covenant and sacrifice. In the context of the Pentateuch, the Levitical sacrifices would be meaningless, even impossible, outside of the covenant relationship within which they exist. As Exodus and Leviticus present the situation, prior to the offering of the Yom Kippur sacrifice, or any of the other Levitical sacrifices for that matter, the covenant had to be inaugurated, the tabernacle had to be set up, and the priests had to be consecrated. One cannot Yom Kippur oneself into a covenant relationship with God. The inauguration of the covenant relationship comes first.

Moreover, Leviticus 26 makes clear that if the covenant should be fractured by ongoing disobedience, then merely offering Levitical sacrifice will not restore it.[24] When the covenant is broken in this way, the people go into exile and God himself turns against them to discipline them. When the covenant is healthy, the sacrifices contribute to the ongoing maintenance of the covenant relationship—God is present in the sanctuary, and the people can approach him in worship because ongoing forgiveness and purification are available; God and his people live in peace. Yom Kippur and the other feasts and sacrifices exist within the context of the covenant. Their purpose is to maintain the covenant relationship, not to inaugurate it or even restore it. The implication of this logic is plain—one cannot simply offer sacrifice to inaugurate or reinaugurate a covenant relationship should it become fractured in the way Leviticus 26 describes. Exodus 24 describes the unique rituals that inaugurated the Mosaic covenant. In a similar way, Hebrews also knows of a unique event that inaugurated the new covenant—Jesus's death.

Jesus's Death in Hebrews: New Passover and New Covenant Inauguration

What then of the death of Jesus in Hebrews? I argue extensively elsewhere that Jesus's death is linked in Hebrews 9:15–21 with the rituals that ratified or inaugurated the Mosaic covenant and the use of the tabernacle.[25] Nevertheless, in Hebrews, as in the Pentateuch, inauguration and initial purification are prerequisite to the use of the tabernacle and so to the offering of the sacrifices that maintain the covenant. Hebrews interprets inauguration in terms of initial purification, as noted above by Haber, but the basic logic that things

24. So Lev. 26:31, where God declares that when the covenant is broken, he will refuse to smell the aroma of the sacrifices.

25. For my arguments on this point see Moffitt, *Atonement and the Logic of Resurrection*, 289–96.

must first be consecrated and set in order and then sacrifices may be offered is affirmed in Hebrews. As the author says in 9:6–7, everything must first be set up and prepared, and then the priests can enter and minister.[26] There is, however, another way in which the role that Jesus's death plays in Hebrews aligns with the larger narrative of the Pentateuch. In Hebrews 2:14–15, Jesus's death is identified as liberating God's people from their bondage to the fear of death and from the one who wields the power of death—the Devil. This passage, I argue, contains an allusion to Passover.[27]

Hebrews' relative silence regarding Passover is well known. The author explicitly mentions it only once, in 11:28, where he states that Moses performed the Passover and the aspersion of blood by faith so that "the destroyer of the firstborn" would not touch the people of Israel. This "destroyer" (ὁ ὀλεθρεύων) clearly alludes to the strange statement in Exodus 12:23. Exodus 12:23 LXX states that, on account of the Passover blood on the doorposts, the Lord would "not permit the destroyer" (οὐκ ἀφήσει τὸν ὀλεθρεύοντα) to enter the houses of the Israelites and strike them. While throughout the Passover story the Lord himself is the one who strikes the Egyptian firstborn (e.g., Exod. 12:13), here in 12:23 some other agent, the destroyer, is identified as the one who does the smiting.

Hebrews' identification of the audience as part of "the congregation of the firstborn" enrolled in the heavens in Hebrews 12:23, together with the author's earlier comment in 2:14 that Jesus defeated the Devil, the one who holds the power of death, suggest the inference that "the destroyer of the firstborn" in 11:28, who was kept away by the paschal blood that Moses sprinkled, is this same malevolent angelic figure referred to in 2:14. That is to say, given that the destroyer targeted the "firstborn," and given that the audience is among the "congregation of the firstborn," it is hardly a stretch to conclude that the author assumes that the audience's enemy—the Devil—is the very destroyer whom Moses in some sense defeated at the first Passover. If this connection is valid, then the author likely alludes to the exodus, if not the Passover itself, when he speaks in 2:14–16 of Jesus's death defeating the Devil and obtaining liberation from the fear of death.

At least two additional arguments further support this conclusion. First, some Second Temple Jewish traditions clearly identify the destroying agent

26. Hebrews 9:1–5 describes many of the preparations and accoutrements that constituted the sancta of the tabernacle. In 9:6–7 the writer affirms that only after everything was prepared could the priests and high priests enter and perform the sacrifices. Interestingly, Josephus makes similar claims regarding Aaron's high-priestly service in the tabernacle relative to God's coming to dwell there (see *Ant.* 3.188–92, 197–98, 201–3).

27. See chap. 2 of this volume for a more sustained and detailed argument justifying the claims of the next few paragraphs.

of Exodus 12:23 with the malevolent angelic being who wields the power of death and who stands in the heavenly court accusing God's people. Jubilees 49:2, for example, states that "all the forces of Mastema were sent to kill every first-born in the land of Egypt—from the pharaoh's first-born to the first-born of the captive slave-girl at the millstone and to the cattle as well."[28] Throughout Jubilees, it is clear that Prince Mastemah is the chief angelic opponent of God's people. In fact, in Jubilees 48 he is identified as the evil spiritual force who motivates Pharaoh and the Egyptians to oppose Moses and the people. It is only when some of the good angels bind Mastemah for a time that Pharaoh finally relents and allows the people to go. Once Mastemah is again released, however, Pharaoh changes his mind and pursues the people. Thus Jubilees allows the inference that at least some Second Temple Jews conceived of the first Passover not only as liberation from Pharaoh but also, if only in a limited way, as liberation from Mastemah, who was at work in Pharaoh. Moreover, in those passages where Jubilees envisions the eschatological future in which the land is ultimately purified and people's sins and impurities are finally done away with, the text affirms that there will also be no more Satan or evil one who destroys (see Jub. 23:29; cf. 50:5). It appears that Mastemah is the primary figure the text thinks of as a Satan and destroyer who will one day be no more.

Evidence such as this strengthens the plausibility of the idea that Jesus's defeat of the Devil in Hebrews 2:14–16 is conceptually linked with the Passover, when Moses sprinkled blood in order to prevent the Destroyer from harming Israel. Indeed, the notion of the seed of Abraham being delivered from bondage (δουλεία) appears to echo the exodus event (every use of the term δουλεία in Exodus and Deuteronomy in LXX refers to enslavement in Egypt).[29]

A second piece of evidence, however, concerns the remarkable similarity between the narrative logic of the first Passover and the exodus in the Pentateuch, on the one hand, and the actual development of Hebrews' argument, on the other. The point can be illustrated as follows: The first Passover marked the liberation of God's people from their enslavement to Pharaoh in Egypt. Once they were liberated, Moses led the people out of Egypt and into the wilderness, where they journeyed to Sinai, ratified the covenant, inaugurated the tabernacle and sacrifices, and moved toward the promised inheritance, only to fail to attain it at Kadesh.

---

28. Translation from J. C. VanderKam, *The Book of Jubilees*, CSCO 511, Scriptores Aethiopici 88 (Leuven: Peeters, 1989), 315.

29. LXX: Exod. 6:6; 13:3, 14; 20:2; Deut. 5:6; 6:12; 7:8; 8:14; 13:6, 11.

Intriguingly, shortly after discussing Jesus's liberation of his brothers and sisters from the Devil in Hebrews 2, the author draws an explicit analogy between the audience and Israel in the wilderness in Hebrews 3–4. This can hardly be an accident. From the perspective of the kind of pentateuchally shaped narrative laid out above, the author's logic here makes perfect sense. If Jesus's death is being conceived of as a new Passover, then Hebrews' emphasis on the wilderness identity of the audience follows nicely. The audience can and must recognize their current position in space and time as analogous to that of the firstborn who have been freed from their slavery and, like Israel under Moses, are now journeying in the eschatological wilderness.

If all this is more or less correct, Hebrews has made some conflations in the larger pentateuchal story. Passover/exodus and covenant inauguration are all directly linked in Hebrews with Jesus's death. Nothing about this conflation is, however, inherently anti-Jewish. This very linkage has biblical precedent. Jeremiah 31:32, for example, directly connects God's act of taking Israel out of Egypt with his making a covenant with them. The new exodus motif of Jeremiah 31 with its emphasis on liberation from an enslaving power and the making of a new covenant with Israel and Judah are, by Jeremiah's comparison to the Mosaic covenant, tightly bound together, even conflated.[30]

More significantly, though, Hebrews' Yom Kippur analogy—the author's discussion of Jesus's presentation of his atoning sacrifice to the Father and his ongoing high-priestly ministry in the heavenly holy of holies—can be seen to stand at some remove from the event of Jesus's death once the role of Jesus's resurrection and bodily ascension in the homily's logic are recognized. The sequence of Jesus's death, resurrection, and ascension suggests that, to return to Haber's argument discussed above, Hebrews has *not* in fact conflated covenant inauguration with covenant maintenance. Jesus's death in Hebrews is not the sum total of his sacrifice. The author does not confuse the presentation of Jesus's sacrifice or Jesus's intercession for his people with the act that liberates his people and inaugurates the new covenant. On the contrary, if the presentation of Jesus's sacrifice occurs after his resurrection, then Hebrews' location of Jesus's Yom Kippur sacrifice and high-priestly intercession on the other side of that event suggests that the author understands that Jesus's sacrifice is meaningful and necessary *within* the bounds of an already inaugurated covenant relationship. Jesus's offering of his sacrifice

---

30. Interestingly, Tg. Zech. 9:11 links Zech. 9:11's language of the "blood of the covenant" (cf. Heb. 13:20) with Israel's deliverance from Egypt. See J. Marcus's discussion in *The Way of the Lord: Christological Exegesis of the Old Testament in the Gospel of Mark* (Louisville: Westminster John Knox, 1992), 157.

and his high-priestly intercession at God's right hand can therefore be understood to be the means by which he maintains the new covenant relationship inaugurated at his death.

In sum, two significant ways that Hebrews conceives of Jesus's death are as the event that liberated God's people from slavery to their spiritual foe, the Devil (2:14–15), and as the act that inaugurated the new covenant between them and God (9:15–18). After this liberating and inaugurating work, however, Jesus rose from the dead and ascended into the highest heaven as the new covenant's great high priest. There he performs his high-priestly service in God's presence, being in himself both high priest and sacrifice. This ministry consists, then, both of the presentation of his atoning sacrifice to the Father—something that is effectively a perpetual reality by virtue of his remaining in the Father's presence—and of his perpetual intercession there for his people.

If the preceding points are granted, it follows that the author thinks about the new covenant and its cult and sacrifice in ways that are strikingly analogous to both the Pentateuch's logic of covenant and cult and its larger narrative arc. In Hebrews, as in the Pentateuch, God liberates his people and inaugurates a covenant with them. That covenant is then partly maintained by way of sacrifice and high-priestly intercession. But how might all of this relate to the question of identity in Hebrews? I turn next to address this question.

Hebrews' Wilderness Identity: Living between Jesus's Ascension and Return

The preceding argument suggests a plausible rationale for why the author of Hebrews compares his readers with the exodus generation who were led into the wilderness. As those whom Jesus has freed from slavery and brought into the new covenant that he inaugurated, they now await his return, when he will bring them fully into their inheritance (cf. Heb. 9:28). The author likens this eschatological situation to Israel in the wilderness.

The wilderness analogy developed does not, then, merely draw upon Israel's story as a moral example. Rather, the author applies this element of the Pentateuch's narrative to his readers because, in addition to the other elements of that larger narrative discussed above, they do not yet possess the fullness of the inheritance God has promised them. They are, like Israel at the edge of their promised inheritance, waiting to enter it.[31]

31. Curiously, this perspective allows another aspect of the analogy to emerge—Israel waiting to hear the report of the spies. According to Num. 13:2 LXX, each of those who was sent to spy out the promised land was a "leader" (Greek: ἀρχηγός) in his tribe (the relevant phrase reads "each a leader from among them"; Greek: πάντα ἀρχηγὸν ἐξ αὐτῶν). Moreover, one of

As Ernst Käsemann noted, the motif of God's people in the wilderness is not limited to Hebrews 3–4 but forms one of the central themes in the epistle.[32] The author's use of the motif of the new covenant, his references to the inauguration of that covenant and of the tabernacle, and the contrast between Sinai and Zion all make good sense on the proposal that the author of Hebrews intentionally works with a narrative about Jesus and his people that is structured by important portions of the Pentateuch, a narrative that implies that the new covenant people are now in the wilderness.

As argued with respect to Passover and covenant inauguration above, Hebrews does conflate elements of the Pentateuch's depiction of the wilderness experience. The author not only likens his readers to Israel about to go into the land but also compares them to the congregation of Israel encamped at Sinai awaiting Moses's return. Thus, in Hebrews 12 the audience is to envision themselves as part of the congregation of the firstborn encamped around Zion. They too have witnessed the signs and wonders of God's liberation (cf. 2:4). They have the divine Spirit present among them. They can, because of the new covenant, rightly worship the Father through the ministry of their high priest precisely because everything has now been set in order and properly prepared for worship.

Now, however, they must wait patiently for their high priest to conclude his session in the heavenly holy of holies and return to bring salvation. Then they, together with all who have gone before them, will finally and fully enter their long-awaited inheritance. All this implies that the wilderness identity of God's people in Hebrews is closely associated with the covenant-inaugurating death of Jesus and the covenant-maintaining high-priestly work made possible by the ascension of Jesus. Specifically, Hebrews' wilderness identity is correlated with the liberation and inauguration of the new covenant made possible by Jesus's death, on the one hand, and with the time of waiting while Jesus performs his high-priestly ministry in the heavenly holy of holies—the time between his ascension and his return—on the other.

those spies was Joshua (Ἰησοῦς, "Jesus"). By locating his readers in the wilderness, the author of Hebrews encourages them to view themselves as poised at the edge of the promised inheritance waiting for their ἀρχηγός (see Heb. 2:10; 12:2), their Ἰησοῦς, to return (9:28; 10:35–37) and lead them into their inheritance.

32. E. Käsemann, The Wandering People of God: An Investigation of the Letter to the Hebrews, trans. R. A. Harrisville and I. L. Sandberg (Minneapolis: Augsburg, 1984). Notably, the argument advanced here stresses the people of God waiting in the wilderness, not wandering there. It seems that Hebrews does not precisely link the new covenant people with Israel's time of wandering in the wilderness. Rather, the author locates them earlier in the story to a point before Israel disobeyed. On Hebrews' own logic, to abandon the community leads to loss of one's inheritance. This is what would put one into a position like those at Kadesh, who disobeyed God's command to go into the land.

Conclusion

The preceding arguments imply that the author of Hebrews developed a pervasive wilderness identity in conjunction with a conception of Jesus's salvific work that recognizes a distinction between his Passover-like and covenant-inaugurating death and his ongoing high-priestly work of covenant maintenance in the heavenly tabernacle. Indeed, this perpetual high-priestly work of covenant maintenance is likely to be among the generative impulses for the wilderness identity in Hebrews. This deduction follows from the author's logic that so long as Jesus remains in the heavenly holy of holies interceding for his people before God, they must wait for him to return to them. Only when their high priest returns will they enter their long-awaited inheritance.

Notably, then, the ultimate goal that both the Pentateuch and Hebrews point toward is the same—the entry of God's people into their promised inheritance. As in the Pentateuch, God's new covenant people are in the position of having been decisively liberated from their former enslavement, but they nevertheless remain in some sense outside their inheritance. Thus, in pentateuchal terms, they are waiting in the wilderness. While they wait, however, they can be assured that their high priest is perpetually maintaining the covenant relationship.[33]

This last point is crucial for Hebrews' understanding of how to live as wilderness people. Because Jesus currently maintains the covenant that he mediates, the people of this covenant can always go to him in times of need. While they wait in the wilderness, they are reminded that they have a high priest who makes atonement for them and who can help them in times of need (2:17–18). They are exhorted during this time to approach God's throne boldly in the midst of their times of testing (4:16). Jesus can always atone for his people. If, however, they turn away from Jesus, they risk losing the very inheritance they have been promised. In short, the author of Hebrews appeals to the larger narrative of the Pentateuch partly as a way of providing his readers with the categories and the identity that they need to faithfully persevere in their present situation. They have been liberated from their slavery, and they are members of the new covenant. They may now be in the eschatological wilderness. But the correlate of this state affairs is that their high priest is presently with the Father interceding for them. If they patiently endure while they wait for him to return, they will ultimately enter fully into the inheritance God has promised them.

---

33. I discuss this feature of Hebrews in more detail in chaps. 8 and 9.

4

Isaiah 53, Hebrews,
and Covenant Renewal

A handful of scholars have argued for broad, thematic connections between Hebrews and the so-called suffering servant figure of Deutero-Isaiah.[1] In general, however, the kinds of links that have been suggested (e.g., the self-sacrifice of both figures,[2] their prophetic roles,[3] the pattern of exaltation followed by humiliation that begins both Isa. 52:13–53:12 and Hebrews[4]) have not been widely embraced by modern commentators on Hebrews. Isaiah is quoted in Hebrews at least once,[5] and a handful of allusions to Isaiah

---

1. O. Cullman's discussion of Hebrews' high-priestly Christology explores possible conceptual connections between the idea and that of the suffering servant (*The Christology of the New Testament*, trans. S. C. Guthrie and C. A. M. Hall, rev. ed. [Philadelphia: Westminster, 1963], 83, 91–107). J. Schaefer picks up and further develops some of Cullman's points, while also arguing for even more thematic connections in Hebrews to the suffering servant figure ("The Relationship between Priestly and Servant Messianism in the Epistle to the Hebrews," *CBQ* 30 [1968]: 359–85).

2. Cullman especially emphasizes this (*Christology of the New Testament*, 91). He also sees a point of contact with the idea that Jesus mediates the new covenant (100). It seems to me he is on much firmer ground on this latter point (see also n. 8 below).

3. Schaefer, "Relationship between Priestly and Servant Messianism," esp. 384–85. Schaefer's bigger argument is that the servant ideas Hebrews invokes are subsumed within the author's more determinative high-priestly Christology.

4. J. C. McCollough notes this similarity ("Isaiah in Hebrews," in *Isaiah in the New Testament*, ed. S. Moyise and M. J. J. Menken, The New Testament and the Scriptures of Israel [London: T&T Clark, 2005], 159–73, here 170).

5. Isaiah 8:18 is quoted in Heb. 2:13b ("Behold I and the children God has given me"). The preceding clause in Heb. 2:13a ("I will put trust in him") is probably from Isa. 8:17. The division

are scattered throughout the homily.[6] But the facts that Hebrews only invokes Isaiah's servant material once (in Heb. 9:28)[7] and that arguments for a broader influence of Isaiah's servant material tend to rely on theological and/or tenuous historical reconstructions help explain why so few have found larger thematic links between Hebrews and Isaiah's servant material persuasive.

There is, however, something to the insights of those who have seen larger thematic points of contact between Hebrews and Isaiah's servant figure. Oscar Cullman perceived a link between the servant's death and the renewal of covenant relationship and suggested that this conceptual connection informed Hebrews' argument.[8] While the Isaianic servant died an atoning death to restore the covenant, Cullman argues that Hebrews further develops servant ideas by linking them with the high-priestly sacrifice of Jesus's death. This sacrifice was the means of bringing about the new covenant.

Cullman's insight that Jesus's death is related in Hebrews to the restoration of a covenant relationship in a way that reflects the death of the servant is essentially correct. However, he is wrong to identify the crucifixion as Jesus's high-priestly sacrifice. I argue instead that, in keeping with some other Second Temple Jewish evidence such as 2 Maccabees, Hebrews does not conflate the reconciliation that results from the singular suffering of the servant on behalf of God's people with the Mosaic covenant's normal means of atonement between God and his people—Levitical sacrifice. Rather, the author recognizes that Jesus's vicarious suffering and death, like those of the servant, have a special *extra-sacrificial* role to play in the dynamics of God's covenant relationship with his people. The servant's vicarious death reboots the covenant relationship when it is so broken that no sacrifices can be offered.

---

created between Heb. 2:13a and b by the phrase "and again" could, however, suggest that the author is drawing from different sources here. Notably, similar wording to 2:13a occurs in Isa. 12:2 and in 2 Sam. 2:23. The contexts of both those verses align well with the preceding citation of Ps. 21:23 LXX in Heb. 2:12—the celebration of God's deliverance.

6. For example, an allusion to Isa. 26:20 appears to be combined with the citation of Hab. 2:3–4 in Heb. 10:37–38. In Heb. 13:20 the author uses language drawn from Isa. 63:11. For a discussion of other possible allusions, see McCollough, "Isaiah in Hebrews."

7. Hebrews 9:28 speaks of Christ being offered once "to bear the sins of many." O. Hofius is surely correct to claim that "there can be no doubt that Isaiah 53:12cα LXX . . . has been taken up here" ("The Fourth Servant Song in the New Testament Letters," in *The Suffering Servant: Isaiah 53 in Jewish and Christian Sources*, ed. B. Janowski and P. Stuhlmacher, trans. D. P. Bailey [Grand Rapids: Eerdmans, 2004], 163–88, here 184).

8. Cullman, *Christology of the New Testament*, 55, 100. Cullman also observed that Hebrews' emphasis on Jesus's present intercession for his people "is Christologically important and ought to be given a more central place also in systematic theology than is usually the case" (102–3). He is absolutely correct on this point, which is still in need of being taken more seriously in much Christian theological reflection.

The servant's role, in other words, is to restore the covenant relationship so that the relationship is healed and sacrificial ministry may resume. Because of the servant's vicarious death, God's momentary anger against his people for breaking his covenant turns to mercy. This turning makes it again possible to offer sacrifices to God. Hebrews understands this distinction between covenant renewal and regular priestly ministry and sacrifice (the latter being significant aspects of covenant maintenance). The author uses the distinction to indicate ways in which the suffering, death, resurrection, and ascension of Jesus all contribute to his siblings' salvation.[9]

Four Central Assumptions

Four important assumptions that inform the following argument require brief explanations. First, I work with the hypothesis that the suffering servant figure of Isaiah represents a divinely ordained means for restoring the covenant relationship when it has become strained to the point that the covenant curses fall upon the people.[10] In addition to confession and repentance, passages such as Isaiah 53 suggest that a certain kind of vicarious suffering, even death, can result in a restored covenantal relationship.[11] God has appointed the servant to suffer vicariously so that his covenant people are not completely destroyed.[12] By bearing the guilt and sin of "many" and eliminating these

9. Schaefer's identifications of other possible thematic points of contact between Hebrews' Christology and the Isaianic servant texts are worthy of more thorough investigation. Exact verbal links are not strong, but thematic ones such as Jesus's sinlessness, prophetic role, and exaltation after death are intriguing.

10. M. Zehnder notes that the servant figure plays "a crucial role in the (re)establishment of the covenant relationship between the Lord and his people" ("The Enigmatic Figure of the 'Servant of the Lord': Observations on the Relationship between the 'Servant of the Lord' in Isaiah 40–55 and Other Salvific Figures in the Hebrew Bible," in *New Studies in the Book of Isaiah: Essays in Honor of Hallvard Hagelia*, ed. M. Zehnder, Perspectives on Hebrew Scriptures and Its Contexts 21 [Piscataway, NJ: Gorgias, 2014], 231–82, here 246).

11. In Isa. 54 God declares that his brief turning away from his people in anger has passed as he turns again to them in mercy and compassion (esp. 54:7–8). He promises in v. 10 that his "covenant of peace" (LXX: ἡ διαθήκη τῆς εἰρήνης) with his people will never be removed (see the similar idea in 55:3, which speaks about an "everlasting covenant" with reference to God's love for David).

12. In addition to the explicit covenant language of Isa. 54:10 and 55:3, W. J. Dumbrell ("The Role of the Servant in Isaiah 40–55," *Reformed Theological Review* 48 [1989]: 105–13) notes that a number of motifs in Isa. 54–55 (e.g., a barren woman having many children, God as the Holy One and husband of Israel, God as redeemer, God's mercy/ḥesed, a reference to Noah, the mention of David) recall language and themes related to the Noahic, Abrahamic, Sinaitic, and Davidic covenants (111–12). The density and variety of these covenant motifs directly following Isa. 52:13–53:12 indicate "the Servant's instrumentality in bringing about the consummation of all previous covenants in a new covenant" (111). He rightly concludes,

problems, the normal covenantal means of dealing with sin and impurity—temple sacrifices—can be reinstituted.[13]

This last conclusion is further supported by the following three facts: (1) The Isaianic servant, who is described at points as being given as a covenant, explicitly restores God's people in Isaiah 42:7 and in 49:5–6, 9–12; (2) these ideas of covenant restoration are embedded in Deutero-Isaiah's new exodus themes, which describe the liberation from Babylon with language and imagery drawn from the exodus from Egypt[14]—that is to say, the Isaianic servant plays a central role in the reconciliation of God and his covenant people because they are in exile and so are experiencing God's anger and the covenant curses; (3) the suffering and death of the servant in Isaiah 52:13–53:12 are part of the means by which the covenant curses are reversed and the relationship is restored to health. The servant's vicarious death contributes to the turning of God's anger to mercy (54:7–8).

Second, I assume that the servant in Isaiah does not function in 52:13–53:12 as some kind of cultic sacrifice or priestly figure.[15] This is obviously a contested point. Some argue that the passage contains numerous cultic allusions.[16] The

---

"The logic of the placement of chapters 54 and 55 suggests that all this has been achieved by the suffering and death of Yahweh's Servant (Is. 53)" (113).

13. These claims naturally entangle one in numerous thorny questions surrounding the original meaning of the servant material and of Deutero-Isaiah. These are not the main concern of this essay. Whatever the original intent and form of Isaiah's servant material, when one reads Isa. 40–55 in its final form it seems natural to identify the amazing blessings of chaps. 54–55 with the promised restoration of God's people from exile/new exodus. The fact that these blessings with their rich covenantal overtones (see n. 11) follow the description of the servant's suffering and death in Isa. 53 suggests that they directly result from the servant fulfilling the purpose for which he was called and chosen, a purpose that includes his terrible suffering and death on account of others' guilt and sins. For a robust defense of the notion that Isa. 53 does, on its own terms, envision a righteous person bearing others' sins and then suffering and dying in their place, see B. Janowski, "He Bore Our Sins: Isaiah 53 and the Drama of Taking Another's Place," in *The Suffering Servant: Isaiah 53 in Jewish and Christian Sources*, ed. B. Janowski and P. Stuhlmacher, trans. D. P. Bailey (Grand Rapids: Eerdmans, 2004), 48–74.

14. Many recognize this. See, for example, B. W. Anderson, "Exodus Typology in Second Isaiah," in *Israel's Prophetic Heritage: Essays in Honor of James Muilenburg*, ed. B. W. Anderson and W. Harrelson (London: SCM, 1962), 177–95; G. P. Hugenberger, "The Servant of the Lord in the 'Servant Songs' of Isaiah: A Second Moses Figure," in *The Lord's Anointed: Interpretation of Old Testament Messianic Texts*, ed. P. E. Satterthwaite, R. S. Hess, and G. J. Wenham (Grand Rapids: Baker, 1995), 105–39.

15. See esp. H. G. Reventlow, "Basic Issues in the Interpretation of Isaiah 53," in *Jesus and the Suffering Servant: Isaiah 53 and Christian Origins*, ed. W. H. Bellinger (Harrisburg, PA: Trinity, 1998), 23–38.

16. E.g., F. S. Thielman, "The Atonement," in *Central Themes in Biblical Theology: Mapping Unity in Diversity*, ed. S. J. Hafemann and P. R. House (Downers Grove, IL: InterVarsity, 2007), 102–27, here 107–8. J. D. G. Dunn thinks the passage "is studded with sacrificial terminology and imagery, and the role of the Servant cannot fully be understood apart from the sacrificial

language of the servant "sprinkling" (נזה) many nations in Isaiah 52:15 is sometimes taken to denote a priestly or sacrificial act.[17] This seems unlikely, however. While the verb is commonly used in the Pentateuch for acts of sprinkling substances such as blood, water, or oil on objects or people to purify them, it is also used twice in non-cultic contexts to refer to blood being spattered. In 2 Kings 9:33 Jezebel's blood spatters the wall and horses, while in Isaiah 63:3 the garments of the one who comes from Edom are spattered with the blood of those upon whom he trampled. No priestly or sacrificial ideas are detectable in these passages. Moreover, Isaiah 52:15 gives no indication regarding what substance is sprinkled, as is typical of the verb's use in cultic contexts. LXX seems to be aware of these difficulties and apparently renders the verb with the idea of "marveling/amazement" (θαυμάζω).[18] The servant does not sprinkle something on the nations, he "startles" or "amazes" them. The later targum of Isaiah takes the clause to refer to the servant "scattering" (בדר) the nations (Tg. Isa. 52:15).[19]

Be that as it may, the other evidence in the near context often adduced to support a cultic meaning for "sprinkling" in Isaiah 52:15 does not definitively require a sacrificial interpretation of either the servant or his role. Thus, while some claim that the depiction in Isaiah 53:7 of the servant being afflicted and led like a lamb to the slaughter implies a sacrifice, there is nothing obviously cultic or sacrificial here. The Hebrew verbs used to describe the various wounds and blows the servant suffers in 53:5, 7 are not cultic.[20] Neither the

---

background of his death" ("Paul's Understanding of the Death of Jesus as a Sacrifice," in *Sacrifice and Redemption: Durham Essays in Theology*, ed. S. W. Sykes [Cambridge: Cambridge University Press, 1991], 35–56, here 43).

17. S. G. Dempster suggests that the verb might allude to the Day of Atonement ritual of sprinkling blood in the sancta ("The Servant of the Lord," in Hafemann and House, *Central Themes in Biblical Theology*, 158). J. J. Williams argues that sprinkling intends to refer to "the sacrificial death of the servant" (*Maccabean Martyr Traditions in Paul's Theology of Atonement: Did Martyr Theology Shape Paul's Conception of Jesus's Death?* [Eugene, OR: Wipf & Stock, 2010], 78). Notably, however, the verb is never used in the MT to describe or represent the slaughter of sacrificial victims. When the verb is used in close connection with someone's death (2 Kings 9:33; Isa. 63:3), it is clear that no sacrificial ideas are being invoked.

18. Assuming the translator's Hebrew *Vorlage* was the same as the MT here, the choice of θαυμάζω suggests the translator saw no reasons in the larger context to link the verb with a priestly or sacrificial act.

19. The targum takes the act of sprinkling metaphorically, such that now the nations themselves are described in terms of being scattered like liquid would be sprinkled (see W. A. Tooman, "The Servant-Messiah and the Messiah's Servants in Targum Jonathan Isaiah," in *Isaiah's Servants in Early Judaism and Christianity: The Isaian Servant and the Exegetical Formation of Community Identity*, ed. M. A. Lyons and J. Stromberg, WUNT 2/554 [Tübingen: Mohr Siebeck, 2021], 318–36, here 322n21).

20. See the discussion in Janowski, "He Bore Our Sins," 67–68.

Hebrew nor the Greek nouns denoting "slaughter" (טבח, MT; σφαγή, LXX) in 53:7 are used with reference to Levitical sacrifices in either MT or LXX.[21] The very next line of verse 7 compares the servant to a sheep before its shearers. Sheep were not taken to the temple to be sheared. The language of 53:7 suggests a pastoral image, not a sacrificial one—this is the kind of thing a shepherd does with sheep. Two other pieces of evidence need to be briefly addressed: the use of the word אשם in 53:10 and the common assumption that Levitical sacrifice involved vicarious substitution.

Taking the last point first, space does not allow for a detailed discussion of the relevant evidence. Some argue that the vicarious suffering and death of the servant are sacrificial because substitutionary death stands at the heart of Levitical sacrifice.[22] A number of related issues are germane (e.g., the function of hand laying, the question of whether transferal of sins was part of Levitical sacrifice, the role of the so-called scapegoat on the Day of Atonement).[23] This much is clear: animals given to God as gifts at the temple were to be "unblemished" (תמים, e.g., Lev. 1:3; 3:1; 4:3). They were not abused or killed in a way that included disfigurement or suffering because this would make them unfit to be given as gifts to God. Levitical sacrifices are also never described as objects of God's wrath. Additionally, the one animal that clearly has sins placed upon it and then bears those sins (the scapegoat; Lev. 16:21–22) goes away from God's presence—an important distinction between this animal and all the other animals offered as sacrifices, which are taken into God's presence.[24] All of these points suggest it is a mistake to assume vicarious and penal ideas attached to the animals given to God as sacrifices.

The word אשם in Isaiah 53:10 often denotes a sacrifice. This is the word used in Leviticus for the so-called guilt offering (e.g., Lev. 5:15–19). As with

21. The Hebrew cognate verb (טבח) is also not used in Levitical contexts for sacrificial slaughter, though it is used for slaughtering animals in other contexts (e.g., Gen. 43:16; Exod. 21:37; Deut. 28:31). The Greek cognate verb (σφάζω) is used in LXX for sacrificial and nonsacrificial slaughter.

22. Thielman identifies these ideas as part of the guilt offering and speculates that they may be in play in Isa. 53 ("Atonement," 107–8).

23. My own detailed study of Jewish sacrifice, which has not yet been published, leads me to agree with those who argue that, apart from the scapegoat ritual, hand laying does not imply either substitution or the transferal of sins. See especially D. P. Wright, "The Gesture of Hand Placement in the Hebrew Bible and in Hittite Literature," *Journal of the American Oriental Society* 106, no. 3 (1986): 433–46.

24. The scapegoat carries sins away from God and the people, thereby eliminating them. C. A. Eberhart notes, "While sacrificial rituals are characterized by a gradual movement toward the sanctuary, . . . the dynamics of elimination rituals are in each case directed away from the human habitat and toward uncultivated territory" (*The Sacrifice of Jesus: Understanding Atonement Biblically*, Facets [Minneapolis: Fortress, 2011], 91).

the term "sprinkle" in Isaiah 52:15, however, this word is also used outside of cultic contexts, where it refers not to a guilt offering but to being guilty or to eliminating guilt (e.g., Gen. 26:10; 42:21; 2 Chron. 19:10 Isa. 24:6). Notions of sinning or trespassing are closely associated with the idea that one is guilty. This is significant because the sins/guilt of others are said to be placed upon the servant figure (Isa. 53:6, 11). Rather than imagining God offering the servant as a sacrifice (a guilt offering), the point seems to be that God planned to eliminate the guilt of the people that was placed upon the servant by having the servant take the guilt and die in the place of the guilty.[25] This is a reconciling act that removes the guilt, but it is not a sacrificial one in terms of the Levitical cult.[26]

My third major assumption concerns the role of sacrifice within the Mosaic covenant relationship. I assume that regular Levitical sacrifice and temple worship function as central means whereby the covenant relationship is *maintained*. These are realities that make sense and work *within* the context of the covenant, not outside of it.

Two pieces of evidence support this third assumption. First, Levitical sacrifice as described in the Pentateuch at the tabernacle and later at the temple makes no sense outside the context of the covenant. According to the Pentateuch, the covenant is established first as the appropriate context within which these realities exist and function. The covenant is inaugurated before the tabernacle is built and before any of the priests are even ordained. The tabernacle, Levitical priests, and Levitical sacrifices are presented in the Pentateuch

---

25. See especially the discussion of Janowski ("He Bore Our Sins," 65–70), whose account I am following here. Those who think the idea of the guilt offering is in play here tend to link this with the sprinkling of Isa. 52:15. This makes little sense, however. There is a blood ritual in the guilt offering. According to Lev. 7:2, the blood is tossed (not sprinkled) around the sides of the outer altar. The guilt offering that forms the final part of the purification of a skin disease involves a priest applying some of the blood of the offering to the right ear, right thumb, and right big toe of the person being purified (14:14). Again, however, the blood is not sprinkled on the person (there is a sprinkling ritual earlier in the process, but this is not part of the guilt offering). Sacrificial ideas simply do not make sense in the context of Isa. 52:13–53:12.

26. C. Breytenbach rightly argues that Isa. 52:13–53:12 contains a notion of a vicarious death bringing reconciliation without concepts of cultic sacrifice being present (*Versöhnung: Eine Studie zur paulinischen Soteriologie*, WMANT 60 [Neurkirchen-Vluyn: Neukirchener Verlag, 1989], 212–15). Similarly, J. A. Groves notes both that the idea of atonement is not limited to sacrificial contexts and that the servant is raised up to do a new thing (suffer vicariously) relative to the function of atoning sacrifices within the Levitical cult ("Atonement in Isaiah 53," in *The Glory of the Atonement: Biblical, Historical, and Practical Perspectives*, ed. C. E. Hill and F. A. James III [Downers Grove, IL: InterVarsity, 2004], 61–89). Curiously, Groves goes on to refer to the servant as a sacrifice (87). He also argues that Isaiah rejects the Levitical cult. Whether or not this is right with respect to Isaiah, in biblical-canonical and historical terms, the return of the exiles to Jerusalem correlated not with the rejection of the cult but with the restoration of the temple and the sacrifices.

as realities that come after the establishment of the Mosaic covenant. Only after these are all set up does regular, Levitical sacrifice commence.

Second, some of the sacrifices are explicitly given for the purpose of solving problems—sin and certain kinds of physical impurities—that jeopardize the relationship between God and his covenant people. These sins and impurities need to be remedied so that the relationship is not threatened. If not corrected, these problems can lead to God's wrath breaking out against the people, the people being unable to approach or dwell near God's presence, and even God's presence departing from his earthly house (the tabernacle/temple). Sacrifice is one of the ways in which the problems that can cause these results are fixed. Significantly, however, when the covenant relationship becomes so damaged that the curses of the covenant fall upon the people, the people lose the ability to offer sacrifices, not least because *God will no longer accept them*. This point is clear in Leviticus 26:31, where God says that he will refuse to smell the odor of the people's sacrifices. Even if sacrifices were to be offered, they would not be accepted by God. Moreover, when the temple itself is defiled or even destroyed, it becomes impossible to offer sacrifices to God.[27]

This last situation is the very one that the servant is raised up to address. The depiction of the servant's suffering and the renewal effected by the servant *do not*, in other words, provide a model of covenant restoration that is sacrificial. Rather, the Isaianic servant serves as the means of restoration needed *precisely when sacrifice is impossible* because the covenant is in breach. When the curses of the covenant have fallen upon the nation, no amount of cultic sacrifice will fix the situation because God will refuse to accept them. Indeed, when the people are in exile and Jerusalem lies in ruins, no sacrifices can even be offered.

My fourth assumption follows from the preceding points and is particularly significant for the following discussion of 2 Maccabees. I assume that the adjectives "sacrificial," "atoning," "reconciling," and "salvific" are not necessarily synonymous. The ease with which some use these terms either interchangeably or as near synonyms, especially with respect to certain discussions around a so-called martyr theology in Second Temple Jewish thought, contributes to confusion when trying to think through questions related to the servant's vicarious death and/or the deaths of the martyrs in 2 Maccabees.[28] These deaths can be envisioned as salvific, especially in the sense of recon-

---

27. Whatever one thinks about M. Noth's larger theory about the Deuteronomist and Deuteronomic History, he rightly drew attention to the importance of these covenantal dynamics, especially in the postexilic period. For the English edition of Noth's earlier German work on the topic (originally published in 1943) see M. Noth, *The Deuteronomistic History*, 2nd ed., JSOTSup 15 (Sheffield: JSOT, 1991).

28. See, for example, J. J. Williams, *Maccabean Martyr Traditions*, esp. 72–84.

ciling, without necessarily being understood as sacrificial.[29] Moreover, given the range of meanings associated with the term "atonement,"[30] it should be clear that the term can rightly be used outside of sacrificial contexts to refer to reconciliation within a relationship. The servant's death in Isaiah 53 is atoning in this sense, but it is not atoning in sacrificial terms.

Before considering Hebrews, a short discussion of 2 Maccabees is in order because, as I argue below, the covenantal logic of this text works along the lines just detailed, and this text offers an instructive example of intertextual engagement with Isaiah 53 that illustrates the points just made. As such, this text provides significant evidence for how the Isaianic servant could be understood in relation to the concerns of covenant and sacrifice in the Second Temple period.

The Martyrs and the Deuteronomic Logic of 2 Maccabees

The text known as 2 Maccabees presents itself as an epitome of a larger work by Jason of Cyrene (2 Macc. 2:19–32). In the course of condensing Jason's account, the epitomist crafts a narrative that traces the covenantal dynamics of blessing and curse often referred to in modern scholarship as the Deuteronomic history.[31] Hellenistic influence on 2 Maccabees cannot be doubted, but at the heart of its narrative lies the distinctively Jewish, covenantal pattern laid out in texts such as Leviticus 26 and Deuteronomy 28–30: blessings for obedience and cursing for disobedience.[32] God protects and blesses Jerusalem, his temple, and his people when they are obedient to his law. When his people disobey his law, he is justly provoked to anger. God expresses this anger by removing his protection from the city, temple, and nation.[33] In pentateuchal

---

29. A number of scholars, especially those who recognize the influence of Greco-Roman ideas in the accounts of the Maccabean martyrs in 2 Macc., have rightly seen that Jewish cultic categories, such as blood purification, are not in play in 2 Macc. (esp. S. K. Williams, *Jesus' Death as Saving Event: The Background and Origin of a Concept*, Harvard Dissertations in Religion 2 [Missoula: Scholars Press, 1975], esp. 76–90; and D. Seeley, *The Noble Death: Graeco-Roman Martyrology and Paul's Concept of Salvation*, JSNTS 28 [Sheffield: JSOT Press, 1990], 87–91). The situation is different in the later text known as 4 Macc.

30. See chap. 1 of this volume for a brief discussion of the history and meaning of this language.

31. D. A. deSilva comments that 2 Macc. seeks "to demonstrate the ongoing legitimacy of Deuteronomy's philosophy of history as . . . traced out in recent events" (*Introducing the Apocrypha: Message, Context, and Significance* [Grand Rapids: Baker Academic, 2002], 266).

32. See esp. J. W. van Henten, "Jewish Martyrdom and Jesus' Death," in *Deutungen des Todes Jesu im Neuen Testament*, 2nd ed., ed. J. Frey and J. Schröter, UTB 2953 (Tübingen: Mohr Siebeck, 2012), 139–68.

33. R. Doran, concluding his literary analysis of 2 Macc., notes that his most important finding is the presence of "the Deuteronomic theme that the invincible God of the Jews protects

terms, this latter state names a situation in which, even if sacrifices could be offered, God would not accept them (Lev. 26:31). Because the covenant is in breach and the curses of the covenant have fallen on the people, sacrifices cannot be offered and the relationship cannot be brought back to a healthy state so that the people can again commune with their God and enjoy the blessings of the covenant. Isaiah speaks of a means for restoring the covenant—the suffering and death of the servant. This, I argue, is significant for understanding how the martyrs contribute to the restoration of sacrifices in 2 Maccabees.

Second Maccabees begins with two letters urging the celebration of the date marking the recent repurification of the temple. These letters are rich with references to covenant motifs, God's salvation, and the restoration of the sacrificial cult at the temple in Jerusalem as a result of the revolt led by Judas Maccabeus. The epitome begins in 3:1, with the narrator's statement that Jerusalem was at peace and the law was being observed. Then follows the story of the gentile Heliodorus being repulsed by angels when he tried to enter the temple. In chapter 4 the situation changes when Jason becomes the high priest by way of bribery. The epitomist notes in 4:13–17 that the neglect of the sacrifices and the turning of the people from God's law led to disaster. Thus, in 5:15–20 Antiochus Epiphanes is able to enter the temple and plunder it. Antiochus was not repulsed like Heliodorus because the LORD was angry with his people on account of their disobedience. This anger is expressed not only by allowing the temple to be defiled but also by the subsequent persecution that falls on the Jewish people more generally (6:1–11).

The narrator describes all this in terms of God's punishment on account of the people's sin (2 Macc. 6:12–17). Then follows the stories of the faithful martyrs—Eleazar and the seven brothers with their mother (6:18–7:42). In chapter 8 the epitomist describes the beginning of the revolt led by Judas Maccabeus. The narrator is careful to explain in 8:5 that the burgeoning revolt was successful because "the Lord's wrath had turned to mercy" (τῆς ὀργῆς τοῦ κυρίου εἰς ἔλεον τραπείσης). Because God's anger had turned to mercy, the gentiles could not stand against Judas's army. Chapters 8–9 go on to depict various victories of Judas's army over larger gentile forces. In chapter 10 Jerusalem is finally recaptured, the temple purified, and the sacrifices reinstated (10:1–4).

As noted above, this narrative is structured around the Deuteronomic idea that God blesses and protects his temple and people when they keep his laws

---

his temple and his people only when they are loyal to him and good" (*Temple Propaganda: The Purpose and Character of 2 Maccabees*, Catholic Biblical Quarterly Monograph Series 12 [Washington, DC: Catholic Biblical Association of America, 1981], 101).

but turns away in anger, allowing the temple and the people to suffer, when they do not. Robert Doran concludes his analysis of the structure of 2 Maccabees by noting that the three main sections of the text (2 Macc. 3; 4:1–10:9; and 10:10–15:36) "are concerned with attacks on the Jerusalem temple and the defense of the temple. In the first section, the attack failed because the laws of God were observed (2 Macc. 3:1). In the second section, the sins of the people brought on the disasters under Antiochus IV. . . . When the anger of the Lord turns to mercy through the suffering of the martyrs, Antiochus' forces are defeated and he himself punished and killed, while the temple is restored. In the final section, further attacks on the temple territory are turned back through God's help" (15:37).[34] Notably, between the outpouring of God's anger and the restoration of God's mercy stands the suffering and deaths of the martyrs. The epitomist, as Doran suggests, implies that the deaths of the martyrs in 2 Maccabees 6 and 7 function as the means for restoring the relationship when God's anger is being poured out upon his people because of their disobedience to his law. The suffering and deaths of the martyrs, together with their intercessory prayers, appear to be instrumental in turning God's anger to mercy.

This last point is unsurprisingly contested, because the epitomist does not explicitly identify the martyrs' deaths as the reason that God's anger turned to mercy.[35] Yet, the connection between the martyrs' deaths and the return of God's mercy rests on more than just the narrative progression from 2 Maccabees 6–7 to the statement of 2 Maccabees 8:5. The pattern of suffering and dying when the people are under the covenant's curses draws from that of the suffering servant in Isaiah 52:13–53:12 and the subsequent statement in 54:7–8 that God's anger against his people will turn to mercy.[36] Five observations lend support to the suspicion that the epitomist intends to associate the martyrs

34. Doran, *Temple Propaganda*, 75.
35. Some argue that there is no connection between the deaths of the martyrs and God's anger turning to mercy. For example, S. K. Williams states that 2 Macc. "does not suggest a direct cause-effect relationship between the death of the martyrs and the deliverance and purification of the temple. That work God effects through the righteous warriors, the Maccabees" (*Jesus' Death as Saving Event*, 89). H. Versnel agrees, writing that there is no "explicit indication of an *effective* causal relationship in that God's mercy indeed has returned *as a result of the death of the martyr*" ("Making Sense of Jesus' Death: The Pagan Contribution," in Frey and Schröter, *Deutungen des Todes Jesu im Neuen Testament*, 260). Williams and Versnel are right to be skeptical about notions of vicarious sacrifice underlying the turning of God's anger to mercy. What they do not adequately grasp, however, is the fact that the pattern of God's anger turning to mercy is derived from that of Isa. 53–55, where the servant is the means of restoring relationship between God and his people precisely when sacrifices cannot be offered.
36. Many commentators note that 2 Macc. 8:5 alludes to Isa. 54:7–8, though not all think Isa. 53 is also significant (see, e.g., D. R. Schwarz, *2 Maccabees*, Commentaries on Early Jewish Literature [Berlin: de Gruyter, 2008], 261).

with the Isaianic servant and therefore views their suffering and deaths as a central element in the restoration of God's mercy.

First, already at the beginning of 2 Maccabees the prayer offered when the sacrifices were restored after the exile under Nehemiah contains language redolent of the servant material in Isaiah 49 (2 Macc. 1:24–29). Jonathan Goldstein notes that, among other points, the prayer's references to the people being enslaved, despised, and an abomination echoes the language in Isaiah 49:7, which speaks of the people as despised, abhorred, and enslaved.[37] From the very start of 2 Maccabees, the ideas of God restoring his people and the temple are linked with allusions to Deutero-Isaianic material.

Second, George Nickelsburg has made a strong case for the influence of Isaiah in the Second Temple period on the developing idea of resurrection as the final and ultimate vindication of God's people.[38] As part of this case, he argues that the Isaianic servant and Isaiah 53 in particular inform elements of 2 Maccabees 6–7. He notes, "In 2 Maccabees 6 and 7 the servant material colors the description of the suffering of the heroes."[39] The brothers are, for example, explicitly called "servants" three times: twice δοῦλοι (7:6, 33) and once παῖδες (7:34). The δοῦλος language in 2 Maccabees 7 most likely comes from Deuteronomy 32:36 LXX, though it is worth noting that in Isaiah 49:3–6 LXX the terms δοῦλος and παῖς are used interchangeably for the servant figure.[40] The suffering of the brothers also mirrors, at times, that of the Isaianic servant. Like the servant, the brothers are beaten with "scourges" and their hair is ripped off. Isaiah 50:4 states that a tongue is given to the servant. The third brother sticks out his tongue to have it cut off claiming that it was given to him from heaven. As with rulers who see the servant figure in Isaiah, the king in 2 Maccabees is astonished as he witnesses the martyrs' fidelity in the midst of their suffering. Moreover, the brothers are severely disfigured, a motif clearly present in Isaiah 53.

Third, in addition to the evidence offered by Nickelsburg, another relevant point of contact between the servant and the martyrs in 2 Maccabees can be identified. The Isaianic servant figure is the one figure in the Hebrew Bible

37. J. A. Goldstein, *II Maccabees: A New Translation with Introduction and Commentary*, AB 41A (Garden City, NY: Doubleday, 1983), 179.

38. G. W. E. Nickelsburg, *Resurrection, Immortality, and Eternal Life in Intertestamental Judaism and Early Christianity*, Harvard Theological Studies 56 (Cambridge, MA: Harvard University Press, 2006).

39. Nickelsburg, *Resurrection*, 132.

40. Goldstein (*II Maccabees*, 294–96) makes the highly plausible suggestion that 2 Macc. 7 stands within a developing interpretive tradition that connected Deut. 32 with Isa. 52–53 (among other texts).

who suffers vicariously on behalf of the sins of others.[41] Martin Hengel cautiously suggests that Isaiah 53, given its singularity, might have influenced 2 Maccabees 7 (esp. 7:32–33, 37–38).[42]

Some argue that neither the Isaianic servant nor the martyrs are likely to be thought to suffer vicariously for the sins and guilt of others, since they are not themselves to be thought of as sinless.[43] But the plain sense of both texts seems to suggest that they do suffer on account of the nation's sins. I see no reason why either the servant or the martyrs have to be thought to be sinless in order to suffer on behalf of others. They doubtless suffer because they, too, are part of the people who have sinned (as with Isaiah, being unclean and living among a people who are unclean does not disqualify one from divine mission). Nevertheless, compared to those whose lawlessness has brought the covenant curses down upon the people, they are faithful and righteous individuals. The martyrs are being persecuted precisely because they refuse to engage in lawlessness (e.g., 2 Macc. 7:1). When one of them says, "We are suffering for our own sins" (7:32), the very next verse makes it clear that "our sins" refers not to the sins of the individual martyrs per se but to the sins of the nation that brought down God's wrath upon all of them (7:33). This is a feature of the Deuteronomic logic: God's anger comes against temple, city, and nation, especially when the priests and other leaders of the people are most at fault (see esp. 4:10–17). The martyrs suffer for the sins of the people detailed earlier in 2 Maccabees (in a way, the temple does as well). Not only, then, are the martyrs described in terms that recall the suffering of the Isaianic servant, but they also do something the servant does—suffer and die on account of the sins of the nation. That Isaiah 53 is the one place in the Hebrew Bible where this idea is found suggests that the epitomist intended for readers to connect the martyrs with the Isaianic servant.[44]

Fourth, the Hebrew text tradition of Isaiah 53:12 suggests that the servant restores God's people not only by suffering and dying on their behalf but

---

41. See K. Koch, "Sühne und Sündenvergebung um die Wende von der exilischen zur nachexilischen Zeit," *EvT* 26 (1966): 217–39, here 237; and M. Hengel, *The Atonement: The Origins of the Doctrine in the New Testament*, trans. John Bowden (London: SCM, 1971), 7, 57.

42. M. Hengel, "The Effective History of Isaiah 53 in the Pre-Christian Period," in Janowski and Stuhlmacher, *Suffering Servant*, 96 (see also Hengel, *Atonement*, 60).

43. See esp. S. K. Williams, *Jesus' Death as Saving Event*, 76–90 and 107–11. The assumption that only a perfectly sinless person could rightly suffer vicariously for the sins of others likely assumes too much conceptually from later Christian reflection on the vicarious death of Jesus.

44. It may also be significant that when the final brother dies, the narrator says he "put his trust completely in the Lord" (2 Macc. 7:40). Given (1) the other Isaianic allusions in the passage and (2) the idea that the people have turned from God and are experiencing his anger, this may be an echo of Isa. 8:17 and/or 12:2.

also by interceding for them.[45] Arguably, the seventh son does precisely this when in 2 Maccabees 7:37–38 he cries out, "I, like my brothers, give up body and life for the laws of our ancestors, appealing to God to show mercy soon to our nation and by trials and plagues to make you confess that he alone is God, and through me and my brothers to bring to an end the wrath of the Almighty that has justly fallen on our whole nation" (NRSV). Moreover, a few verses later Judas Maccabeus also prays that God would be merciful to Jerusalem and "hearken to the blood that cried out to him" (8:3 NRSV). Immediately after this prayer, the epitomist states that God's wrath turned to mercy and that Judas and his army were unstoppable. Some who note the importance of intercessory prayer in 2 Maccabees for the turning of God's anger to mercy do not take seriously enough the fact that this is also an aspect of the servant's ministry in Isaiah 53.[46]

Fifth, nothing in 2 Maccabees 6–7 indicates any connection between the suffering and deaths of the martyrs and Jewish sacrifice.[47] In 2 Maccabees, proper sacrifice is associated with the service of the priests at the Jerusalem temple. The epitome recognizes that sacrifice was, as in the time of the Babylonian exile, suspended for a period of time (1:7–8, 18–22; 2:16–18). As the epitomist states, God's anger at the people's disobedience to his law meant that the temple was violated because God was no longer protecting the temple or his people (4:14–17; 5:17–20). The martyrs die in this period of time. They die when the Deuteronomic curses are falling upon the nation and the temple. Their deaths, that is, occur at a time when no sacrifices can be offered precisely

45. Interestingly, Tg. Isa. 53, a section that B. Chilton argues has roots in the Tannaitic period, expands this idea so that the servant, identified with the Messiah, is said to intercede for God's people in Isa. 53:4, 7, 11, and 12. In 53:4, 11, and 12, this intercession is explicitly said to be for the peoples' sins (see B. Chilton, *The Isaiah Targum: Introduction, Translation, Apparatus and Notes*, The Aramaic Bible 11 [Collegeville, MN: Michael Glazier, 1987], 103–5).

46. See esp. U. Kellermann, "Zum traditionsgeschichtlichen Problem des stellvertretenden Sühnetodes in 2 Makk 7,37f," *Biblische Notizen* 13 (1980): 63–83.

47. For one recent advocate of the view that the martyrs are sacrifices, even a substitute for Yom Kippur, see J. J. Williams, *Maccabean Martyr Traditions*, esp. 43–63. Williams incorrectly associates ideas like reconciliation (καταλλαγ- root words), bearing sins, and vicarious suffering and death with Levitical sacrifices. This language and these ideas are not aspects of Levitical sacrifice (see my brief discussion of atonement in chap. 1 of this volume). Moreover, Williams repeatedly conflates 2 and 4 Macc. While there is a definite link between the martyrs and sacrifice in the latter text, there is no hint of such a connection in 2 Macc. Breytenbach may overstate his case when he concludes that the first clear attestation of Hellenistic traditions of vicarious death and Jewish sacrifice being connected is in the late-first-century 4 Macc. (C. Breytenbach, "Gnädigstimmen und opferkultische Sühne im Urchristentum und seiner Umwelt," in *Opfer: Theologische und kulturelle Kontexte*, ed. B. Janowski and M. Welker, Suhrkamp Taschenbuch Wissenschaft 1454 [Frankfurt: Suhrkamp, 2000], 217–43, here 242). He is, however, correct that these are different and typically distinct conceptual realms that are not conflated in 2 Macc.

because the nation stands under God's anger and the covenant curses. As I suggested above, this is the very kind of situation the Isaianic servant helps to solve. When the people cannot offer sacrifice, the servant is called to fulfill a mission whose goal is the restoration of the relationship. The servant plays a central role in turning God's anger again to mercy.

The preceding points indicate that the suffering, death, and intercession of the martyrs in 2 Maccabees are intentionally modeled on the Isaianic servant. That one of the martyrs explicitly implores God to be reconciled with his people (7:32–33) and that God's anger is subsequently said to turn to mercy (8:5) indicates that their suffering and pleas have contributed to God turning again to his people in mercy. The narrative flow of 2 Maccabees closely correlates here with the pattern of Isaiah 53–54 (esp. 54:7–8). This suggests that the suffering of the martyrs has, like that of the servant, contributed to bringing the time of the covenant curses to an end. After the martyrs die, a time of restoration and renewal arrives. In the case of the Isaianic servant, this renewal partly entails the regathering of God's people and the recovery of the land. In terms of Jewish history, the return of the exiles led to the restoration of Jerusalem and the temple under the leadership of Nehemiah (as is recognized in 2 Macc. 1:19–29). The situation detailed in 2 Maccabees 4–5 had not deteriorated to the level of another exile (though the fact that the second letter affixed to the beginning of the epitome explicitly looks for the regathering of God's people in light of the repurification of the temple is intriguing). The violation of the temple and suffering of the people are clearly identified in 2 Maccabees in Deuteronomic terms. God's anger relents only after the martyrs' deaths. This marks the beginning of Judas's surprisingly successful revolt, and chapters 8–10 detail his victories. All this culminates in the recapture of Jerusalem and the repurification of the temple. At this point, sacrifices can again be offered—God's anger turning to mercy has restored the normal means of worship and covenant maintenance. Given the logic of Isaiah 53–54, the fact that this turning follows the martyrs' deaths can hardly be coincidence. The epitomist has drawn on the Isaianic servant material to explain how the Maccabean martyrs contribute to the restoration of good relations between God and his people, a restoration that eventually leads to the restoration of the temple and sacrificial worship there.

In sum, the Maccabean martyrs are not presented in 2 Maccabees as sacrifices. They can be seen to fall instead under a different category, one needed when sacrifice was not possible—that of the Isaianic servant. Like the servant, their vicarious suffering and intercession for the nation contributes to the restoration of the covenant relationship. In this way their suffering and deaths can be seen as salvific, even atoning: they help to renew the covenant relationship by reconciling God to his people (esp. 2 Macc. 7:33; 8:29). It would be a mistake, however, to confuse this reconciliation with sacrificial atonement. Rather, as in Isaiah 53–54, this reconciliation is needed to restore good relations so that sacrifices can again be offered. These ideas, I suggest, throw helpful light on Jesus's salvific death in Hebrews.

Jesus's Death and the New Covenant in Hebrews

Hebrews nowhere explicitly identifies Jesus with the Isaianic servant. There are, however, a few curious moves in the argument and one clear allusion that suggest the influence of the servant material in the homily. Given the author's grasp of Jewish Scripture, he would likely have recognized the influence of Isaiah 53 on his arguments. Admittedly, however, these elements may underlie aspects of his argument simply because they were already hardwired, as it were, into the preaching about Jesus that he and the congregation to whom he writes had heard (Heb. 2:3). Be that as it may, I argue below that, similar to 2 Maccabees, the logic of Isaiah 53–54 informs both the link in Hebrews between Jesus's vicarious death and exaltation and the association of his death with the inauguration of the new covenant.

I begin by looking at Hebrews' allusion to Isaiah 53. As noted above, most commentators recognize an allusion to Isaiah 53:12 LXX in Hebrews 9:28, when the author states that Christ was offered once "to bear the sins of many."[48] The language of "bearing the sins of many" used in Hebrews (ἀναφερεῖν + ἁμαρτίας + genitive of πολύς) occurs in LXX only in Isaiah 53:12 where the text says that the servant "bore the sins of many" (αὐτὸς ἁμαρτίας πολλῶν ἀνήνεγκεν; see also the similar phrasing in 53:4: οὗτος τὰς ἁμαρτίας ἡμῶν φέρει ["this one bears our sins"]). Hebrews' language in 9:28 calls to mind Isaiah 53:12.

A brief aside here about the verb "offer" (προσφέρω) in Hebrews 9:28 will be helpful for understanding this larger argument. It is worth noting that any number of things can be offered to people and even to God without implying any hint of a sacrifice. Even Hebrews reports that Jesus "offered a loud cry and tears" to God (5:7). This is not likely to be a sacrificial notion but simply a description of giving prayer to God. Nevertheless, "offer" in 9:28 likely has a sacrificial meaning (i.e., the verb here likely refer to "offering" in terms of offering a sacrifice, just as the verb is used in near context of 9:25 and 10:1–2, 8). This is a common meaning of the verb in cultic contexts in LXX when one offers a sacrifice to God.

48. E.g., H. W. Attridge, *The Epistle to the Hebrews: A Commentary on the Epistle to the Hebrews*, Hermeneia (Philadelphia: Fortress, 1989), 266.

There are, however, four reasons why the idea in Hebrews 9:28 that Jesus "was offered to bear the sins of many" should be distinguished from Jesus's high-priestly act of offering himself to God as a sacrifice. First, if one looks to the Levitical cult for the idea of an animal "bearing sins," the nearest parallel is the so-called scapegoat on the Day of Atonement. As noted above, this goat was *not* ultimately offered to God. Rather, after sins were placed upon it, it was led away into the wilderness by someone other than the high priest (Lev. 16:10, 21–22). The point seems to be that precisely because sins were placed on the goat, it must move away from God's house and presence. This goat bears sins *away* from God. By contrast, the goat that does not have sins placed on it is explicitly offered to God (16:9). This is the goat whose blood is taken into the holy of holies by the high priest (16:15–16). Hebrews' reflection on Jesus offering himself to the Father consistently tracks with this latter direction.[49] Like the high priest and the blood of the goat on the Day of Atonement, Jesus moves into the heavenly holy of holies to offer himself to the Father. Conceptually, then, there seems to be a distinction in the Levitical system between a sacrifice that is offered to God and the goat that "bears sins." This goat is not offered to God but moves away from his presence.

Second, Hebrews 9:28's comment about Jesus being offered to bear sins must refer to his death on earth. The following two points suggest this conclusion: (1) The ideas in 9:27 about death being followed by judgment correspond to those of Jesus bearing sin being followed by his appearing a second time to save those waiting for him in 9:28.[50] Death in verse 27 parallels Jesus being offered to bear sin in verse 28, while judgment in verse 27 parallels Jesus's second appearance for salvation in verse 28. (2) The mention of Jesus "appearing a second time" to his waiting people implies an earlier, first appearance. This first appearance must also have been an appearance to those on earth. Moreover, verse 28's characterization of Jesus's second appearance as being "without sin" (χωρὶς ἁμαρτίας) also implies that Jesus's first appearance to those on earth included his being offered "to bear the sins of many." There is, in other words, a contrast between his first appearance on earth (to bear sins) and his second one (without sin and for salvation). Jesus's death, his being offered to bear sins, and his first appearance on earth are tightly bound together conceptually.

Third, if the preceding two points are correct, it follows that Jesus's appearances in Hebrews 9:28 must be different from his singular appearance

---

49. I discuss this feature of the Son's sacrifice in more detail in chap. 10 of this volume.

50. So, e.g., C. R. Koester, *Hebrews: A New Translation with Introduction and Commentary*, AB 36 (New York: Doubleday, 2001), 429.

before God mentioned in verses 24 and 26. Jesus's appearance before the
Father clearly occurs in heaven and is clearly associated with his offering of
himself as a sacrifice to the Father (v. 26). This is unlikely to be understood by
the author as the first appearance assumed in verse 28 because, as just noted,
those to whom Jesus appears a second time are his waiting people *on earth*.
Jesus does not, that is, appear a second time before the Father in heaven; he
appears a second time to those on earth. This is significant evidence for the
conclusion that the time and place where Jesus "was offered" in 9:28 is different from the time and place of his singular self-offering to God in 9:24–26. By
way of contrast to the earthly appearances of verse 28, that of verses 24–26
relates to God and occurs in "heaven itself." This appearance happened when
the Son entered the heavenly tabernacle as the great high priest. In terms of
the larger incarnational narrative that Hebrews presupposes about the Son,[51]
his appearance before God must stand between the two earthly oriented appearances of verse 28. The second appearance of 9:28 and the first one it
presupposes can therefore be described in other terms as the Son's first and
second advents. His first advent includes his death, when he bore sins. His
second advent will be "without sin" and for salvation. Between these two appearances on earth stands Jesus's high-priestly offering and ministry before
the Father in the heavens (9:24–26; cf. 7:25; 8:1–2).

Fourth, in Hebrews 9:25 Jesus actively "offers himself" (προσφέρῃ ἑαυτόν;
note the active voice) to God once as a sacrifice in the heavenly holy of holies
(9:24–26). In 9:28, however, the verb denoting offering is in the passive voice
(προσενεχθείς), as if God were the one offering Jesus. Curiously, the recipient of the offering of 9:28 is not specified.[52] One can nevertheless distinguish
between Jesus's active self-offering, which correlates with his entering the
heavenly tabernacle to appear before the Father (9:24–26) and the time when
Jesus "was offered" once to bear sins, which correlates with his time on earth
where he died (9:28). That is to say, Jesus's active self-offering to God is linked
with his entrance into "heaven itself" to appear before God, while his being
offered to bear sins occurred on earth when he died, *before* he passes through
the heavens and offers himself to God. The passive offering of Jesus is again
distinguishable from Jesus's active high-priestly act of offering himself to
God as a sacrifice.

How are these details to be correlated and held together? I propose the
following solution: In Hebrews 9:24–28 the writer shows that he can move

---

51. See chap. 10 for a more detailed discussion of the incarnation in Hebrews.
52. Conceptually, this idea comes remarkably close to Paul's conviction in Rom. 4:25a that
Jesus "was handed over on account of our transgressions." This may not be purely accidental
since both texts appear to speak of Jesus's death by way of allusion to Isa. 53.

between different elements of the process of offering a sacrifice to God. Jewish sacrifice consisted of a sequence of acts that constituted the process of giving a gift to God. (For a more detailed account of this process, see especially the relevant portions of chaps. 9 and 10 in this volume.) Slaughter was an essential part of many sacrifices. This act, however, occurred away from the altar and was neither the time when nor the place where the sacrifice was ultimately offered to God. The offering to God was a later part of the process. It occurred when the gift was brought by a priest to the altar and thus conveyed into God's house and presence. This latter notion aligns well with the homily's statements in 9:24–26 to the effect that Jesus enters heaven as the great high priest, appears before God, and "offers himself" there as a sacrifice. Yet, if, as I suggest, the writer can move between the different elements involved in offering God a sacrifice, then when in 9:28 he speaks of Jesus's death in terms of his being offered once to bear sins, he is not thereby collapsing the entirety of Jesus's high-priestly ministry and sacrifice into the crucifixion.

Put differently, the author knows that Jesus is the one who died as the sacrifice, rose as the sacrifice, and ascended into the heavenly tabernacle to offer himself to God as the sacrifice. If the author could work with this sort of sequential understanding of the process of sacrifice, then one can plausibly see how he could have referred to Jesus's death as an element of his sacrificial offering without assuming or intending to imply that this aspect of the sacrificial process was the sum total of Jesus's active offering himself to God as a sacrifice. In fact, if the appearance in Hebrews 9:24–26 and those of verse 28 are distinguishable in the ways argued above, it would make sense for the homilist to refer to Jesus's death as an aspect of his offering—it is that part of his sacrifice that occurred before he entered the heavenly tabernacle to offer himself to God, while also emphasizing that the subsequent, active act of self-offering occurred before God in the heavenly tabernacle. Moreover, this sequential account of Jesus's offering opens space for the author to associate Jesus's death with work distinct from that of his heavenly self-offering. This work is that of the Isaianic servant (and possibly also with the scapegoat, which was sent away from God). Hebrews can isolate Jesus's death as part of his sacrifice without collapsing this event or the work it accomplishes into that of his high-priestly presentation of himself to God as the ultimate atoning sacrifice. Without diminishing the person of Jesus—he is the incarnate Son who died, rose, ascended, and now intercedes for his people—the homilist can identify different work being done at different points in the larger narrative about the Son. Jesus's first appearance on earth was for the purpose of bearing sins, a feature of his work that interestingly correlates with his being away from the Father. His appearance before the Father in the heavenly tabernacle allows him, as the great high priest, to offer himself to God as the sacrifice that makes atonement and to intercede on behalf of his people.[53] His second appearance to those on earth will be "without sin" and for the salvation of those waiting for his return to them from the heavens. The Son died on earth bearing sins. He returned to his Father to offer himself as the sacrifice that purifies, perfects, and sanctifies his people while they wait to enter their inheritance.

The preceding discussion of Hebrews 9:28 suggests that the description of Jesus being "offered to bear the sins of many" both refers to his crucifixion and, by way of an allusion to Isaiah 53:12, characterizes that death in terms that recall the Isaianic servant. Jesus's death, in other words, is linked by the homilist in 9:28 with that of the servant figure in Isaiah. This is not, however, the only place in Hebrews where the influence of Isaiah 53 is detectable. Two points suggest that Isaiah 53 also underlies the argument of Hebrews 2, albeit more implicitly than is the case in 9:28.

First, for the author of Hebrews, Jesus's vicarious death is identified in Hebrews 2:9 as the reason that he has been crowned with the glory and honor promised to humanity in Psalm 8. Conceptually, the ideas that Jesus "tastes death" for all and is subsequently exalted, being "crowned with glory and honor," correspond well to the ideas of the servant's vicarious death and exaltation in Isaiah 52:13–53:12.

Second, in Hebrews 2 the homilist aims to show that the Son was exalted above the angels as the particular human being, Jesus. This is in keeping with the preacher's prophetic interpretation of Psalm 8, which he reads as promising that humanity will one day be elevated above the angels. But the argument contains a curious feature: Psalm 8 says nothing about humanity being crowned with glory and honor because of death. Why, then, did Jesus need to suffer death to attain the glory and honor promised in Psalm 8? Moreover, it is clear in the rest of Hebrews 2 that death alone does not lead to being crowned with glory and honor. In fact, the author views death as a tool used by the Devil to keep people enslaved (2:14–15). Humans die (see also 9:27), and the Devil uses fear of death to keep them enslaved. So in Hebrews, dying in and of itself does not lead to the exaltation promised in Psalm 8. Unlike many in the wider Hellenistic world, Hebrews does not envision the fact of death as a possible means by which people are freed from their slavery in the present world.[54]

---

53. Once again, this appears to parallel a notion found in Romans. In Rom. 8:34 Paul appears to think sequentially through Jesus's death, resurrection, and ascension to God's right hand where, as in Hebrews, Jesus now sits and intercedes "for us."

54. This was one of E. Käsemann's great insights. He saw clearly that the author's high-priestly Christology cut across the grain of cultural ideas about death as the means of freeing

The idea of the vindication of the righteous sufferer influences the author's argument here. This conclusion is partly supported by the citation of Psalm 22:22 at Hebrews 2:12.[55] But even Psalm 22 does not fully explain the logic of the move being made in Hebrews 2:9, where the author also states that Jesus tasted death on behalf of others. The apparently vicarious nature of Jesus's death here is neither derivable from Psalm 22 nor easily deducible from the idea that God will vindicate the righteous sufferer. Where, then, does the homilist get this idea?

The logic of the fourth servant song offers a plausible explanation.[56] If Isaiah 53 is in play behind the scenes in Hebrews 2, then it makes sense for the author to inject into his interpretation of Psalm 8 the idea of Jesus being glorified and honored *because* he suffered death for the sake of others.[57] Like the servant figure who suffered death on behalf of others and then is "greatly glorified" (Isa. 52:13 LXX), Jesus can be seen to deserve the glorification promised in Psalm 8 in part *because* he tasted death on behalf of others. Moreover, his singular vicarious death, like that of the servant, sets him apart from his human siblings, a point that fits well with the author's claim in Hebrews 2:10–11 that Jesus was made perfect through his suffering, and thus he is not merely one among his siblings but *the one* who is able to sanctify his siblings.[58]

---

the soul to ascend to heaven (*Das wandernde Gottesvolk: Eine Untersuchung zum Hebräerbrief*, 4th ed., FRLANT 55 [Göttingen: Vandenhoeck & Ruprecht, 1961], esp. 144–54).

55. Interestingly, many recognize that the Isaianic servant tradition has influenced Ps. 22 (see esp. M. A. Lyons, "Psalm 22 and the 'Servants' of Isaiah 54; 55–56," *CBQ* 77 [2015]: 640–56).

56. Schaefer ("Relationship between Priestly and Servant Messianism," 377–78) notes a possible connection between Heb. 2:9 and the Isaianic servant, though he does little to develop the thought.

57. There may also be an allusion to Isa. 41:8–9 in Heb. 2:16. The latter verse states that the incarnate Son does "not take up the angels but he takes up the seed of Abraham" (οὐ . . . ἀγγέλων ἐπιλαμβάνεται ἀλλὰ σπέρματος Ἀβραὰμ ἐπιλαμβάνεται). Similar language occurs in Isa. 41:8–10 LXX, where God says that his chosen servant Israel is "the offspring of Abraam, whom I have loved, you whom I took hold of from the ends of the earth [σπέρμα Αβρααμ ὃν ἠγάπησα οὗ ἀντελαβόμην ἀπ᾽ ἄκρων τῆς γῆς], and I called you from its mountain peaks, and I said to you, 'You are my servant; I have chosen you and not forsaken you'; do not fear for I am with you; do not wander off, for I am your God who has strengthened you, and I have helped you, and I have made you secure with my righteous right hand" (NETS). I have argued elsewhere for significant allusions to the exodus event in Heb. 1–4 (D. M. Moffitt, "Exodus in Hebrews," in *Exodus in the New Testament*, ed. S. M. Ehorn, LNTS 663 [London: T&T Clark, 2022], 174–95). If exodus ideas are prominent in Heb. 1–2, the possible points of contact between Heb. 2:16 and Isa. 41:8–9 extend beyond the verbal similarities between σπέρματος Ἀβραὰμ ἐπιλαμβάνεται in Heb. 2:16 and σπέρμα Αβρααμ . . . οὗ ἀντελαβόμην in Isa. 41:8–9 to the conceptual one of God calling his people out of the nations. Even the contrast between the gods of the nations in Isa. 41:7 and God choosing Abraham's seed to be his servant in 41:8 is remarkable given that Hebrews is contrasting the angels—including the malevolent angel, the Devil—with Abraham's seed in 2:16. God's charge to his people in Isa. 41:10 not to "wander off" also resonates well conceptually with Hebrews' warning not to "drift away" (2:1).

58. These ideas relate back to the claim in Heb. 1:9, drawn from Ps. 44:7 LXX, that the Son has peers above whom he has been anointed.

Second, the motifs of "seeing" and of "inheriting many" found in Isaiah's servant material parallel ideas in Hebrews 2. The language of "seeing" the servant and of "seeing" salvation occurs in Isaiah 52:10, 52:15, and 53:2 (various forms of ὁράω are used in LXX). A comparison of 53:2 and 52:15 suggests the dramatic reversal in the servant's situation just explored above. In 53:2 he is seen to have no "glory" (δόξα), while in 52:15 many nations marvel and kings' mouths are stopped when they see him highly exalted. Conceptually, a similar reversal is evident in Hebrews' reading of Psalm 8 where, interestingly, the author introduces the motif of "seeing" (βλέπω) Jesus as the one who was made low but is now "crowned with glory [δόξῃ] and honor." Moreover, because of what the Isaianic servant endures, he is said in Isa. 53:12 LXX to "inherit many." In context, the masculine plural "many" (πολλῶν) is best understood as "many people." This is clear in 53:11 where the servant is said to "serve many" and bear their sins, an idea repeated in 53:12, where the servant bears the sins of "many." The idea continues to be developed in chapter 54, where the barren one has "many children" (54:1). This seed will "inherit nations" (54:3). One result of the servant's death for others, therefore, appears to be that he gains an inheritance that consists of "many people." In this light, it may be significant that Hebrews 2:12–13 depicts the glorified Jesus declaring, in words taken from Psalm 21:12 LXX and Isaiah 8:18, that God has given him brothers and sisters and children.

One more point should be considered. The links that Hebrews makes between the death of Jesus and the inauguration of the new covenant are well explained if Isaiah 53 stands in the background. In Hebrews 9:15–18 Jesus's death is identified as the event that inaugurates the new covenant. In 9:15 this death is "for the redemption of the trespasses against the first covenant" (εἰς ἀπολύτρωσιν τῶν ἐπὶ τῇ πρώτῃ διαθήκῃ παραβάσεων). Although the Isaianic servant's death is never explicitly said to bring about the redemption of the people, the idea that God will redeem his people from their sins and lawlessness is prominent in Deutero-Isaiah (e.g., 43:1, 14; 44:21–24; 52:3). This redemption is a constitutive element of the promised new exodus: it is central to the release of the people from enslavement in exile and to their return to the land. The way in which the suffering and death of the servant contributes to the restoration of the relationship between God and his people suggests, therefore, that the servant's death is instrumental in redeeming the people. Moreover, as Scott Hahn has pointed out, significant conceptual parallels exist between aspects of Hebrews 9:15–18 and the Isaianic servant. Both the servant and Jesus die, both are instrumental in bringing some kind of renewed covenant relationship, and both also receive an inheritance. That Hebrews does allude to Isaiah 53:12 in the near context (Heb. 9:28) strengthens the suspicion that the author is working with concepts drawn from Isaiah 53.[59]

What many commentators have not seen is the remarkable fact that after Hebrews discusses the inauguration of the new covenant by means of Jesus's death, the homilist goes on to speak about the purification of the heavenly tabernacle, Jesus's entrance into that heavenly space, and Jesus's appearance before the Father to offer himself as a sacrifice (see again 9:24–26). Jesus, in other words, first redeems his people and inaugurates the promised new covenant. These are activities associated with his death or, to use the notion implied in 9:28, with his first appearance on earth to bear the sins of many. He subsequently ascended into the heavenly tabernacle to offer his sacrifice and perform his high-priestly work there in the heavenly holy of holies. After inaugurating the new covenant, Jesus entered the heavenly tabernacle to appear before God and serve there as the great high priest of this very covenant.

Remarkably, this sequence (first covenant renewal, then restoration of the means of maintaining the relationship—offering sacrifice) aligns well with the way in which 2 Maccabees draws on the Isaianic servant to show that the martyrs' deaths for the sins of the nation were instrumental in renewing the covenant relationship. First, they suffer and die for the sins of the nation. Then, the covenant relationship is restored, the temple is purified, and regular sacrifice is reinstated. Hebrews obviously differs from 2 Maccabees in numerous ways. I am not arguing here that Hebrews' use of the servant tradition is dependent on 2 Maccabees.[60] Rather, I am pointing out that both the pattern in 2 Maccabees, which partly depends on the Isaianic servant material, and the presence of a similar pattern in Hebrews suggests that some in the Second Temple period understood the suffering and death of the Isaianic servant to be the prophetically sanctioned mechanism for restoring the broken covenant relationship so that sacrifice could again be offered to and accepted by God.

Clearly, the author of Hebrews thinks that something had gone wrong with the old covenant (so Heb. 8:7–13). The need for the promised new covenant of Jeremiah is equally urgent for the homilist. But how can this new covenant be inaugurated? Hebrews, like other early Christian texts (e.g., Luke 22:20; 1 Cor. 11:25), focuses on Jesus's death as the means by which the new covenant comes about. Doubtless, numerous factors must have been in play

59. S. W. Hahn, "A Broken Covenant and the Curse of Death: A Study of Hebrews 9:15–22," *CBQ* 66, no. 3 (2004): 416–36, here 433. I am not persuaded by Hahn's larger thesis about the meaning of διαθήκη and the dead bodies as sacrifices in this passage, but I do think he is right to suspect the presence of the Isaianic servant here. See also the discussion of Cullman in n. 8 above.

60. Though the author probably did know 2 Macc. At the very least, he seems to allude to the stories of the Maccabean martyrs in Heb. 11:35b–36 (Attridge, *Hebrews*, 349–50).

for Jesus's early followers as they began to argue for this conclusion. I do not mean to reduce or oversimplify the situation by suggesting that Isaiah 53 *fully* explains Hebrews' link between Jesus's death and the inauguration of the new covenant. Nevertheless, the evidence discussed above suggests that Isaiah 53 plays an important role in Hebrews' understanding of the inauguration of the new covenant. The notion that Isaiah 53 offered a means whereby God's covenant relationship could be renewed when things had gone badly wrong helps to explain how Hebrews could argue that Jesus's sin-bearing death functioned as the means by which the new covenant was inaugurated.

In short, just as Psalm 8 on its own terms cannot explain why Jesus had to die in order to be exalted above the angels, so also the idea of the vicarious death of one for many does not on its own suggest the idea of covenant renewal.[61] There is, however, a singular example of a similar idea in the Hebrew Bible—the suffering servant of Isaiah 53. The evidence of 2 Maccabees demonstrates that the servant tradition could be interpreted in terms of restoring the relationship between God and his covenant people. This provides a useful analogy for reflecting on Jesus's redemptive death in Hebrews. If the suffering and death of the Isaianic servant who bears the sins of the many is needed to bring God's people back into covenant relationship with him when the covenant is in breach, and if the one who so suffers is glorified and exalted by God above the siblings he inherits, then one can see how the servant tradition provides the homilist with important, implicit assumptions that help him advance his argument. The one clear allusion to Isaiah 53 in Hebrews 9:28 is only the proverbial tip of the iceberg.

Conclusion

I have argued above that Isaiah 53 was understood by at least some Second Temple Jews as depicting a special means by which God's covenant relationship with his people could be restored and normal temple worship reinstated. This special role was needed when the people had failed in their covenant obligations to the point that they found themselves under the curses of the covenant. To fall under the covenant curses left the people with no means by which to offer sacrifices to God or to expect that he would accept them. This is the situation that the Isaianic servant is called by God to rectify. The vicarious suffering and death of a servant for the sins of the many was, so the

---

61. This is especially true if one presses the influence of Greco-Roman backgrounds on the notion of "dying for others." See, in particular, Versnel, "Making Sense of Jesus' Death." Jewish covenantal categories do not provide good analogues in the Greco-Roman world.

prophet Isaiah had said, the divinely ordained means by which the relationship could be restored.

While Hebrews does not explicitly identify Jesus as the Isaianic servant, the author does apply language from Isaiah 53:12 to Jesus in Hebrews 9:28. Jesus's death functions like that of the servant—he bears the sins of many. Moreover, aspects of the logic of the argument of Hebrews 2 and Hebrews 9 are illuminated if one allows that the servant tradition stands in the background. Jesus was crowned with glory and exalted above the angels *because* he tasted death for everyone. This causal logic does not stem from Psalm 8 but does align well with the exaltation of the servant. Hebrews appears to read Psalm 8 in the light of the servant's death and subsequent exaltation. Perhaps more significantly, the link between Jesus's death and the inauguration of the new covenant makes good sense in light of the move from Isaiah 53 to Isaiah 54. Jesus's suffering and death, somewhat like those of the martyrs in 2 Maccabees 7, function as the means for bringing about a renewed covenant relationship.

If these observations are correct, an important implication may also be close to hand: Hebrews, like 2 Maccabees, distinguishes between the extra-sacrificial means of dealing with sin and the normal cultic/sacrificial ones. If, as I argue in other chapters in this volume, Jesus's high-priestly ministry is primarily understood in Hebrews in terms of the work that he performs as the mediator of the new covenant in the heavenly holy of holies, then it may be that this priestly and cultic activity can and should be distinguished from the special, extra-sacrificial work of Jesus's death. The death of Jesus is salvific. It is redemptive and atoning in the sense that it establishes and makes possible the new covenant context in which Jesus can serve as the interceding covenant mediator. It is not, however, fully equivalent to his subsequent high-priestly and sacrificial ministry in God's heavenly presence. Recognizing ways in which Hebrews correlates Jesus's death with the servant in Isaiah 53 can, to put the point differently, help one identify meaningful distinctions between the work Jesus does to inaugurate the new covenant by way of his death and the subsequent, regular high-priestly and sacrificial work that he does to maintain the new covenant between his siblings and God by way of his ascension into the heavenly tabernacle.

5

"If Another Priest Arises"

Jesus's Resurrection and
the High-Priestly Christology of Hebrews

A near universal consensus in Hebrews' scholarship maintains that the letter says little about the resurrection of Jesus as a distinct moment or category and even less about the theological implications of this aspect of early Christian confession.[1] The tendency is to assume that Hebrews' author, if he reflects on the resurrection at all, does not distinguish between that event and Jesus's exaltation.[2]

Against this assessment, I argue that the category of Jesus's resurrection—as the moment when he took possession of an enduring, indestructible (i.e., perfected) life—both is present in the text and plays an important role in the homily's theological argument. Indeed, the most distinctive christological

I am especially grateful to Richard B. Hays, David A. deSilva, Gabriella Gelardini, and Bernd Janowski for their critical comments on this project. In addition to the Epistle to the Hebrews and Christian Theology conference, a version of this essay was read at the German-English New Testament Colloquium, Eberhard Karls Universität Tübingen. I would also like to thank the German-American Fulbright Commission and the Institute of International Education for funding me to pursue research related to this topic, as well as Hermann Lichtenberger and the Institut für Antikes Judentum und Hellenistische Religionsgeschichte for hosting me in Tübingen.

1. For a couple of examples, see H. W. Attridge, *The Epistle to the Hebrews*, Hermeneia (Philadelphia: Fortress, 1989), 406; F. F. Bruce, *The Epistle to the Hebrews*, NICNT (Grand Rapids: Eerdmans, 1990), 32–33.

2. Cf. Bruce, *Hebrews*, 32–33, 86–87, 388; P. Ellingworth, *The Epistle to the Hebrews*, NIGTC (Grand Rapids: Eerdmans, 1993), 603.

contribution of the epistle—the conclusion that Jesus is the great high priest in the order of Melchizedek—depends on the affirmation that God raised Jesus from the dead. For this author, Jesus's possession of perfected or resurrected creaturely life stands logically and temporally prior to his elevation to the heavenly priesthood and his exaltation to the throne as the royal Son.

Jesus's Resurrection as a Category in Hebrews

The only relatively clear reference to Jesus's resurrection in Hebrews occurs in 13:20, where God is identified as having "brought out of the dead ones [ἐκ νεκρῶν] the great shepherd of the sheep, our Lord Jesus."[3] A more subtle allusion, however, can be identified in 5:7. Here the writer declares that Jesus, "in the days of his flesh, was offering up prayers and requests with a great cry and tears to the one who was able [τὸν δυνάμενον] to save him out of the realm of death [ἐκ θανάτου], and he was heard because of his reverence."[4] In order to fully grasp the implications of this statement, Hebrews 5:7 needs to be read in light of the recognition that Jesus stands as the chief example of a larger pattern that runs right through the letter—namely, that God rewards those who faithfully persevere in times of testing. I argue that in light of this pattern, the mention of Jesus's being "heard" most likely refers to his resurrection.

Jesus as the Paradigmatic Example of Faith in Testing, Part 1

Already in Hebrews 4:15 the writer has presented Jesus as an example of someone who, although tested (πεπειρασμένον) in every respect, was without sin. While the notion of "sin" in this letter entails a great deal more than a mere lack of faith in the face of testing, such faithlessness is closely associated with sin in the near context of 4:15 (see 3:12, 19; and 4:2, where ἀπιστία in the midst of testing is correlated with the sin that prevents one from obtaining God's promises).[5] The comment that Jesus was without sin when tested therefore implies that his own behavior during his time of testing was characterized by

3. Notably, not everyone sees this statement in Heb. 13:20 as a reference to Jesus's resurrection. Attridge, for example, argues that by using the verb ἀνάγω, the writer has deliberately avoided the standard terminology for resurrection (i.e., use of the verb ἐγείρω). Hebrews, he claims, consistently uses "language of exaltation not resurrection for the act whereby Jesus' sacrifice is consummated and he himself 'perfected'" (Attridge, *Hebrews*, 406).

4. The use of ἐκ seems to imply not salvation "from" death but rather salvation "out of" death since, as Heb. 13:20 shows, the author clearly knows that Jesus died and was brought out of that state by God. Cf. Attridge, *Hebrews*, 150; Ellingworth, *Hebrews*, 288–91.

5. According to Ps. 94:8 LXX (see Heb. 3:8), Israel's failure in the wilderness occurred in "the day of testing" (τὴν ἡμέραν τοῦ πειρασμοῦ).

faith. In contrast to Israel's faithless response in the wilderness (cf. 3:7–4:2), Jesus acted in faith during his time of testing.[6]

Hebrews 5:7 clarifies at least one of the ways Jesus's faith expressed itself. In the midst of his ordeal, he cried out to the one who was able to save him out of the realm of death. By highlighting the fact that Jesus cried out to God, the author implicitly presents Jesus as an illustration of the very kind of bold reliance on God in times of need that he has just urged upon his audience in their own times of testing (cf. 4:14–16).[7] Additionally, the identification of God as having the "power to save out of the realm of death" suggests that a key element of Jesus's faith was the belief that God was able to resurrect him out of the realm of death. Two factors further substantiate this interpretation.

First, such an understanding of faith coheres remarkably well with some of the most rudimentary Christian teachings the writer goes on to outline. In Hebrews 6:1–2, faith in God and belief in the resurrection belong to the most elementary principles of "the initial teaching" (see also 11:6 and 11:35, where these same elements are also presented as constitutive of faith). Second, as will be argued in more detail below, in the only other passage in the letter where God is described as having the "power" to save "out of" death, the reference is explicitly collocated with belief in resurrection (cf. 11:17–19). All of this suggests the conclusion that the portrayal of Jesus's own response in the midst of testing in 5:7 illustrates the kind of faith that the author impresses upon his readers.[8] Of particular note, however, is the comment that as a result of Jesus's reverence, he was *heard*.[9]

Hebrews' reference to Jesus's "prayers" (δεήσεις) and "cry" (κραυγῆς) being "heard" (εἰσακουσθείς) echoes the rich biblical tradition of God's people and/or the afflicted righteous one crying out to God in times of dire need and being heard.[10] In such contexts God's "hearing" typically connotes the salvation of those crying out.[11] In view of this background, the author's comment that Jesus's cry "was heard" should be understood as an indication

6. Cf. Ellingworth, *Hebrews*, 292.

7. See D. A. deSilva, *Perseverance in Gratitude: A Socio-Rhetorical Commentary on the Epistle "to the Hebrews"* (Grand Rapids: Eerdmans, 2000), 191.

8. Jesus's role as the paradigm of faith is spelled out more clearly in Heb. 12:1–4 (for a more detailed discussion of this point, see below). Cf. deSilva, *Perseverance in Gratitude*, 191.

9. Given that Jesus's crying out to God is portrayed as an act of faithful obedience, it follows that Jesus's faithful endurance even unto death appears most naturally to be at the heart of what the writer has in view when he speaks in Heb. 5:7 of Jesus's εὐλάβεια.

10. For a few examples, see Exod. 2:23–24; Pss. 4:1–3 (4:2–4 LXX); 6:8–9 (6:9–10 LXX); 18 (17 LXX); 22:22–24 (21:23–25 LXX); 31:19–24 (30:20–25 LXX); 91:14–16 (90:14–16 LXX); Jon. 2:2–9 (2:3–10 LXX); Mic. 7:7–8.

11. Within the biblical narrative, this pattern of God's hearing entailing salvation is also linked with Israel's inheritance of the land (cf. Exod. 3:7–8; 6:4–8; Deut. 26:5–9; Neh. 9:7–15).

that God did in fact save him. Yet in contrast to much of the tradition just mentioned, Jesus's suffering ultimately ends in his death (2:9). Since he is not saved from dying, Hebrews' claim that Jesus "was heard" points to God's salvific action on his behalf as something that occurred *after* death—that is, salvation out of the realm of death (not salvation from having to endure the suffering of death).[12]

Jesus's own faith when tested was therefore rewarded in that God heard him and, by implication, saved him out of the realm of death. If this is basically correct, then the mention in Hebrews 5:7 of Jesus's crying out and being heard is consistent with the author's emphasis throughout the letter on faithful endurance and the reception of God's promises (see, for example, 6:12–15, which anticipates 11:1–12:2). That Jesus's salvation out of death is a reference to his resurrection becomes clearer when one considers other passages in the letter where this pattern of faith and reward is explicitly linked with resurrection.[13]

Abraham's Faith in Testing and Resurrection

One of the few passages in Hebrews that unequivocally refers to resurrection is 11:17–19. Here Abraham stands as a shining example of faith receiving its promised reward from God. In these verses the author depicts Abraham acting faithfully in the midst of being tested (πειραζόμενος). Abraham's offering of Isaac is said to be grounded in his reckoning that if he slew Isaac, God was "able to raise [him] out of the dead" (ἐκ νεκρῶν ἐγείρειν δυνατὸς ὁ θεός). This seems to entail that he believed that since God promised him heirs through Isaac, God would bring Isaac out of the dead so that, as promised, Isaac would be the source of his progeny.[14]

The similarities between this passage and Hebrews 5:7 are striking. First, it is notable that in Hebrews both Jesus and Abraham are explicitly described

---

12. Cf. especially the discussion in W. R. G. Loader, *Sohn und Hoherpriester: Eine traditionsgeschichtliche Untersuchung zur Christologie des Hebräerbriefes*, WMANT 53 (Neukirchen-Vluyn: Neukirchener Verlag, 1991), 99–104. It should be pointed out that this conclusion shows significant development relative to the majority of Psalm texts, in which the righteous are heard and saved *before* they die. There are, however, clues that this tradition is developing toward the notion of resurrection (cf., for instance, B. Janowski, *Konfliktgespräche mit Gott: Eine Anthropologie der Psalmen* [Neukirchen-Vluyn: Neukirchener Verlag, 2003], 336–38).

13. Cf. Ellingworth, *Hebrews*, 288, who also thinks that Jesus's resurrection is implicit here (in spite of his agreement with the consensus that "elsewhere in Hebrews the resurrection of Jesus is not prominent"). Various other interpretations have been offered, but a solid consensus understands Jesus's being "heard" as implying his exaltation (e.g., Attridge, *Hebrews*, 150).

14. See esp. the discussion in Bruce, *Hebrews*, 303–4.

as having been "tested" (cf. 2:18; 4:15; 11:19).[15] Second, in both 5:7 and 11:19 the writer speaks of God as having the "ability" or "power" (cf. the participle δυνάμενον in 5:7 and the adjective δυνατός in 11:19) to deliver someone "out of" (ἐκ) death. Third, this particular belief about God (i.e., that God is able to save people out of death) appears to be the primary element of faith being emphasized in both passages—that is, faith in God's power to save someone out of death motivated the exemplary behavior these individuals demonstrated when tested. Fourth, in both cases the faithful endurance is rewarded. Jesus was heard. Abraham received Isaac back again.

Thus, in both passages faithful perseverance leads to salvation in relation to death. In the case of Abraham and Isaac, the resurrection out of the dead is ἐν παραβολῇ (Heb. 11:19)—only a hint or type of the good things to come.[16] In the case of Jesus, the situation is obviously different because, unlike Isaac, he did die. Nevertheless, the same basic pattern underlies these texts: (1) faith in God as the one who can raise the dead is an essential component of endurance in times of testing, and (2) God rewards such faith with salvation. In 11:17–19 one sees, even if only in a parable, that this reward or salvation is ultimately resurrection.

The linguistic and conceptual parallels between Hebrews 5:7 and 11:17–19 provide good grounds for concluding that when the author states in 5:7 that Jesus's prayer to the one who could save out of death was heard, he is alluding to Jesus's resurrection. In the midst of Jesus's faithful suffering, God heard his cry and did exactly what 13:20 claims—brought him out of the dead.[17] There is, however, yet another important piece of evidence for the presence of Jesus's resurrection in Hebrews. In keeping with the pattern of faith receiving God's commendation, Jesus stands in 12:2 at the very climax of the list of those whose lives exemplify this pattern.

Jesus as the Paradigmatic Example of Faith in Testing, Part 2

Hebrews 11 consists of a list of individuals who, because of their faith, are presented by the author as examples of those who will ultimately inherit God's promises. While the list provides instances of promises fulfilled (i.e., faith already rewarded), there are a few key eschatological promises still unfulfilled and toward which those on the list still look in faith. These promises

---

15. The people of God in the past (Heb. 3:8) and, implicitly, in the present (4:15–16) are said to experience testing, but apart from the mention of God's being tested (3:9), Jesus and Abraham are the only individuals in the letter overtly identified as having been tested.

16. E.g., Attridge, *Hebrews*, 335; Bruce, *Hebrews*, 304.

17. So also J. Kurianal, *Jesus Our High Priest: Ps 110,4 as the Substructure of Hebrews 5,1–7,28* (Frankfurt: Peter Lang, 2000), 70.

are a city built by God (v. 10), a heavenly homeland (vv. 14–16), and a "better resurrection" (v. 35).

Before proceeding, a brief word about this "better resurrection" (κρείττονος ἀναστάσεως) is appropriate. Three factors suggest that the "betterness" of this resurrection has to do with its eschatological and enduring quality.

First, given the direct contrast between the resurrection mentioned in Hebrews 11:35a and the κρείττονος ἀναστάσεως in 11:35c, it follows that the former resurrection is only a return to mortal life (resuscitation), while the latter, better resurrection brings a superior kind of life.[18] Second, this "better resurrection" is one of several eschatological promises listed in this chapter (cf. vv. 9–10 and 13–16). Because these eschatological possessions are heavenly, they are unshakable and enduring (cf. 12:25–29). This suggests that the better resurrection, like the enduring eschatological city and home-land, must be a resurrection to a life that endures. Third, when the author uses a form of κρείττων/κρείσσων, it often carries the connotation of being heavenly and enduring.[19]

The "better resurrection" is therefore the promise of a life no longer subject to mortality. This resurrection ushers in the kind of unshakable life that can inherit the fullness of the other eschatological promises—the enduring city and homeland.

As was noted above, Jesus stands at the pinnacle of the list of faithful ones in Hebrews 11. He is the chief example of someone who faithfully suffered in order to obtain the greater joy promised to him. By placing Jesus at the list's apex, the author holds him up as the main example to be emulated. Jesus, as the ἀρχηγός and τελειωτής of the faith (12:2), is thus presented as the first one to have obtained the eschatological promises noted in chapter 11 (see also 2:10). The joy that Jesus anticipated certainly cannot be reduced to the promises referred to in chapter 11.[20] Yet, given his place in this list and the lengths to which the author has gone to identify him with those who have placed their hope in him, it would be exceedingly strange if the author thought that Jesus himself did not obtain the city, homeland, *and* resurrection promised to those being sanctified (cf. 2:11).

The foregoing discussion suggests that the author of Hebrews has not ignored Jesus's resurrection. But is this category distinct from his exaltation

---

18. This is widely recognized. E.g., Attridge, *Hebrews*, 350; C. R. Koester, *Hebrews: A New Translation with Introduction and Commentary*, AB 36 (New York: Doubleday, 2001), 514.

19. This is especially clear in Heb. 9:23; 10:34; and 11:16 but seems implicit in 7:19, 22; 8:6; and 12:24, where the heavenly nature of Jesus's ministry is central to the better hope, covenant, and promises.

20. For example, the exaltation to the messianic throne at God's right hand and the redemption of his brothers and sisters must also be taken into account.

to the royal throne in heaven for this author? Additionally, does the resurrection play a significant role in the christological reflection of this text? For the balance of this chapter I argue that Jesus's resurrection is not only a moment distinct from his exaltation but one fundamental for the letter's christological claim that Jesus serves as the heavenly high priest.

Perfection and Jesus's Priestly Prerequisites

Hebrews 5:1–10 is generally taken to be the writer's attempt to lay out Jesus's prerequisites for priestly office. The two key qualifications often recognized are (1) his ability to sympathize with those for whom he ministers and (2) his call by God.[21]

Yet Hebrews' use of "perfection" language within the argument for Jesus's priestly status (i.e., in 4:14–8:2) emphasizes another qualification especially pertinent to the particular high priesthood Jesus holds—a life that endures.[22] In 5:8–10 the author claims that Jesus had to undergo suffering as a prerequisite for attaining perfection. Perfection, in turn, is a necessary qualification for him to become the source of everlasting salvation (i.e., to become the everlasting high priest).[23] Thus the writer lays out a logical and temporal sequence of events that culminates in the elevation of Jesus to the office of high priest in the order of Melchizedek. Jesus's possession of perfected life is one of the distinguishing features that qualify him for that priestly office. Perfection, then, is not something inclusive of Jesus's priestly ministry and heavenly exaltation to the throne at God's right hand. It is something he first had to possess in order to then become the heavenly high priest who, after making a cleansing for sin, was exalted to the throne at God's right hand (cf. Heb. 1:3). Two main observations support these claims.

21. See, for instance, Bruce, *Hebrews*, 122–26; E. Grässer, *An Die Hebräer (Hebr 1–6)*, EKKNT 17/1 (Neukirchen-Vluyn: Neukirchener Verlag, 1993), 268.

22. There is little consensus on the meaning of "perfection" language in Hebrews (see the recent summary and discussion in Kurianal, *Jesus Our High Priest*, 219–27). One of the more influential views is that of D. Peterson. Peterson argues that "perfection" language with reference to Jesus is a vocational category closely linked with Jesus's ability to sympathize with his people. As such, perfection involves a process encompassing the entire sequence of events from Jesus's life on earth to his exaltation at God's right hand (*Hebrews and Perfection: An Examination of the Concept of Perfection in the "Epistle to the Hebrews,"* SNTSMS 47 [Cambridge: Cambridge University Press, 1982], 66–73; so also Attridge, *Hebrews*, 86–87). Peterson is right that perfection is related to Jesus's priestly vocation but wrong in when and where he locates it. Jesus's perfection does not include his exaltation; rather it is a prerequisite for his entry into heaven as the great high priest (see also, Kurianal, *Jesus Our High Priest*, 230–33).

23. The author clarifies this in Heb. 7:24–25, where he states that the everlasting salvation obtained by Jesus depends on his having become an everlasting high priest.

First, there is an obvious logical relationship between the process of learning obedience through suffering (Heb. 5:8) and the state of perfection Jesus is said to have attained (5:9)—Jesus's perfection *follows* his suffering. He was made perfect only *after* his suffering had ceased. Jesus was, therefore, not perfect until after his death.

Second, the two aorist passive participles in Hebrews 5:9–10, both of which function adverbially in relation to ἐγένετο, imply a temporal, sequential development from suffering to perfection to being appointed high priest. It was *after* Jesus was perfected that he became the source of everlasting salvation for all those who obey him, being *at that time* appointed high priest by God, according to the order of Melchizedek. The broader argument of Hebrews supplies significant support for this interpretation.

In Hebrews 7:23–25 the writer contrasts the service of priests after the order of Aaron with Jesus's priestly service. The primary point of contrast concerns the respective relationships of Jesus and the Levitical priests to the power of death. Both Jesus and the Levitical priests experienced death. The crux of the distinction is that death prevents the Aaronic priests from "remaining" (παραμένειν). Jesus, however, "remains forever" (μένειν αὐτὸν εἰς τὸν αἰῶνα) and, because of this fact (διὰ τὸ μένειν αὐτόν), possesses an everlasting priesthood—that is, as 7:25 clearly states, Jesus "always lives" (πάντοτε ζῶν) to intercede for his people.

The contrast between these two priestly orders reaches its climax in Hebrews 7:28. On the one hand, the priests in Aaron's order are said to be weak (as has just been shown in vv. 23–25, they die and cannot overcome death's power). The high priest appointed by God to Melchizedek's order, on the other hand, is the Son, who is in the state of "perfection" forever. In keeping with this context, the term "perfection" encapsulates the attribute of enduring life that Jesus has. This is what distinguishes him from the other, weak high priests. All priests, according to the author, are called by God and can sympathize with those for whom they minister. What makes Jesus different and fit for a different priesthood is the fact that unlike the other priests, he is not subject to mortality; rather, like Melchizedek, he "remains" and "lives" (cf. 7:3, 8).

If this is right, then the logic of the argument indicates that Jesus's perfection is the prerequisite that qualifies him to serve as the everlasting high priest.[24] Precisely because Jesus's perfection ensures that he will never forfeit his ministry to death, he can be appointed by God to serve in Melchizedek's

---

24. See, too, the discussion of Kurianal, *Jesus Our High Priest*, 230–33, who also identifies Jesus's perfection with the resurrection.

enduring priestly order.[25] Yet, since Jesus did in fact die, everything the writer has just predicated about Jesus's perfection and ministry can only apply to him *after* his death. Before he died, Jesus, the incarnate Son, was liable to the power of death. He was made like his brothers and sisters in every respect (cf. Heb. 2:17–18). Only at some point after he died, then, did he attain the state of perfection (i.e., possess the kind of life that is not liable to the power of death), and only then could he become the source of everlasting salvation.

The logical and temporal relationships noted above in the discussion of Hebrews 5:8–10 therefore find additional support in the argumentation of 7:23–28. As the writer works out the particulars of the argument he presented *in nuce* in 5:8–10, he emphasizes the importance of Jesus's perfected state. This perfection—which includes Jesus's ever-enduring/ever-remaining life— qualifies him to be a better high priest of Melchizedek's order.

But can a moment be identified when Jesus came into possession of this enduring life and thus became qualified to be the heavenly high priest? Several commentators argue that such an identification is not possible.[26] There are clues in the text, however, that suggest otherwise.

The writer comments in Hebrews 8:4 that if Jesus were on earth he would not even (οὐδ' ἄν) be a priest because there exist those who offer gifts in accordance with the law.[27] In keeping with the discussion above about the relationship between Jesus's perfection and his priestly status, 8:4 recognizes that Jesus was not a priest on earth. In fact, 8:4 clearly locates Jesus's priestly ministry in heaven after his life and death on earth. The writer's logic is clear. The authority of the law remains valid on earth, and on earth there already exists a lawfully appointed order of priests. Therefore, Jesus, being from the tribe of Judah (7:14), cannot serve in that priesthood. What then qualifies Jesus to serve as a priest? As was shown above, Jesus can be a priest because he has the necessary qualification for another order of priesthood—that of Melchizedek, a priesthood that one has not by genealogy but by enduring life.

There was a time, then, before which Jesus, the incarnate Son, could not even be a priest, let alone the great high priest. Before his life and death on earth, he was not perfect and, because of his human lineage, could not serve in the lawful priesthood. Now, however, Jesus is the high priest who passed

25. Kurianal rightly comments that Jesus's eternal life "is the most relevant aspect of the ideal state necessary for being declared High Priest according to the order of Melchizedek. This perfection makes it possible for him to be a priest forever" (*Jesus Our High Priest*, 232).

26. E.g., Attridge, *Hebrews*, 147; Ellingworth, *Hebrews*, 294; and esp. Peterson, *Hebrews and Perfection*, 97.

27. See especially Ellingworth, *Hebrews*, 405.

through the heavens (Heb. 4:14) and, after making atonement, sat down at God's right hand (1:3; 8:1). Perfection, as the requisite qualification for him to become the heavenly high priest, therefore stands between Jesus's death and his elevation to the heavenly priesthood. In light of the discussion above about Jesus's faith when tested receiving the reward of the better resurrection, the most likely candidate for this moment is that of the resurrection. After his death, God brought Jesus out of the realm of death and into a life that will endure forever. Only after this point was Jesus qualified to be the heavenly high priest. If this is correct, then Jesus's resurrection forms a central plank in the priestly Christology of the letter.

The Son Became High Priest: Psalm 110:4 and Resurrection Life

Careful attention to the writer's use of Psalm 110:4 and the argumentation of Hebrews 7 substantiates the conclusion stated above. Specifically, the writer's comment that Jesus "arose" in the likeness of Melchizedek serves as the middle term he relies on to justify his unparalleled christological claim that just as God called Jesus to be Son (Ps. 2:7; Heb. 5:5), God also called him to be priest "forever" (Ps. 110:4; Heb. 5:6).

The related questions of how the writer came to apply Psalm 110:4 to Jesus and how he came to link Psalm 2:7 and Psalm 110:4 have long drawn scholarly attention. Some have speculated about a possible liturgical background for these links.[28] Others have argued that the author understood Jesus's priestly ministry as an aspect of his status as Son.[29] We will probably never know exactly what led the author to make these links. Nevertheless, his argument for the Son's priestly status allows some sound deductions regarding how he set about trying to persuade others to affirm this conclusion—namely, he relies upon the confession of Jesus's everlasting life as a middle term to make the case that Jesus is both Son and priest. Importantly, the extent to which his argument exhibits tension regarding the combination of the offices of reigning Son and high priest in the person of Jesus further indicates that he has not conflated Jesus's coming into possession of enduring life with his exaltation.

---

28. For only a couple of examples, see Attridge, *Hebrews*, 99–103, who argues for a notion of angels as priests possibly influencing liturgical or exegetical traditions known to the author, and E. Käsemann, *Das wandernde Gottesvolk: Eine Untersuchung zum Hebräerbrief*, 4th ed. (Göttingen: Vandenhoeck & Ruprecht, 1961), 124–25.

29. For a few examples, see G. W. Buchanan, *To the Hebrews: Translation, Comment and Conclusions*, AB 36 (Garden City, NY: Doubleday, 1972), 94–97; Grässer, *An Die Hebräer (Hebr 1–6)*, 292.

A High Priest from the Tribe of Judah

The author's argumentative strategy for Jesus's elevation to the priest-hood strongly suggests that he does not conceive of Jesus's priestly ministry as something implicit to his status as reigning Son. As was noted above, his argument highlights a real problem for Jesus's priestly status—his human genealogy. While Jesus's tribal lineage is arguably important for his status as royal Son, the author recognizes that it should prevent him from holding priestly office (cf. Heb. 7:13–14; 8:4).

The fact of Jesus's descent from Judah pushes the writer to demonstrate how Jesus can be a priest in spite of his genealogy. Yet if Hebrews understands Jesus's priestly ministry as an extension of his status as reigning Son, this is a very strange way of defending such a position. That is, if the priesthood is founded upon or an extension of sonship, then Jesus's tribal lineage ought to be a factor working in the writer's favor. Instead, the author seeks to dem-onstrate the very possibility that the royal Son can be a priest *in spite of* his genealogy. Jesus's role as priest here seems therefore to be distinct from—that is, not predicated upon—his status as Son.

In keeping with this assessment, the argument of Hebrews 7:1–8:2 ap-pears designed to show that, irrespective of the law's prescriptions, someone outside of the tribe of Levi can in fact serve as a priest because another priesthood exists. The mention of Melchizedek and his priestly order in the oracle of Psalm 110:4 provides the author with an example of another priesthood, one that depends not on tribal descent but on the quality of life one possesses. Melchizedek—being without father, without mother, and without beginning or end of days—is a priest because he "remains" (μένει, Heb. 7:3) or "lives" (ζῇ, Heb. 7:8). The author finds in Ps. 110:4 a promise that there will be another priest like Melchizedek. Such a priest, he reasons, will have the right to serve in this order not because of tribal genealogy but because he will *arise* (ἀνίστημι) in the likeness (τὴν ὁμοιότητα) of Melchize-dek (cf. Heb. 7:15).

Arising to the Eternal, Heavenly Priesthood

The term "arising" can simply refer to a state of affairs coming into being or to an individual taking an office.[30] This latter sense is almost certainly the meaning in Hebrews 7:11. That the writer uses this language in 7:15 to indicate something more is suggested by his explication of what it means

30. Many commentators argue that this is all the term implies here. E.g., Ellingworth, *Hebrews*, 373.

that "another priest" (that is, a different priest—one outside of the tribe of Levi[31]) will arise in the "likeness" of Melchizedek. He argues in 7:16 that, like Melchizedek, this other priest belongs to this priesthood by virtue of the fact that he possesses the power of an indestructible life (κατὰ δύναμιν ζωῆς ἀκαταλύτου).[32] Over against the qualification of tribal genealogy prescribed by the law, Jesus and Melchizedek are qualified for their priestly offices because they possess the kind of life that remains forever.[33]

Yet, as was noted above, prior to his death, Jesus's life was subject to death's power. He can only be said to have a life that remains, a life that is indestructible, *after* God has saved him out of the realm of death. It therefore follows that the affirmation of his resurrection must underlie the logic of the author's argument here. The language of another priest "arising" in Hebrews 7:15 is thus a reference to Jesus's resurrection.[34] The author has created a brilliant double entendre.[35] Another priest has arisen—namely Jesus, who, in spite of the law's prescriptions with respect to tribal lineage, is qualified to be a priest because God heard his cry and rewarded his faithful suffering with the promise of the better resurrection life.

In sum, the writer's argument suggests that the link between Psalm 2:7 and Psalm 110:4 does not lie in an intrinsic connection between "Son" and "priest," but rather depends on the perception of the coherence between the oracle of God in Scripture about an everlasting priest and the affirmation that God raised Jesus from the dead. Since Jesus has that perfected resurrection life, he is qualified to be the everlasting priest. The one God called as Son is therefore also the one called by God to be priest forever in the order of Melchizedek.

---

31. In this context the classical sense of ἕτερος as "different" is evident. So, e.g., Attridge, *Hebrews*, 200; Bruce, *Hebrews*, 165.

32. Cf. D. M. Hay, *Glory at the Right Hand: Psalm 110 in Early Christianity*, SBLMS 18 (Nashville: Abingdon, 1973), 146–47. Hay suggests it is a "resurrection-exaltation" conviction that lies behind this argument. Yet the tension between Jesus's priestly status and the link between exaltation and royal sonship in Hebrews suggests that this assessment too quickly conflates resurrection and exaltation.

33. This is widely recognized. So, e.g., Attridge, *Hebrews*, 199.

34. In the main, scholars understand the author's comment about Jesus's life as a reference to his ascension and/or exaltation (e.g., Attridge, *Hebrews*, 203). A few commentators, though, rightly detect a resurrection logic in play here (e.g., Bruce, *Hebrews*, 169). Notably, Koester considers the possibility that ἀνίστημι might refer to Jesus's resurrection but concludes that the term probably points primarily to his being elevated to the office of priest (Koester, *Hebrews*, 355; cf. Kurianal, *Jesus Our High Priest*, 111).

35. For an analogous instance of this same word play see Acts 3:22 and 3:26. I am grateful to D. A. deSilva for drawing my attention to this text.

Conclusion

The comment that "Christ's resurrection per se does not figure so centrally in [this] writer's thinking"[36] nicely captures the consensus position regarding Jesus's resurrection in Hebrews. The argument of this essay, however, calls this conclusion into question. I have sought to show not only that the author of Hebrews affirms Jesus's resurrection but also that this category or moment makes a distinctive contribution to his argument for the high-priestly Christology of the text. The assumption of this event underlies the writer's argument for how it is possible that Jesus, the reigning Son from the tribe of Judah, can nevertheless be the great high priest.

36. Peterson, *Hebrews and Perfection*, 70.

6

Blood, Life, and Atonement

Reassessing Hebrews' Christological Appropriation of Yom Kippur

The recent work of several Hebrew Bible scholars on the ways that blood sacrifice functioned has highlighted the importance of the ritual manipulation of blood over the act of slaughtering the victim as the primary means for atonement prescribed by the Mosaic law.[1] Some scholars have tried to apply this understanding of purification to the book of Hebrews,[2] and indeed, no other New Testament text contains such a detailed and consistent application of cultic, sacrificial language to Jesus.

I contend in this chapter that Hebrews' appeal to Yom Kippur needs to be understood in terms of the author's emphasis on the post-crucifixion life of Jesus. To put the issue more bluntly, I argue that Jesus's death on the cross is

Versions of this essay have been presented at various conferences and colloquia. I am grateful for all the critical feedback I have received.

1. E.g., C. A. Eberhart, *Studien zur Bedeutung der Opfer im Alten Testament: Die Signifikanz von Blut- und Verbrennungsriten im kultischen Rahmen*, WMANT 94 (Neukirchen-Vluyn: Neukirchener Verlag, 2002); B. Janowski, *Sühne als Heilsgeschehen: Traditions- und religionsgeschichtliche Studien zur priesterschriftlichen Sühnetheologie* (Neukirchen-Vluyn: Neukirchener Verlag, 2000); J. Milgrom, *Leviticus 1–16: A New Translation with Introduction and Commentary*, AB 3 (New York: Doubleday, 1991), esp. 1031–35; I. Willi-Plein, "Some Remarks on Hebrews from the Viewpoint of Old Testament Exegesis," in *Hebrews: Contemporary Methods—New Insights*, ed. Gabriella Gelardini (Leiden: Brill, 2005), 25–35.

2. Most notably C. A. Eberhart in *Studien zur Bedeutung der Opfer.*

not the place or the primary means of atonement for the author of Hebrews.[3] Rather, when the writer claims in Hebrews 8:4 that Jesus can only serve as a high priest in heaven, he intends to say that the great atoning moment of the incarnation occurred not when Jesus was crucified but after he was resurrected and ascended into heaven. There he presented himself alive and incorruptible before God. Just as Yom Kippur focuses not on the slaughter of the victim as the atoning moment but on the presentation of its blood—that is, its life—before God, so also the author of Hebrews thinks in terms of the presentation of Jesus's indestructible life before God as the central act that effects atonement.

The thesis just presented is likely to trigger a number of critical questions. I cannot address all the possible objections in this brief chapter. I focus instead on three of the main problems a thesis like this encounters in contemporary Hebrews' commentary. These are as follows: (1) the assumption that the cross/death of Jesus is the center of atonement in Hebrews, (2) the general opinion that the author of Hebrews does not consider Jesus's resurrection to be a discrete event that contributes to the Christology and soteriology developed in the epistle, and (3) the view that Yom Kippur consists of two key moments—the slaughter of the victims in the court of the sanctuary and the presentation of their blood in the inner sanctum—that the author correlates with the christological and soteriological agenda of his epistle. I turn, then, to a brief discussion of these points.

3. Jesus's death on the cross is almost universally assumed to be his sacrifice and where atonement occurs in Hebrews. See, e.g., H. W. Attridge, who explains that in Heb. 8–10 the writer interprets Jesus's death "as a sacrifice that effectively atones for sins," adding that "the complex exposition [of Heb. 8–10] will indicate how it is that Christ's death accomplishes [atonement]" (*The Epistle to the Hebrews*, Hermeneia [Philadelphia: Fortress, 1989], 146). P. Ellingworth comments, "The significance of the cross is essentially Christ's once-for-all self-offering in obedience to the will of God; yet that significance can clearly not stand apart from the crucifixion itself" (*The Epistle to the Hebrews*, NIGTC [Grand Rapids: Eerdmans, 1993], 70). W. L. Lane also states, "In the sacrifice of his body on the cross, Jesus freely and fully made the will of God his own. Consequently, his sacrifice embodied the totality of obedience. . . . Because Jesus embraced the will of God in solidarity with the human family, the writer of Hebrews deduced, the new people of God have been consecrated to the service of God" (*Hebrews 1–8*, WBC 47a [Dallas: Word Books, 1991], cxxxiv). He later adds, "The perfection of the new priest is exhibited and is fully accomplished in the offering of himself once for all as the sufficient sacrifice for the transgressions of the people. His own sinlessness . . . required of him no sin offering and assured the unconditional efficacy of his atoning death" (194). B. Lindars writes, "The argument for the permanent efficacy of Christ's sacrificial death is a major contribution [of Hebrews] to the theology of the New Testament. . . . Hebrews alone tackles the subject [of Jesus's death as a sacrifice] comprehensively and systematically, so as to show not only how it can be claimed that the death of Christ was a sacrifice for sins in general, but also how its effect is continually operative" (*The Theology of the Letter to the Hebrews* [Cambridge: Cambridge University Press, 1991], 125).

The Two Great Moments of Yom Kippur and Jesus's Blood in Hebrews

The importance of Yom Kippur as a source for the soteriological and christological reflection of the author of Hebrews goes almost without saying. Jesus's priestly service and blood offering are both depicted in terms of and contrasted with those of the high priest who enters the holy of holies once a year on the Day of Atonement.[4] It has become commonplace in Hebrews scholarship to assume that the author maps Yom Kippur's two great moments—the slaughter of the victim and the presentation of its blood in the holy of holies—onto the two great christological foci of the Son's humiliation (epitomized by his death) and exaltation (epitomized by his entry into heaven). As the great high priest, then, Jesus is both victim and priestly officiant on the cross.

A few citations will illustrate the point. In his commentary on the homily, F. F. Bruce eloquently states,

> It is because of [the writer's] concentration on the priestly aspect of Christ's work that our author has so much to say of [Jesus's] death and exaltation, but so little of his resurrection. The two principal moments in the great sin offering of Old Testament times were the shedding of the victim's blood in the court of the sanctuary and the presentation of its blood inside the sanctuary. In the antitype these two moments were seen to correspond to the death of Christ on the cross and his appearance at the right hand of God.[5]

Similarly, Kenneth Schenck argues that Yom Kippur serves to hold Jesus's death and exaltation together as one atoning sacrifice. He writes, "The author of Hebrews integrates these separate events together by using them to construct a metaphor in which Christ's death is a sacrifice offered in a heavenly tabernacle on a decisive 'Day of Atonement.' The whole movement from Christ's death to his 'session,' or seating, at God's right hand thus functions somewhat as a single event in the plot."[6]

Time would fail me to discuss the many other permutations on this basic position that could be cited.[7] A great many scholars think the writer's appeal

---

4. See, e.g., Heb. 9:7, 11–12. Hebrews draws on other sacrificial imagery in addition to Yom Kippur (e.g., 13:15), but the blood offering on Yom Kippur is the dominant motif.

5. F. F. Bruce, *The Epistle to the Hebrews*, NICNT (Grand Rapids: Eerdmans, 1990), 32–33.

6. K. Schenck, *Understanding the Book of Hebrews: The Story behind the Sermon* (Louisville: Westminster John Knox, 2003), 14–15.

7. E.g., Attridge, *Hebrews*, 147; G. Bertram, "Die Himmelfahrt Jesu vom Kreuz aus und der Glaube an seine Auferstehung," in *Festgabe für A. Deissmann zum 60. Geburtstag 7 November 1926*, ed. K. L. Schmidt (Tübingen: Mohr, 1927), 187–215, here 214; Ellingworth, *Hebrews*, 445; E. Grässer, *An die Hebräer 10,19–13,25* (Zürich: Benziger Verlag, 1999), 402; L. T. Johnson,

to Yom Kippur enables him to explicate the theological meaning of the crucifixion from both an earthly and heavenly perspective. On the one hand, Yom
Kippur allows him to envision the earthly event of the crucifixion in terms
of the slaughter of the sacrificial victim. On the other hand, the imagery of
the high priest's entry into the holy of holies allows the heavenly or spiritual
significance of the crucifixion to be drawn out—Jesus's death can be likened
to the presentation of his blood as an atoning sacrifice to God. Yom Kippur
therefore serves as a theological prism through which some of the manifold
realities of the singular event of the crucifixion can be seen distinctly.

Given this general understanding of the centrality of the cross and the function of the author's appeal to Yom Kippur, it is unsurprising that references to
Jesus's blood in Hebrews are assumed to be self-evident references to Jesus's
death. Scot McKnight, for example, claims that when Hebrews explains the
crucifixion, "The tilt is in the direction of the death of Jesus as a self-sacrifice,
often spoken of as blood."[8] Likewise, while explaining how blood language
helps the author develop the significance of Jesus's death, Luke Timothy Johnson states, "When Hebrews speaks of Christ entering the sanctuary with his
own blood, it means that Christ's entry into God's presence was through the
violent and bloody death on the cross."[9] Again, many others could be quoted,[10]
but the point is clear. The language of "blood," it is generally assumed, functions
in Hebrews as a metaphor for Jesus's obedient, self-sacrificial death on a cross.

One other element of this larger interpretation of Hebrews needs to be
addressed. The perceived correlation between the two-step movement of Yom
Kippur (slaughter-presentation) and what is taken to be the essential substructure of the high-priestly Christology developed in Hebrews (death-exaltation)
explains for most commentators the striking paucity of reference to Jesus's
resurrection in Hebrews.[11]

Hebrews: A Commentary, NTL (Louisville: Westminster John Knox, 2006), 237; R. D. Nelson,
"He Offered Himself: Sacrifice in Hebrews," *Interpretation* 57 (2003): 251–65, here 255; J. W.
Thompson, *The Beginnings of Christian Philosophy: The Epistle to the Hebrews* (Washington,
DC: Catholic Biblical Association of America, 1982), 107–8; H. Windisch, *Der Hebräerbrief*
(Tübingen: Mohr, 1931), 79.

8. S. McKnight, *Jesus and His Death: Historiography, the Historical Jesus, and Atonement
Theory* (Waco: Baylor University Press, 2005), 365.

9. Johnson, *Hebrews*, 237; cf. 256.

10. E.g., Bruce, *Hebrews*, 213; Ellingworth, *Hebrews*, 456; C. R. Koester, *Hebrews: A New
Translation with Introduction and Commentary*, AB 36 (New York: Doubleday 2001), 427; W. L.
Lane, *Hebrews 9–13*, WBC 47b (Dallas: Word Books, 1991), 240; H.-F. Weiss, *Der Brief an die
Hebräer: Übersetzt und Erklärt* (Göttingen: Vandenhoeck & Ruprecht, 1991), 467.

11. Apart from Heb. 13:20, the meaning of which is disputed (Attridge, for example, sees
no reference to resurrection here [Attridge, *Hebrews*, 406]), there is no clear mention of Jesus's
resurrection in Hebrews.

Bruce continues the citation quoted earlier with the following comment: "In this pattern [established by Yom Kippur] the resurrection, as generally proclaimed in the apostolic preaching, finds no separate place."[12] Hans Windisch puts his finger squarely on the problem when he states that Jesus's death and exaltation in Hebrews "encompass . . . the work of redemption. The resurrection is ignored in all the imagery because it would destroy the unity of [Jesus's] high-priestly work."[13] Since the author holds the cross as the place of sacrifice and the Yom Kippur blood offering as a metaphor for that death, the closest possible connection between that event and the writer's language of Jesus's heavenly offering must be maintained. Anything like a claim that Jesus rose bodily from the dead would, in other words, drive a wedge between the necessary unity of Hebrews' high-priestly Christology and theology of atonement by bifurcating Jesus's priestly self-sacrifice on the cross from the atoning act of offering his blood to God. Given this theological reflection on Yom Kippur, the writer understandably ignores the claims of other early followers of Jesus regarding his resurrection.[14]

Jesus's Resurrection in Hebrews

The coherence of the picture sketched above with the apparent lack of explicit reference to Jesus's resurrection in Hebrews and with certain a priori assumptions about the central atoning role of the crucifixion has contributed to the dominance of this consensus. But what if Jesus's resurrection were shown to be present in Hebrews? If such a case could be made, the common understanding of Hebrews' use of Yom Kippur and corresponding christological substructure would need to be rethought.

Given limitations of space, I cannot here mount a complete case for the presence of Jesus's resurrection in Hebrews. Rather, I only lay out five main

---

12. Bruce, *Hebrews*, 33.

13. English translation is mine. Windisch's German: "umschließen . . . das Erlösungswerk, die *Auferstehung* ist bei der ganzen Symbolik ignoriert, weil sie die Einheitlichkeit der hohen-priesterlichen Aktion aufheben würde" (*Der Hebräerbrief*, 79).

14. Many other expressions of this interpretive stance are evident in modern secondary literature (so, e.g., Attridge, *Hebrews*, 86–87, 406; Grässer, *An die Hebräer 10,19–13,25*, 402; O. Hofius, *Katapausis: Die Vorstellung vom endzeitlichen Ruheort im Hebräerbrief*, WUNT 1/11 (Tübingen: Mohr Siebeck, 1970), 181n359; J. Jeremias, "Zwischen Karfreitag und Ostern: Descensus und Ascensus in der Karfreitagstheologie des Neuen Testamentes," ZNW 42 (1949): 194–201; E. Käsemann, *Das wandernde Gottesvolk: Eine Untersuchung zum Hebräerbrief*, 4th ed. (Göttingen: Vandenhoeck & Ruprecht, 1961), 148n1; J. Moffatt, *A Critical and Exegetical Commentary on the Epistle to the Hebrews*, ICC (Edinburgh: T&T Clark, 1924), xxxviii–xxxix; A. S. Peake, *Hebrews: Introduction, Authorized Version, Revised Version with Notes and Index* (New York: H. Forwed, 1902), 32, 242; Schenck, *Understanding the Book of Hebrews*, 37–39.

lines of argument that present a serious challenge to the conclusion that the author of Hebrews ignores Jesus's resurrection.

First, a relatively clear reference to Jesus's resurrection occurs in Hebrews 13:20. Here the writer speaks of the God of peace as "the one who led out of the dead ones . . . Jesus" (ὁ ἀναγαγών ἐκ νεκρῶν . . . Ἰησοῦν). To be sure, commentators are well aware of this point, and several explanations have been offered to show that this mention of Jesus's resurrection is little more than an offhand remark that does not threaten the larger soteriological and christological concerns explicated in the body of the sermon.[15] Attempts to push this comment to the periphery of Hebrews falter, however, in view of other evidence in the homily.

Second, then, the presence of a handful of explicit references to resurrection in Hebrews must be taken into account, not least because these references indicate the author's belief in resurrection. In 6:2 the writer couples belief in the general resurrection with belief in the eschatological judgment, identifying both of these as elements belonging to the foundational teaching about the Christ (ὁ τῆς ἀρχῆς τοῦ Χριστοῦ λόγος, 6:1). That the author affirms some future resurrection finds further confirmation in chapter 11. Here the content of Abraham's faith as he is about to slay Isaac is said to be his belief that "God was able to raise [Isaac] out of the dead" (ἐκ νεκρῶν ἐγείρειν δυνατὸς ὁ θεός, 11:19). That Abraham received Isaac back because he acted on this faith is taken by the writer as a "parable" (παραβολή) that presumably points to the reality of the coming eschatological resurrection.

This last suggestion finds further support in the writer's comment in Hebrews 11:35 that while some dead are known to have been restored by a form of resurrection, others endured great trials hoping to obtain a better resurrection (ἵνα κρείττονος ἀναστάσεως τύχωσιν). The contrast here between a "resurrection" in which women received back their dead and a "better resurrection" most probably points to a distinction between a temporary restoration to life and the hope for the enduring life of the eschatological resurrection. Texts such as Hebrews 6:2, 11:19, and 11:35 therefore provide solid evidence that the author believes in an eschatological resurrection of the dead.

Third, in light of the observations in the previous paragraph, the reference in Hebrews 12:2 to Jesus as the one who stands—or, rather, sits—at

---

15. One way this has been dealt with is to argue that the resurrection here is spiritual and/or has been conflated with the exaltation (see, e.g., Attridge, *Hebrews*, 406; Nelson, "He Offered Himself," 255; Grässer, *An die Hebräer 10,19–13,25*, 402; Schenck, *Understanding the Book of Hebrews*, 38). Others argue that this is a preformed blessing. Thus the reference to Jesus's resurrection is incidental to the argument of the epistle, since the author is simply citing the language of a traditional blessing (e.g., Bertram, "Die Himmelfahrt Jesu," 213–14; Windisch, *Der Hebräerbrief*, 121).

the pinnacle of a litany of examples of faith in Hebrews 11 is striking. If Abraham endured his trial because of his faith in God's resurrection power, and if those who suffered even to the point of death in 11:35 did so in the hope of obtaining the better resurrection, how much more is this likely to be true of Jesus, the author and perfecter of this faith? Put differently, if the list in Hebrews 11 of those lesser examples of faith in the midst of suffering includes explicit references to belief in God's promised resurrection, how likely is it that, when the writer points to Jesus despising the shame of the cross on account of the joy set before him, he imagines that Jesus himself is not a recipient of that hoped-for better resurrection? If Jesus is not here envisioned as the chief example of someone who suffered in the hope that God would raise him from the dead, then the author's appeal in Hebrews 11 to those who endured brutal deaths on account of their belief in resurrection amounts to little more than a cheap rhetorical sleight of hand. If, however, the reference to Jesus at the apex of this list is assumed to include the confession of Jesus's resurrection, then Jesus's exemplary faith perfectly coheres with the faith of those in chapter 11.

Fourth, the conditionals I mention above are more than just suppositions. There is good evidence to suggest that Jesus is identified in Hebrews as enduring his own suffering in the faith that God would raise him from the dead, and that his faith received the object of its hope. In Hebrews 5:7 the author portrays Jesus as being heard when he offered a great cry and tears to "the one who was able to save him out of death" (τὸν δυνάμενον σῴζειν αὐτον ἐκ θανάτου). This depiction of God as "the one able to save from death" is remarkably similar to the content of the reasoning the author attributes to Abraham in the midst of his test. Abraham, it will be recalled, successfully endured his test because he believed God was able to raise Isaac out of the dead. Moreover, just as Abraham's faith led to his receiving Isaac back as a parable of the resurrection, so also the comment about Jesus being heard most naturally implies that the God to whom Jesus cried did not leave him in the realm of death but rather exercised power over death by resurrecting him.

Fifth, when the author makes his case that even though Jesus comes from the tribe of Judah (and not that of Levi) he can nonetheless be a priest (cf. Heb. 7:13–16), he appeals to Jesus's possession of an enduring and indestructible life. Hebrews 7 aims in part to establish the fact that Scripture testifies to a priesthood that is not founded upon Levitical genealogy—that of Melchizedek. The author finds a reference to a non-Levitical priesthood in Psalm 110:4. Here, God swears to the individual addressed, "You are a priest forever according to the order of Melchizedek." The writer's deduction from this instance of divine speech is clear. Scripture attests the existence of a priestly order other than that of Aaron—the order of Melchizedek. Jesus can be a priest in spite of his Judahite genealogy, so long as he possesses the qualifications necessary to belong to that other priesthood. Melchizedek, the writer argues, "remains" (Heb. 7:3) and "lives" (7:8). His priestly status is apparently connected with this quality of enduring or everlasting life. Thus, when the writer speaks of Jesus becoming a priest in the likeness of Melchizedek, he states that Jesus became a priest not according to the commands of the law (i.e., Levitical lineage) but by the power of an indestructible life (7:16). Jesus, in other words, has become a priest because, like Melchizedek, he "remains" (7:24) forever and "always lives" (7:25). His Judahite lineage may prevent him from being part of Aaron's order of priests, but his indestructible life qualifies him to serve in the other biblically attested order of Melchizedek (cf. 7:11). The problem, of course, is that author knows full well that Jesus died (e.g., 2:9; 9:15). How then can he say that Jesus's life is indestructible and everlasting? The most likely answer is that he here assumes that Jesus rose from the dead to an enduring life.

This latter point finds some corroboration in the writer's actual language in Hebrews 7:15. Here, in contrast to the tribe to whom Moses said a priest must belong, Jesus is declared to be another kind[16] of priest, one who has "arisen" (ἀνιστάται) in the likeness of Melchizedek. While the verb ἀνίστημι may simply refer to someone being elevated to an office (cf. 7:11), the explanation of this "arising" here as (1) being in the likeness of the ever-living Melchizedek in 7:15 and (2) having to do with the possession of the power of an indestructible life in 7:16 strongly suggests that the term denotes resurrection.[17]

When taken together, the five arguments just surveyed show that the writer's comment in Hebrews 13:20 is anything but an aberration from major emphases in the rest of the homily. To borrow language from the Ethiopian eunuch: Behold, here is evidence for Jesus's resurrection; what then hinders us from recognizing it? The answer lies, I think, in the a priori assumption that Hebrews locates the place and moment of Jesus's atoning sacrifice on the cross. With Jesus's death as the hermeneutical anchor, it becomes difficult to see how the language of blood and atonement in Hebrews can be distinguished from the crucifixion. Moreover, as noted above, the pattern of Yom Kippur seems to explain how the writer could conceive of Jesus as a high priest while also explaining the atoning significance of the cross. Within this model, the resurrection has no discrete place. Recent scholarly work on Yom

---

16. The sense of ἕτερος here is clearly that of "different," rather than another of the same kind (see the helpful discussion of the word in Attridge, *Hebrews*, 200; Bruce, *Hebrews*, 165).

17. I argue this point in greater detail in chap. 5.

Kippur and blood rites in Scripture, however, suggests that the emphasis on death, which is often assumed to be one of the high points in the Yom Kippur sacrifice, is mistaken.

Death, Blood, Purity, and Yom Kippur

Over the past few decades a number of Jewish and Hebrew Bible scholars such as Jacob Milgrom, Ina Willi-Plein, Bernd Janowski, and Christian Eberhart, to note only a few, have undertaken sustained examinations of the role and effect of blood offerings as detailed in the Jewish Scriptures. These scholars disagree on many points, but significant lines of convergence are clear. First, there is general agreement that it is the life of the sacrifice that is effective for atonement.[18] Thus in Leviticus 17:11 God declares, "The life of the flesh is in the blood; and I have given it to you for making atonement for your lives on the altar; for it is the blood that makes atonement, by means of the life."[19] While this passage does not directly address Yom Kippur, it appears to summarize the basic theology of blood sacrifice—the blood is the vehicle or agent of the victim's life, and that *life* upon the altar effects atonement. The converse of this point is that the death or slaughter of the victim, while necessary to procure the blood, has no particular atoning significance in and of itself.[20]

Second, the ritual manipulation of the life-bearing blood results in purification.[21] The central act of blood manipulation on Yom Kippur occurred when the high priest entered the holy of holies and sprinkled the blood on the

18. E.g., Janowski, *Sühne als Heilsgeschehen*, 247; B. J. Schwartz, "The Prohibitions concerning the 'Eating' of Blood in Leviticus 17," in *Priesthood and Cult in Ancient Israel*, ed. G. A. Anderson and S. M. Olyan (Sheffield: JSOT Press, 1991), 34–66, here 47.

19. This translation follows the RSV with minor modifications. J. Sklar has offered a compelling defense of the translation of בנפש as "by means of the life" (*Sin, Impurity, Sacrifice, Atonement: The Priestly Conceptions*, HBM 2 [Sheffield: Sheffield Phoenix, 2005], 168–73).

20. Willi-Plein, "Some Remarks on Hebrews," 33; Eberhart, *Studien zur Bedeutung der Opfer*, 203–4; C. A. Eberhart, "Characteristics of Sacrificial Metaphors in Hebrews," in *Hebrews: Contemporary Methods—New Insights*, ed. Gabriella Gelardini (Leiden: Brill, 2005), 37–64, here 39–44, 49.

21. Jacob Milgrom, in particular, has argued that the implements and sancta of the tabernacle are the object of purification (*Leviticus 1–16*, 254–58, 1079–84; similarly, Eberhart, "Characteristics of Sacrificial Metaphors in Hebrews," 44; Willi-Plein, "Some Remarks on Hebrews," 32–33). For Milgrom, blood manipulation purifies because the blood comes into contact with certain parts of the tabernacle. Over against Milgrom, however, R. E. Gane has convincingly argued on this point that just as certain impurities could defile the objects in God's house without physical contact (e.g., Lev. 20:3, where offering one's children to Molech defiles God's sanctuary), so also purification of certain objects in the tabernacle by way of sacrificial blood manipulation could lead to purification of the worshipers apart from having blood applied to them (*Cult and Character: Purification Offerings, Day of Atonement, and Theodicy* [Winona Lake, IN: Eisenbrauns, 2005]).

mercy seat. Ensuring the achievement of this purified state was of paramount importance: this purity allowed the human to approach the deity and the deity to remain in contact with humanity.[22] Thus, if there is any focal point of Yom Kippur, it is on the sprinkling of the blood in the holy of holies—that is to say, it is the moment when the life of the animal is taken into God's presence.

As Christian Eberhart notes, these points suggest that in cases of blood offering like Yom Kippur, "sacrificial blood purifies on physical contact, which means when it is actually applied to people or the sanctuary and its sacred objects. But this purification would not happen if the animal . . . were to be slaughtered without the subsequent blood application rite being carried out."[23] The biblical account of Yom Kippur, therefore, does not assume two great moments. To quote Eberhart again, "The moment of slaughter as such . . . has no particular significance."[24] Rather, a more critical or central activity was the presentation of the life of the victim—that is, its blood—in the holy of holies.

Jesus as the Heavenly High Priest in Hebrews

If we assume for the moment that the author of Hebrews understood the basic concepts just discussed—the blood is the life of the victim, and the presentation of that life in the holy of holies by the high priest is when and how atonement happens on Yom Kippur—then a remarkable conclusion follows: the writer is unlikely to have conflated Jesus's atoning work with the crucifixion. On this supposition, he is more likely to stress Jesus's entry into the heavenly holy of holies to present his offering in God's presence than to focus on the death of Jesus on the cross. Moreover, the language of "blood" in this larger conception would probably function for the writer as a metaphor not for Jesus's death (as if one would ever bring death into God's presence) but for his life.

This hypothesis nicely explains several elements in the homily. First, it makes sense of the writer's puzzling comments in Hebrews 8:3–4 that while Jesus had to have something to offer, if he were on earth he would not be able to make any offering or serve in any kind of priestly capacity, because on earth those who offer the gifts according to the law already exist. These verses appear to say that Jesus was not legally eligible to be a priest on earth, let alone the high priest he is confessed to be in 8:1–2. On the one hand, such a conclusion is hard to square with the general assumption that Jesus's crucifixion was

22. Esp. Willi-Plein, "Some Remarks on Hebrews," 33.
23. Eberhart, "Characteristics of Sacrificial Metaphors in Hebrews," 58.
24. Eberhart, "Characteristics of Sacrificial Metaphors in Hebrews," 58.

the moment when he officiated as high priest over his own sacrifice. If that were what happened on the cross, then it would seem that Jesus did serve in a priestly capacity on earth and that the author has merely become muddled in the complexities of his own argument.[25] On the other hand, the claims of 8:3–4 cohere nicely with the argument of Hebrews 7 briefly outlined above. Jesus was not a priest until after his resurrection. Only after he arose to an indestructible life was he eligible to be the great high priest of Melchizedek's order, because the legal prescription regarding Levitical genealogy no longer barred him from serving in a priestly capacity. If, in keeping with the biblical picture of Yom Kippur, the writer has not conflated Jesus's death with Jesus's atoning offering, then his claims in 8:3–4 make perfect sense.

Second, if the writer really thought that Jesus made his offering in the presence of God in heaven and not on the cross on earth, then his consistent emphasis on Jesus making his offering in heaven also makes good sense. That is to say, when the author speaks in Hebrews 6:19–20, 7:26, 8:2, 9:11, 9:23–25, and 10:12 of Jesus's priestly service and offering as occurring in the presence of God *in heaven*, this language does not need to be explained away as referring to the spiritual significance of the cross. Rather, the writer probably meant that Jesus made his offering in heaven, the very place where he was qualified to make it.

Third, the evidence given above for Jesus's resurrection may be recognized. Moreover, the language of Jesus's heavenly presentation of his offering can be seen to function in a way that depends on the atoning role of blood offering as described in Jewish Scripture. The blood language in Hebrews likely functions as a metonymy for Jesus's life, not for his death. In keeping with the role of the blood on Yom Kippur, the entry of Jesus into heaven with his resurrection life and the offering of himself before God there mark the time, place, and agent of atonement in Hebrews.

Conclusion

The offering of blood in the Mosaic cult did not symbolize the entry and presentation of death before the presence of God. This was instead the offering of life. In the same way, Hebrews' emphasis on Jesus's living presence in heaven—the location where the author consistently claims Jesus made his offering—implies that it is not the death/slaughter of Jesus that atones

---

25. Indeed, this is what scholars assume the author thought was the case (see esp. A. J. M. Wedderburn, "Sawing Off the Branches: Theologizing Dangerously *ad Hebraeos*," *JTS* 56 [2005]: 393–414).

but the presentation of his life before God in the heavenly holy of holies. Jesus's resurrection makes this presentation possible not only by informing the Christology of Hebrews—Jesus's resurrection brings him as a human being into possession of the indestructible life necessary for him to become the high priest of Melchizedek's order—but also by providing an explanation for the author's sacrificial soteriology that is intelligible in terms of the biblical account of blood offering.

The case presented above does not, however, suggest that Jesus's death has no importance for the author of Hebrews. While I have focused on the presentation of sacrificial blood as the moment when atonement was effected and on the importance of blood, the agent of atonement, as life, I do not mean to imply that death was not part of blood sacrifice. Nor do I mean to say that Jesus's death is unimportant for the author of Hebrews.

Rather, I have attempted to highlight the fact that blood sacrifice needs to be conceived of as a *process* that involves a whole sequence of events. The slaughter of the victim and the presentation of the blood are both necessary elements of that sequence, but neither of them alone is sufficient to achieve the goal toward which the entire process aims. The mistake of much modern commentary on Hebrews has been to think of these two elements in the process, at least as they apply to the incarnate Son, as essentially interchangeable and coterminous—both occurred when Jesus was crucified. This has contributed to a distorted understanding of the place and importance of Jesus's resurrection in the Epistle to the Hebrews. I am not seeking to reduce everything in Hebrews to Jesus's heavenly presentation while trying to show that everything must not be reduced to Jesus's crucifixion. In my opinion, recognizing that sacrifice is a process helps avoid a reductionistic interpretation by allowing the different elements of the sequence to relate to one another as parts of the whole process without having to collapse these elements or their sequential relationship into one another.[26]

One further conclusion may be drawn from this study. If the arguments above are basically sound, then Hebrews' appeal to Yom Kippur attests to a kind of early Christian Judaism concerned with showing how the purification rites of the Mosaic cult elucidate the confession about and theological implications of Jesus's resurrection and exaltation. That is to say, the incarnation of the Son of God clearly compels substantial rethinking and development vis-à-vis Jewish Scripture and belief, but the reading of Hebrews proposed

26. R. Nelson has already suggested something like this when he spoke about a "sacrificial script," though he still does not grasp, in my view, the way that Jesus's resurrection helps clarify the relationship of the elements of the script (see "He Offered Himself").

above suggests that some early followers of Jesus sought to work out this development in continuity with and even under the pressure of the biblical witness (e.g., Jesus cannot serve as a priest on earth because the law forbids it; the offering of blood emphasizes life, not death). Such a hermeneutic would imply that the discrete voice of Scripture plays as big a role in the writer's understanding of Jesus and the atonement as do confessional elements like those of his resurrection and ascension.

7

Weak and Useless?

Purity, the Mosaic Law, and Perfection in Hebrews

In the opening chapter of the Epistle to the Hebrews, the author approvingly cites Psalm 44:8 LXX with reference to the heavenly Son. God says to the Son in Hebrews 1:9, "You loved righteousness and you hated lawlessness [ἐμίσησας ἀνομίαν]." This very love of righteousness and hatred of lawlessness is identified as the rationale for God's anointing the Son and thereby elevating him beyond his peers. Despite this claim about hating lawlessness, one aspect of Hebrews sometimes identified as a clear indicator of the text's supersessionist character is the author's presumed disdain for the Mosaic law's external rituals. The author avers in Hebrews 9:9–10 that these rituals cannot "perfect the conscience of the worshiper, but deal only with food and drink and various baptisms, regulations for the body imposed until the time comes to set things right" (NRSV). The law, being "weak and useless" (7:18), was never able to perfect anything (7:19). The author's appeal to Psalm 40 in Hebrews 10 even seems to suggest that God has no desire for external, earthly sacrificial rituals.[1] Now that Jesus has offered a better sacrifice than

---

1. For example, W. Eisele argues that Christ's full obedience to God's will in Heb. 10 renders earthly rituals and offerings useless: "For all our attempts at sanctification would be pointless because they remain earthly activities" (my translation; Eisele's German: "Denn alle Heiligungsversuche unsererseits müßten sinnlose, weil irdische Veranstaltungen bleiben"; *Ein unerschütterliches Reich: Die mittelplatonische Umformung des Parusiegedankens im Hebräerbrief*, BZNW 116 [Berlin: de Gruyter, 2003], 105). H. Montefiore suggests that the critique of sacrifice in Heb. 10 cannot be limited to particular rituals but indicates a more general "divine disapproval

anything prescribed by the law, the law and its external rituals have been replaced. Jesus's once-for-all sacrifice means the law and its sacrifices have become outmoded and can be discarded.

Indeed, some have argued that the implications of Hebrews' claims about Jesus's sacrifice so destabilize and subvert the law's sacrificial logic that in the course of making these claims, the author saws off the very theological branch upon which his argument rests when he maintains that Jesus's death was the ultimate sacrifice.[2] On the one hand, the author affirms in 9:22 that the aspersion of blood is necessary for forgiveness. On the other hand, his interpretation of Psalm 40 in Hebrews 10 appears to obviate the whole notion that God wants sacrifice at all.[3] "Hebrews," A. J. M. Wedderburn comments, "seems to persist resolutely with cultic terminology even after it has, to all intents and purposes, dealt the cultic way of thought a *coup de grâce*."[4] For Wedderburn, the fundamental contradictions in Hebrews result from the collision of apocalyptic and Platonic worldviews that are constitutive of the somewhat confused thought world of the epistle. The idea that the preexistent Son could become human and then, at the decisive salvific moment of his death, leave his body and the material realm to return to heaven while still being thought to offer his blood in that heavenly realm deconstructs both the author's sacrificial theology and his supposed Platonic foundations.

Such arguments are clearly supersessionist and antinomian, relegating the very logic of the law with its material concerns and rituals to the dustbin of history. They are also, according to Wedderburn, incoherent. How can Jesus leave the material realm but still have his blood with him? How can the cross be both a historical event and a heavenly/spiritual one? In fact, Wedderburn suggests, the more seriously the author of Hebrews takes his claims that the crucifixion is the heavenly moment of Jesus's high-priestly offering, the more unstable and incoherent his entire theological project becomes.

I have argued elsewhere that this sort of reading of Hebrews is mistaken on several levels (see chap. 8). Hebrews does not presuppose a dualism or cosmology that is essentially Platonic. In my view, the author also does not claim that the atoning sacrifice Jesus offered is reducible to the historical event of the crucifixion. Rather, the author thinks that the atoning sacrifice Jesus offered culminated in the presentation of himself alive in his resurrected

of the Law itself" (*A Commentary on the Epistle to the Hebrews*, Harper's New Testament Commentaries [San Francisco: Harper & Row, 1964], 168).

    2. A. J. M. Wedderburn, "Sawing Off the Branches: Theologizing Dangerously *ad Hebraeos*," *JTS* 56 (2005): 393–414.

    3. Wedderburn, "Sawing Off the Branches," esp. 401–4.

    4. Wedderburn, "Sawing Off the Branches," 409.

humanity when he ascended to the Father and entered the heavenly holy of holies.[5] I will not rehearse those arguments here. I want instead to examine the assumption that the author rejects the law and its sacrificial logic because the rituals required by the law were only effective for earthly, external matters and could not effect internal purification.

Hebrews' claim that the law only produced limited and external purification is shocking. I am persuaded that Susan Haber is correct when she suggests that such a claim limits the purifying force of the cultic elements of the Mosaic economy to the realm of ritual purification.[6]

I am also persuaded, however, that Haber, Wedderburn, and others go wrong when they deduce from this polemic that the author must therefore reject ritual purity concerns, and even the entire logic of Levitical sacrifice, and replace these with a preformed Christology centered on the death of Jesus as the ultimate saving event. I argue here that the author's close connection between perfection, purity, and one's ability to approach God's presence, especially in the case of Jesus, indicates instead that the very concerns of both moral purity and sin, on the one hand, and ritual purity, which does not pertain to sin, on the other, lie at the center of his soteriological reflection. The author confesses that Jesus, although he is the heavenly Son and is without sin, had nevertheless to be made perfect in his humanity in order to become the great high priest, return to the heavenly realms, and minister there on behalf of his brothers and sisters. Such a concept of perfection, I argue, overlaps significantly with Jewish ritual purity concerns.

Yet if this is correct, then the author's arguments about the law's limited powers of purification do not support the further inference that he rejects entirely sacrificial ritual and external purification, replacing or superseding them with something wholly other, something inimical to the Levitical rituals—the claim that Jesus's death is the means of inner, moral purification for others. Rather than rejecting the logic of sacrifice and external purification found in the Mosaic law, the author has instead pushed that logic to what he takes to be its ultimate conclusion—purification that makes one fit to enter fully and permanently into the sacred space of God's heavenly presence. The author of Hebrews, I suggest, speaks of this kind of purification in terms of perfection. Before examining Hebrews directly, however, it will be helpful to consider some of the important work on the

---

5. See, esp., D. M. Moffitt, *Atonement and the Logic of Resurrection in the Epistle to the Hebrews*, NovTSup 141 (Leiden: Brill, 2011).

6. S. Haber, "From Priestly Torah to Christ Cultus: The Re-Vision of Covenant and Cult in Hebrews," *JSNT* 28 (2005): 105–24. For my own detailed engagement with and critique of Haber's essay, see chap. 3.

concepts of Jewish ritual and moral purity that has been done in the last few decades.

Conceiving Ritual and Moral Purity

In his book *Impurity and Sin in Ancient Judaism*, Jonathan Klawans advances the thesis that the biblical conception of purity, as well as the conception found in some expressions of Second Temple Judaism and later rabbinic Judaism, is best understood as consisting of two parallel purity systems—the ritual and the moral.[7] Klawans is engaging in an argument whose full scope lies outside the purview of this study. Nevertheless, a brief summary of his understanding of these two systems will be useful here.

The ritual purity system has to do with those events and activities delineated in the Bible (see esp. Lev. 12–15) that render persons or inanimate objects impure, as well as with the particular ritual means by which this impurity can be rectified. Importantly, ritual impurity is only skin deep. That is to say, this kind of purity has nothing to do intrinsically with the purity of the interior self but only with the purity of one's body.

By the time of the late Second Temple period, a number of situations and activities were considered to render a person or thing ritually impure—for example, stepping over a grave, touching a corpse, or even being in the same "tent" as a corpse.[8] Sexual intercourse, menstruation, and the emission of semen also rendered people and objects they came in contact with impure. The birth of a child made a woman ritually impure. Various skin ailments would make a person impure. Moreover, in many cases persons or objects that were in an impure state could further transmit that impurity to those who came into certain kinds of contact with them.

Notably, none of these activities necessarily involved any kind of sin or moral fault. Birthing a child, preparing a corpse for burial, developing a skin disease, menstruating, emitting semen—none of this was deemed to be sin. All of these things, however, created some kind of contaminating force that infected, as it were, people and things and made them impure, usually by way of direct, physical contact. By the same token, touching a corpse, or a person who had a skin disease, or a woman who was menstruating, or a man who

---

7. J. Klawans, *Impurity and Sin in Ancient Judaism* (Oxford: Oxford University Press, 2000), esp. 21–32.

8. For a well-reasoned discussion on the kinds of activities and circumstances that were likely considered to render one ritually impure in the Second Temple period see E. P. Sanders, *Judaism: Practice and Belief, 63 BCE–66 CE* (London: SCM, 1992), 217–22.

had recently ejaculated made one impure, but again, to touch and thereby contract impurity was not to sin.

The solution for these ritual impurities generally involved the passage of time and washings.[9] Semen emission, for example, made a Jewish man impure. He and those with whom he came into certain kinds of contact could become pure by immersing and waiting until sunset (Lev. 15:1–11). The removal of impurities contracted by the birth of a child or from a skin disease or from a corpse required more complicated and interesting processes. A woman who bore a male child, for example, was impure for a period of seven days, as with her menstruation, and then for an additional thirty-three days, bringing her time of impurity to a total of forty days (12:1–4). At the end of this period she was required to bring a burnt offering and a so-called sin offering (12:6–8). Only then would she be fully purified from the act of giving birth (12:8). The fact that blood sacrifices formed a component of purification in certain cases such as the birth of a child is a matter to which I return below. The central point for the moment is that the preceding examples prove that the contraction of ritual impurities was not necessarily a matter of moral transgression/sin.

This is not to say that ritual impurity matters could not cross over into the realm of sin. They could, particularly in cases where certain actions caused one who was ritually impure to transgress a prohibition. One of the primary places where such transgression became possible was the sacred space of the temple. Leviticus 12:4, for example, makes it abundantly clear that a woman who is impure on account of giving birth must not touch any holy thing or come into the sanctuary while in her impure state.

Corpse impurity was also to be kept out of the sacred precincts. The underlying principle seems to be that ritually impure persons were not allowed to draw near to God's presence.[10] This likely explains the logic behind the curious fact that the high priest was the one person whom Leviticus explicitly says must avoid being contaminated by a corpse (Lev. 21:10–11). Indeed, relative to the average person, the rules for priests were also much more stringent in this regard, though priests are not bound by the strict prohibition that applies to the high priest (21:1–3). The rationale for these stricter rules seems to be that because the priests, and the high priest in particular, came closest to the presence of God, they were required to be far more careful about their ritual purity status.[11] If they were to become impure and then come close to God's presence, they would be guilty of sin.

9. See esp. Sanders, *Judaism*, 72.

10. Sanders, among several others, makes a compelling case that proximity to God's presence in the temple served as the primary rationale underlying purity concerns (*Judaism*, 70–72).

11. So Sanders, *Judaism*, 71–72.

The preceding discussion implies that the primary point at which ritual impurity became a major problem or crossed over into the realm of sin concerned coming into the sacred space of the sanctuary and thus also drawing near to the presence of the God who dwelt there. God did not allow ritually impure persons to come too near his presence. But why was this? Jacob Milgrom, among others, makes a cogent case that a core concern in matters of ritual impurity was the presence and problem of death. Ritual purity concerns often had to do with the presence or appearance of decay. Loss of blood, semen, the deterioration of the body in the case of skin diseases, and, of course, the human corpse all suggest the diminution of the body's life force and thus the presence of death. God will not tolerate death being brought into his presence.[12]

Yet death cannot be the only factor in play. Hyam Maccoby notes that if death were the only concern at the center of ritual impurity then it is strange that while the loss of vaginal blood makes a woman impure (presumably by loss of life force), bleeding from a wound, something that could actually lead to death, does not.[13] Why, moreover, does giving birth make a woman impure? Obviously the process of birth involves the issue of vaginal blood, but if that were all that was going on, it is odd that the woman would be considered impure for several weeks beyond the normal seven days of menstruation impurity. It seems that the birth of the child itself somehow increases the magnitude of the woman's impurity. Maccoby therefore suggests, I think correctly, that the problem is not death alone but the cycles of mortality in general. Sex, birth, decay, and death—functions that relate to and are even definitive of mortality—lie at the center of ritual purity.[14]

The realm of moral impurity, to continue with Klawans's terminology, differs in significant ways from that of ritual impurity. I noted above that Klawans is addressing a much larger argument than can be fully discussed here. Essentially the debate revolves around whether sin produces a real, defiling force as ritual impurity does, or if the language that speaks of sin producing some kind of impurity amounts only to a metaphorical application of ritual impurity language to the abstract realm of moral infraction. Klawans argues, persuasively in my view, that the category of "impurity" should properly be applied to sin because sin, like the ritual matters mentioned above, produces real defilement. Thus, it is appropriate to speak about a system of moral purity,

---

12. See J. Milgrom's discussions of this in, e.g., *Leviticus 1–16: A New Translation with Introduction and Commentary*, AB 3 (New York: Doubleday, 1991), 46, 767, 1002–3.

13. H. Maccoby, *Ritual and Morality: The Ritual Purity System and Its Place in Judaism* (Cambridge: Cambridge University Press, 1999), 31.

14. Maccoby, *Ritual and Morality*, 49–50, 207; cf. Sanders, *Judaism*, 217.

just as it is to speak about one of ritual purity. This system is not, however, identical to that of ritual purity. Whereas ritual impurity need not be—indeed, could not be—ultimately avoided, one was to seek to avoid moral impurity because this kind of impurity resulted from violating a divine prohibition or failing to perform a divine command.

The discussion above showed that ritual impurity was only external and involved a great deal of contagion by physical touch. This is not the case for moral impurity. Sinful acts result in moral impurity that defiles the sinner inwardly, but this impurity does not defile other people. Thus, one cannot pass along moral impurity to another person or thing by contact. This is not to say, however, that moral impurity does not convey defilement. Moral impurity conveys defilement to the land of Israel (see esp. Lev. 18:24–25), something ritual impurity never does. Furthermore, the defilement caused by some sin seems to transfer an impurity directly to the sacred space of the sanctuary, even from a distance (see, e.g., 20:3, where the abominable sin of an Israelite sacrificing a child to Molech, presumably at one of Molech's temples, nevertheless defiles God's sanctuary). Moral defilement therefore attaches to the sinner in some internal sense, to the land, and to the sanctuary simply by the commission of the prohibited act. This defilement is not external and not visible to the human eye, but it is nevertheless real and brings real consequences.

In yet another way this kind of defilement differs from that of ritual impurity: neither time nor washing can purge the stain of sin. Moral purification involves repentance, recompense, and the offering of sacrifices. Ultimately, however, the defilement of the land and temple that results from moral impurity can build to the point that the land reacts by "vomiting out" the people who dwell upon it (e.g., Lev. 18:26–30), and the presence of God can depart from the sanctuary.[15]

Thus, there are key differences between these two systems, but there are also key parallels. Klawans summarizes the situation well when he writes, "We ought to understand that with both kinds of impurity, we are dealing with perceived effects that result from actual physical processes. In the case of ritual impurity, a real, physical process or event (e. g., death, menstruation) has a perceived effect: impermanent contagion that affects people and certain objects within their reach. In the case of moral impurity, a real, physical process or event (e. g., child sacrifice or adultery) has a different perceived effect: a noncontagious defilement that affects persons, the land, and the

---

15. This last point is made with particular force in J. Milgrom, "Israel's Sanctuary: The Priestly 'Picture of Dorian Gray,'" *Revue biblique* 83 (1976): 390–99.

sanctuary."[16] In short, both systems of purity have to do with real impurities that convey to real objects, even if the ways in which these impurities convey and the things to which they are conveyed differ markedly from each other.

There is, however, a curious fact about these two systems of purity that Klawans says little about: while many cases of ritual impurity require no sacrifice for purification, some cases do. Also curious is the fact that the sacrifices for purification in both the ritual and moral systems are the same—the so-called sin offerings. That is to say, when a moral infraction needed to be rectified, the guilty party had to offer a "sin" offering. This sacrifice was essential for atonement (see, e.g., Lev. 4:27–35). In certain cases of ritual impurity, however, the person in need of purification also had to offer a "sin" offering that also effected atonement for them (see esp. 12:6–8, where a woman who has given birth has to offer a "sin" offering by which the priest makes atonement for her).

Jacob Milgrom's theory about ritual impurity mentioned above accounts for this strange situation by positing that, like moral impurity, some ritual impurities also convey a stain to the sanctuary. While not universally accepted,[17] this theory makes a great deal of sense at this point. Milgrom argues that both severe ritual impurities (such as giving birth and corpse impurity) and sins or moral impurity defile the sanctuary and its altars even from a distance. The more serious impurities penetrate more deeply into the sacred precincts than the more minor ones. This would explain the need for blood sacrifices in cases of sin and of certain ritual impurities such as birth. Blood, Milgrom argues, has the power to cleanse or purify the altars and the sacred precincts from the impurities that cling to them as a result of moral and ritual impurities.[18]

As evidence Milgrom points to cases where sacrificial blood is applied to an altar or other part of the sanctuary and the object of the verb for atonement, *kipper*, is the sanctuary or the altar to which the blood is applied. In Leviticus 16:15–20, for example, the holy place, the tent of meeting, and the altars are "atoned for" by way of blood application. The atoning action, in other words, is that of purification. The detergent or agent that effects that purification is blood.

Importantly, Leviticus 16:16 identifies both the uncleanness (i.e., ritual impurity) and the sins of the people as the sources of defilement that make the annual purification necessary. The clear implication of this is that the peoples' ritual and moral impurities have both defiled the sacred precincts, which are consequently in need of cleaning/purification. This regular cleansing

---

16. Klawans, *Impurity and Sin*, 34.
17. See, e.g., the multiple criticisms of Milgrom's theory in Maccoby, *Ritual and Morality*.
18. See esp. Milgrom, *Leviticus 1–16*, 254–58, 711–12.

is essential to the covenant relationship. If this ongoing maintenance were not performed, the level of impurity would build to the point that God's presence would depart (see, e.g., Ezek. 5:11). Blood application in this sacred space is a necessary means for effecting the sanctuary's purification.

Where Milgrom's theory seems weakest, however, concerns the relationship between the purification of the altars and sacred spaces, on the one hand, and that of the people for whom sacrifices are being offered, on the other. Milgrom argues that blood purifies objects by way of direct, physical application. Since blood is not applied to the person bringing the sacrifice, Milgrom reasons that sacrifice does not play a role in purifying the offerer. Sacrifice is necessary only to purify the altars contaminated by the peoples' sins and ritual impurities. The offerer, in the case of sin, is purified from the defilement of sin by experiencing guilt and repenting.[19] In ritual matters, the offerer is purified by time and washings.

Roy Gane has leveled a trenchant critique against Milgrom at just this point.[20] Gane points to texts that do in fact link the offering of sacrifice with the purification of the offerer. In Leviticus 12:7, for example, the woman who gave birth is finally rendered pure from (*min*) her ritual impurity by means of the sacrifices she offers. Similarly, in Numbers 8:12, 21 the Levites are purified by their sacrifices. Sacrifice, in other words, does seem to remove impurity from the offerer. This evidence suggests that Milgrom's theory is only half right. Milgrom's theory of the conveyance of impurities to the holy places from a distance is correct, but it suffers from being unidirectional. Just as one need not be in contact with the sacred spaces to convey impurity to them, so also, Gane argues, the purity effected by blood application to the altars can have the effect of purifying the offerers too. Blood, that is, need not be applied directly to the people in order for the purity it effects on the sacred appurtenances to be reciprocally conveyed to them.

One more conversation partner is worthy of mention here. In his book *Sin, Impurity, Sacrifice, Atonement: The Priestly Conceptions*, Jay Sklar notes that while Klawans rightly highlights distinctions between the systems of ritual and moral impurity, the fact that the same sacrifices (esp. the "sin" offering) are required in the case of some ritual impurities as are required for moral impurities suggests that at this point the two systems converge.[21] This becomes even clearer when one considers the end results of both kinds of impurities.

---

19. Milgrom, *Leviticus 1–16*, 254–56, 1056–58.

20. R. E. Gane, *Cult and Character: Purification Offerings, Day of Atonement, and Theodicy* (Winona Lake, IN: Eisenbrauns, 2005), esp. 106–43.

21. J. Sklar, *Sin, Impurity, Sacrifice, Atonement: The Priestly Conceptions*, HBM 2 (Sheffield: Sheffield Phoenix, 2005), 144–50, esp. 149.

That is to say, both ritual impurity and moral impurity create defilement that puts the people in danger with respect to God, and both threaten God's willingness to remain present in the sanctuary.

Sklar argues further that the term *kipper*, which is used to resolve both kinds of impurity, should not be pressed too hard to mean only purification in matters of ritual purity and only ransom in matters of moral purity. In sacrificial contexts, the means for effecting both ransom and ritual purification is the application of sacrificial blood, especially the blood of the "sin" offering. Thus, Sklar suggests, sacrificial atonement cannot be reduced to either ransom or purification but should be understood as including both ransoming and purifying effects.[22]

This cursory discussion of the ritual and moral purity systems depicted in the Hebrew Bible can now be summarized. Ritual purity is primarily a matter of one's external condition. This kind of defilement is contagious and usually spread by contact. At its core, ritual impurity appears to be about matters of mortality. Further, ritual impurity is a major obstacle when one tries to come close to God's presence. God does not permit ritually impure persons to come close to his presence. To bring impure mortality into God's sacred space is to be guilty of sin. The need for people to be in a ritually pure state therefore appears to be primarily about rendering mortal humanity fit to draw near to God's presence.

Moral purity has to do with obeying God's commands. The violation of divine directives results in moral defilement. A person's moral impurity is not external and is not contagious. Nevertheless, while ritual and moral purity are distinct, both problematize the relationship between God and his people. Ritual impurity prevents the people from approaching God. Moral impurity threatens their ability to dwell in the land, which is defiled by sin, and threatens them with God's punitive wrath. Both kinds of impurity further stand in the way of God and his people dwelling together because both convey defilement to the sanctuary. The sanctuary needs regular purification if God's presence is to remain there.

It further appears to be the case that sacrificial atonement in the fullest sense—that is, the state that results from solving the problems of moral and ritual impurity such that God and humanity can dwell together—requires the removal of the threat of God's wrath by way of redemption or ransom *and* the purification of the people, the land, and the sanctuary. Full atonement,

---

22. For a condensed version of his argument, see J. Sklar, "Sin and Impurity: Atoned or Purified? Yes!," in *Perspectives on Purity and Purification in the Bible*, ed. N. S. Meshel et al., LHB/OTS 474 (London: T&T Clark, 2008), 18–31.

in other words, is effected when the defilement from both moral and ritual impurities is purged.

But what does any of this have to do with Hebrews? I demonstrate next that the meaning of perfection language in Hebrews overlaps at points with both of these concepts of purity. To be more specific, the author at times uses perfection language to mean the complete and enduring rectification of the impurities that separate God and humanity. If this is right, then the fact that Jesus needed to be perfected suggests that the writer has purity concerns in view. Yet the fact that Jesus, who was without sin/moral impurity, nevertheless needed to be perfected implies that, even though he is the heavenly Son, his mortal humanity required purification before he could approach the Father in the sacred heavenly space and serve there as the high priest for his people. This, however, implies that the writer has not dismissed the importance of the kinds of external matters so central to the ritual purity system detailed in the law.

Perfection as Purity in Hebrews

That the author of Hebrews thinks in terms of moral purity is abundantly clear in Hebrews 1:3. There he states that "after making purification for sins" (καθαρισμὸν τῶν ἁμαρτιῶν ποιησάμενος), the Son took his place at God's right hand. Given Hebrews' portrayal of Jesus as the high priest who enters the heavenly holy of holies, the collocation of the terms "purification" and "sin" probably signals an allusion to the statement in Leviticus 16:30 LXX that the high priest's atoning work on the Day of Atonement serves to purify the people from all their sins (καθαρίσαι ὑμᾶς ἀπὸ πασῶν τῶν ἁμαρτιῶν ὑμῶν).

Equally clearly, the writer employs a concept similar to that described above as ritual purity. As was noted, one of the oddities in Hebrews is the author's claim that the sacrifices prescribed in the law did not effect moral purification but only brought about a limited purification of the body. Hebrews, as Haber has stated, appears to have reduced purification in the law to ritual purification. But does this mean that the author goes on to reject the logic of ritual purification and its concern for external and bodily things? The author's use of perfection language indicates that this is not the case.

The close link between perfection and immortal life made by the author in Hebrews 7 is, as I have argued elsewhere, one among many clues that the author assumes Jesus's bodily resurrection in his argument.[23] The logic of the argument in this chapter works by way of a contrast between the law,

---

23. Esp. Moffitt, *Atonement and the Logic of Resurrection*, 194–208.

which links priestly legitimacy and authority with Levitical tribal lineage, and the power of Jesus's enduring resurrection life. The law's linkage of tribal lineage/genealogy and legitimate priestly succession is bound up with the reality of death. The writer stresses this point explicitly in Hebrews 7:8 and 7:23, and implicitly gestures toward it when he argues that the kind of life that Melchizedek and Jesus have legitimates their priestly status in spite of their genealogies (cf. 7:3, 16, 24–25). The point seems to be that Jesus, as a human being, became the great high priest he is confessed to be when, in his humanity, he was raised from the dead never to die again.

As the author wraps up the argument of Hebrews 7 and transitions to another point, he restates this critical contrast between the law and Jesus's enduring life in different terms when he says, "The Law appoints men as high priests who have weaknesses, but the word of the oath, which came after the Law, appoints as high priest a Son who has been made perfect forever" (7:28). Given the contrast in the preceding argumentation of chapter 7, one can gloss 7:28 as follows: the law appoints as high priests men who are subject to death, while the oath of Psalm 110:4 appoints Jesus, the Son, who is not subject to death and thus lives forever. The law's emphasis on genealogy as much as proves that the Levitical priests could not escape death, because the very logic of genealogy presupposes the reality of death. This is a major element of their and the law's "weakness." By way of contrast, the perfection of the Son means he does not share this weakness. He now lives in such a way that he will never again be subject to death.

By linking the law with death and Jesus with life, the author makes a move analogous to that of Paul as he thinks about the law. It appears that both Paul and Hebrews agree that the law was unable to bring life to God's people. Paul goes beyond Hebrews when he argues that the law, though good, became a tool of death. Like Paul, however, Hebrews seems to be working with an apocalyptic dualism that views the created realm as somehow separated from God's presence because it is tainted with sin, death, and corruption. The law is inextricably connected to the pole of this dualism that is subjected to death and the one who holds the power of death—the Devil (cf. Heb. 2:14).

If this is basically right, then when the author of Hebrews argues that the law never made anything perfect, he is claiming that the law was never able permanently to move God's people from their present condition into the fullness of God's presence. The law, to put the point differently, never fully solved or dealt with the problem of death. In fact, the problem of death is in some sense hardwired into the very logic of the law, particularly in the ritual purity codes and the genealogical stipulations regarding priestly service. This further means that the law never purified people to the point that their subjection to mortality was no longer a problem that prevented them from entering the fullness of God's presence. This, I suggest, is what the author means when he says that the law's regulations regarding genealogy and priesthood are "weak and useless." What the law in its weakness could not do, however, the author of Hebrews argues the Son has accomplished by rising again and ascending into the heavens as the great high priest.

I do not intend to imply here that the meaning of perfection in Hebrews is exhausted by or reducible to the idea of enduring life. I am, however, suggesting that these nuances in the author's argument indicate that ritual purity concerns lie close to hand in some of his uses of perfection language. Indeed, the presence of a notion of purity is already hinted at in his contrast in 7:19 between the law's inability to perfect anything and the better hope in Jesus that enables his followers *to approach God*. As noted above, the ritual purity codes in Leviticus are designed to enable people to approach God by rendering their mortality fit to draw near to his presence.

Hebrews 9:9 and 9:14 provide substantive confirmation that perfection and purity overlap for the author. In these verses the terms "perfection" and "purification" are used interchangeably. In 9:9 the author claims that the gifts and sacrifices offered under the law could not perfect the conscience of the worshipers. In 9:14, by way of contrast, he points out that the blood of Christ purifies the conscience. This is solid evidence that perfection and purity can be used synonymously in Hebrews. Equally clearly, though, these statements imply a concept of moral purity (as in 1:3), not ritual purity.

Yet the situation is different in the case of Jesus himself. The author characterizes Jesus's life as being "without sin" (Heb. 4:15). In the midst of his testing, Jesus was sinless. Jesus, in other words, was morally pure. He had no need to offer any sacrifice for himself in order to deal with his own sin (7:27). Nevertheless, the author plainly states throughout the epistle that Jesus was perfected, implying a need for this perfecting (2:10; 5:9; 7:28). What could it mean that Jesus, the preexistent Son of God, had to be made perfect?

Many arguments have been offered in the past to explain this language.[24] Given the linkage of perfection and purity in Hebrews noted above, I suggest

---

24. E. g., P. J. Du Plessis argues that perfection language in Hebrews primarily relates to Jesus's priestly consecration, though not to the exclusion of his subjective, existential development as a human being (ΤΕΛΕΙΟΣ: *The Idea of Perfection in the New Testament* [Kampen: J. H. Kok, 1959], esp. 212–17, 243). D. Peterson pushes back on this and other ideas by suggesting instead that Jesus's incarnate suffering, saving death, and exaltation should be viewed as a process that makes Jesus fit for the vocation of being a merciful high priest who can fully save his people (*Hebrews and Perfection: An Examination of the Concept of Perfection in the "Epistle to the Hebrews,"* SNTSMS 47 [Cambridge: Cambridge University Press, 1982], esp. 49, 67, 73, 103). D. A. deSilva links Jesus's perfection with his "arrival at his heavenly destiny"

that perfection language as applied to Jesus also verges into the realm of purity.[25] Yet, in the case of Jesus, the Son of God, the purity in play is not in the moral realm but in the realm of ritual. If, as I have argued, Jesus's perfection has to do with his resurrection to immortal humanity,[26] then the concept of purity that does apply to Jesus would have to do with the purity of his body. Although he was the Son, in his humanity he was fully mortal and, as such, was subject to ritual impurity. Prior to his resurrection, Jesus, the Son of God, was subject to death and did in fact die as a human being.

To put the point differently, the ultimate problem of mortality and the way in which death hindered humanity from fully entering God's presence applied to Jesus's imperfect/mortal humanity. This logic looks remarkably similar to the logic of ritual purification. Thus when, after his death, Jesus was perfected, the point seems to be that he was made fully, *ritually* pure. Jesus's humanity was, in other words, given the better resurrection promised in Hebrews 11:35. At this moment of perfection, Jesus's humanity was no longer mortal, no longer subject to death. Jesus is, therefore, never again subject to the problem of ritual impurity. Because of this perfection, that is to say, because his humanity has been fully and irrevocably purified, he is able to do what no other high priest has done—ascend into the sacred space of the heavenly sanctuary, draw close to the fullness of God's presence, and importantly, remain there.

Hebrews, the Law, and Supersessionism

If the preceding conclusions are properly tapping into the author's logic, then they hold important implications for the larger questions of supersessionism in Hebrews and for the author's apparently disparaging language about the law. I have already suggested that for the author of Hebrews the law's limitations follow from the fact that the law is, in some sense, itself subject to

---

(*Perseverance in Gratitude: A Socio-Rhetorical Commentary on the Epistle "to the Hebrews"* [Grand Rapids: Eerdmans, 2000], 199; see also 197–99). K. B. McCruden, on the basis of the documentary papyri, has more recently argued that "perfection" language could carry the notion of public, definitive/official attestation of a transaction (*Solidarity Perfected: Beneficent Christology in the Epistle to the Hebrews*, BZNW 159 [Berlin: de Gruyter, 2008], 26–37). In the context of Hebrews this implies that perfection language is mainly language intended to comment in a public and definitive way on the beneficent, personal character of Jesus's high-priestly sacrifice (69, 117–21, 139).

25. This has been noted at various times. W. G. Johnsson, for example, argues that from a cultic perspective, perfection language in Hebrews has partly to do with allowing access to the heavenly cult (*Defilement and Purgation in the Book of Hebrews*, Studies in Jewish and Christian Literature [Dallas: Fontes, 2020], 120–21, 260–63).

26. Moffitt, *Atonement and the Logic of Resurrection*, 198–214.

death and corruption. Hebrews seems to work with an understanding that the law's sphere of authority and legitimacy is circumscribed by the fact that it is bound up with an age that will pass away once the world/age-to-come arrives.

This is a significant point, because it implies that the author's comments about the law's limitations with respect to perfection are not a dismissal of the legitimacy and authority of the law *within its proper sphere*. In fact, in one of the more overlooked verses in modern Hebrews commentary, the writer notes that the law's authority prevents Jesus from being a priest on earth. Hebrews 8:4 reads, "If he [i.e., Jesus] were on earth, he would not even be a priest because there exist those who offer the gifts in accordance with the Law." The writer takes seriously the fact that Jesus has now passed through the heavens and entered God's presence. This is one of the reasons that Hebrews so consistently locates Jesus's priestly work in the heavens. On earth, the law forbids him from legitimately holding priestly office and thus serving in priestly ministries.

Such a claim indicates that the author has not simply dismissed the authority of the law. In the heavenly sphere and in the coming age, the law's limitations, particularly in the realm of ritual purity, do not apply. In a way not unlike Paul in Galatians 3, this argument relies on Jewish apocalyptic periodization to bracket the law by locating it within a particular period/age, a circumscribed place and time that precedes the eternal age. At least some of the law's regulations will, therefore, go the way of the rest of the corruptible realm with which it is so closely bound (cf. Heb. 1:13–14; 8:13; 12:27). When the earthly realm is finally shaken for the last time, such that only the unshakable realities remain, the law will be "metathesized" or changed (cf. 7:11–12, 18–19; 8:13).

But the language of "supersessionism" does not accurately describe this kind of logic. The idea that perfection entails the purified and enduring life of the resurrection and the eternal age to come would obviate the law's ritual purity codes in some notable ways. What contamination by death and corruption is present or even possible for one who lives in such an immortal state? When there is no possibility of impurity from mortality, the need for rituals of bodily purification disappears.

Conclusion

Within the Mosaic economy, both moral and ritual impurity prevented full communion and fellowship between God and his people. These problems were mitigated by way of sacrifice and other rituals. But, the author of Hebrews reasons, how much better would be the situation in which moral defilement/ sin was fully erased never to accrue again, and in which ritual impurity could never even be contracted? This situation is at points called "perfection" in Hebrews. Sacrifices are good in their time and place. God was pleased with the sprinkled blood that Abel offered him (Heb. 12:24). So also, God is pleased with the sacrifice that the Son offered him. But how much better would the situation be in which sacrifices for forgiveness and purification were no longer necessary because the problems they solve are no longer problems at all? This, I suggest, is the logic of Hebrews' argument. The ritual elements of the law are surely relativized, but that does not mean that they are somehow bad or inherently negative, or that Hebrews does not apply the logic of such sacrifices to Jesus. The Mosaic rituals are limited but nevertheless good. The point for the author of Hebrews seems to be that once one has been perfected and has been able to enter fully into the fullness of God's presence, the need for the law's rituals of purification and forgiveness disappears.

In sum, Jesus was the sinless Son of God but nevertheless was bound by the limitation of the law when on earth and had to be perfected in his humanity before he could return to the heavenly realms. Therefore, the links between perfection, purity, and resurrection in Hebrews suggest that the concerns that lie at the center of ritual purity as detailed in the law are foundational for, not in opposition to, the Christology and soteriology of Hebrews. There is here a polemic against viewing the law in absolute or eternal terms but not one that dismisses or denigrates the law. As with the angels, Moses, Aaron, and the priesthood, the law is good and revelatory for the author of Hebrews, but neither the law nor these other figures opened the way for God's people to enter the fullness of the inheritance the writer of Hebrews thinks they were ultimately promised. This is a central aspect of what the author means when he highlights Jesus's perfection and the ways in which what Jesus offers is better than what came before.

8

Serving in the Tabernacle in Heaven

Sacred Space, Jesus's High-Priestly Sacrifice, and Hebrews' Analogical Theology

In her book *Sacred Space: An Approach to the Theology of the Epistle to the Hebrews*, Marie Isaacs argues that Hebrews, in response to the destruction of Jerusalem, seeks to shift its audience's focus away from the physical and external notions of sacred space associated with the promised land of Israel, the city of Jerusalem, and the temple. These, the author of Hebrews argues, need to be replaced by "the only sacred space worth having—heaven."[1] Through his death, Jesus has gained access to that realm. The crucifixion and, specifically, the corresponding access to God that it acquired are used by the author to reorient the traditional Jewish concept of "sacred territory as located geographically on earth" by redefining this space as "a beatific state in heaven."[2] Thus, the author's task is fundamentally hermeneutical. Beginning with his belief that Jesus's death can be metaphorically understood as a sacrifice that cleanses one's interior person, he attempts to show further how the concrete physical locales and external rituals that constituted sacred space in the Mosaic economy on earth can serve as metaphors that point to

1. M. E. Isaacs, *Sacred Space: An Approach to the Theology of the Epistle to the Hebrews*, JSNTSup 73 (Sheffield: JSOT Press, 1992), 67.
2. Isaacs, *Sacred Space*, 82.

the abstract, immaterial realities of being in God's presence. Hebrews, in other words, transforms sacred physical space into a sacred spiritual state.

While Isaacs seeks to work these ideas out in Hebrews with respect to the spatial language of the text, she is far from alone in applying to Hebrews the assumption that the author's language about Jesus's entering heaven and ministering there is best understood as part of an extended metaphor that depicts the spiritual significance of Jesus's death in terms of the atoning ministry of the Jewish high priest—particularly, though not exclusively, with respect to his entry into the holy of holies on the Day of Atonement.[3] Along these lines, one also finds references in the modern secondary literature to the author's "high-priestly metaphor."[4]

I argue here that this approach to Hebrews misconstrues the text in two interrelated ways. First, the view that Hebrews develops metaphors out of the biblical depictions of the earthly cult and its sacred space as a way of reflecting on the abstract spiritual realm of heaven assumes the wrong model for heaven and for how the author relates earthly sacred space and high-priestly ministry to their corresponding heavenly counterparts. Second, such an interpretation of Jesus's salvific work mistakes Hebrews' analogical reasoning for metaphor. The affirmation and depiction of Jesus's high-priestly status and heavenly work in Hebrews, together with the author's conception of "the heavens" as progressively sacred space that contains a heavenly tabernacle/temple, suggest instead that the author assumes a cosmology that allows him to draw analogies between the atoning offering of blood in the holy of holies on earth and Jesus's atoning offering of himself in the ultimate sacred space, the holy of holies in heaven.

Given the language of "metaphor" and "analogy" that has just been used, a few caveats are in order before proceeding. First, I am not suggesting that those who argue that Hebrews' high-priestly Christology and conception of sacred space are metaphors necessarily claim that such metaphors do not refer to realities and/or that these metaphors would not have been understood as referring to realities by the author or the intended audience. Second, I am not

---

3. So, for example, H. W. Attridge, *The Epistle to the Hebrews*, Hermeneia (Philadelphia: Fortress, 1980), esp. 260–66; K. Backhaus, "Per Christum in Deum: Zur theozentrischen Funktion der Christologie im Hebräerbrief," in *Der Sprechende Gott: Gesammelte Studien zum Hebräerbrief*, WUNT 240 (Tübingen: Mohr Siebeck, 2009), 68–71; C. A. Eberhart, "Characteristics of Sacrificial Metaphors in Hebrews," in *Hebrews: Contemporary Methods—New Insights*, ed. Gabriella Gelardini (Leiden: Brill, 2005), 37–64; J. Smith, *A Priest Forever: A Study of Typology and Eschatology in Hebrews* (London: Sheed & Ward, 1969), esp. 112–14.

4. For example, K. L. Schenck, *Cosmology and Eschatology in Hebrews: The Settings of the Sacrifice*, SNTSMS 143 (Cambridge: Cambridge University Press, 2007), 45–46, 144–81, esp. 145, 168.

suggesting that Hebrews contains no metaphors. Hebrews is shot through with metaphor (see, e.g., 2:1; 3:4; 4:12; 5:12–14; 6:7–9; 12:29; 13:20). The central question I address is how the basic model or conception of heaven implicit in the text is related to the notions of sacred space and Jesus's high-priestly sacrifice developed by the author. These, I argue, are neither conceived of nor primarily described in terms of metaphor. Third, I am not attempting to engage the larger philosophical debates around the centrality of metaphor for structuring human language, understanding, and engagement with reality.[5] The terms "metaphor" and "analogy" are tightly defined below. They are intended to indicate linguistic tropes that would be recognized within a given linguistic system, not to point to larger categories for conceiving of the very possibility of language and thought. To say that Hebrews' high-priestly soteriology and correlated conception of heavenly sacred space are primarily analogical, not primarily metaphorical, is not, therefore, to make a claim about either the nature of theological reasoning in general or the essential structures that underlie language and rationality. Rather, when viewed synchronically, Hebrews' ways of speaking about the relationship between heavenly and earthly cultic realities work by drawing analogies between assumed heavenly realities and biblically depicted earthly ones, not by creating metaphors from biblical descriptions of earthly structures and practices in order to explain spiritual abstractions or name the significance of the author's own experience of salvation.

Models, Metaphors, and Analogies

The majority of modern interpreters of Hebrews would agree, I think, that Hebrews' reflection on heaven and Jesus's high-priestly work depends on an appeal to the biblical depictions of the sacred space of the tabernacle (and perhaps also to any knowledge the author had of the sacred space of the temple in Jerusalem) and depictions of the high priest's activity in that space on the Day of Atonement as a model of some kind. The crucial question is, What kind of modeling and corresponding hermeneutic ground the author's project?

In her trenchant and helpful monograph *Metaphor and Religious Language*, Janet Martin Soskice carefully distinguishes homeomorphic models from paramorphic ones and examines the ways that these models, especially

---

5. G. Lakoff and M. Johnson, *Metaphors We Live By* (Chicago: University of Chicago Press, 1980); S. McFague, *Metaphorical Theology: Models of God in Religious Language* (Philadelphia: Fortress, 1982), esp. 15–16.

the latter, relate to metaphors.[6] According to Soskice, a homeomorphic model is a model whose subject is also its source. This kind of model represents its subject by imitating its source. A model airplane or a cardboard globe would be an example of a homeomorphic model. The various elements that constitute the model are so arranged as to be related in an "analogy of structure" to the subject being modeled.[7] That is, the elements of a homeomorphic model are structured to one degree or another such that they are located in relation to one another according to the structural relations among the elements of the source being depicted. Obviously such models are not metaphors, not least because they are not linguistic acts.

Moreover, linguistic descriptions of these sorts of models may well apply terms that belong to the associative network of the source—that is, the set of terms, ideas, and relations that one takes to be fitting/natural for the original object or state of affairs—to the model. Yet even these linguistic acts are not metaphors. An example will illustrate the point. If one tells a child to be a good "pilot," to "fly" his or her model plane over to its display case, and to "land" it there, the terms "pilot," "fly," and "land" are not being used metaphorically. This is speaking analogically, by noting fitting parallels between aspects from the associative network of a real airplane—the model's subject and source—and the model itself. The use of the terms "pilot," "fly," and "land" with reference to the model is therefore understood by the language user to correspond in a fitting way to the model's source. These terms are deemed appropriate to juxtapose with the model, even though no one would mistake the child's moving the plane around for literal flight.

The preceding points are not intended to reduce analogy to use with or to derivations from homeomorphic models, for analogies need not be model based at all.[8] More central to the trope is the recognition that "analogical relations all refer to the same thing, they all have the same *res significata* but they refer to it in different ways."[9] Thus, speaking analogically is speaking in a way that while recognizing differences also recognizes that the application of certain terms is fitting or appropriate to an object or state of affairs. Analogy may stretch the meaning of a term by using it in a new way, but such usage does not generate a fundamentally new perspective or picture relative to the subject,

6. J. M. Soskice, *Metaphor and Religious Language* (Oxford: Clarendon, 1985), esp. 101–3.

7. Soskice, *Metaphor and Religious Language*, 64.

8. Soskice states that her use of the term "analogy" is not model related (*Metaphor*, 66, 74). I suspect that she means here that analogy is not related to paramorphic modeling. Regardless, I can see no reason why analogy would necessarily be inappropriate to linguistic expressions related to homeomorphic models that apply terms from the associative network of the model's source to the model itself.

9. Soskice, *Metaphor*, 65.

since the new application of the term does not invoke what is understood to be a fundamentally different set of associative networks relative to the object or state of affairs being described.[10] Analogy works by noting comparisons that, in a particular linguistic and cultural context, would be understood to identify fitting correspondences between the things being compared.

Here, too, one can helpfully see the distinction between speaking analogically about a model and speaking literally about an exact copy or replica. To speak about an exact replica, which is by definition identical to its source apart from its relative position in space and time, in terms appropriate to the source is to use literal language. To speak of a homeomorphic model, which is not an exact replica, in those same terms is not to speak literally. The small plastic plane mentioned above cannot literally fly and land the way a replica that is a copy of its source in every (or virtually every) respect can and, assuming it has been built to the same standards of quality, does. Analogical speech applied to a model, as here defined, is not, then, to be confused with literal speech applied to an exact copy or replica of a source or prototype.

A metaphor, by way of contrast, speaks of one thing in terms of another thing whose associative network is recognized to be fundamentally different. A metaphor, in other words, construes a unified subject matter by way of "a plurality of associative networks."[11] Speaking in this way necessarily generates a new picture or perspective on the subject matter.[12] To say, for example, that the brain is a computer is to construe the brain in terms otherwise foreign to it precisely because "computer" is a term whose associative network is fundamentally different from that of "brain." The metaphor may eventually become a dead metaphor, at which point the language is taken by the speaker to be fitting or natural. At its origin, however, the metaphor is recognizable as a metaphor precisely because of the obvious juxtaposition of different associative networks inherent in the comparison.

Soskice argues that this sort of metaphor proposes a paramorphic model for understanding the subject being described. Unlike a homeomorphic model, which could be conceived of as a model *of* an object or state of affairs, a paramorphic model is a model *for* an object or state of affairs. Such models often, therefore, correlate with abstract reflection.[13] Additionally, whereas the subject of a homeomorphic model is the same as its source, that of a paramorphic model necessarily differs from its source, and thereby introduces elements from different associative networks as constitutive of the model. Because of

10. Soskice, *Metaphor*, 64–66.
11. Soskice, *Metaphor*, 53.
12. Soskice, *Metaphor*, 49–53; cf. 64–66.
13. Soskice, *Metaphor*, 103.

these dynamics, the original "theory constitutive metaphor"—that is, the central metaphor that proposes the paramorphic model (e.g., the brain is a computer)—can fruitfully generate additional metaphors by comparing elements of the plurality of associative networks latent within the model (e.g., the "brain is a computer" model might also suggest metaphors like the brain receives "input" and "processes" it).[14] Such construal can be of immense use for theorizing about objects and states of affairs that are not directly accessible or understood.

But how does this discussion relate to the topic at hand? Many modern interpreters of Hebrews have, I think, tended to assume that the depiction found in Hebrews of Jesus serving in the heavenly tabernacle in high-priestly terms is, to use Soskice's categories, part of a theory-constitutive metaphor that proposes a paramorphic model for understanding an abstract state of affairs—namely, the salvation one feels or believes oneself to have as a result of Jesus's crucifixion. The central metaphor (Jesus's death is the ultimate atoning sacrifice) is understood to propose a model whereby an abstract subject (the salvific benefits one receives as the result of Jesus's crucifixion) is construed in terms of an associative network that is fundamentally different from the historical reality of Jesus's crucifixion by the Romans. The different associative network at the heart of the metaphor is that of Jewish rituals of blood sacrifice, especially those performed on the Day of Atonement.

G. B. Caird illustrates the preceding point well when he writes, "The language of sacrifice is metaphorical when used of the death of Christ. Literally the death of Christ was no sacrifice, but a criminal execution, regarded by the one side as a political necessity and by the other as a miscarriage of justice."[15] To depict the historical event of Jesus's crucifixion in terms of Jewish blood sacrifice is to speak metaphorically, because such an account brings together two different associative networks (crucifixion and Jewish sacrifice) and thereby enables the historical subject (Jesus's death as a criminal) to be understood in terms of something else entirely (the atoning sacrifices performed in the Jewish temple). The central metaphor proposes

---

14. Soskice, *Metaphor*, 102.

15. G. B. Caird, *The Language and Imagery of the Bible* (London: Duckworth, 1980), 157. E. W. Stegemann and W. Stegemann highlight the fundamentally modern assessment of reality that underlies such a distinction between the brute fact and our interpretation of the meaning of the fact ("Does the Cultic Language in Hebrews Represent Sacrificial Metaphors? Reflections on Some Basic Problems," in Gelardini, *Hebrews*, 13–23). They argue that on its own terms Hebrews does not use cultic language as a substitute or metaphor for the real meaning of the death of Jesus. As will be clear, I agree with them that Hebrews is not using cultic language metaphorically but for the very different reason that I do not think Hebrews equates Jesus's death with the atoning event of offering his sacrifice to God in heaven.

a model that helps one conceive of how Jesus's death could have resulted in salvation for humanity.[16]

This model is thought to be especially powerful for the author of Hebrews precisely because he presses the associative networks it brings together (Jesus's suffering and death, on the one hand, and Jewish sacrificial practice and theology, on the other) to generate so many other illuminating metaphors. These additional metaphors further contribute to reflection on the abstract existential or spiritual aspects of the historical subject. Thus, when viewed as a sacrifice, Jesus's crucifixion can be construed in terms of the act of blood ablution that effects purification and redemption like the sprinkling of blood in the holy of holies on the Day of Atonement. Jesus himself can further be construed as the great high priest whose work is to offer himself to God by dying as a sacrifice. Jesus's death, particularly when understood as the moment of the release of his spirit from his body, can further be conceived in terms of his high-priestly approach to God. The separation of his spirit from his body and his passing into heaven upon his death can even be construed as the high priest's annual act of passing through the inner veil of the temple and into the holy of holies. The author no doubt thinks that from the perspective of the central metaphor, the biblical depiction of the tabernacle offered fertile ground from which many other secondary metaphors could be generated (cf. Heb. 9:5). If the writer's real subject is "the death of Jesus is the ultimate atoning event," then this sort of metaphorical understanding of Hebrews' theological project is almost certainly correct.

The picture shifts dramatically, however, if the author's soteriological center of gravity does not revolve around the supposed "crucifixion as ultimate atoning event" metaphor. I have argued elsewhere that Hebrews attempts to correlate the basic, protocreedal narrative of early Christian proclamation—the heavenly Son of God became the incarnate Jesus, suffered and died, rose again, ascended into heaven, has taken his place at God's right hand, and will return to bring salvation to those who wait for him—with the irreducible process of Jewish blood sacrifice.[17] This account suggests that the central

16. While the category of metaphor has become somewhat fashionable in the last forty or so years, something like the understanding of Hebrews just described seems to be in play in much modern interpretation of Hebrews as a way of relating Jesus's death to his exaltation and high-priestly work even though the term "metaphor" is not used to describe such interpretations. So, e.g., J. F. McFadyen, *Through Eternal Spirit: A Study of Hebrews, James, and 1 Peter* (New York: Doran, 1925), 129, 136, 147–48; S. Nomoto, "Herkunft und Struktur der Hohenpriestervorstellung im Hebräerbrief," *NovT* 10 (1968): 1–25, esp. 17–18, 23–25; J. W. Thompson, *The Beginnings of Christian Philosophy: The Epistle to the Hebrews* (Washington, DC: Catholic Biblical Association of America, 1982), esp. 107–8.

17. D. M. Moffitt, *Atonement and the Logic of Resurrection in the Epistle to the Hebrews*, NovTSup 141 (Leiden: Brill, 2011), esp. 43, 292–96, 300–303. See also chap. 5 in this volume.

event that effects atonement—that is, the ultimate purification and redemption of humanity—cannot be reduced to or collapsed into the death of Jesus
any more than the atoning effects of the Levitical sacrifices can be reduced to
the act of slaughtering the victim. Rather, the focal point is, for the author,
centered on the return of the resurrected, and therefore still incarnate, Son
back into the heavenly presence of the Father and the angels.

These observations alone are not enough to substantiate the claim being
advanced here, that Hebrews is not driven by a paramorphic model whose
core is a theory-constituting metaphor, for one could simply move the center
of the model to something like the ascension or exaltation of Jesus.[18] The
crucial piece that would significantly alter the assessment of the author's
basic hermeneutic concerns the cosmology that underlies his argumentation.
Once this issue is raised, one comes face-to-face with the long and much-
debated question of whether Hebrews is at its core driven more by something
like a Platonic or Philonic cosmology or by some permutation of a Jewish
apocalyptic understanding of the structure and stuff of the universe. I will not
rehearse the variety of views regarding this long-standing scholarly divide.[19]
Instead, as I also argue elsewhere,[20] I assume here that the dualities one finds
in Hebrews are more heavily dependent on and influenced by some form of
Jewish apocalypticism than by some kind of Platonic idealism.

The contribution I seek to make here has to do with the assessment of the
underlying model the author assumes when reflecting on the heavenly tabernacle and Jesus's high-priestly service there. If Hebrews imagines reality to
consist of the earth and multiple heavens—the highest of which contains the
heavenly tabernacle and holy of holies, where God sits enthroned—populated
by angelic priests who minister there, and if those heavenly realities legitimate
and structure the earthly cult, then the possibility of a thoroughly different
model for understanding Hebrews' application of cultic language to Jesus
emerges. Such an understanding of heavenly space would suggest that the
author of Hebrews, as is the case with some other apocalyptic Jews, under-

---

18. See D. Farrow, *Ascension and Ecclesia: On the Significance of the Doctrine of the Ascension for Ecclesiology and Christian Cosmology* (Grand Rapids: Eerdmans, 1999), esp. 33–40.

19. Although it is now dated, see L. D. Hurst, *The Epistle to the Hebrews: Its Background
of Thought*, SNTSMS 65 (Cambridge: Cambridge University Press, 1990). See, more recently,
E. F. Mason, "'Sit at My Right Hand': Enthronement and the Heavenly Sanctuary in Hebrews,"
in *A Teacher for All Generations: Essays in Honor of James C. VanderKam*, ed. E. F. Mason
et al., 2 vols., JSJSup 153 (Leiden: Brill, 2012), 2:901–16.

20. Moffitt, *Atonement and the Logic of Resurrection*, esp. 145–81, 300–303. See also my
essay "Perseverance, Purity, and Identity: Exploring Hebrews' Eschatological Worldview, Ethics,
and In-Group Bias," in *Sensitivity to Outsiders: Exploring the Dynamic Relationship between
Mission and Ethics in the New Testament and Early Christianity*, ed. J. Kok et al., WUNT 2/364
(Tübingen: Mohr Siebeck, 2014), 357–81.

stands the relationship between the heavenly and earthly cults in terms of a homeomorphic model that allowed for numerous analogies to be drawn, not in terms of a paramorphic model that enables metaphorical reflection. I turn, then, to a brief examination of Hebrews' conception of heaven and the heavenly tabernacle.

Hebrews' Cosmology, the Heavens, and the Heavenly Tabernacle

Edward Adams has recently argued that Hebrews' worldview assumes a cosmology not easily squared with the kind of Platonic cosmology that scholars such as James Thompson[21] have sought to link with the text.[22] Adams points out, rightly in my view, that Hebrews does not embrace an anti-materialist dualism, nor does the author ever judge creation to be inherently negative.[23] Additional critiques of interpretations of Hebrews that rely too heavily on Platonic or Philonic cosmological commitments have recently been made by, among others, Eric F. Mason[24] and Scott D. Mackie.[25] Both Mason and Mackie highlight the similarities between Hebrews and Jewish apocalyptic texts, especially the important motif of Jesus's enthronement in the heavenly sanctuary. Hebrews' emphasis on Jesus's heavenly enthronement raises the question as to how the author conceives of the heavenly tabernacle where he says Jesus has entered and now ministers (cf. Heb. 7:25–26; 8:1–2; 9:11–12, 23–24).

In a 1978 article in *Semeia*, George MacRae argues for the importance of recognizing two different conceptions of the relationship between heaven and

21. J. W. Thompson, *Beginnings of Christian Philosophy*, esp. 152–62; more recently, J. W. Thompson, "What Has Middle Platonism to Do with Hebrews?," in *Reading the Epistle to the Hebrews: A Resource for Students*, ed. E. F. Mason and K. B. McCruden, SBLRBS 66 (Atlanta: Society of Biblical Literature, 2011), 31–52. Similarly, see, e.g., W. Eisele, *Ein unerschütterliches Reich: Die mittelplatonische Umformung des Parusiegedankens im Hebräerbrief*, BZNW 116 (Berlin: de Gruyter, 2003); L. T. Johnson, *Hebrews: A Commentary*, NTL (Louisville: Westminster John Knox, 2006).

22. E. Adams, "The Cosmology of Hebrews," in *The Epistle to the Hebrews and Christian Theology*, ed. R. Bauckham et al. (Grand Rapids: Eerdmans, 2009), 122–39.

23. I have also argued that the duality in Hebrews between heaven and earth does not track out in terms of a material versus spiritual or intelligible realm (see Moffitt, *Atonement and the Logic of Resurrection*, esp. 301–2).

24. He makes the point in several publications, but see especially E. F. Mason, *"You Are a Priest Forever": Second Temple Jewish Messianism and the Priestly Christology of the Epistle to the Hebrews*, STDJ 74 (Leiden: Brill, 2008). In a more recent study Mason highlights the fact that Hebrews makes a connection, common in apocalyptic texts, between the heavenly sanctuary and the divine throne ("'Sit at My Right Hand,'" esp. 907–16).

25. See esp. S. D. Mackie, "Ancient Jewish Mystical Motifs in Hebrews' Theology of Access and Entry Exhortations," *NTS* 58 (2011): 88–104.

the heavenly temple at play in Hebrews.[26] MacRae draws attention to the important point that the conception of heaven as temple is different from that of a temple in heaven. The former, he claims, is more associated with a Platonic or Philonic cosmology, and the latter with more apocalyptic cosmologies. For reasons I discuss below, I do not find his claim that Hebrews combines these two notions compelling. The importance of highlighting the distinction between these two concepts of the heavenly temple, however, is hard to overstate.

More recently, Jonathan Klawans has focused attention on this same distinction.[27] Klawans notes that scholars sometimes conflate the notion of a temple in heaven (upon which the temple in Jerusalem is modeled) with that of heaven as a temple (where the Jerusalem temple complex—that is, the forecourt and temple sancta together—serves as a microcosm of the universe), even though Second Temple and early Common Era texts that speak of a heavenly sanctuary typically attest either one conception or the other.

Klawans also notes that in cases where the Jerusalem temple is taken to be a microcosm of the cosmos, the entire universe is spoken of as God's temple. The earth is likened to the forecourt of the temple complex, while heaven is the temple itself—God's sanctuary. In the other model, the temple complex on earth is in some way conceived of as a representation of an actual structure in heaven. In this latter case the earth is not viewed as the forecourt of the cosmic temple complex, and heaven is not identified with the temple or the inner sanctuary. Rather, just as there is an especially sacred space on earth that is divided into various spaces and sancta that grow progressively more sacred until one comes to the inner sanctuary where God's presence dwells on earth most fully, so also in heaven there is an especially sacred space divided into various spaces and sancta that grow progressively more holy until one reaches that most holy place where God's presence dwells in heaven most fully (see, e.g., 1 En. 14; 2 En. 20:1–21:6). Unsurprisingly, this latter idea correlates with a highly developed understanding of angels as God's heavenly priests and human priests as their corresponding ministers on earth. There is also here a common conception of the heavenly realm consisting of multiple tiers or "heavens" (e.g., 2 En. 3–22; T. Levi 3:1–10). One of the key biblical grounds for this conception of reality is a particular interpretation of God's repeated admonishments to Moses in Exodus 25:9, 40 (see also 26:30 and 27:8) to make the earthly tabernacle and its accoutrements in accordance with what he had seen on the mountain.

26. G. W. MacRae, "Heavenly Temple and Eschatology in the Letter to the Hebrews," *Semeia* 12 (1978): 179–99.

27. J. Klawans, *Purity, Sacrifice, and the Temple: Symbolism and Supersessionism in the Study of Ancient Judaism* (Oxford: Oxford University Press, 2006), 111–44.

Indeed, how one interprets these passages in Exodus and the revelation given to Moses on the mountain becomes critical at precisely this point. Philo provides a particularly clear example of a Platonic interpretation of Exodus 25:9 in his *Quaestiones et solutiones in Exodum* II. When speaking of Moses being "shown" the pattern for the tabernacle on the mountain, Philo says that Moses did not literally "see" anything, since human eyes cannot see the intelligible, immaterial forms. The language of "seeing" is only a symbol to indicate that his mind or soul had a clear perception of the intelligible realities (*QE* 2.52, 82; cf. *Mos.* 2.74–76).

Because Moses had this "vision" of the forms imprinted in his mind, he was able to build the tabernacle complex as a microcosm of the universe. Philo, therefore, shows how elements of the earthly tabernacle represent aspects of the cosmos (*Mos.* 2.80–107). He emphasizes, for example, that certain numbers of pillars represent, respectively, the source from which the stuff of earth was formed and the senses that humans use to interact with the material world (2.80–81). The four kinds and colors of material used for the woven coverings correlate to the four elements out of which the world was made (*Mos.* 2.88; *Congr.* 116–17). The altar of incense is in the middle of the first sanctum and therefore stands between earth and water (*Mos.* 2.101) and is itself a symbol of the earth (2.104), while the seven-branched candelabra is a symbol of heaven with its seven planets (2.102–3).

Hebrews also appeals to this section of Exodus. The author cites Exodus 25:40 in Hebrews 8:5, just after saying that Jesus has entered the true tabernacle where God is enthroned in heaven (8:1–2), and shortly before he lists some of the details of the earthly tabernacle and draws comparisons between them and Jesus's ministry (9:1–10:22). Notably, however, nothing like Philo's cosmological explanations of the construction of and items in the tabernacle occurs in Hebrews. Rather than show how elements from the outer part of the earthly structure represent, for example, the elements from which the earth is fashioned, Hebrews sets out to demonstrate that just as the earthly tabernacle had certain implements, necessary rituals, and sancta in which the priests and high priests performed their ministries (9:1–10, 19–22), so also must Jesus perform certain rituals in the sancta in heaven where he engages in his high-priestly ministry (9:11–14, 23–26; cf. 5:1; 7:27; 8:1–5).

In Hebrews 8:4–5 this point is made with some clarity. The author states in 8:1–2 that Jesus is the great high priest in heaven. In 8:4 he notes that if Jesus were on earth, he would be disqualified by the law from serving as even a priest. Jesus, he appears to say, cannot minister as one of the regular priests on earth, let alone as a high priest. Given that the author refers in 8:4 to the regular priests who ministered only in the forecourt and the first sanctum of the tabernacle, his comment in 8:5a that those priests serve in a copy and shadow of the heavenly things implies that the forecourt and initial tent correspond in some way to heavenly realities. The forecourt and initial sanctum, in other words, are conceived of not as representing the lower, earthly, or material elements of the cosmos but as copies of things in heaven. The earthly priests are not said to serve in that part of the tabernacle that primarily represented the lower parts of the cosmos while the high priest alone enters that space that represents the realities that cannot be seen (cf. Philo, *Spec.* 1.72). Instead, the author of Hebrews speaks of the whole tabernacle complex as being related to the structure Moses saw in the heavenly realm. Philo's view that the earthly temple complex symbolizes the entire cosmos, which is the true temple (so, e.g., *Spec.* 1.66; *Somn.* 1.215; *Mos.* 2.194), therefore differs markedly from that of the author of Hebrews, who looks to the whole structure of the earthly tabernacle as reflecting realities located in heaven. This is an important contrast between these two authors.

This last observation suggests that Hebrews works with a more straightforward, nonmetaphorical interpretation of Exodus 25:40 in Hebrews 8:5 than the one given by Philo regarding Exodus 25:9 (see also his interpretation of Exod. 25:40 in *QE* 2.82). If the author of Hebrews assumed, as at least some apocalyptic Jews did, that Moses looked into heaven (or even ascended into heaven[28]) and saw the heavenly tabernacle/temple structure there, then the language of Exodus 25:40 concerning the pattern of the heavenly realities being "shown" (τὸν δεδειγμένον, Exod. 25:40 LXX; τὸν δειχθέντα, Heb. 8:5) to Moses is not a metaphor for mental apprehension of intelligible and immaterial forms, as is clearly the case in Philo.

Moreover, this more literal interpretation of Exodus 25:40 would further imply that the spaces of and practices carried out in the earthly tabernacle would be properly organized and composed along the lines described above as "an analogy of structure." Rather than conceiving of the totality of the universe itself as the true temple complex, this kind of cosmology would assume that two legitimate temples, as well as two legitimate priesthoods,[29] existed in the universe. One of these, the one in heaven, is the source. The other one, on earth, is a (homeomorphic) model that reflects the heavenly source.

---

28. For evidence for this view see Moffitt, *Atonement and the Logic of Resurrection*, 150–62.

29. The argument for the legitimacy of Jesus's high-priestly status in Heb. 7 presupposes, I have argued, the legitimacy of both the earthly, Levitical priesthood and the heavenly priesthood. See D. M. Moffitt, "Jesus the High Priest and the Mosaic Law: Reassessing the Appeal to the Heavenly Realm in the Letter 'To the Hebrews,'" in *Problems in Translating Texts about Jesus: Proceedings from the International Society of Biblical Literature Annual Meeting 2008*, ed. M. Caspi and J. T. Greene (Lewiston, NY: Mellen, 2011), 195–232.

As the contrast between Hebrews and Philo already implies, Hebrews attests to the temple-/tabernacle-in-heaven concept. Other evidence also points toward this conclusion. I will not here repeat the arguments I have outlined elsewhere for the significance of Hebrews' angelology and contrasting anthropology with respect to the idea of a temple complex in heaven or for the idea that the tabernacle structure Jesus entered is laid out in a way similar to the earthly one.[30] Instead, I focus on another aspect of the language in Hebrews that contrasts with Philonic language and cosmology but correlates well with the concept of a tabernacle in heaven—namely, the fact that the author believes in the existence of multiple heavens.

In Hebrews 4:14 the writer describes Jesus passing through "the heavens" (τοὺς οὐρανούς). Jesus is said to be higher "than the heavens" (τῶν οὐρανῶν) in 7:26. In 8:1 the author claims that Jesus is seated on the throne at the right hand of the Most High "in the heavens" (ἐν τοῖς οὐρανοῖς). The sacred heavenly things that Jesus's sacrifice purifies are identified in 9:23 as being "in the heavens" (ἐν τοῖς οὐρανοῖς). The congregation of the firstborn mentioned in 12:23 is enrolled "in the heavens" (ἐν οὐρανοῖς). According to 12:25, in language evocative of Jewish apocalyptic texts, Jesus is presumably (cf. 1:2) the one who admonishes the readers "from the heavens" (ἀπ' οὐρανῶν).[31]

Were these the only references to heaven in Hebrews, there would likely be less argument over the points being addressed here. The *crux interpretum*, however, lies in Hebrews 9:24, where the author not only refers to Jesus entering the singular "heaven itself" (αὐτὸν τὸν οὐρανόν) but also puts this language in apposition to the idea that Jesus entered the heavenly sanctuary. This break from the author's usual pattern is sometimes taken as evidence that he thinks of the cosmos as the true temple complex—the earth is the cosmic forecourt and heaven itself is coextensive with the cosmic temple, as in the Philonic model. Indeed, MacRae appeals to this verse as evidence that the author thought of heaven as cosmic sanctuary, like Philo.[32] But does this singular reference to "heaven itself" demand a Platonic or Philonic interpretation?

In addition to Hebrews 9:24, two other uses of οὐρανός in the singular form occur in Hebrews (11:12 and 12:26). Both of these latter instances of the term occur, however, in the context of biblical allusions. The singular

30. See Moffitt, *Atonement and the Logic of the Resurrection*, esp. 118–44 and 220–25, respectively.

31. The plural form of οὐρανός also occurs in Heb. 1:10, though this is obviously due to the author's biblical *Vorlage*.

32. MacRae argues that both concepts are found in Hebrews because the author, who believed in the cosmos-as-temple model, accommodated his language at points to his audience, who embraced the more apocalyptic concept of a temple in heaven ("Heavenly Temple and Eschatology," 186–88).

form of the word at these points most likely reflects the direct influence of the versions of the biblical passages as the author knows them. This recognition is nevertheless important because it highlights the fact that the dependence of someone, like this author, on a Greek version of Jewish Scriptures might allow them to use the word "heaven" in both plural and singular forms without necessarily implying that the change in number entails any change in the reality to which they assume the term refers.[33]

In fact, one commonly finds precisely this switching between the plural and singular forms of the word in apocalyptically oriented early Jewish and Christian texts written in Greek. Thus Paul, who clearly believes in at least three heavens (2 Cor. 12:2), often refers to heaven in the singular (e.g., Rom. 1:18; 10:6; 1 Cor. 15:47; Gal. 1:8). He can even use οὐρανός in the singular and plural forms back-to-back in 2 Corinthians 5:1–2 with apparent reference to the same reality (cf. 1 Thess. 1:10; 4:16).[34] This variation between forms stands in marked contrast to nonapocalyptic Jewish authors such as Philo and Josephus. The latter hold the view that the cosmos is God's temple complex—with heaven itself being the cosmic sanctuary/temple. In keeping with this cosmology, both of these authors use the singular οὐρανός consistently throughout their writings. This usage agrees with Greek philosophical speculation about the nature of the cosmos, where the singular form is by far the norm.[35]

33. I have asserted elsewhere (*Atonement and the Logic of Resurrection*, 231n36) that the author distinguishes between created heavens and uncreated heavens. I am no longer confident that this view is correct. The evidence presented here—and particularly the fact that the author speaks of the "heavens" being changed (Heb. 1:10–11) and of the "heaven" being shaken (12:26)—seems to suggest instead that he is merely adopting biblical language and assuming that the plural and singular forms are interchangeable ways of referring to the same reality. There are things that are "unshakable" and that "remain" after the final shaking (12:27), but such distinctions do not correlate neatly in Hebrews with a "heaven" and "earth" dualism. It seems to be that just as some of the heavenly things, like the earthly things, require purification (9:23), so also at least some of the heavenly things, like the earthly things, will be subject to the final, eschatological transformation (1:10–11; 12:26).

34. Here I provide only some of the clearer references, not an exhaustive list. In the New Testament see Mark 1:10–11; 11:25; 12:25; 13:25, 32; Col. 1:5, 16, 20; 4:11; 1 Pet. 1:4, 12; 3:22; 2 Pet. 1:18; 3:5. The phenomenon occurs in the Greek translation of Jub. 2:2, 16; 11:8, as well as of 1 En. 18:3–10. See also throughout the T. 12 Patr. (e.g., T. Levi 2:6, 9; 5:1); Apocr. Ezek. 2:1; 5:1; Apoc. Ezra 1:7, 14; Apoc. Sedr. esp. 2:3–5; 3 Bar. 2:5; 11:2 (along with clear references to a first heaven, second heaven, etc., throughout); T. Ab. 4:5; 7:4.

35. As is well known, the plural form of οὐρανός is extremely rare in Greek literature before the Septuagint (see, e.g., F. Torm, "Der Pluralis Οὐρανοί," *ZNW* 33 [1934]: 48–50; P. Katz, *Philo's Bible: The Aberrant Text of Bible Quotations in Some Philonic Writings and Its Place in the Textual History of the Greek Bible* [Cambridge: Cambridge University Press, 1950], 141–46). A search of the Thesaurus Linguae Graecae turns up the following evidence. The pre-Socratic philosopher Anaximander is attributed with having conceived of multiple heavens in the

Given that Hebrews' use of the plural and singular forms of οὐρανός fits with the practice of others of the same time period who believed in multiple heavens and often also attest the idea of a temple in the heavens, the use of the singular in 9:24 cannot bear the weight that MacRae tries to place upon it. More plausible is the interpretation advanced by Otfried Hofius that "heaven itself" in 9:24 refers to the highest of the heavens, the place where the heavenly holy of holies of the tabernacle/temple was thought to be located (see, e.g., T. Levi 5:1).[36] That Jesus has entered the highest heaven coheres well with the language of Jesus passing "through the heavens" (4:14) and being now higher "than the heavens" (7:26) while still also being "in the heavens" (8:1). Jesus, that is, has not left the heavens, as one might imagine someone in Philo's or Plato's universe having to do were that person able to be absorbed into the ultimate realm of the divine that exists outside the cosmos. Instead, Jesus has been invited to ascend to the highest place in the heavens, the place above all the other heavens, where the heavenly holy of holies and the heavenly throne of God are.

The preceding points suggest that the author of Hebrews held to a cosmology along the lines attested in Jewish apocalyptic texts that imagine multiple heavens with a tabernacle or temple structure located in the highest heaven. As his interpretation of Exodus 25:40 in Hebrews 8:5 indicates, the heavenly tabernacle served as the source for the earthly structure. These points support the conclusion that the author of Hebrews works with something like what was identified above as a homeomorphic model when he reflects on the relationship between the earthly and heavenly sacred spaces. In the author's view, the real subject of the earthly sacred space is also its source—the heavenly tabernacle. Thus the earthly space neither is an exact replica of the heavenly tabernacle nor represents the entirety of the cosmos. Rather, because Moses saw the pattern of the heavenly edifice, he built the earthly one in such a way as to have an analogous structure, even if the earthly structure is only a shadowy sketch. This analogy of structure further implies, however, a fitting set of correspondences or analogies between, on one hand, the earthly tabernacle and the activities that take place within it and, on the other hand, the heavenly tabernacle and the activities that occur there.

---

cosmos. Idaeus may have thought along similar lines. Aesop's fable about the Peacock and the Crane uses the plural form once. Aristotle, in a handful of passages, entertains the possibility that more than one οὐρανός exists, only to dismiss the idea (so also Theophrastus). The plural form occurs one time in the *Catasterisimi*, attributed to Eratosthenes.

36. O. Hofius, *Der Vorhang vor dem Thron Gottes: Eine exegetisch-religionsgeschichtliche Untersuchung zu Hebräer 6,19f. und 10,19f.*, WUNT 1/14 (Tübingen: Mohr, 1972), 70–71. A number of commentators follow his lead to one degree or another (e.g., Attridge, *Hebrews*, 263; W. L. Lane, *Hebrews 9–13*, WBC 47b [Dallas: Word Books, 1991], 248).

Hebrews and Analogy

The preceding discussion suggests that the author of Hebrews has a more concrete conception of heavenly space than is sometimes thought. Some have argued that, while Hebrews does speak in terms of a heavenly sanctuary and multiple heavens, there is nevertheless a strong Hellenizing bent to this language similar to what one finds in Philo, in that the author ultimately conceptualizes these spaces in terms of the interior realm of the human being.[37] If, however, the author thinks of the resurrected Jesus ascending bodily through the multiplicity of heavens and appearing before God in the holy of holies in the highest heaven, this reduction of heavenly space to the interiority of the human being is no longer tenable.

A better solution likely lies in the arguments of some recent work, such as that of Loren Stuckenbruck, that takes seriously the fact that in some of the apocalyptic material at Qumran, the cosmological dualism between the heavenly and earthly realms—together with the spiritual battles being fought between the good and evil angels—is viewed as being directly related to the interior realm of human existence.[38] Hebrews may well think in more concrete terms about atonement as occurring when Jesus ascended bodily into the sacred space of the heavenly holy of holies *and* recognize that this has direct implications for the interior purification of the human being (e.g., Heb. 9:14) without having to reduce the former to the latter.

Be that as it may, the cosmology of Hebrews and the correlated conception of the tabernacle in heaven suggest that if a human being were to ascend into that heavenly space, then the application of language from the realm of earthly priestly service to that figure would not be a matter of metaphorical reflection. Rather, it would be fitting to appeal to the associative network of the earthly tabernacle/temple as a way to describe an ascent to the uppermost heavenly things because that ascending person would be entering the inner sanctum of the heavenly tabernacle, the very source that determines the structure of the earthly model. In other words, one would be speaking by analogy, not metaphor.

The author of Hebrews goes even a step further when in Hebrews 7 he presents an extended argument to demonstrate the legitimacy of Jesus's high-priestly status even though Jesus comes from the tribe of Judah, not that of

37. See esp. Attridge, *Hebrews*, 222–24.
38. L. T. Stuckenbruck, "The Interiorization of Dualism within the Human Being in Second Temple Judaism: The Treatise of the Two Spirits (1QS III:13–IV:26) in Its Tradition-Historical Context," in *Light against Darkness: Dualism in Ancient Mediterranean Religion and the Contemporary World*, ed. A. Lange et al., JAJS 2 (Göttingen: Vandenhoeck & Ruprecht, 2011), 145–68; see esp. 166–68.

Levi. Such an argument not only indicates that the author is aware that he is not working in metaphor (why would it be necessary to go to these lengths to demonstrate the legitimacy of a metaphor?) but also goes even beyond analogy. Jesus is literally a high priest for the author of Hebrews.

The author's analogical reasoning is evident, however, when he speaks about Jesus presenting himself to God in the heavenly tabernacle in sacrificial terms. As was noted above, the general trend in the modern period has been to read Hebrews in terms of a paramorphic model driven by the constitutive metaphor "Jesus's death is the ultimate atoning sacrifice." If instead the author thinks in terms of the ascension and appearance of the resurrected Jesus as the great high priest in the presence of God in the highest heaven—in the heavenly holy of holies of the heavenly tabernacle—then the author is working not metaphorically, but analogically. Just as (1) the high priest in the earthly tabernacle brought the blood of the sacrificial victim into the earthly holy of holies and offered it to God once a year, and just as (2) it was the power of the life of the victim contained within that blood that effected atonement (see Lev. 17:11; cf. 16:15–16), so also, by analogy, (1) Jesus, the heavenly high priest, entered the heavenly holy of holies once and offered himself alive to God, and (2) it is his resurrection life, his now indestructible human life, that has the power to do what the life of animals could not—provide ultimate atonement.

To apply these terms and categories to the resurrected and ascended Jesus is not metaphor, because the associative field of Jewish blood sacrifice is fitting for the context of Jesus's high-priestly ministry in the heavenly tabernacle, the source and subject of the earthly model. Yet this language is also not literal. That is to say, Jesus does not literally sprinkle, smear, or pour out his blood at God's throne in heaven. The fact that Hebrews describes Jesus's offering in terms of himself (Heb. 7:27; 9:25–26), his body (10:10), and his blood (9:12, 14; 12:24) shows that the author is not at these points thinking literally of Jesus manipulating his blood in heaven. Rather, he is thinking in terms of analogy to the blood rituals. Just as blood, as the substance that contained life, was brought by the earthly high priest into God's presence in the holy of holies on Yom Kippur and was sprinkled there to effect a limited atonement, so Jesus, the heavenly high priest, took himself into God's heavenly presence and offered himself to God to effect ultimate atonement. Hebrews' sacrificial language of Jesus offering his body, blood, and self to God is often thought to be part of a metaphor in which these terms are all ways of describing Jesus's death. This language is instead, I am arguing, analogy that highlights the central importance of Jesus's resurrection life as that sacrifice that Jesus presents and God accepts. Jesus's life, by analogy to sacrifice of animal blood in the earthly tabernacle, has been offered to the Father in the heavenly holy of holies to make atonement for sins.

Conclusion

The larger point of this study has been to explore the possibility that sacred space and sacrificial language in Hebrews are not driven by a metaphorical theology that attempts to unpack the spiritual, heavenly, or existential significance of Jesus's crucifixion. The ideas that there is a tabernacle/temple in heaven, that this tabernacle is the source for the earthly structure, and that Jesus rose, ascended bodily, and entered that heavenly tabernacle allow for a theological model that has analogy at its core, not metaphor. Indeed, the relationship between the earthly and heavenly tabernacles the author assumes, described here in terms of a homeomorphic model, appears to ground an analogical hermeneutic that allows him to explore the biblical depictions of the earthly sacred space and the priestly service done there in order to better understand what Jesus is doing in the heavenly space and how his heavenly service effects atonement.

In Hebrews Jesus's death is one element of a larger ritual process that culminates in his entry into the heavenly tabernacle. There he presents himself before God as the offering that makes full atonement for God's people. The Epistle to the Hebrews is not, therefore, structured around an extended metaphor that focuses exclusively on Jesus's death, something that is in any case hard to square with the actual ritual process of sacrifice as described in Leviticus. Rather, the author takes sacrificial practice in the earthly sacred space of the tabernacle/temple to offer analogies for the way things must be in the heavenly tabernacle precisely because the earthly space is a model of that heavenly space. In this way the author correlates the larger early Christian story of Jesus with the biblical pattern of sacrifice and shows, by analogy, how Jesus's death, resurrection, and ascension into God's presence in the heavenly holy of holies effect ultimate atonement.

9

It Is Not Finished

Jesus's Perpetual Atoning Work as the Heavenly High Priest in Hebrews

Even at this moment, as a human being, [Jesus] is making intercession for my salvation, for he continues to wear the body that he assumed.

Gregory of Nazianzus, *Oration 30*, 14

The ongoing high-priestly ministry of Jesus in the heavenly tabernacle stands among the more neglected aspects of New Testament Christology and soteriology in much modern biblical and theological reflection. Jesus's cry in John's Gospel, "It is finished" (19:30), has taken on a life of its own, becoming a proof text in certain circles for the view that the full and final completion of Jesus's sacrificial and salvific work occurred as he expired on the cross. Alan Stibbs makes this case particularly clearly in the introductory paragraph to his book *The Finished Work of Christ*. Stibbs claims, "The idea that Christ's atoning work is 'finished' is Scriptural in origin: it is indeed based on a word uttered by our Lord Himself before His death on the cross."[1] This word is, of course, Jesus's cry in 19:30—Τετέλεσται (It is finished!). Stibbs continues, "Clearly, therefore, when Jesus at last reached the point of departure from this present earthly life, the work to which this word τετέλεσται referred was

1. A. M. Stibbs, *The Finished Work of Christ* (London: Tyndale, 1954), 5.

already fully accomplished."[2] Whether or not this is the proper interpretation of John 19:30,[3] the witness of Hebrews differs in kind from such an account of Jesus's priestly and sacrificial work precisely because Hebrews stresses more emphatically and explicitly than any other New Testament text that Jesus is currently the great high priest, who now ministers for his people in the heavenly holy of holies (Heb. 8:1–4; see also 7:25).

But what comprises Jesus's heavenly ministry? Hebrews suggests that upon his passing through the heavens as the one appointed by God to the position of high priest in Melchizedek's order, Jesus drew near to the Father in order to appear in his presence (see esp. 4:14–16; 5:8–10; 9:24–26). There, as the great high priest, he presented to God nothing less than himself as the ultimate atoning sacrifice on behalf of his brothers and sisters. He thereby made purification for sins and sat down at the Father's right hand, where he waits for all his enemies to be made his footstool (esp. Heb. 1:3; 10:12–14). His once-for-all offering has been presented and accepted. He has no need to re-present or re-offer himself to the Father.[4]

But is this the sum total of Jesus's heavenly ministry? Moreover, does the once-for-all-ness of his sacrifice mean that his atoning work is fully and finally finished even now? If this were the case, one might wonder why Hebrews emphasizes the need to have a high priest who presently serves as a minister in the heavenly holy of holies (8:1), particularly one who continually intercedes for his people (7:25). If all sin and impurity is fully and finally taken care of by the singular entry of Jesus into the Father's presence, why is his ongoing

---

2. Stibbs, *Finished Work*, 5. Stibbs states the thesis of his book as follows: "Christ's work of offering Himself for men's salvation is unmistakably represented in Scripture as *exclusively* earthly and historical, the purpose of the incarnation, wrought out in flesh and blood, in time and space, under Pontius Pilate; that by this once-for-all finished happening the necessary and intended atoning work was completely accomplished" (8, emphasis added). It is worth pointing out here that such an account of Jesus's death as the sum total of his atoning sacrifice cannot be made to square with the actual scriptural depictions of atoning sacrifices detailed in Leviticus. Stibbs may be aware of this issue. He tellingly labels approaches that emphasize Jesus's heavenly presentation of his atoning sacrifice to the Father as "more Jewish than fully Christian" (22). One of the problems Stibbs does not engage, however, is the very real historical one of how the first Christians, who were Jews, could have thought about sacrifice in such new and different "fully Christian" categories rather than the "Jewish" ones that they believed God gave them in Scripture.

3. For a few examples of commentators who argue the case see, R. V. G. Tasker, *The Gospel according to St. John*, Tyndale New Testament Commentaries (Grand Rapids: Eerdmans, 1960), 211; L. Morris, *The Gospel according to John*, rev. ed., NICNT (Grand Rapids: Eerdmans, 1995), 720n77; cf. 130–31.

4. I detail the case for this interpretation of Hebrews' understanding of Jesus's sacrifice in D. M. Moffitt, *Atonement and the Logic of Resurrection in the Epistle to the Hebrews*, NovTSup 141 (Leiden: Brill, 2011).

intercession, presumably a constituent element of his high-priestly ministry, still necessary?[5]

This study reexamines these questions and offers the following three conclusions: (1) Jesus's work of high-priestly intercession implies the need for ongoing forgiveness and purification—some kind of ongoing work of sacrificial atonement[6]—for his followers; (2) if this is correct, Hebrews does not conceive of Jesus's atoning, high-priestly work as completed on the cross or even upon his ascension, though his singular act of presenting himself to the Father is clearly unrepeatable;[7] (3) the atoning work that Jesus continues to perform now is that of maintaining the new covenant relationship between God and his people, work that is necessary while the covenant people are still in the process of being sanctified and have not yet been perfected.

In short, the author reflects on Jesus's ongoing work of sacrificial atonement in ways that are remarkably analogous to the ministry of the old covenant priesthood—especially that of the high priests—and the Levitical sacrificial system. As the high priest of the new covenant, Jesus now ministers in the heavenly tabernacle by offering to the Father the ongoing worship that maintains God's new covenant relationship with his people and mediates the blessings and promises associated with that relationship. This act of ongoing offering consists in the very presence of the interceding Son, Jesus, with the Father. The author of Hebrews, in other words, neither embraces a logic of sacrifice that stands against that of the Levitical system, which God ordained, nor works with a new covenant logic that differs radically from that of the Mosaic covenant. Instead, as one might expect given that the earliest Christians were Jews, he draws insights about who Jesus is and how Jesus saves his followers from the very Scriptures and practices he takes to be inspired and revealed by God (cf. Heb. 1:1–2). The logic of the new covenant and the

---

5. As one might guess from the quotation of Gregory of Nazianzus in the epigraph to this chapter, a rich history of reflection on this question can be found in patristic literature (I survey some of this literature in chap. 11). See also the fascinating late nineteenth-century study of W. Milligan, *The Ascension and Heavenly Priesthood of Our Lord: The Baird Lecture 1891* (London: Macmillan, 1892), esp. 113–65. Though my own account of Hebrews differs in significant ways from Milligan's, our questions and interpretations of Hebrews are similar at many points. (I am grateful to Michael Kibbe for bringing Milligan's volume to my attention.)

6. I define this term later in this chapter. See also D. M. Moffitt, "Hebrews," in *T&T Clark Companion to Atonement*, ed. A. J. Johnson (London: Bloomsbury T&T Clark, 2017), 533–36.

7. This does not mean that Jesus's death/work on the cross is not salvific. The point, rather, is that Jesus does more to effect salvation than simply die. The tendency to speak of the atonement as if it were equal to a systematic account of Christian soteriology creates confusion when the wide variety of problems that early Christians believed Jesus solved in order to save humanity are lumped together into one concept and event. I discuss this issue more later in this chapter.

sacrificial and high-priestly ministry Jesus performs within in it relate organically for this author to those of the old covenant.

Some Key Assumptions

The arguments advanced here depend in part upon six working assumptions and one caveat concerning Jesus's high priesthood, sacrifice, and atonement in Hebrews. I have explored and defended these conclusions in other publications, but some acknowledgment and elaboration of my working conclusions are necessary for the sake of the case being advanced here.

First, I assume that the author of Hebrews has thought carefully through the problem of Jesus's tribal lineage for the legitimacy of the claim that Jesus is a high priest. The author and the original audience likely shared a confession that identifies Jesus as a high priest (see Heb. 3:1). This identification may be a central element of the confession that some have begun to call into question.[8] The writer presents his apologetic reflection on the validity of Jesus's high priesthood in 5:1–7:28, and especially in chapter 7. His main goal in chapter 7 is to show how Jesus, a Judahite by birth, can legitimately be the high priest he is confessed to be. The problem the author faces concerns Jesus's humanity.[9] This latter point has at times not been properly explored in the commentary literature due to the misguided assumption that Hebrews derives Jesus's high-priestly status from the fact of his divine Sonship.[10] Thus,

8. G. H. Guthrie conclusively demonstrates the structural links between Heb. 4:14–16 and 10:19–23, arguing that these verses form an inclusio (*The Structure of Hebrews: A Text-Linguistic Analysis*, NovTSup 73 [Leiden: Brill, 1994], 79–80). This is relevant for reflecting on the confession the author urges the congregation to maintain. While he never gives the content of the shared confession he wants his intended readers to continue to affirm, the fact that the bulk of the material that stands between his two explicit calls to hold fast to this confession (4:14; 10:23) revolves around the topic of Jesus's high priesthood (with the author first defending the legitimacy of Jesus's high priesthood in 5:1–7:28 and, second, discussing the covenantal context, location, and nature of Jesus's high-priestly ministry in 8:1–10:20) implies that the affirmation of Jesus's high-priestly status is one of the central elements of the common confession that he thinks his readers are in danger of surrendering (see also the explicit reference to Jesus's high priesthood in the author's first reference to a shared confession in 3:1). E. Käsemann advances a similar conclusion, though via a different route, locating the confession of Jesus's high priesthood in early Christian liturgy that predates Hebrews (*Das wandernde Gottesvolk: Eine Untersuchung zum Hebräerbrief*, 4th ed. [Göttingen: Vandenhoeck & Ruprecht, 1961], 108–10).

9. For my detailed arguments on this subject see Moffitt, *Atonement and the Logic of Resurrection*, esp. 200–214.

10. So, for example, B. F. Westcott, *The Epistle to the Hebrews: The Greek Text with Notes and Essays*, 3rd ed. (London: MacMillan, 1903), 124; J. Moffatt, *A Critical and Exegetical Commentary on the Epistle to the Hebrews*, ICC (Edinburgh: T&T Clark, 1924), 64. Other accounts that do not look to Jesus's divinity but nevertheless think Jesus's priesthood is a

it bears repeating that the issue of Jesus's priestly status is in Hebrews chiefly a question of his humanity, not one of his status as divine Son per se.

A few observations help to clarify the point. If the author thought that Jesus's high priesthood was a function of Jesus's divine nature rather than one of Jesus's humanity, he has done a particularly poor job laying out his case. One could well imagine him reducing the complex argument of Hebrews 7 to a simple statement that Jesus is high priest *because* he is the Son. Instead, however, the logic of the author's argument aims to show that, *although* Jesus is the Son, he suffered, died, and, after being made perfect (τελειωθείς), *became* (ἐγένετο) the source of eternal salvation (5:8–10). That is to say, although Jesus is the royal and divine Son, he nevertheless became the high priest that he is confessed to be. This logic implies that simply being the Son does not qualify Jesus to be a high priest.

Unpacking this concessive logic requires sustained and careful argumentation on the part of the author precisely because he knows that as the Son Jesus lacks the proper qualification to be a priest at all, at least on earth, where the Mosaic law has authority (compare Heb. 7:14 and 8:4). To put the point differently, when the divine Son took up the blood and flesh of Abraham's seed, he took up the blood and flesh of the line of Judah. The Son came into the world in the tribe and lineage of Judah. While this coheres well with the Son's royal role as the Christ, the reigning Messiah, the fact of the incarnation creates a problem for Jesus's elevation to service in the priesthood. According to the Mosaic law, no one from the tribe of Judah can legitimately serve as a priest. To be a priest of God who serves in the earthly sanctuary, one must belong to the tribe of Levi (esp. Deut. 18:1–5). Thus, even though Jesus is the Son and, like Aaron, he was called by God to the office of high priest, his elevation to that office faces a problem created by the incarnation itself, precisely because the incarnation placed the Son in the wrong tribe for priestly service. The issue the author therefore has to solve when looking at both the confession of Jesus's high-priestly status and God's revelation through Moses revolves around his status as the incarnate Son in Judah's tribe.[11]

The author must have seen a number of possible solutions to this issue. He has already ruled out a simple deduction from the Son's divine preexistence,

---

function of his sonship are present in the secondary literature (e.g., Käsemann, *Das wandernde Gottesvolk*, 141). D. W. Rooke suggests that Hebrews draws on the ancient Israelite notion of sacral kingship ("Jesus as Royal Priest: Reflections on the Interpretation of the Melchizedek Tradition in Hebrews 7," *Biblica* 81 [2000]: 81–94). Among other considerations, the fact that Hebrews does so little to develop the royal office of Melchizedek works against Rooke's thesis.

11. One wonders if this difficulty with confessing Jesus as both royal Son from Judah's tribe and high priest may be one of the points under contention among those who might be tempted to abandon the community and its confession.

taking seriously the need for high priests to be human beings (Heb. 5:1). Still, he could have merely reasserted in Hebrews 7 God's call of Jesus to the role (5:5–6), a fact he obviously thinks is fundamental for Jesus's elevation to high-priestly status. Divine fiat would seem to offer sufficient warrant to allow for an exception to the Mosaic law. The writer does not, however, center his argument in Hebrews 7 on the fact of Jesus's divine appointment. He could have simply appealed to Melchizedek, the priest-king, as offering a model from Psalm 110 that justifies the application of both roles to Jesus. Here, too, he is clearly aware of Melchizedek's dual offices (Heb. 7:2–3), and his passing comment on Melchizedek's kingship seems designed to highlight the fact that this figure holds both royal and priestly offices. Yet after pointing this out, he surprisingly does not develop Melchizedek's royal role as his argument in Hebrews 7 unfolds.

The author adopts instead a different solution, one that takes Jesus's death, bodily resurrection, and ascension into account. In the process, he highlights his respect for the authority of the Mosaic law. Rather than appealing to the Son's divinity as something that simply trumped the particularity of Jesus's humanity, rather than playing out the mention of God's call of the Son to the high priesthood in terms of divine fiat that simply supersedes the law, rather than developing Melchizedek's royal status and explaining how this is a model for Jesus, the tack he takes both (1) recognizes that the law forbids Jesus to serve as a priest on earth (Heb. 7:14; 8:4) and (2) develops the claims that Jesus's high-priestly office is heavenly and that the high-priestly service he performs occurs in the heavenly tabernacle (8:1–4).

Second, I assume that the bodily resurrection of Jesus from the dead, which Hebrews correlates with the Son's perfection and which also pertains to the incarnate Son's humanity, provides the author with the solution to the Mosaic problem of Jesus's tribal descent barring him from priestly ministry. The bodily resurrection of Jesus perfects his Judahite humanity. Since he is a perfected Jew from the tribe of Judah, Jesus's humanity is now immortal, no longer corruptible and no longer subject to death, as it clearly was when he died on the cross. The indestructible life he now has as a human being qualifies him to serve in another legitimate priesthood, the heavenly one to which the ministering spirits belong.[12] As noted above, the author does not resolve the problem of the Mosaic law's stipulations on tribal descent by dismissing the law tout court. Indeed, the law's authority regarding priestly legitimation appears to be the presupposition that necessitates his defense of the legitimacy of Jesus's high priesthood. The logic of the argument in

12. For additional argumentation see chap. 5.

Hebrews 7 seizes on the transformation of Jesus's particular Judahite humanity in the resurrection such that, as a human being, Jesus now has life that is
like that of Melchizedek. This indestructible life into which he arose qualifies
him to serve as the priest of Melchizedek's order spoken of in Psalm 110 (see
esp. Heb. 7:15–16).[13] Further, this implies that Jesus became the high priest
he now is at the resurrection, when his human lineage no longer barred him
from priestly service.[14] The author has, then, constructed a careful and precise

13. In an excellent essay G. Gäbel has recently argued against this conclusion ("'[. . .] inmit-
ten der Gemeinde werde ich dir lobsingnen' Hebr 2,12: Engel und Menschen, himmlischer und
irdischer Gottesdienst nach dem Hebräerbrief," in *Gottesdienst und Engel im antiken Judentum
und frühen Christentum*, ed. J. Frey and M. R. Jost, WUNT 2/446 [Tübingen: Mohr Siebeck,
2017], 185–239, esp. 212–15). I continue, however, to be persuaded that the writer assumes
that Melchizedek is an angelic priest, one of the ministering—that is, priestly—spirits (see
Heb. 1:7, 14), above whom Jesus has been elevated in his resurrected humanity. This means,
contra Gäbel, that Hebrews is interested both in Melchizedek himself—particularly because
of the kind of life this mysterious figure possesses—and in how Jesus relates to him (as well
as how Melchizedek relates to the eternal Son). The conclusion that Melchizedek is an angel
not only explains why the author can identify him in immortal terms, which is surely the most
straightforward reading of the language about him in Heb. 7:3 and 7:8, but also coheres well
with the writer's identification of Jesus as the great *high* priest even though this fact (that is,
his *high* priesthood) cannot be deduced from Ps. 110:4, which speaks only of a priest. Gäbel
is right to note that the priestly order to which Jesus belongs has only one high priest—Jesus
himself. But why is the Son the high priest of an order named after Melchizedek? In my view,
the Son has become the sole high priest of Melchizedek's order because the Son, unlike any
of the other priests currently serving in the heavenly priesthood, is the first perfected human
being elevated to serve in this priestly order. As such, he has been exalted above *all* the angels/
ministering spirits and has taken his place at God's right hand, just as the argument of Heb.
1–2 demonstrates. Melchizedek is *priest* of God most high (the author follows the language of
Genesis, which speaks of Melchizedek only as a priest), but the perfected Jesus, who has been
elevated above all the angels (including, on this hypothesis, Melchizedek), is the *high* priest of
God most high. For more detailed argumentation, see Moffitt, *Atonement and the Logic of
Resurrection*, 204–7.

14. It is common in the secondary literature to read that Hebrews does not identify a moment
when Jesus became high priest (e.g., H. W. Attridge, *The Epistle to the Hebrews*, Hermeneia
[Philadelphia: Fortress, 1989], 146–47). In arguing for this view, D. Peterson provides an excellent
discussion of some of the main issues that are at stake. Interestingly, Peterson himself notes,
"[Jesus's] death on the cross must be included in our view of his priestly work, *though our
writer nowhere explicitly states this*" (*Hebrews and Perfection: An Examination of the Concept
of Perfection in the "Epistle to the Hebrews*," SNTSMS 47 [Cambridge: Cambridge University
Press, 1982], 193, emphasis added). What the literature shows is that the twinned assumptions
(1) that the death of Jesus must be the locus of his high-priestly sacrifice and (2) that Hebrews
has little concern for Jesus's resurrection, bodily or otherwise, are among the major drivers
of this conclusion. Thus, many continue to assume that the author of Hebrews did not think
with precision about when Jesus became a high priest in spite of the following facts: Hebrews
(1) predicates Jesus becoming a high priest (ἵνα . . . γένηται . . . ἀρχιερεύς) on his full participation
in the human condition, something that must include his suffering and death (2:17), (2) locates
Jesus becoming the source of eternal salvation after (or upon) his being made perfect (τελειωθεὶς
ἐγένετο . . . αἴτιος σωτηρίας αἰωνίου, 5:9), (3) implies that Jesus entered the heavenly holy of
holies after having become a high priest (ἀρχιερεὺς γενόμενος, 6:20), (4) says Jesus arose in the

argument that takes seriously both the particularity of the heavenly Son's incarnation and the authority of the divinely given law of Moses.

Third, I work with the assumption that this author believes that the resurrected Jesus ascended through the heavens into the highest heaven, where he entered the inner sanctum of the heavenly tabernacle. This is the location where he serves as high priest. Moses saw this heavenly structure while he was on Sinai and therefore patterned the earthly tabernacle on the heavenly exemplar he saw. For the author of Hebrews, the priority of the heavenly tabernacle implies that the structure of and worship within the earthly tabernacle brim with analogies to their heavenly counterparts. Analogies of structure, activity, and function naturally hold between the earthly and heavenly realities because Moses obeyed God and made everything according to the pattern that was shown to him on the mountain (see Exod. 25:40; Heb. 8:5). These analogies imply a hermeneutical corollary: one can learn something of the heavenly structure and its cultic service, and so also about where Jesus is and what Jesus is presently doing, by looking at its earthly model.[15]

Fourth, this last assumption implies further that Hebrews not only reads Jewish Scripture, or the Old Testament, in the light of Christ but also learns about Christ by reading him in the light of Scripture. The relationship between Christology and Scripture in Hebrews is dynamic and dialogical. The author even suggests that given space and time he could have said more about the significance of the earthly tabernacle for understanding the realities that Christ entered and the service that he performs there (Heb. 9:5).

Fifth, a note on my working assumptions about Jewish sacrifice is in order. I assume that a sacrifice consists of an irreducible ritual process. Roy Gane has compellingly argued that the rituals that constitute the process of sacrifice as presented in Leviticus relate to each other hierarchically.[16] This means

---

likeness of Melchizedek and has become a priest (ὃς . . . [ἱερεὺς] γέγονεν) by the power of his indestructible life (7:15–16), and (5) states clearly that Jesus could not be even a priest on earth (εἰ . . . ἦν ἐπὶ γῆς, οὐδ' ἂν ἦν ἱερεύς), let alone a high priest (8:4).

If, however, the author did think carefully about this and did not, like so many of his interpreters, assume that Jesus had to be a high priest on the cross but concluded instead that Jesus became a high priest at his resurrection in order to pass through the heavens and serve in this capacity in the heavenly holy of holies, then the data from Heb. 2:17, 5:9, 6:20, 7:15–16, and 8:4 fall neatly and consistently into place. If this interpretation is correct, it is not the author of Hebrews who is confused and imprecise on when Jesus became a high priest. Rather, interpreters create confusion by continuing (1) to assume that the author of Hebrews must identify the cross as the primary if not exclusive place and time of Jesus's atoning, high-priestly sacrifice and (2) to downplay or deny the importance of Jesus's bodily resurrection for the argument of Hebrews.

15. I argue this point at length in chap. 8.

16. R. E. Gane, *Cult and Character: Purification Offerings, Day of Atonement, and Theodicy* (Winona Lake, IN: Eisenbrauns, 2005), esp. 3–24.

that some elements of the process hold more importance or weight than do others relative to achieving the goals of a given sacrifice. This also implies that a sequence of ritual elements is necessary, but no one of these elements is alone sufficient for the sacrifice. That is to say, a sacrifice involves several ritual events and cannot, therefore, be reduced simply to one element within the sequence. Contrary to the assumption of many today, therefore, neither the verb nor the noun "sacrifice" is, in biblical terms, self-evidently synonymous with the ritual act of slaughtering a victim.[17] The word "sacrifice" does not mean "to slaughter or kill something." If one only slaughtered a victim, even at the temple, but did not bring the body and blood of the victim to the altars and offer them to God, no sacrifice would occur.

This last point partly explains why killing the victim is an essential element of some, but not all, sacrifices.[18] Additionally, slaughter is a constitutive part of some sacrifices, such as Passover and peace offerings, that are not offered for the purpose of sacrificial atonement. There are also examples of ritual acts that can atone but do not entail any act of slaughter (e.g., Num. 16:46–50 MT). These facts suggest that death is not central to the logic of atonement in the Levitical system. Moreover, in those cases where an animal is slaughtered as part of a sacrifice, including but not limited to atoning sacrifices, there is no hint that the animal is made to suffer, nor that the victim is an object of abuse or wrath. Inflicting suffering on the sacrificial victim is not a part of the biblical sacrificial system, and, while sacrifices can serve in part to protect the people from the danger of God's wrath breaking out against the guilt they have incurred (e.g., Num. 18:5), the items offered to God are never themselves depicted as objects of that wrath. The common assumption that suffering and dying for someone else is an act of sacrifice, which clearly is a denotation of the term "sacrifice" in contemporary English, leads to a category mistake when read back into the biblical accounts of Levitical sacrifice. To maltreat a sacrificial animal would be to render it ineligible to be offered to God, since a sacrificial victim that suffered physical damage from abuse would no longer be ἄμωμος (without blemish).[19]

17. The point can be shown from another angle. In, for example, Lev. 2:1–15 LXX, flour, loaves, and the firstfruits of the grain are all identified with the noun θυσία. Plainly the noun "sacrifice" cannot here denote a slaughtered thing. The term is used because the basic elements of a priest bringing something to an altar on behalf of a supplicant are in play. The logic of "sacrifice," in other words, revolves around giving a gift to God, not around the act of slaughter, which may or may not be a constitutive part of a particular θυσία.

18. On this issue see esp. C. A. Eberhart, *The Sacrifice of Jesus: Understanding Atonement Biblically*, Facets (Minneapolis: Fortress, 2011), 60–101.

19. It is interesting to note that the author of Hebrews locates Jesus's perfection after the completion of his suffering and death. If, as I have argued, the author correlates Jesus's perfection

Rather than being abused or made to suffer, the requirement that sacrificial animals be unblemished implies that they were treated with care prior to their being handed over to God. Further, the supplicant is the one who "pays" for the sacrifice by supplying the actual gift that is offered. It hardly seems a stretch to imagine the cost being borne joyfully when the gift offered is given in thanks; solemnly, even gratefully, when offered to make atonement for an impurity; or sorrowfully and as a penalty when, with repentance, the gift is given to atone for a moral infraction.

Be that as it may, within the series of elements that constitute an atoning sacrifice, the priestly work of applying blood to the various altars and burning portions of the victim on the outer altar (the acts whereby the sacrifice is ultimately offered or given over to God) are weightier than other elements for effecting atonement—they are higher up, as it were, in the hierarchically structured process. This conclusion follows from the fact that these elements of the process, in contrast to that of slaughtering of the victim, (1) occur at and upon the various altars and (2) can only be performed by priests.[20] To reduce Levitical sacrifice to the act of slaughtering a victim, which is not done on any of the altars, is a mistake.[21]

These points imply that one can speak about a sacrificial death/slaughter as an essential, constituent part of much Levitical sacrifice. To speak, however, of a sacrificial death is not to identify the death or slaughter itself as the sum total of a sacrifice.[22] Furthermore, the data of Leviticus suggest that the central aspects of the sacrificial process, the weightier elements in the hierarchy, have to do with the priest moving through progressively more sacred space in the tabernacle/temple precinct in order to approach the various altars and thereby bring the material of the sacrifice into God's presence. Bringing the

---

with his resurrection (*Atonement and the Logic of Resurrection*, esp. 198–200), then it makes good sense to interpret him as speaking of Jesus as the one who offered himself without blemish (ἄμωμος; Heb. 9:14). Such language should not be reduced simply to moral categories. What is needed for Jesus, who is the high priest and the sacrifice, to approach God and offer himself is for him to be not only morally pure but also ritually pure—to have a purified body. The resurrection, which on this reading of Heb. 9:14 would be the work of the eternal spirit (cf. Rom. 8:11), renders Jesus's humanity perfect so that he can ascend to the Father and offer himself "without blemish." By virtue of his resurrection the morally pure Jesus, who was without sin (Heb. 4:15), now has ritually pure humanity.

20. So, e.g., Eberhart, *Sacrifice of Jesus*, 85; Gane, *Cult and Character*, 67.

21. In an attempt to avoid confusion, I try to speak consistently of "slaughter" or "sacrificial death/slaughter" when referring to the act of killing the victim, reserving the term "sacrifice" either for the larger process as a whole or to identify either the acts of presentation or the actual materials offered.

22. It seems reasonable to assume that one could speak metonymically about sacrifice, taking one of the various elements of the process to stand in for the whole, but such utterances would not ultimately abstract the named element from or set it against the process as a whole.

blood and parts or all of the body of the victim, depending on the sacrifice, into the presence of God by doing things with these elements at altars is at the center of the process. Sacrifice, in other words, is about giving the material of an offering—that is, the required elements of a particular offering—over to God. God's willingness to accept the gift stands at the conceptual and effectual core of the process.[23] When the biblical data about sacrifice are so understood, Hebrews' emphasis on Jesus's entrance into the heavenly tabernacle, where he appears before the Father in the heavenly holy of holies and presents himself as a sacrifice—that is, offers the Father himself, his living blood and flesh—coheres remarkably well with the accounts and logic of sacrifice as depicted in Leviticus. As modern people we may balk at such ideas, but that is hardly a concern of the author of Hebrews.

Sixth, I assume that the author works with a sustained, pentateuchally shaped narrative throughout his homily. The narrative singles out the death of Jesus as the event that frees the seed of Abraham from slavery. Like Moses's use of the blood at the first Passover, Jesus's death liberates the people of God from the one who enslaved them.[24] This is clearly a salvific act, one of the necessary events that constitute the people's salvation. In pentateuchal terms, however, it is not true either that the act of liberation/exodus itself is the sum total of salvation for God's people or that Passover is a Levitical offering for sacrificial atonement. The story of salvation, if one may put it that way, moves forward from the exodus to the inheritance. Thus, the basic outline of the pentateuchal narrative in Hebrews involves a new Passover-like event in which Jesus defeats the Devil, liberates his people, and inaugurates the new covenant for them.[25] These are the primary salvific functions of Jesus's death in Hebrews.[26] In keeping with these past events, the original

23. The real problems with the sacrificial system occur when God refuses to receive or accept sacrifices that are offered to him (e.g., Lev. 26:31; Jer. 14:10–12; Hosea 8:13–14; Amos 5:20–27). This is a curious datum if the center or effective mechanism of sacrifice has to do with a penalty being borne by a substitute victim by way of its death. To point this out is not necessarily to suggest that some notion of penal substitution should therefore be removed from Christian accounts of Jesus's suffering and death but rather to highlight that such a notion is not likely, in historical terms, to have developed out of or to have been assumed to function within the sphere of Jewish blood sacrifice. To attempt to read suffering and the centrality of death back into Jewish sacrifice leads to all manner of misunderstanding about sacrifice as Leviticus portrays it.

24. I developed this argument in chap. 2.

25. For more detailed argumentation for this claim see chap. 3.

26. J. Compton has characterized my accounts of Jesus's elevation to his priestly office and of the function of Jesus's death in Hebrews as "reductive" and "overcooked" ("Review of *Atonement and the Logic of Resurrection in the Epistle to the Hebrews*," *TJ* 36 [2015]: 133–35). Compton repeatedly intimates that I "reduce" Jesus's death "simply" to an act of preparation for Jesus's atoning work. In fact, while I focus on Jesus's resurrection and entrance into the heavens, I state clearly in the book that "the death of Jesus can be seen as an event that

readers have become members of the new covenant who find themselves in a new wilderness-like period, simultaneously gathered around Mount Zion and waiting at the edge of their promised inheritance for their new Joshua to return to them. When Jesus appears again, he will bring salvation to his people (Heb. 9:28), and they will receive the fullness of the inheritance and rest God has promised them (cf. 1:14).

These six assumptions provide the stepping-off point for the current study. Before I proceed, however, one caveat is in order about the word "atonement." Atonement is a theological term, not a biblical one. As such, the word encapsulates a number of biblical terms and concepts relating to how Jesus brings God and humanity back into full fellowship (e.g., ransom, redemption, reconciliation, forgiveness, purification, propitiation). I work with a narrower notion of sacrificial or Levitical atonement, a qualification I make for the cultic language in Hebrews because the author himself so often highlights the high-priestly and sacrificial person and work of Jesus.[27] Sacrificial atonement has to do with offering God a gift in order to effect purification and/or bring about forgiveness for sins.[28]

---

accomplishes more than one thing in the argument [of Hebrews]" (Moffitt, *Atonement and the Logic of Resurrection*, 285; see also the subsequent discussion on 285–95).

27. I speak explicitly in *Atonement and the Logic of Resurrection* about "Levitical atonement" (see esp. 256–57). I intentionally sought to avoid speaking in the book about "*the* atonement." I did this in order to focus attention on Hebrews' engagement with the Levitical logic, pattern of atoning sacrifice, and priestly work when explaining when and where Jesus offers his high-priestly sacrifice and why, on Levitical-sacrificial terms, this offering correlates with his entrance into the heavenly holy of holies and appearance in God's presence. This is not to say that Jesus's high-priestly sacrifice is the sum total of the author's soteriology (as if everything he says about salvation revolves solely around Jesus's high-priestly work) but to point out that the author is not working with a broad, synthetic-/systematic-theological account of *the* atonement when he explains Jesus's high-priestly and sacrificial ministry. I reemphasize the point here because some reviewers appear to think that highlighting Hebrews' attention on Jesus's act of bringing the elements of his sacrifice—that is, himself—into God's presence is a reductive account of atonement easily disproven by pointing to nonsacrificial occurrences of the language of "atonement" (e.g., Compton, "Review," 134).

28. To limit atonement only to what was accomplished when Jesus suffered and died leads to a reduction of the significance of the incarnation to the crucifixion (see, e.g., Stibbs, who identifies Jesus's death as *the* purpose of the incarnation [*Finished Work*, esp. 28]). This reduction also leads to a confusion of biblical categories. The wide array of problems identified in Scripture that prevent fellowship between God and humanity are, on such an account, all imagined as being solved solely by means of Jesus's suffering and death. Reconciliation, redemption, propitiation, purification, and forgiveness, to name some of the major biblical categories, basically become indistinguishable (if not in terms of the problems they address, then in terms of the solutions given in Scripture to those problems). If, instead of trying to load everything onto the cross, we allow that Jesus is in himself the center of atonement (Jesus is the solution to all the problems that separate God and humanity, not the death of Jesus), then the entirety of the incarnation— Jesus's birth, life, suffering, death, resurrection, ascension, session, and return—can be seen to

Purification and forgiveness needed to occur in order for God's people to enter into covenant with him and, importantly, for them to remain in covenant relationship with him.[29] Central to the cultic system of the Mosaic covenant were those who crossed the boundaries between God and his people—that is, the priests—and drew near to God's presence to present the gifts and offerings they brought on behalf of the supplicants. The one who came closest to God was the high priest, who, on Yom Kippur, entered the most holy place and thereby came more fully into God's earthly presence than any other human being. These elements are central to sacrificial atonement, which primarily aims to effect forgiveness and purification in order to maintain the covenant relationship, not least by enabling impure and guilty humans to approach God's presence and by fulfilling the terms God himself has given whereby he condescends to be in covenant relationship with and to dwell among his people.

Jesus's High-Priestly Maintenance of the New Covenant

As just noted, the Levitical priests and sacrifices were essential to the maintenance of the covenant relationship between God and his people. They are key elements of the mechanism, as it were, that helps to ensure the continued health of the relationship between God and his people such that the people can dwell close to God and God condescends to remain in the midst of his people. So long as God accepts these sacrifices, the covenant relationship remains healthy.

Hebrews, I suggest, understands these Levitical concepts and reflects on the new covenant and its high priest and sacrifice in terms that cohere with—are even informed by—the old covenant and its priests and sacrifices. Because Jesus ascended into the heavenly holy of holies and remains there, it follows for the author that Jesus is *the* high priest who can guarantee that the new covenant relationship is perpetually maintained, something no earthly high priest could do because of death and because the law never brought about

---

contribute in particular ways to *the* atonement. Importantly, such an account would allow for distinct biblical problems to be solved by distinct aspects of the larger sweep of the incarnation. In the case of atoning sacrifice, rather than forcing this to be fundamentally about suffering and death, which Leviticus simply does not support (something that should matter if one wishes to avoid theologies that are essentially Gnostic and/or Marcionite), one could identify ways in which the logics of Jewish sacrifice and high-priestly ministry resolve particular problems that hinder divine-human relations without assuming that these solve all the problems.

29. In keeping with Leviticus, these problems would particularly relate to the ongoing maintenance of the covenant relationship between God and his people. This appears to be Yom Kippur's raison d'être.

perfection. The law, in other words, never made it possible for someone to enter the earthly holy of holies and remain there in God's presence, to say nothing of making it possible for a high priest to pass through the heavens and remain in the heavenly holy of holies. Moreover, as Hebrews 7:25 states, because Jesus is the high priest who always lives and is always at God's right hand, he is always able to intercede for his people and so is able to save them completely (εἰς τὸ παντελές).[30]

The logic of Hebrews 7:25 implies that, if Jesus were not actively interceding for his people, their complete salvation would not be possible. Yet this implication suggests another: Jesus's followers need ongoing atonement. The very work that the high priests on earth could do only once a year is done by Jesus perpetually. In contrast to the old covenant high priests, who were prevented by death from remaining in their office, Jesus, because of his resurrection, is able to not only serve as the heavenly high priest but to do so *without interruption*. Thus, Jesus's high-priestly ministry brings a level of purity and forgiveness that exceeds that of the old covenant. Jesus's ministry ensures that the new covenant relationship is fully maintained. Because he is in himself both high priest and sacrificial offering, his very presence in the Father's presence secures the covenant relationship and ensures the salvation of its members.

This kind of activity is the sort of thing one might expect of a high priest in the holy of holies on Yom Kippur, at least in the late Second Temple period.[31] This is where and when the high priest makes annual supplication for the people as he offers the sacrificial blood. Indeed, supplication on behalf of the people and the other ritual acts performed in the holy of holies, including the offering of the blood, would be inseparable on Yom Kippur. The author of Hebrews conceives of the ongoing high-priestly work of Jesus along remarkably analogous lines. Jesus's ongoing high-priestly intercession works in

---

30. Given that Hebrews views salvation not as something one presently possesses but as something one receives in the future (e.g., 1:14; 9:28), Jesus's continual intercession appears to be an essential part of his work that ensures that his people will be fully saved—they will successfully enter the promised inheritance. In all probability, this full salvation has to do with all God's people being resurrected when they are all made perfect together (11:39–40).

31. Philo identifies offering sacrifices and prayers on behalf of the people as the main responsibilities of the priest and especially of the high priest (see the evidence and discussion in J. Leonhardt, *Jewish Worship in Philo of Alexandria*, TSAJ 84 [Tübingen: Mohr Siebeck, 2001], 228–33). Thus, Philo assumes that the high priest offers prayers when he goes into the holy of holies on Yom Kippur (*Legat.* 306; see also Leonhardt, *Jewish Worship*, 128–29). I offer a more detailed defense of this point in D. M. Moffitt, "Jesus as Interceding High Priest and Sacrifice: A Response to Nicholas Moore," *JSNT* 42 (2020): 542–52, esp. 548–51. For additional evidence that the ministry of the high priest included offering sacrifices and prayers on behalf of the covenant people see Josephus, *Ant.* 3.189–91.

ways that follow the pattern and logic of the annual work of the high priest in the earthly holy of holies.[32] Insofar as the author reflects on Jesus in light of this Jewish holy day, he does so by highlighting both Jesus's presentation of himself to the Father in the heavens, where there is presumably an altar (cf. Heb. 13:10), and Jesus's ongoing work of intercession before the Father (compare 7:25 and 8:1–4). This also makes good sense of the metaphor in Hebrews 12:24 of Jesus sprinkling his blood. Here Jesus's role as covenant mediator is correlated with the act of offering his blood by way of sprinkling, an act that the author says "is speaking" (λαλοῦντι) a better word than Abel.[33]

The preceding account of Hebrews' sacrificial and high-priestly reflection on Jesus's entrance into the heavenly holy of holies has the benefit of offering a historically plausible explanation of the development of early Christian reflection that deduced aspects of christological and soteriological reflection from the very Jewish Scriptures and practices it cherished.[34] On this sort of

32. Milligan recognized this, too, writing with respect to Jesus's heavenly session:
What is [Jesus] about [i.e., doing]? He is not simply interceding on the strength of a past gift or sacrifice. He is presenting an offering on which his intercession is based, and in which it is involved. The idea of offering . . . cannot be separated from the action of our Lord after His Ascension, unless we also separate the thought of offering from what was done by the high-priest of Israel in the innermost sanctuary of his people. Such a separation the ceremonial of the law does not permit. The Jewish high-priest ministered in that sanctuary with more than the recollection or the merit of an offering already made. He had to sprinkle on the mercy-seat and before the veil the blood which he carried in along with him; he had to complete the reconciliation of Israel to God. . . . And all of this was part of the offering, not merely something done after the offering was ended. . . . As, therefore, the Jewish priest continued his work of offering after he had gone within the veil, so, in similar circumstances, we must connect with [Jesus] in whom the economy of Judaism is fulfilled the idea of offering. (*Ascension and Heavenly Priesthood of Our Lord*, 122–23)

33. The comparison and contrast with Abel in this verse probably does not intend to highlight Abel's death, as if Abel's death were somehow compared to the sacrificial act of sprinkling blood in God's presence. Rather, the parallel intends to recall Abel's actual act of offering a sacrifice to God. Abel, in contrast to Cain, was the first one to offer a blood sacrifice to God. In Jewish terms, Abel was the first one to sprinkle sacrificial blood as an offering to God. God looked favorably on Abel and the sacrifices he offered (Gen. 4:4; cf. Heb. 11:4). The point of Heb. 12:24, in other words, is that God is more pleased by the better offering of Jesus than he was with the blood offering made by Abel (and by implication, with the Levitical sacrifices). Abel's offering from the firstborn of his flocks was good and was motivated by faith, and God looked upon it with favor, but Jesus's act of presenting himself to God is even better.

34. Stibbs appears not to see the historical problem with an interpretation of Jesus's sacrifice and high-priestly ministry that bifurcates his high-priestly intercession from his act of presenting his sacrifice. Against those who highlight the need to hold the two together, he argues that Jesus's sacrifice "is unmistakably represented in Scripture as exclusively earthly and historical, the purpose of the incarnation . . . ; [so] that by this once-for-all finished happening the necessary and intended atoning work was completely accomplished" (*Finished Work*, 8). He later adds

reading, in other words, the confession of Jesus's ascension into the heavens and the identification of Jesus as high priest has real content that would make sense to the earliest Christians in terms of their Jewish background. To assume that new and different conceptions of a high priest and of the way in which sacrifice functioned are at the roots of the earliest reflection on Jesus is not impossible, but such an account is much harder to explain historically.[35]

Additionally, the work of covenant maintenance by Jesus the heavenly high priest assumes, at least from the perspective of the author of Hebrews, that Jesus has not stepped outside of space and time, even if these are not precisely the same in the heavens as they are on earth. The central points to note here are (1) the reality and ongoing nature of the incarnation, which the resurrection guarantees, and (2) the confession in Hebrews that Jesus will return to bring salvation to those who are waiting for him (Heb. 9:28). To take seriously the bodily resurrection and ascension of Jesus, as I have argued the author of Hebrews does, allows the inference that Jesus continues to be an embodied human being located in a particular place. For the author of Hebrews this place is the heavenly holy of holies at God's right hand. Furthermore, Hebrews looks ahead to a future time and place when Jesus is no longer absent from his brothers and sisters but will return to them, bringing their salvation with him.

This last point is worthy of more reflection. There has been a tendency in Hebrews' scholarship, especially after Ernst Käsemann's influential book *Das wandernde Gottesvolk: Eine Untersuchung zum Hebräerbrief*, to assume that

---

that the idea that Jewish concepts of sacrifice and high-priestly ministry in the holy of holies suggest that offering and intercession belong together fails "to give due consideration to certain new facts in the New Testament fulfilment of the Old Testament figure, which completely alter the situation. Such a view is, indeed, more Jewish than fully Christian, because it fails properly to appreciate the true . . . perfection, and the consequent surpassing glory, of the priesthood of Christ compared with that of the Levitical system" (22). Hebrews, he later affirms, demands the separation of offering and intercession in the case of Jesus (32). In historical terms (to say nothing of the potential theological problems such a view raises), Stibbs's account is highly implausible. He places the cart of a certain kind of later soteriological reflection before the horse of the actual appeal on the part of the earliest Christians to biblical and Second Temple sacrificial practice as they sought to understand and explain the saving work of Jesus in terms of God's prior revelation.

35. One needs, too, to take seriously the possibility that the self-evidence of a reduction of all of Jesus's sacrificial and atoning work to the cross is both anachronistic and in danger of leading to a kind of diminution of the importance of Jewish Scripture and practices for early Christian understandings of Jesus. This is still a long way from Marcion, but there are nevertheless real theological concerns that need to be borne in mind if one wants to confess that the God who revealed the tabernacle, priesthood, and sacrificial system to Moses is the same God who appointed Jesus to the status of sacrifice and high priest according to the order of Melchizedek but that that God meant something entirely different by the terms "sacrifice" and "high priest" than what he revealed to his people in the Mosaic law.

Hebrews is about pilgrimage, forward motion that leads one out of the world and into God's presence, where Jesus is. God's people wander through this life but are ultimately headed toward their inheritance. The goal is for God's people to endure their earthly suffering and be released into the salvation of the heavenly inheritance. They will one day join Jesus where he sits in the heavenly world to come.

But such a conception struggles to incorporate Hebrews 9:28, where the author does not say that Jesus will bring his people to himself by leading them out of the wilderness and through the heavens to where he is, but rather says that Jesus will appear again to be present with his people, who are waiting for him, ready to receive him back (ἀπεκδέχομαι). Hebrews does not envision the wandering people of God but the waiting people of God.[36] This coheres with the directional metaphor in the writer's admonition for the readers to exhort each other as they see the day "drawing near" (ἐγγίζουσαν, 10:25), and with his reminder that in just a little while, the one for whom they wait "will come" (ὁ ἐρχόμενος ἥξει, 10:37). In Hebrews 11:10 the author even describes Abraham as "waiting" (ἐξεδέχετο) for the city without foundations. The English translation tradition mutes the point, tending to render the verb ἐκδέχομαι in terms of "looking for/forward to" (KJV, RSV, NIV, ESV). The notion of expectation is plainly present, but as several commentators note, the Jewish apocalyptic idea of waiting for the heavenly Jerusalem is the chief point in play here (see Heb. 11:16; 12:22).[37] This does not prove that Hebrews envisioned the descent of the heavenly Jerusalem as in, for example, Revelation 21:2, 10. The idea is hardly implausible, however, when considered in light of Hebrews 9:28, particularly given the close collocation in Hebrews of salvation

---

36. Otfried Hofius made this point forcefully in his volume titled *Katapausis: Die Vorstellung vom endzeitlichen Ruheort im Hebräerbrief*, WUNT 1/11 (Tübingen: Mohr Siebeck, 1970). With respect to this very point he writes, "The congregation is not portrayed as wandering as it journeys to heaven but portrayed as God's people who are *waiting* for the consummation of their salvation, and with all urgency the author seeks to exhort this people not to abandon their patient expectation, which is the very thing that ensures the fulfillment of the promise" (my translation; Hofius's German: "Die Gemeinde [ist] nicht als das zum Himmel wandernde, wohl aber als das auf die Heilsvollendung *wartende* Gottesvolk gesehen, und der Verfasser will dieses Volk . . . mit aller Dringlichkeit dazu aufrufen, die Erwartung nicht preiszugeben, der allein die Erfüllung verheißen ist"; *Katapausis*, 150).

37. For example, Attridge, *Hebrews*, 323–24; C. R. Koester, *Hebrews: A New Translation with Introduction and Commentary*, AB 36 (New York: Doubleday, 2001), 486. Erich Grässer agrees that Abraham is here depicted as waiting for the heavenly city, but Grässer argues that the city's ultimate transcendence in Hebrews means that even here the idea of wandering rather than waiting is primary (*An die Hebräer*, EKKNT 17 [Zurich: Benziger, 1997], 3:127; see also E. Grässer, "Das wandernde Gottesvolk Zum Basismotiv des Hebräerbriefes," in *Aufbruch und Verheißung: Gesammelte Aufsätze zum Hebräerbrief*, ed. M. Evang and O. Merk [Berlin: de Gruyter, 1992], 231–50).

and obtaining the promised inheritance (e.g., 1:14). If the promised inheritance includes receiving the heavenly city, and if receiving this inheritance is at least part of what the writer considers to be constitutive of salvation, then it seems plausible to interpret the idea of Jesus appearing a second time for the salvation of those who wait for him in terms of his bringing the heavenly city to his waiting people. All of this coheres well with the author's claim that the audience does not have a permanent city here but seeks instead the one that is coming (τὴν μέλλουσαν, 13:14).

Furthermore, it is unclear why the idea of a final shaking of the earth and heavens and the removal of created things (Heb. 12:27) cannot cohere with the idea of Jesus returning to his people and bringing them their inheritance. The very fact that the author says in 12:27 that the removal of the shakable things is done in order to allow the unshakable things to remain (ἵνα μείνῃ) implies that these unshakable things are not Platonic, eternal realities. If the author meant something like the latter idea, his statement would be nonsensical. How can the removal of the present creation impinge in any way on the ability of the unshakable things to remain?[38] A more satisfying account of the verse would seem to be foreshadowed in Hebrews 1:12, where the citation of Psalm 102:26 implies that the present created things will be changed, like a garment. The image is not one of simple removal but of replacement (cf. Rev. 21:1).

Be that as it may, the waiting motif of Hebrews 9:28 correlates well with the pentateuchal narrative the author develops in his epistle. It may be tempting to assume that being in the wilderness must imply the forty years of wandering. The author, however, locates his audience in a time and place in the wilderness narrative prior to the failure of the exodus generation at Kadesh Barnea.[39] Even as he discusses that generation as a negative example in

38. Most commentators recognize that Hebrews, if it works with a version of a Platonic dualism, does not do so in a thoroughgoing way (e.g., Attridge, *Hebrews*, 383; J. W. Thompson, *Hebrews*, Paideia [Grand Rapids: Baker Academic, 2008], 268–69). I continue, however, to maintain that Hebrews' confession of Jesus's bodily resurrection and ascension suggests that the author does not work with a dualism between what's earthly material or flesh and what's heavenly or spiritual (see Moffitt, *Atonement and the Logic of Resurrection*, esp. 300–303).

39. Albert Vanhoye places more emphasis on Hebrews' call to enter the promised rest than on the motif of waiting for salvation ("Longue marche ou accès tout proche? Le contexte biblique de Hébreux 3,7–4,11," *Biblica* 49 [1968]: 9–26). Nevertheless, he recognizes that wandering is not the right conceptual category for Hebrews: "The religious situation of Christians is compared to that of the Israelites arriving at the border of the promised land. It is not so much a question of an interminable path as of the last steps to be taken: the moment has come to leave the wilderness and enter the kingdom of God" (my translation; Vanhoye's French: "La situation religieuse des chrétiens est comparée à celle des Israélites arrivés aux portes du pays. Il n'est plus question d'un chemin interminable, mais des derniers pas à franchir: le moment est venu de passer du désert au royaume de Dieu"; "Longue marche," 17).

3:15–4:7, he focuses not on their wandering but on their failure to obtain the promised inheritance,[40] a failure that resulted in the forty years of wandering and that generation's loss of the inheritance. The equivalent act of unbelief for the contemporary audience would be falling away from the community of the faithful and its confession about Jesus. For this author, to wander in the wilderness would appear to be tantamount to having lost already the opportunity of the "today" of Psalm 95.[41]

None of this is to suggest a neat one-to-one correspondence between the broad narrative of the Pentateuch and the wilderness metaphor the author of Hebrews develops. Hebrews works more freely with the pentateuchal narrative than that and does not have trouble conflating elements from these texts and from other scriptural passages. But there is a macrolevel structure here. As stated above, the broad pentateuchal narrative of liberation from the enslavement, inauguration of the covenant and the tabernacle, establishment and inauguration of the means and practices of ongoing worship, and waiting in the wilderness to receive the promised inheritance forms the structure the author uses to locate followers of Jesus in relation to their past, present, and eschatological hope.

Just here, however, in the waiting in the wilderness, the notion of covenant maintenance and ongoing high-priestly intercession makes so much sense. In the wilderness, even before the forty years of wandering, God's people

40. Hofius notes that the author's use of Ps. 94 LXX does not even emphasize the journey from Egypt to the edge of the promised land but rather emphasizes the actions and judgment of the people at Kadesh Barnea: "With respect to the wilderness generation, the author is only concerned with the events of Kadesh Barnea. The preceding journey through the wilderness, as such, lies entirely outside his interest. Even in the two places, 3:9 and 3:16, where he recalls the time of the exodus, he makes no reference to the wandering itself" (my translation; Hofius's German: "Ihn beschäftigt im Hinblick auf die Wüstengeneration einzig und allein das Geschehen bei Kades-Barnea, während die voraufgegangene Wüstenwanderung als solche für ihn gänzlich außerhalb des Interesses liegt. Auch an den beiden Stellen 3,9 und 3,16, wo an die Zeit des Exodus erinnert wird, ist auf die Wanderung selbst kein Bezug genommen"; *Katapausis*, 144).

41. Again, Hofius saw the point clearly, commenting that the wilderness generation "serves for the author of Hebrews as a vivid example of *the impossibility of a second repentance*. For those who have fallen away from God, there is no longer any possibility of return" (my translation; Hofius's German: "ist . . . dem auctor ad Hebraeos ein eindringlichen Beispiel für die *Unmöglichkeit der zweiten Buße*. Für den, der von Gott abgefallen ist, gibt es keine Möglichkeit der Umkehr mehr"; *Katapausis*, 137). Vanhoye similarly observes that the wandering Israelites "rather than being presented as an example for the faithful illustrate the punishment of unbelievers—those who refused God's invitation to enter. These are the ones who are sent back into the wilderness to wander indefinitely until they die. . . . They do not represent the Christian life, but that of damnation" (my translation. Vanhoye's French: "loin d'être proposées en exemple aux fidèles, elles constituent le châtiment des incrédules, de ceux qui refusent l'invitation divine à entrer. Ceux-là sont renvoyés dans le désert pour y errer indéfiniment jusqu'à y mourir. . . . Leur sort ne représente pas la vie chrétienne, mais la damnation"; "Longue marche," 17–18).

experienced tests and trials.[42] The readers of Hebrews continue to face the problems of sin, death, and persecution. What is needed above all else in this wilderness moment is ongoing intercession, some way in which they are being made perfect and being sanctified while they wait for their inheritance.[43] This is part of the hermeneutical dynamic in play in Hebrews. Hebrews, more than any other New Testament text, shows both how the high-priestly work of Jesus is now keeping God's people safe in the wilderness, ensuring that they can approach their exalted high priest boldly in times of need, and how Jesus now intercedes for them such that they will be saved completely and will be able to enjoy the inheritance God has promised his people.

To summarize thus far, the affirmation in Hebrews 9:28 that Jesus will appear again to bring salvation to those waiting for him implies, as one can also deduce from 7:25, that aspects of Jesus's work of salvation are presently ongoing. Jesus is appealing to God for his brothers and sisters. This intercession ensures their full salvation. Not only can this be inferred from 7:25, but the language in 2:11 that speaks of Jesus as the one who sanctifies those who are being sanctified (οἱ ἀγιαζόμενοι) appears to hint at this dynamic too. I suspect further that this offers the best interpretation of 13:20–21, where, unlike the NIV's incomprehensible translation to the effect that the blood of the covenant brought Jesus back from the dead, the point is more likely to be that the blood of the covenant is the means by which God's people are being equipped to please God by doing his will. Jesus's ongoing high-priestly intercession is making God's people perfect—doing what the sacrifices and ministry of the priests in the old covenant aimed to do but ultimately could not do in such a way as to bring perfection (see 7:11, 19; 9:9; 10:1).

The Once-for-All-ness of Jesus's Sacrifice and the Inability to Return to the Covenant

The preceding discussion is likely to raise a number of questions, but two are especially obvious. First, how does this account cohere with the "once

---

42. See Exod. 15:25; 16:4; 20:20; Num. 14:22.

43. If this is correct, it suggests that Jesus's continuing absence from his people was not primarily a problem to be solved but an opportunity for creative christological reflection. If one knows where Jesus has gone—to God's right hand in the highest heaven, or into the heavenly holy of holies—then one can deduce things about who he is and what he is doing: he must be a high priest and he must be performing priestly service on behalf of his people. All of this deduction was in dialogue with Scripture. Texts like Ps. 110 would naturally rise to the foreground, but, at least for the author of Hebrews, so did biblical notions of priestly service and priestly legitimation as one places the confession of Jesus's high-priestly status up against God's past revelation in the Mosaic law.

for all" language in Hebrews and the language of Jesus sitting at God's right hand after having accomplished purification and forgiveness for sins? Texts like Hebrews 1:3 and 10:10–18 might appear, prima facie, to disallow the arguments made above. Second, if Jesus is interceding for his people and thereby maintaining the covenant, how is it that the author can envision the possibility of some falling away from this relationship without any means for restoration?

To take the initial question first, two points can be made. The failure of the old covenant to fully remove sin implies that there are numerous sins of the past that need to be dealt with in order for the new covenant to be made with the house of Israel and the house of Judah. The Jeremiah 31 text cited in Hebrews makes this very point—in the new covenant, the sins and lawless deeds of the past are no longer remembered. At the very least, Jesus's act of sacrificial presentation aimed at dealing fully with certain past sins.[44]

More, however, seems to be implied in the unqualified language of Hebrews 1:3 and 10:10–18. I suggest that the resolution of the apparent tension between these texts and 7:25 is to be found in the recognition that Jesus is, in his resurrected self, both the high priest and the sacrifice of the new covenant. Given that the covenant people are continuing to be sanctified (2:11; 10:14), continue to wait for their perfection (11:39–40), and will ultimately be saved completely, Hebrews assumes that there continues to be a need for their ongoing forgiveness and purification even after their initial purification upon entering the covenant.[45] This is part of the dynamic of their present status as those who wait in the wilderness for Jesus to return to them.

Jesus performs this ongoing ministry by being in himself both the high priest and the sacrifice who sits at the Father's right hand. Because he remains in the Father's presence and intercedes for his people, his sacrificial, atoning work is perpetual. This is partly why there can be no repetition of Jesus's sacrifice—he never has to leave the presence of the Father and then return again in order to present himself again. The once-for-all-ness of Jesus's presentation of himself is correlated with the once-for-all-ness of his death, resurrection, and ascension. There can be no repetition of the process of his sacrifice within the once-for-all-ness of the incarnation, for the risen Jesus cannot leave the Father in order to again take up blood and flesh, die, rise again, and return again to the heavenly holy of holies.

44. One wonders if this may be one of the aspects of Jesus's sacrificial work that are implied in the author's comment in Heb. 9:23 that the heavenly things themselves required purification.

45. This initial purification may well be what the author has in mind in 10:29 when he speaks of apostates in terms of counting the blood of the covenant by which they were sanctified as profane.

Further, the idea in Hebrews 10:14 that Jesus makes perfect those who are being sanctified appears to restate the claim made in 2:11. Jesus is the one who, by means of his one sacrifice, perfects those who are in the process of being sanctified. If this is right, then the point of 10:14 is not, as in many English translations, that this work of perfection is fully completed for all time, but rather that Jesus is now in the state of making his people perfect. This would correlate perfectly with the idea that he is the high priest who now intercedes for his people. Similarly, in 10:10, his people are said to be in the state of being sanctified by means of his one offering. The idea that his brothers and sisters are being sanctified coheres well with the interpretations of 2:11, 7:25, 12:24, and 13:20–21 offered above. If, as I have argued elsewhere,[46] the author of Hebrews thinks the perfection of humanity lies ultimately in the eschatological resurrection of the body and reception of the eternal inheritance, as is also the case with Jesus's own perfection, this again coheres with the resolution of the apparent tensions between these texts. Jesus is the sanctifier who is making his people perfect. His people are being sanctified while they wait for him to perfect them and bring them the inheritance of their salvation. This ongoing work of making his people holy and perfect follows directly from Jesus's ongoing work of interceding for them as their high priest.[47] This high-priestly work is the means by which they will be saved completely such that they will receive the fullness of the inheritance promised to them. Jesus's high-priestly ministry, in other words, ensures that the great narrative of salvation in the Pentateuch will come to its intended denouement and God and his people will dwell together in the unshakable inheritance.

As for the impossibility of restoring those who fall away, Hebrews appears to take a different approach than does Paul, for example, on the question of

---

46. See my discussion of perfection and purity in chap. 7 of this volume as well as my arguments in Moffitt, *Atonement and the Logic of Resurrection*, esp. 195–214.

47. Hebrews is not a unique witness in the New Testament to Jesus's ongoing work of forgiveness and purification for his people in the Father's presence. The idea appears in 1 John 1:7–2:2 as well. The collocation of Jesus's blood, confession of sin, forgiveness of sins, and purification in 1:7–9 suggests the author reflects on Jesus's ongoing work of forgiveness and purification in terms of Jewish sacrificial categories. That the author thinks believers need ongoing forgiveness and purification from sins becomes particularly clear in 2:1. He states there that he is writing to believers ("my little children") in order to encourage them not to sin, the obvious aim or ideal. If, however, they do sin, their sins can be dealt with by means of Jesus's ongoing advocacy for them before the Father. This ongoing advocacy is possible because, the author suggests in 2:2, Jesus is the atoning sacrifice (ἱλασμός) for their sins. The point appears to be that Jesus is the advocate who can intercede for his people when they sin because he is the atoning sacrifice for their sins who is alive and with the Father right now. This looks remarkably like the notions of Jesus's high-priestly ministry and ongoing work of covenant maintenance that one finds in Hebrews.

being able to be removed from the covenant relationship. Paul also seems to have a concept of Jesus performing high-priestly work at God's right hand. He says in Romans 8:34 that Christ Jesus, who died but, even more, who was raised, is now at the right hand of God interceding for his people. On the basis of this intercession, those who follow Jesus, presumably those who confess that Jesus is Lord and believe that God raised him from the dead (10:9), cannot be condemned. Paul goes on to affirm in 8:35–39 that therefore nothing is able to separate those whom Christ loves from God. Jesus's ongoing intercession means that the saving relationship between God and his people cannot be broken. This looks like a concept of covenant maintenance, the mechanism of which is nothing less than Jesus's ongoing intercession. Hebrews, however, seems to argue that the people of the new covenant can effectively remove themselves from the covenant relationship. They can repudiate their confession (4:14; 10:23). They can give up meeting together with the rest of the community (10:25). They can go on sinning willfully (10:26). Should these things happen, they could find themselves in a position like the generation of Israelites after their failure at Kadesh Barnea—wandering in the wilderness without hope of receiving the promised inheritance. It appears to be the case in Hebrews that just as Jesus's work of liberating his people, inaugurating the new covenant, and entering into the Father's presence is unrepeatable, so also one's entrance into this covenant and community cannot be repeated.

Conclusion

If the preceding arguments are correct, Hebrews assumes that the new and living way to God opened by Jesus consists in a life of ongoing cultic relationship within the context of the new covenant. This relationship revolves around worship that involves and is made possible by the perpetual ministry of the great high priest Jesus, the Son of God, in the heavenly tabernacle. This high priest, who is always also in his crucified and resurrected body the sacrifice offered to God, intercedes on behalf of his brothers and sisters. Because of his resurrection and passing through the heavens, Jesus, who is always the crucified one, is interceding for his brothers and sisters. He, as Gregory of Nazianzus puts it, continues even now to wear that body that died and was resurrected.[48] This is why even now he can intercede for his people's salvation. In this sense, the sacrificial work of Jesus is not finished. The fact of his ongoing presence with the Father and physical absence from his people means that he is working on their behalf as their high priest mediating and maintaining

---

48. See the epigraph at the beginning of this chapter, quoting *Oration 30*, 14.

the new covenant relationship. So long as Jesus remains in the heavenly holy of holies and so long as his people are waiting in their own new wilderness state for their perfection and are in the process of being sanctified, Jesus's high-priestly intercession continues. For the author of Hebrews, the return of the high priest to his waiting people will mark the point at which they finally obtain the salvation that all of Jesus's incarnate work guarantees them.

10

Observations on Directional Features of the Incarnation and Jesus's Sacrifice in Hebrews

Hebrews and the Incarnation of the Divine Son

At the core of the Epistle to the Hebrews lies a conviction about the incarnation of the eternal Son of God. Hebrews does not speak explicitly about the eternal Word becoming flesh and dwelling among us in the way John's Gospel does. Nevertheless, the logic of the argument for the elevation of the Son above the angels in Hebrews 1–2 is one of several aspects of the homily that presuppose the incarnation.[1]

The central argument of Hebrews 1–2 can be summarized as follows: The Son, through whom the Father created the ages (1:2) and whose powerful word sustains all things (1:3), was made for a little while lower than the angels (2:6–8). Because he suffered, died, and rose, he has returned to his Father as the first fully perfected and exalted human being. The Son of Hebrews 1 is,

1. For example, Heb. 10:5 describes words from Ps. 40 spoken by Christ as he comes "into the world" (εἰς τὸν κόσμον). This seems clearly to presuppose his preexistence and subsequent incarnation. The statement in Heb. 5:7 that the Son suffered "in the days of his flesh" (ἐν ταῖς ἡμέραις τῆς σαρκὸς αὐτοῦ) most likely also assumes the Son's preexistence and incarnation. There was a time before which the Son did not have flesh and so could not suffer. This changed when he became a human being. As mortal human, he was he liable to suffering and even death. For more detailed argumentation for this interpretation of 5:7, see D. M. Moffitt, *Atonement and the Logic of Resurrection in the Epistle to the Hebrews*, NovTSup 141 (Leiden: Brill, 2011), 208–10.

in other words, now seen in Hebrews 2 to be the exalted human being, Jesus (2:9)—the very human being who has suffered, been crowned with glory and honor, and been elevated to God's right hand. Jesus is the Son who has been elevated above and is now worshiped by the angels.[2]

This argument rests on two implicit and initially paradoxical premises. First, the Son must have existed before creation. How else could he be the one who created the ages and the one who sustains all things? Yet, second, this same Son was at some point lower than the angels and only later was exalted above them. What else can the author mean when he says the Son "became" (γενόμενος, 1:4) greater than the angels, inherited a name greater than any of them, and was invited by God to sit where none of them have ever been invited to sit (1:13)? One of the main issues to be solved in the interpretation of Hebrews 1–2 is this: How can both these premises and the author's explicit claims about the Son be true? How can the very Son who created and sustains all things have ever been lower than and then exalted above any created thing? The incarnation provides the most plausible answer and must be among the chief convictions that the author assumes. That is to say, the homilist assumes that the Son who created all things was made lower than the angels by *becoming* a human being. He was then elevated above all the angels precisely because he continues to be a human being.

The point snaps into focus in Hebrews 2 when the homilist describes the position of humanity in creation in terms of Psalm 8. Human beings were made "for a little while lower than the angels" (ἠλάττωσας αὐτὸν βραχύ τι παρ᾽ ἀγγέλους; Ps. 8:6 LXX; Heb. 2:7). The psalm is read in Hebrews not only as saying something about humanity now but also as predicting that one day

---

2. This summary of the main line of the argument of Heb. 1–2 is contested. Many argue that Hebrews describes the Son in terms of his divine ontology or identity (see, e.g., R. Bauckham, "The Divinity of Jesus Christ in the Epistle to the Hebrews," in *The Epistle to the Hebrews and Christian Theology*, ed. R. Bauckham, et. al [Grand Rapids: Eerdmans], 15–36), while others argue the Son is not presented as a divine being but as a human being elevated to the highest place in heaven (see, e.g., G. B. Caird, "Son by Appointment," in *The New Testament Age: Essays in Honor of Bo Reicke*, ed. W. C. Weinrich, 2 vols. [Macon, GA: Mercer, 1984], 1:73–81). Those who read Hebrews primarily in terms of the Son's divine ontology or identity tend not, it seems to me, to be able to offer compelling accounts of how it is that the Son's status relative to the angels can actually be thought to have changed. Those who read the text primarily in terms of the Son's real elevation above the angels as a human being rightly grasp Hebrews' claim that the Son's status relative to the angels actually changed. They struggle, however, to show how the divine aspects (not least vis-à-vis creation) can be explained. For my own detailed arguments in favor of an incarnational understanding of Hebrews' Christology and in support of the interpretation of Heb. 1–2 I have offered, see esp. Moffitt, *Atonement and the Logic of Resurrection*, 43–144. I note as well that several early readers of Hebrews had little trouble seeing the incarnation of the eternal and divine Son and the bodily resurrection and ascension of Jesus as central presuppositions for the homily's argument (see chap. 11 of this volume for more detailed discussion).

humanity's status relative to the angels will change. At some point, humanity will be crowned with glory and honor and exalted above the angels. This is how the creator Son *became* both lower than and then subsequently exalted above the angels: the creator Son *became* a human being and thus was, for a little while, made lower than the angels only later to be exalted above them (Heb. 2:9).

When the Son "shared in" (μετέσχεν, Heb. 2:14) the blood and flesh of the "seed of Abraham" (2:16; specifically, as 7:14 makes clear, as a member of the tribe of Judah), he was, like all humans, made lower than the angels. Psalm 8, which the author interprets as promising that humanity's current subjection to the angels is only "for a little while" (βραχύ τι), imagines that this status will one day be reversed. Thus, by becoming a human being, the eternal Son was made—for a little while, like all human beings—lower than the angels. As such, he suffered and died. He has subsequently, however, been crowned with glory and honor and so, as Psalm 8 predicts, exalted above the angels (Heb. 2:6–9). The eternal Son is the first human being to have received the promise of Psalm 8 and been exalted above the angels. His being crowned with glory and honor as a human being explains the claims made about the Son's exaltation above the angels in Hebrews 1. The interpretation of Psalm 8 in Hebrews 2 explains the claims in Hebrews 1 regarding the Son's being worshiped by the angels and invited to sit at his Father's right hand.

If the preceding points correctly grasp the flow of the argument in Hebrews 1–2, then another important premise for Hebrews' argument is close to hand: the Son's elevation above the angels is a feature of the incarnation. It is precisely as a human being that the Son is exalted above and worshiped by the angels. That is to say, in keeping with the promise of Psalm 8, the Son is crowned with glory and honor, invited to sit at God's right hand, and worshiped by the angels *because* he returned to the heavenly realms not just as the preexistent Son but also as a human being. Hebrews assumes not only the incarnation of the eternal Son but also the death, resurrection, and ascension of the incarnate Son. Hebrews 2 makes the following point clear: the creator Son of Hebrews 1 is the one who was for a little while made lower than the angels and who can now be seen to be crowned with glory and honor and exalted above them—the creator Son is now also *the* exalted human being, Jesus.

Thus, the incarnation is the implicit assumption that brings the argument of Hebrews 1–2 into focus. The incarnation resolves (by way of the author's interpretation of Ps. 8) the tension inherent in the premises identified above: (1) that the preexistent, creator Son was also (2) in a position lower than his angelic creatures such that he could then *become* greater than them. Moreover, this argument must presuppose Jesus's bodily resurrection precisely because the Son must now remain a human being even as he has returned to the realms where the angels worship him. It is, in keeping with Psalm 8, only as a human being that the Son, Jesus, can be elevated above the angels. The incarnation must, in other words, continue beyond Jesus's death and is, in keeping with Psalm 8, the reason for his exaltation above the angels to the seat at God's right hand.

I have taken the time to lay the preceding points out because they are significant for understanding some important features of Jesus's sacrifice in Hebrews. I focus attention in this chapter on some oft-overlooked implications about the nature and timing of Jesus's sacrifice contained within the movement inherent in the incarnation of the divine Son of God. Specifically, I argue that the dynamic of the Son being made for a little while lower than the angels and then returning to his Father's heavenly presence as the resurrected human being, Jesus, correlates conceptually with the directional movement inherent in bringing a sacrificial gift to God. Within the direction of movement in the incarnation, the Son's return to the Father as the human being Jesus—the moment when, as the great high priest, he "passed through the heavens" (Heb. 4:14) and entered the heavenly holy of holies in order to "appear before the face of God" (9:24)—traces the Levitical pattern of a priest bringing a sacrifice into God's presence. The Son's incarnate ascension and return to the Father are, in other words, mapped by the homilist onto the spaces and directionality that blood and flesh traverse at the temple when the priests offer animals on the altar, and even more directly, when the high priest offers blood in the holy of holies on the Day of Atonement (see esp. 9:7; 13:11).

I begin by making three basic points about Jewish sacrifice that are often missed or misunderstood in modern interpretation of Hebrews (to say nothing of modern theological reflection on sacrifice). These points are that (1) sacrifice moves in a particular direction—specifically, sacrifice involves bringing a gift into God's house and so into his presence; (2) the gift moves from the offerer in the mundane realm into God's holy space and presence by going through a series of hierarchically related steps—sacrifice involves a process; and (3) within that process no animals are slaughtered upon any of the Levitical altars, either as these sacrifices are depicted in the Pentateuch's tabernacle texts or in the actual practice of sacrifice in the Second Temple period at the temple in Jerusalem. I do not here offer substantial evidence or argumentation for these claims but only sketch out in a summary fashion the findings of a much more detailed study on sacrifice in the Second Temple period that I have not yet published. After presenting these larger points, I return briefly to explore their significance for reflecting on the return of the incarnate Son to the Father in Hebrews, paying particular attention to the logic and details of central verses in Hebrews 9–10.

The Direction of Sacrifice: Bringing a Gift into God's House

A careful reading of Leviticus and of relevant Second Temple and rabbinic texts indicates that the act of offering a sacrifice at the Jewish temple involved a process in which the items being offered to God moved in a particular direction. One gave a sacrificial gift to God by bringing it to his house. According to the Pentateuch's depictions, Levitical sacrifice involved bringing gifts to the wilderness tabernacle. Later, as Deuteronomy anticipates, sacrifices were brought to the temple in Jerusalem. Upon arriving at God's house, the sacrifice was taken by God's specially selected servants, the priests, to his altars. By bringing the sacrifice to the appropriate altar, the priests conveyed the gift into God's presence. Sacrifices ultimately moved from the offerer *into* God's house and so *into* his presence by way of the priests. Roy Gane puts the former point well, writing,

> In Hebrew, the idea of "sacrifice" in general is conveyed by the noun *qorban*. . . . The meaning of *qorban* is associated with that of the Hiphil verb from the same root *qrb* (lit., "cause to come near"), which can refer not only to preliminary conveyance of offering material to the ritual location (e.g., [Lev.] 1:3), but also to formal ritual presentation to the Lord (e.g., 1:5, 13). This formal presentation *transfers something to the holy God for his utilization*. So a *qorban* (sacrifice, sacrificial offering) *makes* something *holy* by giving it over to the holy domain of God.[3]

Thus, a certain direction of travel, as it were, is involved in the transferal of the item (the sacrifice) to God by bringing it into his presence. This transferal stands at the heart of Levitical sacrifice. This directional movement and the conveyance of a gift into God's presence are, that is, a constitutive part of Jewish sacrifice. Indeed, as Gane's comments indicate, an essential aspect of what makes the gift holy or sacred consists in this movement of the item offered from the mundane world of the offerer into the presence of God. Something becomes a "sacrifice" (the English word derives from the Latin verb *sacer*, "to make holy") by being dedicated to and then moving into God's house and presence as it is given over to him.

In light of these dynamics, it is hardly surprising that this transferal closely correlates with the idea of giving a gift. That this idea is central to the

---

3. R. E. Gane, *Leviticus, Numbers*, NIV Application Commentary (Grand Rapids: Zondervan, 2004), 78. See also C. A. Eberhart, *The Sacrifice of Jesus: Understanding Atonement Biblically*, Facets (Minneapolis: Fortress, 2011), 71; J. Klawans, *Purity, Sacrifice, and the Temple: Symbolism and Supersessionism in the Study of Ancient Judaism* (Oxford: Oxford University Press, 2006), 69.

conception of sacrifice in the Second Temple period is confirmed by the fact that LXX commonly translates the Hebrew term קרבן with the word δῶρον (gift; see esp. Lev. 7:37–38, where all the various sacrifices to be offered by the Israelites as detailed in Lev. 1–6 are called in v. 38 "their gifts" [קרבניהם, MT; τὰ δῶρα αὐτῶν, LXX]). In the movement (1) of offerers going to God's house, (2) of their gifts entering his house, and (3) of the gifts being conveyed into his presence lies a profoundly relational dynamic. The giving of these gifts is associated with motivations and expressions of gratitude and joy (see, for example, Pss. 54 and 66: burnt and peace offerings could be especially suited for celebration, thanksgiving, freewill offerings, and the fulfillment of vows) but also of sorrow, repentance, and confession (e.g., Lev. 16:29–31; 23:27–32: sacrifices on the Day of Atonement were correlated with the people afflicting themselves).

Subsequent biblical and later Second Temple texts simply assume this all-important conceptual point about sacrifices being brought to God by coming into his house and presence. To note only a few examples, the temple is designated in 2 Chronicles 7:12 as God's "house of sacrifice." In Jeremiah 17:26, God promises through the prophet that if his people will keep his sabbaths, Jerusalem will remain inhabited and the sacrifices will be able to be brought "into his house" (εἰς οἶκον κυρίου, LXX). Jubilees stresses that Levi and his descendants were appointed as priests in order to approach God to minister to him and to serve at his table, from which they are also privileged to eat (31:14–16). The table metaphor used to depict the altar being served by priests in God's presence presupposes the idea of sacrifice being brought into God's house—the metaphor participates in the larger concept of the temple as God's house since this is where God's table would be located. Thus, too, 1 Enoch 89:50 envisions the temple as a house built for "the Lord of the sheep" where his sheep constantly spread an abundant table before him. These latter texts highlight another important feature of gift giving in relation to God: only priests can actually enter his house and convey the gifts into his presence or bring them to his table.

The Hierarchical Process of Sacrifice: Transferring a Gift to God

As just noted, sacrifice involves conveying a gift from an offerer to God by way of priests who bring the gift into God's house. This movement does not, however, occur by way of a singular act, such as killing an animal (killing an animal does not make it holy, nor is this act coterminous with bringing the gift into God's presence—not least because, as I discuss below, no animals are killed on the temple's altars). Instead, by way of a series of activities, the offerer gives the gift to the priests and the priests take it to the altar. The fact of the process allows the possibility that the various elements that constitute the process might relate to each other in structured and potentially hierarchical ways.[4] That only the priests can take the gifts to the altars and that this is frequently correlated with a conception of drawing near to God's presence by entering and serving in his house (even at his table) implies that those priestly activities at the altars are the most significant and effectual acts in the entire process; these are the primary people by whom and the primary places and ways whereby the gift is transferred into God's presence.

That these are the most effectual aspects of the process is particularly clear in those cases where the process achieves the benefits of purification or creates the conditions for forgiveness (i.e., sacrificial atonement). In several cases where atoning sacrifices are described in Jewish Scripture, these benefits are most closely associated with the completion of the priestly activities at the outer altar (see, e.g., Lev. 4:20, 25–26, 30–31, 34–35). The application of blood to the outer and sometimes inner altar (depending on the sacrifice and on who must give it) and the burning of the choice parts on the outer altar are the weightiest and most effective aspects of the process.[5] Moreover, Deuteronomy 12:27 explicitly singles out "blood and flesh" as the elements *offered upon the altar* as the sacrifice. Blood and flesh constitute the gift (at least in the case of animal sacrifices), and the altar is the place where these elements are conveyed to God.

The preceding points further imply that a gift is fully transferred to the Lord when a priest takes various elements of the gift to an altar. By manipulating the blood (in the case of animal offerings) and by burning part (in the case of burnt offerings, nearly all) of the offering, the priest conveys the gift into God's presence, not least by way of the smoke and pleasing aroma ascending to him. The goals of the sacrificial process, both in terms of giving the gift

---

4. R. E. Gane clearly and helpfully describes this feature of sacrifice in his book *Cult and Character: Purification Offerings, Day of Atonement, and Theodicy* (Winona Lake, IN: Eisenbrauns, 2005), esp. 1–24.

5. Leviticus 17:11, especially as it is interpreted in the Second Temple period, singles out the application of blood to the altars as the most effective element within the process of offering atoning sacrifices. The act of burning upon the altar is still, however, significant, not least because this is an element in the process shared by sacrifices of grain, of incense, and of animals. For a detailed defense of the importance of burning, see esp. C. A. Eberhart, *Studien zur Bedeutung der Opfer im Alten Testament: Die Signifikanz von Blut- und Verbrennungsriten im kultischen Rahmen*, WMANT 94 (Neukirchen-Vluyn: Neukirchener Verlag, 2002). He offers a helpful summary of some of the chief points of his argument in "Sacrifice? Holy Smokes! Reflections on Cult Terminology for Understanding the Hebrew Bible," in *Ritual and Metaphor: Sacrifice in the Bible*, ed. C. A. Eberhart, SBLRBS 68 (Leiden: Brill, 2011), 17–32.

and in terms of any benefit that the act of giving confers on the worshipers, are attained if God condescends to accept the gift. The priests, by performing the ritual appropriately, appear to have been given authority to judge that the goals (e.g., sacrificial atonement) have been attained.

Because sacrifice entails multiple acts, some of which are more effectual and central with respect to the goals of the sacrifice than others, it follows that isolating one act from the others or performing only one act from the series in abstraction from the others neither constitutes a sacrifice nor attains the benefits one anticipates from offering the gift. Thus, for example, if one simply killed an animal, even if this happened at the temple, but did not subsequently take any of its parts or its blood to the appropriate altar, no sacrifice would occur and no benefits would accrue to the offerer. This is so because the gift would not have been conveyed into God's presence. Slaughtering an animal does not make a sacrifice. Slaughtering an animal does not convey its body and blood into God's presence. This conveyance happens *after* the slaughter when a priest brings the appropriate elements to the appropriate altar.

By the same token, the gift is given wholly over to God, even when only parts of the gift are actually burned on or used by a priest at an altar. When one sacrifices an animal to God, one cannot simply give some of the animal's blood to God or cut off and burn only some part of the animal—say, its fatty tail—returning the rest of it to the offerer or to the priest to continue to own and use. Giving the gift is costly for the offerer not least because the entire animal, and especially *all* of its blood, belongs entirely to God. The blood of the animal is the element of the sacrifice identified with its life (see esp. Lev. 17:11).[6] The blood must be entirely drained from the flesh and then entirely used at the altar(s) in specific ways. Thus, none of the blood can be given to anyone other than God. In this way all the life of any animal sacrifice is always entirely given to God even in those cases where some of the animal may be eaten by the priests or, in the cases of peace offerings and the Passover sacrifices alone, by the lay offerers.

Thus, when sacrifice involves an animal, slaughtering the animal and draining all its blood (so that all the blood itself and all the appropriate parts of the gift can be given to God, especially at the outer altar) are necessary for the

6. Blood does not represent the animal, nor does manipulating blood on the altar symbolize the giving of life to God. Blood and the manipulation of blood are not symbols or metaphors in the context of biblical sacrifice (see W. K. Gilders, *Blood Ritual in the Hebrew Bible: Meaning and Power* [Baltimore: Johns Hopkins University Press, 2004], esp. 186). Blood is, rather, identified with life (נפש, MT; ψυχή, LXX), which most likely means something like "life force" or "animating principle." To offer blood is not to offer a representation of the animal or a symbol of its life but to give the life itself.

process of sacrifice. Bringing the blood and parts of the animal being given to God to the altar stands at the center of sacrifice. Apart from these elements of the larger process, especially those aspects that involve the appropriate altar, the gift has not been given to God and no sacrifice has occurred. In the cases of sacrifices given to achieve sacrificial atonement, the offering of blood upon the altar is paramount, not least because Leviticus 17:11 states that God has allowed blood/life applied to the altar to effect atonement.

Slaughter and the Levitical Altars

The significance of applying blood to the altars within the hierarchy of activities involved in giving certain gifts to God requires a bit more clarification in light of some modern misconceptions about animal sacrifice and the altars at the temple. A careful reading of Leviticus makes the following point clear: no animals were slaughtered on any of the tabernacle's (and, *mutatis mutandis*, the temple's) altars. Yet many scholars mistakenly assume that the outer altar, sometimes referred to as the altar of sacrifice, was the place where the animal was sacrificed (often assumed to mean "slaughtered")—that is, the place where its blood was shed (i.e., where it was killed).

Consider a handful of examples of how this assumption affects the interpretation of Jesus's death in the Epistle to the Hebrews. Marie Isaacs argues that the altar mentioned in Hebrews 13:10 must refer to the crucifixion of Jesus.[7] The Levitical altar of sacrifice, she rightly notes, was outside the tabernacle sancta in the courtyard. The author of Hebrews metaphorically describes Jesus's current location in heaven in terms of the high priest within the tabernacle's holy of holies. The metaphor likens the earth to the tabernacle's courtyard and the tabernacle itself to heaven. Therefore the altar of 13:10 must be a reference to Jesus's earthly death outside the tabernacle because, in keeping with the metaphor, this is where "the altar of sacrifice" was located.[8] Thus she states, "'Altar' in 13:10 is a metonym for the sacrificial death of Jesus. It is therefore located neither in heaven, nor on earth at the eucharist, but represents the death of Jesus understood in terms of ancient Israel's sacrificial cult."[9] Isaacs here assumes that altar of sacrifice was the place in the courtyard where the animal was slaughtered. Since this altar stood outside the tabernacle sancta, it makes sense to identify the altar in 13:10 with the place where Jesus was killed (i.e.,

---

7. M. E. Isaacs, "Hebrews 13.9–16 Revisited," *NTS* 43 (1997): 268–84.
8. Isaacs, "Hebrews 13.9–16," 275.
9. Isaacs, "Hebrews 13.9–16," 280.

on earth outside of Jerusalem). After Jesus died on the altar of the cross, like animals were sacrificed on the outer altar, he entered the sancta like the priests.

Isaacs is far from alone in this assumption. Norman Young also writes of Hebrews 13:10, "The altar which 'we [Christians] have' is clearly Calvary, for an altar is a place of sacrifice, and that for the writer is outside the gate/ camp, where Jesus suffered in order to sanctify the people by means of his own blood."[10] As with Isaacs, the language of "sacrifice" is here assumed to be equivalent to that act of slaughtering the victim. Thus the outer altar, the place of sacrifice, can be easily correlated with the cross, suggesting that the altar of 13:10 is a way of speaking about Jesus's crucifixion on earth.

Gareth Cockerill similarly states, "The shed blood of 'goats and calves' represented the lives of those who offered them poured out in death. Thus, when [Hebrews] would explain Christ's death by analogy with the sacrifices of the Old Covenant, he describes it as Christ's 'own blood.' His shed 'blood' is his willing offering of his life through death on the cross."[11] Concerning the procedures followed by the Levitical high priests Cockerill elaborates, "After shedding the blood on the altar, those high priests carried it into the Most Holy Place, where they stood sprinkling it on the Mercy Seat above the Ark."[12] Here, then, is the analogy with Jesus's death: just as first the Levitical high priests "shed the blood" of the animals upon the outer altar and then entered the holy of holies, so also Christ's "sacrifice was accomplished on the cross and was the means of his entrance into heaven as High Priest."[13] Cockerill plainly understands "shedding blood" in terms of slaughtering the animal. Thus, as the animal was first slaughtered on the outer altar and then the blood was taken into the tabernacle, so too Christ's blood was first shed when he was sacrificed on the altar of the cross and then he entered heaven.

One last example will suffice. In a lengthy article William Loader has responded to some recent discussion on the topic of Jesus's high priesthood

10. N. H. Young, "'Bearing His Reproach' (Heb. 13.9–14)," NTS 48 (2002): 243–61, here 248.
11. G. L. Cockerill, The Epistle to the Hebrews, NICNT (Grand Rapids: Eerdmans, 2012), 393–94.
12. Cockerill, Hebrews, 394.
13. Cockerill, Hebrews, 394. The conclusion that Cockerill here uses "shedding blood" as synonymous with slaughter is confirmed by the fact that while the slaughter and collection of the blood naturally occurred before the high priest went into the sancta, the act of "pouring out" blood (language that could be rendered "shedding" blood) only occurred at the base of the outer altar after he came out from the sancta and disposed of any blood that remained in the bowl he had carried into the holy of holies. While this latter act is not explicitly mentioned in Lev. 16, the pattern is clearly identified in, e.g., 4:7. Thus by "shedding blood" Cockerill must mean to refer to the prior act of killing the animal, just as by "the shedding of Jesus' blood" he means to refer to the crucifixion.

in Hebrews.[14] It is clear throughout that Loader associates Jesus's death with his sacrifice. In the article, Loader takes issue with those who, on the basis of language in Hebrews associating Jesus's high priesthood with his entering the heavenly realm to intercede there for his people, try to separate Jesus's death from his high-priestly offering. Those who hold this latter view must, Loader says, "explain away" Hebrews' use of the high priesthood motif with respect to the event of Jesus's death. He suggests that this is a problem because the motif of Jesus's death includes a correspondence between that salvific event and "the high priest's sacrifice of the animal on the altar before the Holy Place and the Holiest of Holies."[15] Much better, Loader argues, is a both/and conclusion: "Jesus was high priest on earth offering himself as a sacrifice and he was appointed high priest to the continuing role of intercessor as in the author's received tradition to exercise the ministry of intercession on behalf of his own."[16] As with the other examples noted above, Loader here assumes that just as the animals were sacrificed on the altar in the courtyard in front of the holy place and the holy of holies and before the high priest took the blood into the sancta, so, too, Jesus was sacrificed on earth before he subsequently entered the heavenly tabernacle to intercede there for his siblings.

Whatever one thinks about the larger claims about Jesus's death in Hebrews in the preceding comments, each of these examples works with a patently mistaken assumption—that the outer altar of sacrifice was the place where animals were slaughtered. This assumption allows for what looks like a relatively straightforward, almost self-evident, comparison in Hebrews between Jewish sacrifice on the altar and the subsequent priestly entrance into the sancta, on the one hand, and Jesus's death and subsequent exaltation to heavenly ministry, on the other. Just as at the temple the animal's blood was first shed on the altar—that is, the animal was sacrificed on the outer altar and then the high priest went into the tabernacle/temple to minister on behalf of the people, so also Jesus's blood was first shed on the cross on earth and then as the great high priest he entered the heavenly tabernacle to minister there on behalf of his people.

The problem with these examples, however, is that *no* animals were *ever* slaughtered on the outer altar. The altar of sacrifice was not the place of slaughter. Animals were slaughtered either in the courtyard before the outer altar and sancta or in a special place to the north of the outer altar, depending on the sacrifice (see, e.g., Lev. 1:11; 3:2). It is therefore a mistake to assume

---

14. W. Loader, "Revisiting High Priesthood Christology in Hebrews," *ZNW* 109 (2018): 235–83.

15. Loader, "Revisiting High Priesthood Christology," 266.

16. Loader, "Revisiting High Priesthood Christology," 266.

that the language of sacrificing, immolating, offering, or shedding the blood of an animal *on* the Levitical altars refers to the act of slaughtering/killing the victim. This kind of language does not refer to the slaughter; rather, it must be understood to relate instead to the conveyance of the gift into God's presence by doing things with blood and flesh on the altar. Doing things at the altars with the blood and flesh of the animal was how that gift was ultimately transferred or offered to God (and similarly how grain, incense, etc. were given). *To sacrifice* on the outer altar means to offer the blood and flesh of the animal to God, not to slaughter the animal there.

This fact, in keeping with my preceding observations, already suggests that the act of killing the sacrifice was lower down in the hierarchy of the process discussed above. With respect to Jewish sacrifice, the act of slaughter was not the focal point or center of the sacrifice. Rather, it was among the preparatory and less important elements.[17] This conclusion follows from the fact that the slaughter was not an act that occurred upon any of the altars. While the slaughter stands among the necessary and essential elements of the process of sacrifice when the process involved an animal (i.e., slaughter stands among other elements such as selecting the right item, preparing the item, butchering the animal), the act of killing the animal is less weighty or significant *with respect to achieving the goals* of the process than are those aspects of the process that actually did occur at and upon the altars. The slaughter of the animal had less significance in the process of sacrifice than the priestly acts of manipulating blood and burning flesh upon the altar.

Biblical evidence indicates that the act of slaughter was less important for sacrifice than the acts of offering the elements of the gift on the altar. Ezekiel 44:10–16 draws a distinction between the service of the Levites in general and that of the Zadokite priests in particular. The text details a telling judgment against the Levites, who were unfaithful to God. Because they served idols and led Israel astray, God declares that their ministry in the temple will be significantly curtailed. God will graciously allow them to continue to serve at the temple in certain ways, but their punishment is to be excluded by God from approaching his presence. That is to say, *they are not allowed to serve at the altars* (44:13). Their service is limited to less significant acts that can be performed *without* drawing near to God and *without* entering his presence— that is, *without* approaching the altar. Explicitly noted among these lesser acts that they are permitted to perform is slaughtering some of the sacrificial victims (44:11). The Levites may slaughter these victims and undertake many

---

17. So, e.g., Eberhart, *Studien zur Bedeutung der Opfer*, 399; Gilders, *Blood Ritual in the Hebrew Bible*, 122–23, 184–45, and many others.

of the other necessary tasks of sacrifice. Only the priests, the sons of Zadok, however, will be allowed by God to offer the fatty parts and to manipulate the blood of the sacrifices at his altars. Only the Zadokite priests will be able to draw near to God and enter his presence. The honor of serving at God's table and entering his sanctuary (44:15–16) belongs only to the priests, not to the Levites in general.

The logic of God's judgment on the Levites assumes the very kind of hierarchy among the elements that constitutes the process of sacrifice explored above. This is clear from the Levites' punishment. Their punishment consists in the fact that they are relegated to those roles of temple service that, while necessary, are not as significant for sacrifice as those acts that involve entering God's presence in order to serve at his table and minister before him. It is therefore noteworthy that Ezekiel states explicitly that the Levites *are allowed to slaughter* some of the animals being given as sacrifices, but, as part of their punishment, they *are not allowed to draw near to God to offer the sacrifices to him.* The Levites can slaughter the gifts, but they cannot approach God's presence and serve him at the altars. Ezekiel is hardly the only evidence for this idea.[18] Ezekiel does, however, present clear biblical evidence of an important conceptual distinction among the elements of the process of sacrifice. The Levites' punishment, which relegates them to slaughtering animals while forbidding them from drawing near to God by approaching and serving at the altars, well illustrates the larger point.

One final observation about the location and significance of the slaughter of the gifts in relation to the altar must also be noted in light of the persistent idea in many modern imaginations that animals were actually killed on the temple's altar.

The fire on the outer altar would have made it unsuited for the slaughter of animals. This fire is always to be kept burning. It is a perpetual fire (Lev. 6:12–13). Yet the presence of perpetual fire on the altar makes the act of slaughter there, at least in anything like a decorous and orderly fashion, impossible.

---

18. See also 2 Chron. 30:16–17, where the distinction is evident, though not in terms of punishment. 11QT^a 22.4–5 also distinguishes between the Levites who perform the slaughtering of certain sacrifices and the priests who manipulate the blood at the altar. Later rabbinic texts also imply that the slaughter is less important than blood manipulation. M. Zebaḥ. 3.1 states that even if someone who is technically ineligible to slaughter a sacrifice does the slaughter, this does not invalidate the sacrifice. The reason given for this judgment is the fact that the act of slaughter is *not* one of the sacrificial acts restricted only to the priests (as is the case with acts of blood manipulation at the altar). In other words, a sacrifice is not necessarily invalidated if an ineligible person performs the slaughter, because this act is less significant for the process of offering the sacrifice than are those acts that can only be performed by the priests. But if someone other than a priest receives the blood, an act that is a priestly prerogative, the sacrifice is deemed not to be valid (see m. Zebaḥ. 2.1).

One needs only a little imagination to see this. How would a live animal placed on the fire then be slaughtered? How would its blood be collected from the midst of the conflagration so that it could then be manipulated at the altar? What would it mean to have to collect the blood from the animal killed upon the altar, in the midst of the flames, in a bowl to then throw around the sides or apply to the altar's horns? The indecorous image of trying to kill a living animal after placing it in the fire on the altar shows how nonsensical it is to assume that the temple's outer altar was the place of slaughter for Jewish sacrifices.

Sacrifice entailed bringing a gift to God's house so that it could be given to him. This consisted of a process in which the gift was transferred to God by priests, who were the only individuals allowed to bring the blood and flesh of the gift to the altars in God's house. The sacrificial process included, in the case of animals, the act of slaughter—but the activities at the altars and the entrance into God's house were the most significant elements of the process. One additional point should also be noted: the effective center of sacrifice depended on God's choice to accept or reject the gift being offered to him. No amount of sacrifice or proper procedure could induce God to accept the gifts, a point that the prophets make abundantly clear. Sacrifice was not, in other words, some sort of magical set of rituals that somehow bound or obligated God to act in particular ways.[19]

The preceding points call into question what many take to be a natural progression with respect to Jesus's death in Hebrews. Many assume that just as animals were slaughtered on the altar of sacrifice in the courtyard in front of the tabernacle/temple sancta, and then the priests (and on the Day of Atonement, the high priest) took the blood into the sancta, so too Jesus was sacrificed on the altar of the cross on earth and subsequently entered the heavenly tabernacle to minister there as high priest in the heavenly holy of holies. If in fact animals were not slaughtered on the altar of sacrifice but were instead offered by having priests bring blood and flesh to the altar (and on the Day of Atonement, having the high priest bring blood into the holy of holies to offer to God, as Heb. 9:7 actually states), then the apparently natural association of Jesus's death with the sacrifice of animals upon the outer altar becomes incoherent. There would seem to be three options to explain this oddity. Either (1) the author of Hebrews has no idea how actual sacrifice at the temple worked, or (2) the author has radically redefined sacrifice in a way that contradicts the biblical evidence (perhaps because he means only to develop

---

19. R. E. Gane, speaking about the fact that applying blood to the altars makes purification and allows for the possibility of forgiveness (see Lev. 17:11), rightly observes, "Purification offerings are not magic" (*Cult and Character*, 195).

metaphors that explain the salvific effects of Jesus's death, not to draw more careful analogies between sacrifice and Jesus), or (3) the real problem is one of contemporary misunderstanding about how Jewish sacrifice was actually performed. If the last option is correct, it may be important to reevaluate certain elements of Hebrews' claims about where, when, and how Jesus offered himself to the Father as a sacrifice. Here some more careful reflection on the incarnation of the Son as discussed earlier proves illuminating.

The Incarnation and Jesus's Sacrifice in Hebrews 9–10

The directional movement of a gift into God's house and presence (which is at the heart of the Jewish sacrificial process) and the distinction between the slaughter of an animal and the offering of its blood and flesh by a priest upon an altar have potential import and implications with respect to early Christian claims about Jesus's sacrifice. In modern theological reflection, these implications have tended to go unnoticed at least in part because the crucifixion is often simply assumed to be the sum total of Jesus's sacrifice. His sacrifice is also typically assumed to correlate with the act of slaughtering animals upon the outer altar.

However, certain facts significantly complicate these assumptions—namely, the facts that sacrifice involved an entire process whereby the gift is conveyed into God's presence, and that within the process the presentation of blood and flesh upon an altar were weightier activities than were those activities, such as slaughtering the animal, not done upon the altar. If early Christians, especially those of Jesus's earliest Jewish followers who had participated in temple worship, understood these aspects of sacrifice, then the possibility emerges that their own categories for understanding Jesus in relationship to temple sacrifices might have been far broader in scope than modern assumptions about the crucifixion tend to allow.

The preceding points particularly suggest the possible significance of Jesus's ascension for early Christian reflection on his sacrifice. If early Christians understood sacrifice in terms of conveying a gift into God's house and presence, it seems prima facie plausible that they could have aligned the tradition of Jesus's ascension into God's house and presence with his act of offering himself to God as a sacrifice. By moving into God's heavenly presence, Jesus would be moving in the same direction that priests and sacrifices moved when they offered the gifts to God—into his house.

Could the author of Hebrews, especially given his incarnational assumptions, be thinking in this way? Key pieces of evidence, especially in Hebrews

9–10, suggest that this is precisely how the homilist is thinking about Jesus's offering of himself to the Father as a sacrifice.

First, Hebrews envisions Jesus's ascension (his "passing through the heavens," 4:14) in terms of his entering into the heavenly tabernacle (see esp. 8:1–2; 9:24) and into the heavenly holy of holies in particular. The author not only speaks of Jesus passing through "the veil" or "curtain" (6:19–20; see also 10:20), a reference to the curtain that divided the holy place from the holy of holies in the tabernacle (e.g., Exod. 26:31–35; Lev. 16:15), but also, as I argued in chapter 8, conceives of the heavenly tabernacle—the reality Moses saw when he ascended Mount Sinai (Heb. 8:5–6)—as the true, preexistent analogue for the wilderness tabernacle.

Second, it hardly needs to be said that Hebrews' identification of Jesus as a high priest stands as its most distinctive christological claim within the New Testament. No other text in the New Testament explicitly identifies Jesus as a high priest. Thus, when Hebrews draws parallels between the earthly high priest's entrance into the holy of holies to offer blood (9:7; 13:11) and Jesus's entrance into the heavenly tabernacle to appear before God and minister there as the great high priest (4:14–16; 6:19–20; 9:24–26; 10:19–22), the analogy is clear: Jesus has entered the heavenly holy of holies to offer his own sacrifice before God.[20]

Third, the preceding points all indicate that, at his ascension, Jesus travels in the same direction relative to God's presence as do the gifts given to God as sacrifices at the temple. Jesus is able to enter God's house because, as the argument of Hebrews 7 demonstrates, he is the great high priest of the order of Melchizedek. The direction that sacrifices move (into God's house and presence) and the individuals who can bring them (priests and, on the Day of Atonement, the high priest) correspond to the direction of travel and

20. The directional component of the high priest's annual ministry on the Day of Atonement is commonly recognized in the commentary literature as a feature emphasized in Hebrews. There is, however, a tendency not to follow the analogy Hebrews sets up with respect to this high-priestly offering of blood and Jesus's offering of himself as a sacrifice. Often categories such as "metaphor" or "fulfillment" are invoked to explain how, in effect, Hebrews draws on biblical language (such as the high priest offering blood in the holy of holies to sanctify the people) while filling this language with a new logic and new content—the crucifixion of Jesus (for an especially clear and consistent assertion of this view see Young, "'Bearing His Reproach'"). If, however, Hebrews thinks in terms of the ascension of the incarnate Son of God by way of analogy to the entrance of the high priest into the holy of holies in order to offer sacrifice there, plenty of new content can still be identified. For example, Jesus is both the eternal Son of God and a high priest from the tribe of Judah, elements of Hebrews' Christology unparalleled in the Mosaic law and that the author feels the need to defend and explain in Heb. 4:14–8:6. But the basic logic of the analogy aligns with central aspects of sacrifice—especially in terms of the direction the sacrifice travels—in the way that the process is described in Jewish Scripture. Priests offer animal sacrifices to God by taking the blood and flesh to altars and thus into his house and presence.

identity of Jesus that we find described in Hebrews. The author knows, in other words, that this is how Jewish sacrifice, especially on the Day of Atonement, is performed. As noted above, he says this in 9:7 when he emphasizes that the high priest goes through the veil into the holy of holies once a year in order to offer blood (see also 13:11). The high priest moves in a particular direction, into God's presence, in order to offer blood in the holy of holies.

While it may not be self-evident to modern interpreters that this offering of blood *is* sacrifice, the use of προσφέρω with blood in Hebrews 9:7 denotes the act of offering blood to God. As noted above, modern notions that conflate the terms "sacrifice," "slaughter," and "shedding of blood" are simply mistaken with respect to Levitical offerings. Thus, Jesus traverses a path (into the heavenly tabernacle, through the veil, and into God's presence in the heavenly holy of holies) similar to the one followed by the earthly high priest when he offers blood on the Day of Atonement (into the temple, through the veil, and into God's presence in the earthly holy of holies). The direction the earthly high priest moves relative to God's presence in the process of offering atoning sacrifice on this day is the direction that Hebrews 6:19–20, 9:24–26, and 10:19–20 all presuppose Jesus is moving relative to God's heavenly presence.

If Hebrews assumes the incarnation and the bodily resurrection of Jesus, and if the author knows that sacrifice moves in a particular direction when a priest, and especially the high priest on the Day of Atonement, takes sacrifices into God's house and into his presence (as the homily affirms is the direction of travel for the atoning blood on Yom Kippur), then the conclusion that naturally follows is that Jesus presented himself as an atoning sacrifice when he ascended into God's heavenly presence. Moreover, if the preacher thinks of Jesus "passing through the heavens" in terms of his entrance into the heavenly tabernacle to minister there for his people as their great high priest, then when the homilist says in 9:24 that Jesus entered heaven itself "now to appear before the face of God for us" (νῦν ἐμφανισθῆναι τῷ προσώπῳ τοῦ θεοῦ ὑπὲρ ἡμῶν), he is working with an analogy that compares Jesus's goals and direction of travel with the goals and direction of travel of the earthly high priest on the Day of Atonement. Just as the earthly high priest went into the earthly holy of holies in order to sanctify the people by offering blood (9:7; 13:11), so also the risen Jesus ascended into the heavenly holy of holies in order to offer himself to God as a better sacrifice that provides better sanctification.[21]

21. One might object that Heb. 13:11–12 compares the earthly high priest's act of carrying blood into the holy of holies with Jesus's death outside the gate. But the homilist does not directly compare taking blood into the holy of holies with Jesus's death outside Jerusalem. Rather, he compares what happens to the bodies of the animals whose blood is taken into the holy of holies—they are taken outside the camp and burned—with Jesus's crucifixion. He

When the homilist says in 9:26 that Jesus has "now appeared once-for-all-time at the consummation of the ages to remove sin by his sacrifice" (νυνὶ δὲ ἅπαξ ἐπὶ συντελείᾳ τῶν αἰώνων εἰς ἀθέτησιν ἁμαρτίας διὰ τῆς θυσίας αὐτοῦ πεφανέρωται), he most plausibly means that the sacrifice Jesus offers (ἡ θυσία αὐτοῦ) to the Father consists of his incarnate self—*he*, the risen and ascended Son, *is* the sacrifice that he offers to the Father.[22] This offering deals with sins better than (but still like) the way the act of taking the blood into the holy of holies sanctified the people under the Mosaic covenant. Similarly, at 10:10, when Hebrews speaks of God's people being sanctified by the once-for-all offering of Jesus's body, the most likely referent for this language is not the cross or Jesus's death but his ascension—his entering into God's house and presence as high priest to present himself, his blood and his flesh, before God as the ultimate sacrifice. This is how and when he offers his body to the Father.

This same direction of travel is assumed in Hebrews 10:19–22, where Jesus's siblings are called to trace the path he has already taken into the heavenly holy of holies. The structural elements shared between 10:19–23 and 4:14–16, which are indicative of an inclusio, strongly imply that Jesus's act of "passing through the heavens" as the great high priest in 4:14 is the way in which he passes through the veil and enters the heavenly holy of holies in order to come into God's presence in 10:19–23. That the author imagines this act of Jesus's heavenly self-offering to correlate with drawing near to an altar is implied in 13:10. Here the author says that the congregation has an altar from which those who serve in the tent have no right to eat. This altar, the place where Jesus offers himself, would, in keeping with the direction that Jesus travels and the notion of a tabernacle in the heavens assumed by Hebrews, be the heavenly one. This is the altar where Jesus has gone to serve as high priest and to offer himself to the Father as a sacrifice. The return of the eternal, divine Son to the Father—now as the incarnate Jesus, the human being elevated above the angels and invited to sit at God's right hand—is when and where the Son offers himself to the Father as the ultimate and once-for-all atoning sacrifice.[23]

---

links the crucifixion here with part of the Yom Kippur ritual. He does not directly identify the cross with the act that sanctifies the people. It makes more sense to understand the author in 13:12 connecting Jesus's death with an aspect of the Day of Atonement (an act that occurred away from the temple), while still affirming the principle that taking blood into God's presence sanctifies the people. The offering of Jesus's sacrifice in the heavenly holy of holies corresponds to the high-priestly act that makes atonement (as 13:11 has just reaffirmed). His death corresponds to the burning of the bodies of the animals whose blood went into God's presence and made atonement.

22. One might even imagine him speaking the words of Isa. 8:18 LXX: "Behold, I and the children God has given me" (Heb. 2:13).

23. The Son's royal position as the Messiah on the heavenly throne at the right hand of the Father, which is probably also the "throne of grace" the congregation is exhorted to approach

There is yet one more point to be made in light of the incarnational dynamics explored earlier in this chapter. If the divine, preexistent Son is thought in some sense to be away from the Father's presence when he is on earth—if the directionality inherent in the incarnation involves the Son in some way being sent from the Father, being made lower than the angels, and then subsequently returning to the Father's heavenly presence by passing through the heavens (a journey and destination explicitly depicted in terms of the great high priest entering the heavenly tabernacle)—then the idea that he offers his sacrifice to the Father as he dies on the cross (that is, *prior* to his passing through the heavens in order to enter the heavenly tabernacle and appear before his Father) borders on incoherent.

This is true not only from the perspective of Levitical sacrifice as described in the Old Testament, where the offering of animals is not synonymous with their slaughter, an act that occurred away from the altar. It is also true from the perspective of the subsequent ascension of the Son into the Father's presence. The sacrifices are first slaughtered and subsequently brought by priests to the altar and into God's presence. It would be exceedingly odd for the Son to be thought to return to the Father's presence *after* he offered his sacrifice to the Father. That is to say, if commonplace modern readings of Hebrews are correct and Jesus is thought to offer himself as a sacrifice on the altar of the cross (as noted in the examples given on pp. 167–69), it is exceedingly strange that Hebrews imagines the incarnate Son offering himself as a sacrifice to God at a time when he is away from God's heavenly presence only then to return to God's presence when he passes through the heavens after having made his offering on earth/outside the heavenly tabernacle.

Appeals to concepts like metaphor or poetic language can hardly resolve these fundamental issues with respect to the Son's movement in relation to God if in fact the author of Hebrews imagines the incarnation to continue beyond the crucifixion. The use of high-priestly and sacrificial language with respect to Jesus makes good sense, however, if Hebrews thinks of Jesus's ascension in terms of the incarnate Son passing through the heavens to appear before the Father. If, per Psalm 8, this is also how the creator Son is elevated above the angels, the royal and high-priestly claims about Jesus made throughout Hebrews not only sit well together; they are inherently connected. The Son of God is both the reigning Messiah and the high priest as he enters the heavenly holy of holies to take his seat on the heavenly throne.

---

boldly (4:16), draws upon the association of the ark of the covenant as God's throne in the inner room of his temple—the holy of holies. For passages that describe the cherubim over the lid of the ark as the place where God is enthroned see, e.g., 1 Sam. 4:4; 2 Sam. 6:2; 1 Chron. 13:6.

This is a more coherent interpretation of Hebrews than those that imagine the author explaining the event of Jesus's death metaphorically *as if it were* an act in which the Son can be thought to be a high priest offering himself (even "shedding his blood") as a sacrifice to God when he died on the cross. If Jesus's death is his high-priestly sacrifice, the metaphor in play stretches the conceptual realm of biblical sacrifices beyond recognition, both in terms of where Jesus is sacrificed and in terms of the directions in which the Son travels in the incarnation. If the Son offers himself to the Father on the altar of the cross, he offers himself away from the Father's presence. In incarnational terms, he first moves away from God's heavenly house and presence to offer himself as a sacrifice on earth—outside the heavenly tabernacle. He subsequently moves back into the Father's presence when he enters the heavenly tabernacle as the great high priest *after* having offered his sacrifice on earth. If this is the direction of the incarnate Son's self-offering in Hebrews, it is difficult to understand what the terms "sacrifice," "high priest," "ministry," and "altar" actually mean in the homily. This language seems to have little to do either with the Old Testament or with actual sacrificial practice in Jerusalem, if the homilist thinks Jesus's death is the totality of his sacrifice.

Conclusion

The points made above about the incarnation and the Son's directions of travel in Hebrews—his being made lower than the angels as a human being and then his movement into the heavenly tabernacle to appear before the Father, minister as high priest, and be exalted to God's right hand above all the angels—are not unique to my interpretation of Hebrews. Many interpreters recognize these dynamics in one way or another. Hebrews plainly speaks of the Son passing through the heavens, entering the heavenly tabernacle, and being invited by God to sit on the heavenly throne.

The preceding arguments diverge from much modern commentary on Hebrews by correlating the movement inherent in this sequence, especially with respect to the risen Jesus, with the movement inherent in Jewish sacrifice as described in biblical and Second Temple texts. Commonplace modern assumptions about sacrifice being centered on the act of slaughter/death, which many simply assume happened on the outer altar in the courtyard of the temple, have obscured this correlation. The assumption that the cross is the altar of Jesus's sacrifice because the outer altar was where animals were slaughtered at the temple contradicts the biblical and Second Temple evidence. "Slaughter" and "sacrifice" are, moreover, not synonymous terms with respect to Jewish sacrificial practice. Rather, the former is part of the process that constitutes the latter. Slaughter precedes the offering of the sacrifice on the altar. Only after the slaughter of the victim does a priest take the elements of the gift to the appropriate altar and convey them into God's house and presence. This reevaluation of the evidence of the Old Testament and of the travel of the incarnate Son in Hebrews allows two theologically and historically significant problems regarding common understandings of Jesus's sacrifice to be clearly identified and one constructive counterpoint to be advanced.

First, the fact that the temple's outer altar was not the place where sacrifices were slaughtered complicates the seemingly self-evident identification of the cross and the temple's outer altar. Interpretations of Jesus's death in Hebrews that take the crucifixion to be the sum total of his sacrifice often rely on this mistaken notion about the outer altar. The preceding arguments imply that more careful assessment and description of Jesus's sacrifice are needed.

Second, if Hebrews does identify the cross as the place and time of Jesus's sacrifice, then in incarnational terms, the author does something strange: he depicts the Son moving *in precisely the wrong direction* relative to God's presence in order to offer himself to his Father as a sacrifice. This is a curious fact that often goes unnoticed in modern theological reflection on Jesus's sacrifice. Rather than imagining the Son of God as the great high priest who brings his sacrifice into God's house and presence, these interpretations must imagine the Son of God offering his sacrifice to God *outside of* God's house, at a point when he is away from his Father's heavenly presence. Such an account is historically suspect to the extent that it contravenes the logic, location, and direction of sacrifice as actually practiced at the temple. It is odd that early followers of Jesus would describe his sacrifice in these terms when trying to show how it aligned with biblical depictions and temple practice. This view of Jesus's sacrifice is theologically problematic to the extent that it assumes an account of sacrifice that strips the biblical texts of the sacrificial logic, location, and direction they consistently attest.

Third, and by way of contrast, if Hebrews envisions the incarnate Son's return to the Father as the time and place of his offering, then a natural set of correspondences between Jewish sacrificial practice and Jesus's death, resurrection, ascension, and ongoing intercession falls into place. The incarnate Son first dies outside of God's house. He then rises and ascends back into God's house and presence there to offer himself to God as a sacrifice and to serve as his siblings' great high priest. This sequence maps remarkably well onto the direction that the Old Testament depicts the priests and sacrifices traveling relative to God's house and presence. Hebrews does not imagine Jesus's sacrifice in terms that set it at odds with those of the old covenant. Rather, the homily works with broadly coherent analogies that are informed by, even depend upon, significant aspects of the logic and direction of Jewish sacrificial practice. In Hebrews we see the divine Son, who was for a little while made lower than the angels, now exalted above them, Jesus—the great high priest who, like the Old Testament's depictions of the Levitical priests and sacrifices, enters God's house and presence there to offer himself to his Father as the atoning sacrifice and to minister on behalf of his people.

11

Jesus's Heavenly Sacrifice in Early Christian Reception of Hebrews

A Survey

When one's reading of an ancient text challenges widely held assumptions, one necessarily wonders whether others in the long history of that text's interpretation have unpacked its inner logic in anything like the same way. One worries, moreover, if no one else has read the text in this way, why have they not done so? Is the proposed reading simply a *novum* cooked up by an overactive scholarly imagination looking for something new to say?

In my 2011 book, *Atonement and the Logic of Resurrection in the Epistle to the Hebrews*, I argue for a reading of Hebrews largely absent from the most influential secondary literature of the last century. I show, first, that Jesus's bodily resurrection is affirmed in the homily and seek, second, to demonstrate that this conviction holds significant implications for the author's apology for Jesus's high-priestly identity and for how he conceives of the nature and timing of Jesus's atoning sacrifice. Specifically, I suggest that the author identifies the center of the offering of Jesus's atoning sacrifice as

A substantial portion of the material on Origen below was read as part of an invited response to I. Howard Marshall's critique of my book at the 2013 meeting of the Evangelical Theological Society. I am grateful to Howard for his generous spirit and critical engagement. Like many, I was saddened to learn of his sudden death. I am also grateful for the insightful critiques of several friends and colleagues, especially Adam Johnson, Tom McGlothlin, Bryan Stewart, Matthew Thiessen, Tom Wright, and the anonymous reviewer.

Jesus's act of presenting himself to the Father *after* his resurrection. As the great high priest, Jesus offered himself to the Father as a sacrifice when he ascended through the heavens and entered the holy of holies in the heavenly sanctuary. For the author of Hebrews, Jesus's presentation of himself in his perfected, resurrected human body—including his now immortal blood and flesh—is the consummation of the high-priestly sacrifice that he offers to the Father and that effects sacrificial atonement (i.e., effects forgiveness of sins and purification for the people for whom he perpetually intercedes).[1]

This reading of Hebrews, however, naturally raises the question stated above. Have others read this early Christian text in anything like this way? A handful of reviewers of the book have rightly highlighted this very question.[2] I intend here to demonstrate that something like this interpretation of

1. A note on sacrifice may be in order here. Several recent studies on Levitical sacrifice have pointed out in fresh ways that such sacrifice is best viewed as an irreducible ritual process wherein some elements are more important for effecting the goals of the sacrificial process than others. R. E. Gane, for example, helpfully points out that the rituals constitutive of the process are hierarchically structured (*Cult and Character: Purification Offerings, Day of Atonement, and Theodicy* [Winona Lake, IN: Eisenbrauns, 2005], esp. 3–24). Thus, while the various ritual elements are necessary, none of them are alone sufficient for the sacrifice—the whole process constitutes a given sacrifice. Moreover, some of the elements are more central/weighty than others for achieving the goals of the sacrifice. All of this means that sacrifice entails a great deal more than killing an animal. The slaughter of a victim is clearly one constitutive element of some, but not all, sacrifices (see esp. C. A. Eberhart, *The Sacrifice of Jesus: Understanding Atonement Biblically*, Facets [Minneapolis: Fortress, 2011], 60–101).

Yet the most central elements of atoning sacrifices—that is, the elements most directly connected with obtaining the atoning benefit of these sacrifices—are the acts of blood manipulation and burning. These activities, by way of contrast to the act of slaughter, are exclusively the prerogatives of the priests and occur at and upon the various altars (see, e.g., Eberhart, *Sacrifice of Jesus*, 85; Gane, *Cult and Character*, 67). In terms of Levitical sacrifices, then, it is a category mistake to reduce or conflate the meaning of the term "sacrifice" with the act of slaughtering a victim since this act does not occur on any of the altars and, therefore, is not one of the elements directly linked with effecting the goals of the sacrifice. In the context of the Levitical sacrificial system one can speak about a sacrificial death/slaughter as an essential part of some of the sacrifices, but—and this is an important qualification—*to speak of a sacrificial death is not to speak of the death or slaughter itself as the sum total of sacrifice*. The priestly actions around and upon the altars are the primary elements of the process. This further suggests that the use and conveyance of the elements of the sacrifice into the sacred space of God's presence (i.e., the *offering* of these things to God) is the conceptual core of Jewish sacrifice.

2. See esp. N. J. Moore's careful review and critique of the book (review of *Atonement and the Logic of Resurrection in the Epistle to the Hebrews*, by D. M. Moffitt, *JTS* 64 [2013]: 673–75, here 675). S. J. Wilhite helpfully suggests that ancient readings of Hebrews should be examined as a way of probing the book's claims (review of *Atonement and the Logic of Resurrection in the Epistle to the Hebrews*, by D. M. Moffitt, *Fides et Humilitas* 1 [2014]: 72–83, here 82). Michael Kibbe thinks the book's argument is weakened by not pursuing the history of reception (review of *Atonement and the Logic of Resurrection in the Epistle to the Hebrews*, by D. M. Moffitt, *Themelios* 37 [2012]: 69–70), though, of course, the book is not a study in the reception history of Hebrews.

Hebrews is in fact present within the larger exegetical tradition. The kind of interpretive engagement with Hebrews that results in conceptions of the nature, timing, and location of Jesus's presentation of his atoning sacrifice similar to those that I argue are present in Hebrews can also be detected in the earliest centuries of Christianity.

Significantly, Hebrews' influence on these accounts, especially beginning with Origen, is not only plain and pervasive but also clearly synthesized with the voices of other authoritative, scriptural texts and confessional ideas. These interpreters are, in other words, allowing Hebrews to contribute to their understanding of Jesus's identity (Christology) and salvific work (soteriology). Rather than setting Hebrews' peculiar witness to these matters against those of other texts (as if everything to be said about Jesus and salvation were reducible only to the account of one authoritative text or tradition), they attest holistic and nonreductive accounts of Jesus's identity and atoning work.

These findings suggest not only that the kind of reading of Hebrews I argue for has a long history (one that has not been adequately taken into account in most contemporary theological and exegetical reflection on the epistle) but also that such a reading of Hebrews, no matter how strange it may seem to us today, has in the past been assumed by some to stand together with and even inform other accounts in the wider biblical witness to and theological reflection on Jesus's identity and salvific work.

Obviously, the presence of these sorts of readings of Hebrews does not prove that the reading of Hebrews for which I argue is necessarily correct (nor is it intended to do so).[3] My goals here are instead to demonstrate that the reading of Hebrews I present in that study (1) is not alone in the wider interpretive tradition and (2) has the potential to highlight some ways in which Jesus's bodily resurrection and ascension have informed past theological reflection on Jesus's soteriological work. Attention to this past reflection, I conclude, may suggest openings for contemporary reflection on Jesus's sacrifice and atonement that recover the high-priestly and sacrificial significance of the confession of Jesus's incarnate ascension into heaven.

Jesus's Heavenly Sacrifice: Surveying Past Interpretations of Hebrews

In a 2014 article, Michael Kibbe argued that my interpretation of Jesus's high-priestly ministry and atoning work in Hebrews has a precursor in the

---

3. I leave such judgment to the relative merits (and demerits) of the exegetical arguments I present in my earlier study.

Reformation-era figure Faustus Socinus. According to Kibbe, my view can rightly be labeled "Socinian," particularly because of my emphasis on the sequence of events that constitute Jesus's atoning work in Hebrews.[4]

There are some interesting ways in which Socinus's interpretation of Hebrews parallels my own.[5] Yet the emphasis I find in Hebrews on Christ as the eternal, preexistent Son who became the incarnate human being Jesus (to say nothing of the fact that my own project never claims to posit a theory or a synthetic, systematic theology of either *the* atonement or Christology, as the term "Socinian" implies) suggests that the claims of the book are misunderstood when linked to those of Socinus, or indeed when read as positing systematic theological claims, in the way Kibbe attempts to do.[6]

Socinus's interpretation does prove that at least one other reader interpreted aspects of Hebrews' language of Jesus's sacrifice along somewhat similar lines. But was Socinus unique in this regard? Further, if others read Hebrews in this way, did they do so in tension with or at the expense of Hebrews' affirmation of the Son's heavenly preexistence?[7]

4. M. Kibbe, "Is It Finished? When Did It Start? Hebrews, Priesthood, and Atonement in Biblical, Systematic, and Historical Perspective," *JTS* 65 (2014): 25–61, here 25; cf. 60–61. Kibbe claims that my interpretation of Hebrews' depiction of Jesus's atoning work "adheres closely to the Socinian view" (25). He writes, "It is the *location* and *timing* of [Jesus's] sacrifice that distinguish [Moffitt's interpretation] from traditional notions of atonement" (46n93; cf. 47). J. R. Treat makes a similarly mistaken connection between my interpretation of Hebrews and Socinus's synthetic theology of the atonement (*The Crucified King: Atonement and Kingdom in Biblical and Systematic Theology* [Grand Rapids: Zondervan, 2014], 216–17).

5. I point this out in a pair of footnotes in the book. See Moffitt, *Atonement and the Logic of Resurrection*, 199n130, 257n76.

6. Kibbe's description of my interpretation as "Socinian" appears to have led him to miss the central importance of Hebrews' incarnational Christology in my study, although I highlight this point repeatedly throughout. For just a few of the more obvious examples, see the statement of my larger thesis in my introductory chapter: "The robust narrative substructure of the singular Christology and soteriology developed in [Hebrews] should be identified as encompassing, in a proto-credal sequence, the full sweep of the significance of the Son's incarnation. For the author of this homily, the heavenly Son came into the world, suffered and died, rose again, ascended into heaven, made his offering for eternal atonement, and sat down at the right hand of God the Father Almighty. . . . This is the outline of the author's Christology and the context in which he works out his understanding of how Jesus effected atonement" (*Atonement and the Logic of Resurrection*, 43). Additionally, see my argument regarding the centrality of this aspect of Hebrews' Christology for understanding the author's defense of Jesus's high-priestly status in Heb. 7 (*Atonement and the Logic of Resurrection*, 207–10; *pace* Kibbe, "Is It Finished?," 47–49).

7. Kibbe states that he is not aware of anyone "prior to Socinus [who] suggested that Christ's priesthood and the atoning sacrifice offered by Christ as priest were specifically post-resurrection realities" ("Is It Finished?," 26n1). He further questions whether one could read Hebrews in such a way and affirm Jesus's deity (47–48). As I demonstrate below, there is clear evidence in early Christian texts that (1) Christ's high-priestly sacrifice could be conceived of as a post-resurrection reality and (2) this was not understood to stand in tension with the confession of the Deity and preexistence of the Son.

The simple answer to both questions is no. A sequential interpretation of Jesus's sacrificial work in Hebrews that identifies Jesus's post-crucifixion offering of his resurrected body to the Father in sacrificial terms was not the innovation of Socinus but has ancient roots in the exegetical traditions of early Christianity. Leaving the evidence of Hebrews itself aside, the idea that Jesus's heavenly presentation of his resurrected flesh and blood to the Father upon his ascension was a sacrifice that effected atonement (that is, an understanding of Jesus's atoning sacrifice as a post-resurrection reality) is positively in evidence as early as the third century CE. The texts examined below also demonstrate that such a conviction could depend both upon the Epistle to the Hebrews and upon the prior conviction that the preexistent, divine Son became incarnate.

In the discussion that follows I survey a select handful of ancient texts that, via allusions to and citations of Hebrews, comment on the subject of Jesus's heavenly sacrifice. An important caveat, however, is in order. I make no claim here to present a comprehensive survey or systematic account of early Christian conceptions of Jesus's identity, Jesus's sacrifice, the atonement, or even of the reception history of Hebrews. The point I seek to establish is more modest: I intend only to show that as early as the late second to early third centuries CE, passages from Hebrews were being interpreted as presenting a post-crucifixion and post-resurrection account of Jesus's sacrificial work. These texts assume or confess that, after the resurrection, the eternal Word ascended back to the Father with his now immortal human body. Further, the fact of Jesus's bodily ascension is taken by some to imply that he continually ministers at the heavenly altar as the great high priest by way of perpetually offering the sacrifice of his resurrected humanity to the Father. Hebrews' emphasis on the once-for-all-ness of the atoning sacrifice that Jesus offers is even understood by some in terms of Jesus's ascension—his singular return to the heavenly realms to perform his perpetual high-priestly service in the Father's presence at the heavenly altar.

Hippolytus's Against Noetus

Already in a few ante-Nicene texts Jesus's presentation of himself alive before God in heaven after his crucifixion and resurrection is interpreted along sacrificial lines.[8] At the beginning of the third century, Hippolytus of

---

8. Irenaeus refers to Jesus offering his resurrected humanity to God in heaven as a kind of sacrifice. In *Against Heresies* he affirms that Jesus "descend[ed] into the lower parts of the earth, searching for the sheep that was lost—which really was his own handiwork—and ascend[ed] into the heights above, offering [*offerentem*] and recommending to his Father that human

Rome, alluding to Hebrews, applies sacrificial categories to describe Jesus's heavenly offering to the Father.

In his *Against Noetus*, Hippolytus argues against Noetus's Patripassianism on the grounds that it cannot account for the fact that the "fleshless Word" (λόγος ἄσαρκος), who was eternally with the Father in heaven, became flesh and, after his resurrection, returned to heaven in his flesh.[9] How, Hippolytus reasons, can the eternal Word of the Father be identical with the Father himself, given that Jesus, who is the eternal Word, returned to heaven in order to present to the Father his very own flesh as an offering? Since the Father has no flesh, there should be no flesh in heaven when the Word returned to heaven, were it the case that Jesus is the Father.

Yet, Hippolytus argues, now there *is* flesh in heaven. In his words, "There is the flesh presented [προσενεχθεῖσα] by the Word of the Father as an offering [δῶρον], the flesh that came by the Spirit and the virgin, demonstrated to be the perfect [τέλειος] Son of God. It is evident, therefore, that he offered himself [ἑαυτὸν προσέφερε] to the Father. But before this [πρὸ δὲ τούτου] there was no flesh in heaven."[10] That is to say, since the Word of the Father was fleshless, took on human flesh to be born of the virgin, was shown to be the perfect Son of God, and then ascended back to heaven, where he offered that very flesh he assumed to the Father, it must be the case that the eternal Word, who continues even now to have his flesh in heaven, is distinguishable from the eternally fleshless Father.[11] For Hippolytus this means the Father did not suffer because the Father is not the incarnate Son.

Of particular note for this chapter is Hippolytus's claim that before Jesus presented the offering of his flesh to the Father ("before this," πρὸ δὲ τούτου), there was no flesh in heaven. Hippolytus here conceives of Jesus's presentation of himself as a gift (δῶρον) to the Father in terms of the presentation of his resurrected body/flesh upon his ascension.[12] Hippolytus does not refer to

---

nature which had been found, making in himself the first-fruits [*primitias*] of the resurrection of humankind" (*Haer.* 3.19.3.67–72; English translation modified from *St. Irenaeus of Lyons: Against the Heresies, Book 3*, trans. D. J. Unger, Ancient Christian Writers 64 [New York: Newman, 2012], 94).

9. PG 10:809b–c.

10. PG 10:809b. English translation lightly modified from *ANF* 5:225.

11. The creedal narrative that structures the logic of Hippolytus's reasoning here is noteworthy. One further suspects that his comment about the Word's being demonstrated to be the perfect Son of God alludes to Jesus's resurrection.

12. In a fragment from the text known as *Discourse on Elkanah and Hannah*, Hippolytus again links the offering of Jesus's humanity to God with his ascension. In reference to Pentecost, he claims that when Jesus first ascended into the heavens (αὐτὸς πρῶτος εἰς οὐρανοὺς ἀναβάς), he presented (προσενέγκας) humanity (τὸν ἄνθρωπον) as an offering to God (δῶρον τῷ θεῷ) (PG 10:864c).

Hebrews explicitly, but his comment that the Son "offered himself" (ἑαυτὸν προσέφερε) to the Father in heaven appears to allude to the homily. Indeed, among the texts that became the New Testament, only Hebrews describes Jesus's sacrifice with the collocation of the verb προσφέρειν + the direct object ἑαυτόν (9:14, 25). Additionally, only Hebrews refers to Jesus's sacrifice with the terms προσφέρειν + δῶρον (8:3–4; cf. 9:9–14). Hippolytus's comment that Jesus was shown to be the perfect (τέλειος) Son of God is also highly suggestive of Hebrews, a text that speaks repeatedly about God's Son being perfected (e.g., 2:10; 5:8–10; 7:28).

One might, however, question whether Hippolytus intends a sacrificial meaning when he speaks of Jesus presenting his flesh in heaven as a δῶρον. The collocation of προσφέρειν + δῶρον can be used in the context of offering tribute to an important and powerful figure.[13] In Septuagint texts, however, the phrase occurs most frequently in sacrificial contexts that assume or explicitly identify God as the recipient of the δῶρον.[14] In these contexts the collocation functions as technical language for sacrificing something to God (e.g., wine, grain, blood).[15] The frequency of the collocation in sacrificial contexts in Septuagintal texts does not conclusively prove that Hippolytus uses προσφέρειν + δῶρον here in a technical sense to designate Jesus's gift as a sacrifice. Given, however, that he read the Scriptures in Greek, the frequent use of this language in sacrificial contexts makes this conclusion highly plausible.

More definitive is the evidence presented above that Hippolytus's language echoes that of Hebrews. In Hebrews, the depiction of Jesus as the high priest who offers himself to the Father is clearly intended to be sacrificial. Given that Hippolytus alludes to Hebrews here, there can be little doubt that he envisions Jesus's heavenly offering of his flesh to God in sacrificial terms. Moreover, while he does not explicitly say that this heavenly sacrifice is atoning, and one must be careful not to push the silence of his text too far, the use of language from Hebrews lends credence to such a conclusion.

Hippolytus's statements in this text provide, then, a clear expression of an incarnational Christology wherein the eternal, divine Word/Son of the Father descended from heaven, became flesh, was born of a virgin, and, after his crucifixion and resurrection, ascended again into heaven with that flesh in

---

13. In nonsacrificial contexts in LXX texts, the collocation tends to mean "bring a tribute/ gift" to a ruler/dignitary (e.g., Gen. 43:26; Judg. 3:17; 3 Kgdms. 2:46b; cf. Matt. 2:11).

14. The collocation of προσφέρειν and δῶρον is rare in LXX texts outside the sacrificial contexts of Leviticus and Numbers. The most common meaning of the phrase is to offer a sacrifice to God (see, e.g., Lev. 1:2, 3, 14; 2:1, 4, 12, 13; 3:6; 4:23, 32; 6:13; 7:13, 29, 38; 9:15; 21:6, 8, 17, 21; 22:18, 25; 23:14; 27:9, 11; cf. Matt. 5:23; 8:4).

15. This, it seems to me, coheres well with the conception of sacrifice discussed in n. 1 above.

order to present it to the Father. Further, with sacrificial language that alludes to Hebrews, Hippolytus says that the Son of God presented that flesh to the Father as a sacrificial offering.[16] Robert J. Daly summarizes Hippolytus's view here well when he writes, "In heaven Jesus offered Himself—His flesh—to the Father. In terms of [a] physically realistic conception of the self-offering of the Word Incarnate, nothing more could possibly be desired."[17] While reflecting more broadly on Hippolytus's conception of Jesus's sacrifice, Daly argues further that Hippolytus "combines his incarnational Christology and soteriology with the gift idea of sacrifice in such a way as to produce a new moment in the development of the Christian idea of sacrifice."[18] This new moment includes, Daly explains, the notion that "the eternal Word of God became man in order to be able to rise again to heaven and offer to the eternal Father not only His flesh, His manhood, but also man himself."[19] My only quibble with Daly's helpful interpretation of Hippolytus is that he does not appear to notice Hippolytus's allusion to Hebrews in the course of developing this sacrificial theology. Yet if Hippolytus's conception of Jesus's sacrifice in terms of a δῶρον offered to the Father upon his heavenly ascension does indeed draw upon Hebrews, it seems likely that the "new moment in the development of the Christian idea of sacrifice" that Daly attributes to Hippolytus is something Hippolytus already found in Hebrews.

Be that as it may, Hippolytus provides substantive evidence for an early appropriation of Hebrews that affirms the narratival and incarnational sweep of Jesus's life, death, resurrection, and ascension and that correlates this nar-

---

16. A clear link with Hebrews and this kind of thinking about the ascended Christ can also be found later in the writings of Photius of Constantinople. Commenting on Heb. 1:13, Photius depicts the Son's exaltation to God's right hand in terms of Jesus presenting the first-fruits offering (τὴν ἀπαρχήν) of humanity to the Father. In language reminiscent of the Mosaic regulations that a sacrificial offering (δῶρον) from the flock must be blameless (ἄμωμον; see, e.g., LXX: Lev. 1:3, 10; 3:1, 6; 4:23, 32), Photius also speaks of Jesus presenting his flesh to the Father as an offering (he uses both δῶρον and substantival participles of προσφέρω) that was blameless (ἄμωμον). The Father, he says, marveled at the offering and placed it close to himself by inviting the offering—that is, the ascended Jesus—to sit at his right hand (see Karl Staab, ed., *Pauluskommentare aus der griechischen Kirche*, 2nd ed., Neutestamentliche Abhandlungen 15 [Münster: Aschendorff, 1984], 639). One wonders if this kind of idea of Jesus's heavenly sacrifice and high-priestly work might also help explain Gregory of Nazianzus's enigmatic reference to the "sacrifice of the resurrection" (*Letter 171*), as well as his comment in *Oration 30*, 14, that "even at this moment, as man, [Jesus] is making representation for my salvation; for he continues to wear the body that he assumed." (I am grateful to Peter Martens for drawing my attention to the latter text.) Certainly these sorts of ideas are evident in other early Christian texts (see below).

17. R. J. Daly, *Christian Sacrifice: The Judaeo-Christian Background before Origen*, Studies in Christian Antiquity 18 (Washington, DC: Catholic University of America Press, 1978), 362.

18. Daly, *Christian Sacrifice*, 372.

19. Daly, *Christian Sacrifice*, 372.

rative, especially its last element, with Jesus's offering of himself—that is, his resurrected flesh—as a sacrifice to the Father in the heavens.

An important question remains open, however: Does Jesus's heavenly offering accomplish anything vis-à-vis atonement? While Hippolytus plainly identifies Jesus's post-crucifixion and post-resurrection presentation of himself to the Father in heaven in sacrificial terms, he does not clearly state here that Jesus's heavenly sacrifice is an *atoning* sacrifice.[20] The situation is different, however, with Origen.

Origen's Homilies on Leviticus

In his *Homilies on Leviticus*, Origen provides extensive and clearly sequential accounts of Jesus's sacrificial work. In several of these *Homilies* he identifies Jesus's heavenly presentation of himself to God as a sacrifice that makes atonement. Further, Origen's reflections on Jesus's heavenly offering in these *Homilies* show obvious and pervasive dependence on Hebrews. Along the lines of the caveat noted above, this survey does not intend to offer either a systematic or comprehensive account of Origen's Christology, cosmology, views on Jesus's sacrifice, understanding of atonement, or even his interpretation of Hebrews. I present instead a discussion narrowly focused on how Origen addresses these issues as they relate to Jesus's atoning work in his *Homilies on Leviticus*, particularly because he repeatedly appeals to Hebrews.[21]

Throughout these *Homilies*, Origen identifies two altars and two sacrifices where and when Jesus offered his blood—one on earth and one in heaven.[22] He writes in *Homily 1* that Jesus's "blood was poured out *not only in Jerusalem*, where that altar and its base and the Tent of Meeting were, *but also*

20. Daly rightly argues that Hippolytus's emphasis on Jesus's heavenly offering derives from the Old Testament idea of sacrifice as a gift given to God (*Christian Sacrifice*, esp. 372). This accords well with the most central aspects of sacrifice as it is depicted in Leviticus (see n. 1 above). What is less clear, however, is how this gift functions for Hippolytus. While Levitical sacrifice generally involves giving something over to God, not all such giving aims to achieve purification and/or forgiveness.

21. H. Crouzel, summarizing J. A. Alcain's study *Cautiverio y rendención del hombre en Orígenes* (Bilboa: Mensajero, 1973), identifies five distinct but overlapping "schemes" that Origen employs to explain the various facets of Jesus's salvific work (*Origen*, trans. A. S. Worrall [Edinburgh: T&T Clark, 1989], 194–97). Among these, Crouzel notes that Origen's ritual or sacrificial scheme is heavily dependent upon Hebrews and primarily oriented around Christ's humanity (though never exclusively). This assessment aligns well with Origen's emphases in the *Homilies on Leviticus*.

22. I speak throughout of Origen, though of course we have Rufinus's translation of these homilies. Whether an idea comes solely from Origen or has been added by Rufinus, however, matters little to the larger conclusions of this study.

that same blood itself was sprinkled on the celestial altar, which is in heaven, where 'the church of the firstborn' [cf. Heb. 12:23] is."[23]

This fascinating comment raises questions regarding how this dual-sacrificial work of Jesus should be conceived. Are these sacrifices assumed by Origen to be one and the same event; are they coterminous? That is to say, is the earthly sacrifice also simultaneously a spiritual, heavenly one? Or, alternatively, are the two sacrifices related to each other sequentially such that one precedes the other? Is the cross, in other words, an initial offering on earth, whereas the sprinkling of Jesus's blood is another sacrifice in heaven that occurs subsequently, after the crucifixion? Moreover, what is the nature and effect of these sacrifices? As Origen continues to reflect on these sacrifices in the course of his exposition of Leviticus, he provides answers to these questions.

At first blush, some of Origen's language might lead one to conclude that these two sacrifices are really one coterminous event. That is to say, one might initially infer that Origen here envisions Jesus's death on the cross as being at the same time his timeless spiritual/heavenly sacrifice of himself to the Father.[24] When, for instance, he explains the heavenly offering of Jesus's blood in *Homily 1*, he writes that on earth Jesus "poured out the very bodily matter of his blood for humanity; but in heavenly places, if there are those who minister as priests there, he offered the vital strength of his body as some kind of spiritual sacrifice."[25] The idea that Jesus offers a spiritual sacrifice could suggest that he offered one sacrifice on the cross that had both an earthly and a spiritual/heavenly dimension.

Origen's dualism between heaven and earth might appear to provide further support for such an interpretation. Indeed, he speaks later in *Homily 1*

---

23. *Hom. Lev.* 1.3.19–23. English translation lightly modified from G. W. Barkley, trans., *Origen: Homilies on Leviticus 1–16*, FC 83 (Washington, DC: Catholic University of America Press, 1990), 34 (emphasis added).

24. So, e.g., P. J. Gorday, "Becoming Truly Human: Origen's Theology of the Cross," in *The Cross in Christian Tradition from Paul to Bonaventure*, ed. E. A. Dreyer (New York: Paulist Press, 2000), 93–125, esp. 103–4, 110–11. Cf. Crouzel, *Origen*, 197. Crouzel's claim that Jerome misunderstood Origen when Jerome said that Origen thought Jesus offered two sacrifices seems to me to be itself confused. Crouzel appears to assume that the language of "sacrifice" is synonymous with "death/slaughter." Thus, Crouzel concludes that for Origen Jesus offered one sacrifice when he died on the cross, though this sacrifice has both earthly and heavenly dimensions. Whatever Jerome's understanding of Origen, in these *Homilies* Origen appears genuinely to posit that Jesus offered two distinct sacrifices, one on earth, which frees humanity from the Devil, and one in heaven, which propitiates God and allows for humanity to be purified (see below). Such a conception of Jesus's sacrificial work seems to draw upon a model of sacrifice that puts more emphasis on the transfer of the elements of the sacrifice into the presence of the recipient of the sacrifice than on the act of slaughter per se (see again n. 1 above).

25. *Hom. Lev.* 1.3.29–33; Barkley, *Origen: Homilies*, 34.

about Jesus's flesh hiding his divine nature on earth. Now, however, Jesus has returned to heaven, "where again his fiery nature is evident."[26] Perhaps, then, Origen thinks of Jesus leaving his flesh behind when he returned to heaven and assumed again the purely spiritual, fiery nature he has eternally had as the preincarnate Word. Were this true, it might follow that Origen applies the category of sacrifice to the historical, earthly event of the crucifixion as a kind of metaphor intended to explain the spiritual, heavenly significance of Jesus's death.

A wider glance at these *Homilies*, however, points to a different conclusion. Whatever Origen thought of the precise nature of the ascended Jesus's resurrected body,[27] in these *Homilies* he stresses that Jesus's resurrection means that this body continues to consist of human flesh and blood, even as the Lord's fiery nature is now clearly manifest in heaven again. Jesus's resurrected body is a transformed, purified body, but for Origen it is no less a human body for that. Moreover, Origen states plainly that the two altars he has already mentioned—the altars where Jesus offers his two sacrifices—are temporally and spatially distinct.

Temporally, they are separated by the resurrection. The first sacrifice occurred before Jesus's resurrection; the second one occurs after it. Spatially, they occur in two different locations. The first one on earth took place outside of Jerusalem—that is, on the cross. The second one perpetually occurs now at the altar in God's heavenly presence. There, at the heavenly altar, Jesus, by virtue of being in God's presence, is continually present to God as a sacrifice. That is, he perpetually offers the Father the sacrifice of his resurrected humanity. Origen does not, in other words, conflate or collapse the time and place of Jesus's offerings at these two altars, as one would expect were he envisioning them as different aspects of the singular event of the cross. Rather, he sets them out in a temporal and spatial sequence—first the cross on earth, then, after the resurrection, the sacrifice at the altar in heaven when Jesus returns to the Father as a glorified human being.

This latter point can be seen clearly in *Homily 3*. Here Origen again speaks of Jesus's pre-resurrected flesh hiding the secret of his divinity while he was on earth. Origen nevertheless claims that Jesus placed the bodily matter of his flesh "to be sacrificed on the holy altars [*sanctificandam . . . altaribus*] and to be illuminated by the divine flames *and to be retained with himself in heaven*."[28]

---

26. *Hom. Lev.* 1.4.49–53; Barkley, *Origen: Homilies*, 36.
27. For a detailed and systematic discussion of Origen's conception of the resurrection of the body see M. J. Edwards, *Origen against Plato*, Ashgate Studies in Philosophy & Theology in Late Antiquity (Aldershot: Ashgate, 2002), 107–14.
28. *Hom. Lev.* 3.5.15–19; Barkley, *Origen: Homilies*, 62 (emphasis added).

Here he plainly affirms that Jesus continues to have the bodily matter of his flesh with him in heaven. But what can he mean when he says that the bodily material of Jesus's flesh was sacrificed on multiple holy "altars" (note the plural *altaribus*)?

The explanation for this idea lies in Origen's conviction, noted above, that Jesus took his resurrected human flesh with him when he returned to the heavenly realms. In *Homily 7* he again affirms this point when he identifies the cross as one altar, the altar where Jesus offered his flesh on earth (*Hom. Lev.* 7.1.110–21), but then goes on to speak of Jesus's ongoing sacrificial service at another altar, the one located in heaven (*Hom. Lev.* 7.2.37–57; cf. 7.2.14–16). In language that alludes to Hebrews 7:25 and 9:24, Origen claims that Jesus "now stands before the face of God interceding for us. He stands before the altar to offer a propitiation to God for us."[29] Jesus's present, perpetual work of intercession is occurring *now*, and this work is a work of atonement/propitiation.[30]

Origen further explains this last notion in *Homily 9*, where he claims that the sacrifice that Jesus presently offers to God is none other than his resurrected body—the very body he took with him when he ascended into heaven. Reflecting on the high priest's activities on the Day of Atonement as detailed in Leviticus 16, Origen ponders the fact that the earthly high priests had to put on consecrated linen garments before their annual entrance into the earthly holy of holies. That tunic, he notes, was made of linen, not animal hide. He finds this detail important because linen, unlike leather, comes from flax, which grows out of the earth. In keeping with the model of the earthly high priests in Leviticus 16, Origen concludes that Jesus also had to put on a consecrated "linen" garment before he ascended into heaven and entered the heavenly holy of holies—the sanctified tunic is his resurrected, earthly body. In Origen's words: "It is 'a sanctified linen tunic' that Christ, the true high priest, puts on when he takes up the nature of an earthly body; for it is said about the body that 'it is earth and it will go into the earth.' Therefore, my Lord

29. Barkley, *Origen: Homilies*, 134. Rufinus has translated the last clause as follows: *adsistit altari, ut repropitiationem pro nobis offerat Deo* (*Hom. Lev.* 7.2.38–39). One suspects that *repropitiationem* renders a ἱλασ- root word, possibly ἱλασμός (cf. the citation of 1 John 2:2 in *Hom. Lev.* 9.5.103).

30. Origen's depiction of Jesus standing at the heavenly altar is interesting given his allusion here to Hebrews. Hebrews, by way of contrast with the standing posture of the Levitical high priests, clearly states that Jesus is presently sitting at God's right hand (see esp. Heb. 8:1; 10:12). One suspects that Origen's conception of Jesus's high-priestly ministry is not only informed by Hebrews but also supplemented with evidence from Leviticus and New Testament texts outside of Hebrews that depict the risen and ascended Christ standing in the heavens (e.g., Rev. 5:6–7; cf. 1:12–18; Acts 7:55–56).

and Savior, *wanting to resurrect that which had 'gone into the earth,' took an earthly body that he might carry it raised up from the earth to heaven.*"[31]

For Origen, then, one of the essential reasons that the Son of God became a human being was so that he could raise that earthly, human body from the dead and ascend with it back into heaven. Moreover, Origen appears to infer, at least partly on the basis Leviticus 16:4, that Jesus's resurrection was a necessary prerequisite for his high-priestly ministry at the heavenly altar. Thus, just as the earthly high priest had first to put on a sanctified linen garment before entering the earthly *sancta sanctorum*, so Jesus also had first to be clothed in sanctified human flesh (flesh that, like linen, comes from the stuff of the earth) before he could serve as the true high priest and enter the heavenly holy of holies. The ascension, Origen here implies, was one of the central purposes of the incarnation. Be that as it may, Origen clearly identifies Jesus's "sanctified linen tunic" as his resurrected human body. But why would Jesus need to take his resurrected flesh into heaven?

Origen's answer coheres with, but also moves beyond, the language noted above in Hippolytus—Jesus took his humanity into heaven in order to offer it to the Father as an *atoning* sacrifice. Commenting on the individual tasked with performing the Day of Atonement's scapegoat ritual—the "prepared man" (Lev. 16:21)—and on the high priest's handling of the goat whose blood is taken into God's presence, Origen explains,

> It was necessary for my Lord and Savior not only to be born a man among men but also to descend to Hell that as "a prepared man" he could lead away "the lot of the scapegoat into the wilderness" of Hell. And returning from that place, his work completed, he could ascend to the Father, and there be more fully purified at the heavenly altar *so that he could give a pledge of our flesh, which he had taken with him, in perpetual purity*. This, therefore, is the real Day of Atonement when God is propitiated for men; just as the Apostle also says, "Since God was in Christ reconciling the world to himself."[32]

The preceding passage provides strong evidence that Origen does not conflate the earthly altar of the cross with the heavenly altar in these *Homilies*, nor is the earthly offering of Jesus thought to be coterminous with the heavenly one. On the contrary, Jesus's death performs a particular salvific role: defeating the powers (leading away the "lot of the scapegoat"; see *Hom. Lev.* 9.2.20–33) by way of his descent into and return from hell. His subsequent resurrection and ascension are prerequisites that then enable him to perform atoning service

---

31. *Hom. Lev.* 9.2.26–32; Barkley, *Origen: Homilies*, 178–79 (emphasis added).
32. *Hom. Lev.* 9.5.47–57; Barkley, *Origen: Homilies*, 185 (emphasis added).

as the high priest at the heavenly altar, where he now offers the sacrifice of his purified human flesh to God.

As Origen continues to reflect on Jesus's ascension as the true high priest who perpetually serves at the heavenly altar on the real Day of Atonement, he also considers how Jesus, like the high priest in his annual act described in Leviticus, left his people behind him and entered alone into the holy of holies to make propitiation. Origen likens the period of Jesus's earthly ministry to Jesus's "year" serving among his people. Jesus's entry *once*, at the end of that "year," into the heavenly holy of holies marks the beginning of the "true Day of Atonement." Origen, however, identifies this one-time entry not with Jesus's crucifixion but with his post-resurrection ascension. Origen understands Jesus's once-for-all-time entrance into the heavenly holy of holies as occurring—and here again he invokes Hebrews—"when with his dispensation fulfilled [that is, his year among the people] he 'penetrates the heavens' [cf. Heb. 4:14] and goes to the Father to make atonement for the human race and prays for all those who believe in him [cf. 7:25]."[33]

Interestingly, in other New Testament texts as well Origen finds corroborating support for the idea that Jesus, after his resurrection and ascension, perpetually offers his atoning sacrifice to the Father in heaven. Thus to his comments from Hebrews he adds, "Knowing this atonement by which [Jesus] propitiates the Father for humans, the Apostle John says, 'I say this, little children, that we may not sin. But if we should sin, we have an advocate before the Father, Jesus Christ the Just; and he himself is the propitiation for our sins' [1 John 2:1–2]."[34] In this same context Origen even links Paul's statement in Romans 3:25 that God appointed Jesus "as a propitiator by his blood through faith" with Jesus's ongoing sacrificial work of atonement in heaven.[35]

Fully consistent with the notion that Jesus's heavenly sacrifice constitutes his high-priestly work on the real Day of Atonement, Origen, in language replete with allusions to Hebrews, goes on to identify the present age—that is, the time between Jesus's ascension and his return to his people—in terms of Christ's perpetual atoning work of intercession in heaven.[36] "Therefore," he writes, "the Day of Atonement remains for us until the sun sets; that is, until the world comes to an end. For let us stand 'before the gates' waiting for our high priest who remains within 'the holy of holies,' that is, 'before

---

33. *Hom. Lev.* 9.5.96–98; Barkley, *Origen: Homilies*, 187.
34. *Hom. Lev.* 9.5.99–103; Barkley, *Origen: Homilies*, 187.
35. *Hom. Lev.* 9.5.103–6; Barkley, *Origen: Homilies*, 187.
36. "Perpetual" should not here be confused with "eternal." Origen seems to say that Jesus's atoning work in heaven began with the ascension and is continually ongoing and necessary until the point when he returns.

the Father;' and who intercedes not for the sins of everyone, but 'for the sins' of those 'who wait for him' [cf. Heb. 7:25; 9:24, 26, 28]."[37]

As noted above, I am not here seeking to reduce all of Origen's thinking on sacrifice and atonement to these passages from his *Homilies on Leviticus*. Remarkably, though, these *Homilies* show Origen reading parts of Hebrews as teaching that Jesus offered himself as an atoning sacrifice to the Father when, after his crucifixion and resurrection, he ascended into heaven. Moreover, Jesus's perpetual intercession for his people is, on the basis of the Levitical high priest's entrance into the holy of holies to offer sacrifice and intercede on Yom Kippur, partly constituted by his perpetual offering of his resurrected self/body to God as a propitiating sacrifice.

Origen derives this interpretation, at least in part, by reading Leviticus together with Hebrews under the conviction that Jesus rose and ascended bodily into heaven. Thus, the instructions for the Day of Atonement in Leviticus 16 provide him with models or analogies both for understanding the significance of Jesus's ascension and for conceiving of what Jesus is presently doing in the heavenly realms. It may even be the case that his comment about Jesus offering "the vitality of his body" in heaven in *Homily 1* is a way of speaking about Jesus's resurrected body and blood constituting the offering of his resurrected *life* as the atoning sacrifice he presents to the Father in heaven.[38]

Origen also plainly sees Jesus's resurrection as the moment that prepares him for his heavenly high-priestly service insofar as this is the moment when he imagines Jesus, by analogy with the high priest in Leviticus 16, putting on the consecrated garment of his now purified earthly human body, the very "linen" garment he needs to wear before he enters God's presence in the heavenly holy of holies and serves there as the great high priest.

The preceding evidence therefore indicates that, at least in his *Homilies on Leviticus*, Origen conceives of Jesus's atoning work in terms of an incarnational sequence wherein, after his resurrection, the ascended Jesus perpetually offers himself to the Father as an atoning sacrifice while interceding for his brothers and sisters. For Origen, this narrative or sequence of Jesus's atoning work consists of the following elements: the eternal Word of God became flesh, dwelt among his people, died, descended into hell, rose again bodily, and ascended into heaven with his transformed humanity. Jesus's post-resurrection ascension marks his entry into the heavenly holy of holies, where he now ministers on behalf of his people as their great high priest. Thus,

---

37. *Hom. Lev.* 9.5.107–12; Barkley, *Origen: Homilies*, 187.
38. This comment coheres remarkably well with the emphasis in Leviticus on the power of the life in blood as the agent that effects sacrificial atonement (see 17:11).

Jesus's ascension constitutes the beginning of the "real Day of Atonement." At the heavenly altar Jesus now/perpetually offers his purified humanity to the Father. Moreover, Origen states that the offering of Jesus's humanity in heaven—which is perpetually occurring so long as Jesus remains in the Father's presence—and his ongoing intercession are the means by which God is propitiated and atonement is made. His many allusions to and citations of Hebrews show the important influence of this epistle on his thinking in these matters.

Origen, however, is not a lone voice in the larger tradition. Theodore of Mopsuestia also conceives of Jesus's offering himself to the Father as involving a post-resurrection, heavenly sacrifice at the heavenly altar. By this point, it should not be surprising to discover that he also relies heavily on Hebrews when expounding the point.

Theodore of Mopsuestia's Homily on Eucharist and Liturgy

In his *Homily on Eucharist and Liturgy* Theodore of Mopsuestia discusses Eucharist in terms of a sacrifice offered by a duly appointed priest of the new covenant. He makes a direct connection between the sacramental actions of this earthly, new covenant priest and the reality of the heavenly service that this priest and these actions represent. Eucharist, he notes, represents the real sacrifice that Jesus offers. Through Eucharist "the new covenant appears to be maintained (*qwym'*)."[39]

Drawing on Hebrews 8:4, Theodore claims that "now" (*hš'*, "at present") Christ "performs the priestly service in heaven and not on earth, because he died, rose, ascended into heaven in order to raise us all up and cause us to ascend into heaven."[40] He adds that Jesus "performs a real high priesthood and offers to God no other sacrifice than himself, as he had delivered also himself to death for all. He was the first to rise from the dead, and he ascended into heaven and sat at the right hand of God in order to destroy our adversaries."[41] Theodore, citing Hebrews 10:12, further claims that "[Jesus] offered one sacrifice for our sins forever, sat on the right hand of God, from henceforth expecting till his enemies be made his footstool."[42] He continues,

---

39. A. Mingana, ed., *Commentary of Theodore of Mopsuestia on the Lord's Prayer and on the Sacraments of Baptism and Eucharist*, WS 6 (Cambridge: Heffer & Sons, 1933), 79. For the Syriac text see p. 214. The idea that the new covenant requires a sacrifice to be maintained is remarkable. Theodore appears here to think that Eucharist participates in Jesus's ongoing heavenly sacrifice perpetually offered to the Father and that this sacrifice is the means for keeping the new covenant relationship intact.

40. Mingana, *Commentary of Theodore*, 80. For the Syriac see pp. 215–16.

41. Mingana, *Commentary of Theodore*, 80.

42. Mingana, *Commentary of Theodore*, 80.

"The work of a high priest consists in his drawing nigh unto God first, and then in drawing also the others to him through himself." Theodore then reflects at length on Hebrews 8:1–5. As part of this exposition he claims, "The apostle [Paul, whom Theodore assumes to be the author of Hebrews] said that Christ is the minister, as he ascended into heaven and there performs service for all of us, so that he might draw us unto him by all means."[43]

When Theodore returns again to explain the actual process of performing the Eucharist, he states that as the priest performs the rituals on earth, "we must picture in our mind that we are dimly in heaven, and, through faith, draw in our imagination the image of heavenly things, while thinking that Christ who is in heaven and who died for us, rose, and ascended into heaven is now [hš'] being sacrificed [mtnks]. In contemplating with our eyes, through faith, the facts that are now being reenacted: that he is again dying, rising, and ascending into heaven, we shall be led to the vision of the things that had taken place beforehand on our behalf."[44] When, therefore, the priest draws near to the altar, he offers a visual depiction of Christ's perpetual heavenly service, service that issues from and directly depends on the full sweep of the Son's incarnation—especially the past events of his death, resurrection, and ascension. The priest's approach to the earthly altar is a "figure" that "dimly represents the image of the unspeakable heavenly things and of the supernatural and incorporeal hosts."[45] This appears to explain how Theodore can say that Jesus is "now" being sacrificed in the Eucharist—that is, the Eucharist participates in the perpetual reality of Jesus's heavenly offering, a sacrifice that is always "now" being offered to the Father by virtue of Jesus "now" being in heaven at the Father's right hand.

Clearly, Theodore does not abstract Jesus's death from Jesus's sacrifice. Jesus's death is sacrificial, and Eucharist is a remembrance of that sacrificial death.[46] Yet, equally clearly he does not reduce Jesus's high-priestly service and atoning sacrifice to the crucifixion. The resurrection and ascension are also constitutive elements of Jesus's sacrifice. Theodore appears, therefore, to take seriously the notion that Jesus's sacrifice consists in a process whose climactic moment is not reducible to Jesus's death but includes his ascension into heaven where he "now" (hš') ministers as the great high priest. That ministry involves Jesus presenting himself to the Father as the ultimate and fully sufficient atoning sacrifice. Eucharist, then, partly functions for Theodore as a visualization of the entire process that culminated in the heavenly

43. Mingana, *Commentary of Theodore*, 81.
44. Mingana, *Commentary of Theodore*, 83. For the Syriac see p. 219.
45. Mingana, *Commentary of Theodore*, 83.
46. Mingana, *Commentary of Theodore*, esp. 74, 78, 79.

offering of that atoning sacrifice. As such, the ritual helps one to remember, even to visualize, not just Jesus's death but also his resurrection, ascension, and approach to the heavenly altar, where, Theodore seems to aver, he now perpetually presents the sacrifice of himself to the Father.

Theodore, then, conceives of the full sweep of Jesus's death, resurrection, ascension, and session at God's right hand as constituting Jesus's sacrifice. When, therefore, he speaks of the "now" of the eucharistic sacrifice, he identifies the actions that the earthly priest performs as temporally representing and participating in the singular past events that climaxed in Jesus's present, perpetual, high-priestly presentation of himself to the Father in heaven. This sacrifice—that is, both Jesus's actual, primary sacrifice and the eucharistic sacrifice, which represents and participates in that one real sacrifice—is the means by which the new covenant relationship is maintained.

In a way similar to Origen in his expositions of Leviticus, Theodore also seems to think in terms of Jesus entering heaven as the event of his once-for-all/perpetual presentation or offering of his sacrifice to the Father. Because of Jesus's ongoing presence in heaven at the Father's right hand, Eucharist helps maintain the restored relationship between God and his people that Jesus, as the mediator of the new covenant, accomplishes.[47] Jesus's heavenly, high-priestly ministry, in other words, provides the ongoing covenantal maintenance that ensures the relationship between God and his new covenant people. Moreover, Hebrews makes an essential contribution to his understanding of these matters.

Theodoret of Cyrus's Questions on Leviticus

While less developed than Origen and Theodore, Theodoret of Cyrus also at points attests a similar conception of Jesus's sacrifice. In the course of discussing Leviticus 16 in question 22 of his *Questions on Leviticus*, Theodoret argues that the entire Yom Kippur ritual "prefigures the incarnation of our Savior; as the high priest entered the holy of holies and performed this rite once a year, so Christ the Lord endured the saving passion and ascended to heaven once, 'thus effecting eternal redemption' [Heb. 9:12] as the holy apostle says."[48]

Commenting on Hebrews 8:1–3, he suggests, somewhat like Origen, that the reason Christ assumed humanity was in order to offer that nature to God on behalf of humanity when he ascended into the tabernacle (i.e., heaven).

---

47. Cf. Apos. Con. 8.13.7–10 for the similar idea that Christ is the priestly mediator who now presents the eucharistic offering to the Father at the heavenly altar.

48. R. C. Hill, trans., *Theodoret of Cyrus: The Questions on the Octateuch*, Library of Early Christianity (Washington, DC: Catholic University of America Press, 2007), 2:57.

There, the very one who created heaven now ministers as a human being.[49] He further explains that the annual entry of the earthly high priest into the holy of holies served "as a type of Christ, who was the first to ascend into heaven and disclose access to us."[50]

When reflecting on Hebrews 9:24–26, Theodoret affirms that Jesus, as the great high priest, entered heaven to appear before God. The verb "to appear" in Hebrews 9:24 means, Theodoret explains, that Jesus appeared before the Father as a fleshly human being so that "now for the first time human nature went up to heaven."[51] He also links Jesus's once-for-all offering with the ascension when he notes that just as the earthly high priests entered the holy of holies once every year with the blood of animals, so Christ entered heaven with his own blood in order to offer himself once for all, thereby dealing decisively with sin and promising immortality to his followers.[52]

The Homilies of Narsai and Jacob of Sarug on Jesus's Ascension

Yet more evidence for this kind of interpretation of Hebrews and Jesus's heavenly sacrifice can be found in the writings of the Syriac theologians Narsai and Jacob of Sarug. In his *Homily on the Feast Day of the Ascension*, Narsai reflects on the significance of Jesus's ascension. Narsai speaks repeatedly about Jesus's ascension as the moment when the molded and corrupted "clay of our bodily structure" and the "humble dust of Adam" put on glory and were exalted into heaven.[53] Further, via a host of allusions to themes and language found in Hebrews, he speaks of the "Self-Existent" and "hidden One" who put on a human body and, by taking our dust into heaven, "opened the way to the kingdom on high and entered to serve in the holy of holies as the high priest. Into the sanctuary on high he arrived to serve spiritually in (that) resplendent place, undefiled by things earthly."[54] His "visible body mounted the wind and arrived on high."[55]

Narsai is keen to stress that Jesus did not lose his human body of flesh and bone as he ascended. He even interprets the angelic admonition to the

---

49. R. C. Hill, trans., *Theodoret of Cyrus: Commentary on the Letters of St. Paul* (Brookline, MA: Holy Cross Orthodox Press, 2001), 2:169.

50. Hill, *Theodoret of Cyrus: Commentary*, 2:172–73.

51. Hill, *Theodoret of Cyrus: Commentary*, 2:175.

52. Hill, *Theodoret of Cyrus: Commentary*, 2:175.

53. F. G. McLeod, trans., *Narsai's Metrical Homilies on the Nativity, Epiphany, Passion, Resurrection and Ascension: Critical Edition of Syriac Text*, PO 40 (Turnhout: Brepols, 1979), e.g., 163, 167, 179.

54. McLeod, *Narsai's Metrical Homilies*, 167. Cf. Heb. 8:1–2; 9:24; 10:19–21.

55. McLeod, *Narsai's Metrical Homilies*, 169.

disciples in Acts 1:11 as intended to allay any doubts that Jesus might have left his body behind when he ascended. Since the angel says that Jesus will return in the same way as he ascended, Narsai reasons that Jesus must "remain unaltered in body and soul. Under that (very) appearance, he will remain in ineffable glory" until his return.[56] In this way Jesus can actually return just as he ascended—as a blood-and-flesh human being. In Jesus, then, "a member of our race" has "entered to minister in the holy of holies on behalf of [our] life."[57]

Narsai, not unlike Origen and Theodoret, also appears here to interpret Hebrews' "once for all" language in terms of the singularity of Jesus's ascension. He states that Jesus "entered heaven to atone (*dnḥs'*) for all by the sacrifice of himself (*bdbḥ' dnpšh*). *He made one entrance* and was received in the sanctuary above. . . . He entered and appeared before the All-seeing One to whom everything was visible."[58] Narsai adds, again with language redolent of Hebrews, that when Christ entered the heavenly holy of holies, God "welcomed him and conferred on him the crown belonging to the name of the Divine Essence."[59] Jesus, he states later, "secured the peace and renewal of the universe through his ascent."[60] Through the victory of his ascension Jesus "made restitution for the bond of our guilt."[61] By this sacrifice he "reconciled the height and the depth" with God.[62]

In a similar vein, and equally reminiscent of Hebrews (especially of the author's argument in Hebrews 1–2 regarding the Son being elevated above the angels in his humanity), Jacob of Sarug says in his *Homily on the Ascension of Our Lord* that, after rising from the dead and spending forty days with his disciples, Jesus ascended to a place above all the ranks of the angels. Indeed, he left the angels below him as he entered the heavenly holy of holies. Jacob avers, "To the holy of holies, the high priest bore himself magnificently. Towards that awesome interior tabernacle where the Father is, for the Son alone can enter towards the Father. Outside the door the angels stayed like the Levites, and Christ, the high priest, alone entered."[63] He later adds, "To the place where the Son was exalted with his Father neither Cherubs nor Seraphs with their hallowings were raised. There are [many]

56. McLeod, *Narsai's Metrical Homilies*, 171.
57. McLeod, *Narsai's Metrical Homilies*, 175.
58. McLeod, *Narsai's Metrical Homilies*, 175. Cf. Heb. 9:24–26.
59. McLeod, *Narsai's Metrical Homilies*, 175. Cf. Heb. 1:3–4; 2:9.
60. McLeod, *Narsai's Metrical Homilies*, 181.
61. McLeod, *Narsai's Metrical Homilies*, 185.
62. McLeod, *Narsai's Metrical Homilies*, 187.
63. Thomas Kollamparampil, trans., *Jacob of Sarug's Homily on the Ascension of Our Lord*, TCLA 24 (Piscataway, NJ: Gorgias Press, 2010), 50.

priests but the high priest is only one; and into the holy of holies, only one enters, not many."[64]

Moreover, drawing from Hebrews 8:1–2 Jacob adds that the Son advanced beyond the angels "to the hidden place which is not at all part of creation. . . . The tabernacle which is not made, nor has it any like it among created things. . . . He alone entered into that inner holy of holies."[65] "The high priest," he continues, "has entered the holy of holies, with his own blood (*bdm'*) he will reconcile his Father with humanity. He is the offering (*dbḥ'*), the high priest, and the libation (*nwqy'*) too and he himself entered so that the whole creation might be pardoned through him."[66] Jesus "descended, visited us and ascended redeeming us."[67]

Conclusion

The preceding survey, though limited, has demonstrated conclusively that the idea that Jesus offered himself—specifically his resurrected human body—to God as an atoning sacrifice in heaven upon his post-resurrection ascension is well attested in some of the earliest reception of Hebrews. Most of the texts explored above explicitly affirm the view that the Son of God, as the eternal Word, took upon himself human flesh and blood, died, rose, and ascended bodily into heaven in order to present his humanity to the Father and perform his sacrificial, atoning ministry there at God's right hand. This, it should be noted, is a model of Jesus's high-priestly sacrifice that coheres well with, is even directly informed by, key elements in the depictions of sacrifice and high-priestly service found in Leviticus.

Moreover, it is also worth highlighting that although this understanding of Jesus's heavenly atoning work is often directly linked in the texts discussed to passages from Hebrews, the figures surveyed above also reflect synthetically on a wide range of texts and traditions. Hebrews makes a distinctive contribution to their thinking because Hebrews, more than any of their other authoritative texts, explicitly focuses on the high-priestly sacrifice of the ascended Christ in the heavenly holy of holies.

These findings suggest two concluding comments. First, some may object that the kind of interpretation of Hebrews detailed above implies that the

---

64. Kollamparampil, *Jacob of Sarug's Homily on the Ascension*, 52.

65. Kollamparampil, *Jacob of Sarug's Homily on the Ascension*, 54.

66. Kollamparampil, *Jacob of Sarug's Homily on the Ascension*, 56, 58 (for the corresponding Syriac text, see pp. 57, 59, lines 481–84).

67. Kollamparampil, *Jacob of Sarug's Homily on the Ascension*, 58.

crucifixion of Jesus becomes merely preparatory for atonement and is thus
no longer central to Jesus's sacrifice and atoning work. Such a critique, however, wrongly assumes both the meanings of and the relationship between
sacrifice and atonement just to the extent that it already presupposes that
Jesus's sacrificial, atoning work is reducible to his suffering and death. None
of the figures discussed above would dispute the unique and indispensable
importance of the suffering and death of Jesus for the salvation he obtains.
Were one to query them on these points, one would find that they have a
great deal to say about the ways that Jesus's death contributes to salvation.[68]

Nevertheless, by thinking sequentially through the whole sweep of the
incarnational narrative, they are able to work with a broad perspective on
Jesus's atoning work. The cross is essential for them, particularly for the
defeat of death and the Devil, but they do not view it as the sum total of
Jesus's atoning sacrifice. Ultimately the full, incarnational story of Jesus,
not the cross per se, is truly central to their understanding of atonement.
The author of Hebrews is understood by these voices in the tradition to be
making a particular contribution to this larger concept of Jesus's sacrifice
and atoning work precisely because of the attention he places on Jesus's resurrection, ascension, and heavenly session. Hebrews informs their accounts
of atonement by explaining more clearly and explicitly than any other New
Testament text how the ascension of the risen Jesus is constitutive of his
atoning sacrifice and high-priestly ministry.

Second, Gustav Aulén clearly perceived the centrality of the full sweep
of the incarnation for atonement in the early church when he posited his
Christus Victor concept, or "Classic Idea" of the atonement. Thus he stated,
"The organic connection of the idea of the Incarnation with that of the
Atonement is the leading characteristic of the doctrine of redemption in the
early church."[69] Nevertheless, this study suggests that even with the "double-
sidedness" of Aulén's theory, his view that atonement is fully the work of
God (as opposed to his account of the "Latin theory" wherein Jesus's death
is a sacrifice offered by humanity to God) is hobbled by his own reductive
understanding of sacrifice. His assumption that Jesus's death *is* Jesus's sacrifice led him to downplay the full contribution Jesus's humanity makes for
atonement along the lines affirmed by the texts discussed above.[70] The texts
studied above clearly allow that, specifically as a human being, the divine Son
offers his sacrifice to the Father.

---

68. For examples from Origen, see Crouzel, *Origen*, 194–97.
69. G. Aulén, *Christus Victor: An Historical Study of the Three Main Types of the Idea of
the Atonement*, trans. A. G. Hebert (London: SPCK, 1931), 58.
70. See, e.g., Aulén, *Christus Victor*, 73–74.

Since Aulén's important work, a number of studies have helpfully expanded the discussion by emphasizing the varieties of sacrifice and of sacrificial ideas and images at play within early Christianity.[71] Frances Young, in particular, has rightly stressed from this fact the dangers of over-systematizing early Christian reflection on atonement.[72] Even Young, however, continues to work with a reductive conception of Jesus's sacrifice wherein Jesus's death is the real subject that the different early Christian sacrificial metaphors seek to explain. This leads her to miss the possibility that some of the tension/dualism she identifies between Jesus's defeat of evil and his offering of his humanity to God might be resolved by paying more careful attention to how sacrifice works when conceived of as a process whose center rests on bringing the material of the sacrifice into God's presence. Specifically, it may be the case that such attention could identify ways in which different figures understand Jesus's death, resurrection, and ascension to make distinct contributions to the atonement (broadly conceived) that they believe he achieves.

Be that as it may, I hope the preceding survey will contribute to a renewed recognition of the importance of sacrifice and sacrificial categories for reflection on the full scope of the atoning work of Jesus not only for contemporary interpretation of biblical texts but also for the interpretation of the texts and communities that came later in the development of the Christian tradition. It may be that such study will lead to a recovery of insights that might themselves prove useful for contemporary theological reflection on sacrifice and atonement.

---

71. E.g., Daly, *Christian Sacrifice*; F. M. Young, *The Use of Sacrificial Ideas in Greek Christian Writers from the New Testament to John Chrysostom*, Patristic Monograph Series 5 (Philadelphia: Philadelphia Patristic Foundation, 1979).

72. See esp. F. M. Young, *Sacrifice and the Death of Christ* (London: SPCK, 1975), 88–95.

12

Righteous Bloodshed, Matthew's Passion Narrative, and the Temple's Destruction

Lamentations as a Matthean Intertext

Jesus's so-called cry of dereliction in Matthew 27:46 serves as the climactic finale for a series of clear allusions to and citations of Psalm 22 in Matthew's passion narrative. This psalm's extensive presence throughout Matthew's depiction of the crucifixion often leads scholars to conclude that Matthew's use of the phrase "wagging the head" in 27:39 also derives from Psalm 22 (v. 7). Yet this same derisive idiom occurs at several other points in Jewish Scripture,[1] most notably in Lamentations 2:15, a verse that contains language remarkably similar to Matthew 27:39. While many commentators note the resemblance between Matthew and Lamentations at this

I wish to express special thanks to Richard B. Hays and Bart D. Ehrman for their encouragement with respect to various stages of this project and for their thoughtful critiques of this chapter. A version was presented in the Matthew section of the annual meeting of the Society of Biblical Literature in San Antonio, Texas, on November 2004. I am appreciative of those attendees who offered encouragement and critical advice. I also want to thank J. R. Daniel Kirk and my wife, Heather, for her support and willingness to employ her editorial skills proofreading versions of this manuscript.

1. See in LXX: 4 Kgdms. 19:21; Pss. 21:8; 43:15; Job 16:4; Sir. 12:18; 13:7; Isa. 37:22; Jer. 18:16; Lam. 2:15.

point,[2] demonstrating an allusion to Lamentations here has proven elusive. Relatively few scholars posit any actual influence from Lamentations, and even fewer have attempted to explore the implications of such an allusion.[3]

In this chapter I argue that Matthew 27:39 does in fact allude to Lamentations 2:15.[4] I show, moreover, that Matthew explicitly draws on Lamentations in his account of the events leading up to the crucifixion in order to portray Jesus's death as the primary act of righteous bloodshed by the hands of the religious authorities in Jerusalem that results in the destruction of Jerusalem and the temple. To see this, it will be necessary to demonstrate the way in which Matthew employs Lamentations as an important and relatively pervasive intertext[5] in his depiction of Jesus's lament over Jerusalem, trial, and passion (especially in chaps. 23 and 27). If it can be shown that Matthew utilizes Lamentations in this way, then this observation suggests first that the textual

2. For example, W. D. Davies and D. C. Allison think that an allusion to Lamentations here is "probable" (*A Critical and Exegetical Commentary on the Gospel according to Saint Matthew*, ICC [Edinburgh: T&T Clark, 1997], 3:618). D. J. Moo discusses the allusion but thinks that the primary background is Ps. 22. In fact, Moo argues that Ps. 22 aligns so well with the context of Lam. 2:15 that Mark's and Matthew's use of the psalm probably led them to include "those who pass by" from Lam. 2:15 (*The Old Testament in the Gospel Passion Narratives* [Sheffield: Almond Press, 1983], 258).

3. S. L. Graham suggests that the term "passersby" may be an allusion to Lam. 2:15 that calls attention to the "wickedness of those in power [who] caused the [temple's] destruction" ("A Strange Salvation: Intertextual Allusion in Mt 27,39–44," in *The Scriptures in the Gospels*, ed. C. M. Tuckett, BETL 131 [Leuven: Leuven University Press, 1997], 504). M. P. Knowles argues more confidently for the Lamentations allusion, claiming that Matthew's use of the allusion "highlights the mocking of Jesus . . . as having ironic reference to the impending fate of the vaticid[al] Jerusalem" (*Jeremiah in Matthew's Gospel: The Rejected Prophet Motif in Matthean Redaction*, JSNTSup 68 [Sheffield: JSOT Press, 1993], 204). As will become clear, I think Graham and Knowles are correct to see the allusion to Lam. 2:15 here, though neither of them presents a sustained argument for the allusion or for the more extensive role Lamentations itself plays in Matthew's passion narrative.

4. In making this claim I am not suggesting that an allusion to Lam. 2:15 excludes the possibility of an allusion to Ps. 22:7. Matthew may have skillfully crafted a double allusion. For the purposes of this chapter, however, I make a case for the generally overlooked allusion to Lamentations.

5. Graham argues that the term "intertext" goes beyond the term "allusion" in that an intertextual study will note the effects of the recontextualization of an allusion. Methodologically this means that by "thinking intertextually . . . we may be able to see how Matthew appropriates a text, for which Jewish Scriptures provide an important intertext, and turns it to Christian polemical use" ("Strange Salvation," 501–2). This use of the word "intertextuality," as U. Luz has recently pointed out, represents only one of the many ways it can be employed (see especially Luz's very helpful delineation of the various models of intertextual analysis in "Intertexts in the Gospel of Matthew," *HTR* 97 [2004]: 119–37). The kind of intertextual thinking Graham calls for seeks, to use Luz's terms, to identify and analyze "intertexts that are consciously invoked by an author and that are part of the rhetorical strategy of the text" and part of "a specific historical and cultural situation" (122). I here engage in this kind of descriptive, textually oriented study. Thus, by suggesting that Matthew uses Lamentations as an intertext, I mean to say that his allusions function polemically. That is, Matthew finds in Lamentations scriptural warrant for drawing clear connections between the crucifixion of Jesus, the Jewish authorities in Jerusalem, and the destruction of the temple.

variants in Matthew 27:4 and 27:24, in which various manuscripts apply the adjective δίκαιος (righteous) to Jesus, need to be reassessed. Second, and more importantly, recognizing Matthew's use of Lamentations in passages related to and including his passion narrative calls into question the commonly held view that these portions of Matthew represent early Christian anti-Judaism and further corroborates the work of those who have cautioned against jumping too quickly to such an interpretation.[6] Rather than anti-Judaism, Matthew's appeal to Lamentations and thus also to Jeremiah to explain the link between the temple's destruction and Jesus's crucifixion is better characterized as an instance of intra-Jewish polemic deliberately modeled on the prophetic tradition in Jewish Scripture.[7]

Lamentations and the Destruction of Jerusalem in 70 CE

If Lamentations formed a significant part of the "cultural framework" or "encyclopedia"[8] for the Jewish community during the time that Matthew

---

6. See, e.g., A.-J. Levine, *The Social and Ethnic Dimensions of Matthean Salvation History*, Studies in the Bible and Early Christianity 14 (Lewiston, NY: Mellen, 1988). In a later essay on the subject of Matthew and anti-Judaism, Levine states that while the "Gospel of Matthew need not be . . . read as anti-Jewish," the text's christocentric reorientation of Jewish symbols and its orientation toward both Jews and Gentiles leads her to conclude that it represents "more than prophetic polemic" and must ultimately, in her reading, be considered "anti-Jewish" ("Anti-Judaism and the Gospel of Matthew," in *Anti-Judaism and the Gospels*, ed. W. R. Farmer [Harrisburg, PA: Trinity Press International, 1999], 36). As will become apparent, I differ with Levine on this point. In keeping with her persuasive conclusion that Matthew's polemic is aimed primarily at figures in positions of authority (see *Social and Ethnic Dimensions* and, to a lesser degree, "Anti-Judaism and the Gospels," 27–35), I demonstrate that Matthew's constant critique of the religious leadership of his day follows directly from his understanding of prophetic polemic. Jewish prophecy provides him with a scriptural paradigm for criticizing Jewish religious leadership, particularly in the face of the destruction of Jerusalem and the temple. Naturally this critique places him at odds with some forms of Judaism, but it seems to me to make more sense to locate the logic of this polemic within the framework of Jewish prophetic discourse than to suggest that Matthew has moved beyond the bounds of Judaism as he knows it.

7. E. P. Sanders points out that Psalms of Solomon provides one example of Jews criticizing other Jews, and especially Jewish religious authorities, in the Second Temple period ("Reflections on Anti-Judaism in the New Testament and in Christianity," in Farmer, *Anti-Judaism and the Gospels*, 268–69). Sanders highlights Pss. Sol. 8:9–22 and labels the critique found there "intra-Jewish sectarian polemic" (269). I would also draw attention to Pss. Sol. 2, which establishes links between the sins of religious leaders in Jerusalem and the temple's desecration (2:3–4) and, intriguingly, appears to echo Lamentations (compare Pss. Sol. 2:11 and 2:19–21 with Lam. 2:15 and 2:1–4, respectively). In any event, I suggest that Matthew's polemic against the religious leadership, and especially the links he makes between what he takes to be the sins of those leaders and the destruction of Jerusalem and the temple, makes the most sense when read as a variation on this kind of intra-Jewish polemic.

8. I have taken these terms from U. Eco (see *A Theory of Semiotics* [Bloomington: Indiana University Press, 1979]). With the word "encyclopedia," Eco attempts to capture the kind of

penned his Gospel, then the likelihood increases that Matthew—and those
to whom he wrote—could have known this text well enough for meaningful allusions to the book to be recognized and understood. Since Matthew
probably wrote his Gospel for Jewish Christians after the momentous events
of 70 CE,[9] there is good reason to think that Lamentations would have been
a prominent part of the "encyclopedia" of Matthew's community. After the
destruction of the temple in 70 CE, one would expect mourning Jews to turn
to Lamentations with renewed interest. It would likely be in the religious
cultural "air."[10]

---

competent signification that occurs in the concrete day-to-day environment of a culturally
constructed code of meaning (see 98–100). Competent use of such a code could include, but is
certainly not limited to, activities like making an appropriate utterance in a given language and
a given context. In such instances the speaker can rightfully expect others who are also competent in the code to understand the utterance precisely because the code is a cultural convention.
That is, the meaning of the utterance is dependent on, among other things, the contextual,
circumstantial, and semantic presuppositions that competent users of the code share owing to
what are, in terms of statistical probability, the common experiences, events, facts, beliefs, and
so on that make up the culture in which they all participate (105–12).

This "encyclopedia" model or theory of codes envisions the phenomena of signification
in terms of a "cultural framework" (111–14). For example, a competent user of the English
language living in America in the middle of the first decade of the twenty-first century can
rightfully expect others in her cultural context to understand her when she speaks of "the
events of September the eleventh." This example helpfully illustrates Eco's point, since the
phrase "September the eleventh" is meaningful in the specified social setting because it occurs
within a "cultural framework" shaped, in part, by the events that occurred on that day in 2001.
The location or meaning of the phrase within the "encyclopedia" as it exists on September the
twelfth, 2001, is radically different than it was on September the tenth, 2001. In the latter case,
the phrase most probably denoted the next day in the calendar year (though within a more
localized context it could have denoted the speaker's birthday, dental appointment, etc.). After
September 11, 2001, the place of the phrase "September the eleventh" (or even simply 9/11) in
the "cultural framework" shifts such that it takes on all manner of associations with such previously unrelated things as airplanes, terrorism, New York City, the World Trade Center, fear,
loss, xenophobia, and so on. The term "encyclopedia," then, nicely captures what, in terms of
statistical probability, a competent individual in a given culture at a given time might be expected
to know and thus also to mean when utilizing the code of her social location.

9. See Davies and Allison, *Gospel according to Saint Matthew*, 1:127–33.

10. Eco provides a helpful thought experiment that illustrates how this might work (*Theory
of Semiotics*, 124–26). He describes a box of magnetically charged marbles, where the box represents the "Global Semantic Universe" (or "encyclopedia"), each marble represents a meaningful
unit, and the magnetic charges represent the ordered relationships (or "cultural framework")
pertaining among the units. If the box were to be shaken, the relative positions of the marbles
would be altered more or less dramatically depending on the force with which the box is shaken.
I suggest that Lamentations and the temple are two of the "marbles" that one can rightly expect
to have been present within the "box" that existed for most Jews in Matthew's time (and perhaps
for almost any Jew living at any point after Lamentations was penned). These two marbles were
likely to have already been strongly attracted to each other and so probably lay relatively close
to one another within the imagined box. I suggest that the destruction of the temple in 70 CE
is exactly the kind of event that would have shaken the box in such a way that these marbles

Two observations support this expectation. First, Josephus provides evidence that after the Romans destroyed Jerusalem, people connected that event with the writings of Jeremiah. In his *Jewish Antiquities* (10.79), Josephus writes of Jeremiah,

οὗτος ὁ προφήτης καὶ τὰ μέλλοντα τῇ πόλει δεινὰ προεκήρυξεν, ἐν γράμμασι καταλιπὼν καὶ τὴν νῦν ἐφ' ἡμῶν γενομένην ἅλωσιν τήν τε Βαβυλῶνος αἵρεσιν

This prophet also publicly proclaimed the sufferings to come to the city [Jerusalem], by leaving behind in writings both the capture [of Jerusalem] that has come about in our time, and the taking [of it] by Babylon. (my translation)

Josephus probably refers here to the book of Lamentations.[11] Yet even if his reference looks more generally to the corpus of Jeremiah, this comment clearly establishes that links were being made between Jeremiah and the first destruction of Jerusalem, on the one hand, and the second destruction in 70 CE, on the other.

Second, while dating traditions found in post–70 CE Jewish literature (e.g., the Targumim, the Talmud) is difficult, in this literature Lamentations is often connected with both the first and the second destructions of Jerusalem. The Targum for Lamentations, for example, identifies clear parallels between Lamentations and the Romans' sack of Jerusalem. In the Targum for Lamentations 1:19, one finds explicit links between the first destruction of Jerusalem and the second.[12] The pertinent section of the verse reads: "When she was delivered into the hands of Nebuchadnezzar, Jerusalem said, 'I called to my friends among the nations, those with whom I had established treaties, to support me. But they deceived me, and turned to destroy me.' These are the Romans who came up with Titus and Vespasian the wicked, and erected siege works against Jerusalem."[13] As with Josephus, the Targum is illustrative of an interpretive move that juxtaposes the first and second destructions of Jerusalem. Additionally, the Targum clearly utilizes Lamentations to facilitate this connection.

---

would be brought into the closest semantic proximity (along with a good many others—e.g., Rome, Titus, and so—that were, prior to that point, much "further away").

11. In the immediate context Josephus has just spoken of the lament Jeremiah composed concerning the death of Josiah. According to R. Marcus, the translator of *Ant.* 10 in the Loeb series, this lament is commonly associated with the book of Lamentations (Josephus, *Jewish Antiquities: Books IX–XI*, trans. R. Marcus, LCL 326 [Cambridge, MA: Harvard University Press, 1937], 200, notes *b* and *c*).

12. Similar connections between Lamentations/Jeremiah, the first destruction of Jerusalem, and the second may be found in Lam. Rab. 39.i.2–4 and Pesiq. Rab. 29.

13. E. Levine, *The Aramaic Version of Lamentations* (New York: Hermon Press, 1976), 65.

Passages such as these exemplify the kinds of readings of Lamentations one would expect after the events of 70 CE, and while these sources do not allow for a conclusive judgment regarding just how early the association was made, it seems reasonable to assume that such a correlation would have arisen during the immediate aftermath of the Romans' razing of Jerusalem. Indeed, it seems likely that neither Josephus nor the Targum make original linkages at this point. Rather, both probably reflect a connection made by Jews struggling to understand the fall of Jerusalem relatively shortly after its devastation. In both cases Lamentations provides Jews reflecting on Jerusalem's demise with a scriptural resource for a theological interpretation of these momentous events.

Lamentations in Matthew's Textual Universe

Having briefly considered the plausibility that Lamentations could have been a significant part of Matthew's cultural encyclopedia, I now turn to the heart of this project—showing that Lamentations forms a significant part of Matthew's textual "universe."[14]

First, of all the Synoptics, only Matthew refers to Jeremiah by name.[15] As Michael Knowles has pointed out, this fact suggests prima facie the importance of Jeremiah for Matthew, particularly when one considers that his references to the prophet are unique to his redaction of the Jesus traditions.[16] Indeed, in his book *Jeremiah in Matthew's Gospel: The Rejected Prophet Motif in Matthean Redaction*, Knowles makes a compelling case that one of the many figures Matthew patterns his narrative on is Jeremiah.[17]

14. S. Alkier, developing a concept he finds in the work of C. S. Peirce, describes the "syntagmatics, semantics and pragmatics of a given text as a world for itself, a possible world" ("From Text to Intertext: Intertextuality as a Paradigm for Reading Matthew," *HTS Teologiese Studies/Theological Studies* 61 [2005]: 1–18, here 3). He labels this possible world the text's "universe of discourse" (3). To speak of Matthew's "textual universe," then, is to make reference to the knowledge of Matthew that one has primarily from a text-internal analysis. The reader of Matthew, for example, can be expected to know, or at least strongly anticipate—even before coming to chap. 28—that Jesus will rise from the dead because Jesus's resurrection has been predicted at several earlier points in the text (see 16:21; 17:9, 22–23; 20:18–19; 26:32). Within the universe of Matthew, the reader learns of Jesus's resurrection well before the event occurs within the narrated world of the text.

15. In fact, Matthew is the only book in the New Testament to mention Jeremiah by name; see Matt. 2:17; 16:14; and 27:9.

16. In the first chapter of his book, Knowles argues persuasively that these three references to Jeremiah betray a "unitary redactional purpose" (*Jeremiah in Matthew's Gospel*, 95).

17. Interestingly, Knowles discusses several allusions to Lamentations (especially in Matt. 27:34 and 27:39). Although his arguments are brief and primarily redaction-critical, his conclusions in favor of the presence of allusions to Lamentations in Matt. 27 agree with my own. Lamentations, though, is only a subpoint to his larger concern—showing that Matthew patterns Jesus's life on Jeremiah in order to portray his death as yet another example of Jerusalem killing the prophets and therefore falling under judgment.

The observation that Matthew partially patterns his Gospel on Jeremiah does not by itself prove that he also alludes to Lamentations or uses the book intertextually. Yet the fact that Lamentations was assumed during the Second Temple period to be one of several works written by Jeremiah,[18] coupled with Matthew's explicit use of the Jeremian motif, further increases the likelihood that he knew and could have utilized Lamentations in his Gospel.

Lamentations as an Intertext in Matthew 23 and 27

With these points in mind, I now examine some specific texts in Matthew in order to demonstrate that Matthew both alludes specifically to Lamentations and employs the book intertextually in order to establish biblically his conviction that Jesus's crucifixion led to the temple's destruction.

One of Matthew's clearest allusions to Lamentations occurs at the end of his account of Jesus's pronouncement of woes on the religious authorities of Jerusalem in chapter 23. Matthew 23:35 reads:

> ὅπως ἔλθῃ ἐφ' ὑμᾶς πᾶν αἷμα δίκαιον ἐκχυννόμενον ἐπὶ τῆς γῆς ἀπὸ τοῦ αἵματος Ἅβελ τοῦ δικαίου ἕως τοῦ αἵματος Ζαχαρίου υἱοῦ Βαραχίου, ὃν ἐφονεύσατε μεταξὺ τοῦ ναοῦ καὶ τοῦ θυσιαστηρίου

> So that all the righteous blood that has been shed upon the land may come upon you, from the blood of righteous Abel to the blood of Zechariah the son of Barachiah, whom you murdered between the temple and the altar.

The phrase πᾶν αἷμα δίκαιον ἐκχυννόμενον (all the righteous blood that has been shed) is particularly interesting for the purposes of this chapter. The exact phrase αἷμα δίκαιον occurs three times in the Septuagint: Joel 4:19; Jonah 1:14; and Lamentations 4:13. Curiously, the marginal cross-reference list for this phrase in NA[27] fails to note Lamentations 4:13 as a possible allusion.[19] This is a striking oversight in light of the fact that not only do Matthew 23:35 and Lamentations 4:13 share exact lexical and formal correspondence (i.e., the phrase αἷμα δίκαιον), but both texts also collocate αἷμα δίκαιον with a form of the verb ἐκχέω/ἐκχύννω. Of the three Septuagint texts I have noted, only Joel 4:19 and Lamentations 4:13 contain this collocation.[20] If, however,

---

18. See, e.g., the Septuagint's explicit identification of Jeremiah as the author of Lamentations, an identification not found in our extant Hebrew manuscripts of Lam. 1:1.

19. All of the prior editions also fail to make any mention in the marginal notes of the similarity between Lam. 4:13 and Matt. 23:35. I note, further, that no reference to Lam. 4:13 has been added to Matt. 23:35 even in the more recent NA[28].

20. Though see also Prov. 6:17, which contains the very similar phrase ἐκχέουσαι αἷμα δικαίου.

Matthew alludes to the Jewish Scriptures at all in 23:35, one would hope to find more than lexical and formal correspondence with the suspected source of the allusion. Interestingly, of these two passages, Lamentations 4:13 also shares themes that align closely with the context of Matthew 23–24.

Lamentations 4:13 addresses one of the main issues that the book is so concerned to deal with—the reason for the destruction of Jerusalem by the Babylonians. The answer offered in 4:13 is this:

ἐξ ἁμαρτιῶν προφητῶν αὐτῆς ἀδικιῶν ἱερέων αὐτῆς τῶν ἐκχεόντων αἷμα δίκαιον ἐν μέσῳ αὐτῆς

because of the sins of her prophets and her unrighteous priests, those who shed righteous blood in her midst.

By placing the phrase τῶν ἐκχεόντων αἷμα δίκαιον (those who shed righteous blood) in apposition to ἀδικιῶν ἱερέων αὐτῆς (her unrighteous priests), the Greek translation of Lamentations singles out the act of shedding righteous blood, particularly on the part of the religious leadership, as one of the primary reasons that judgment fell upon Jerusalem in 586 BCE.

In Matthew 23:1–24:2 Jesus, while in the temple, pronounces a series of woes upon the religious leaders in Jerusalem that culminate in his declaration that all the righteous blood shed from Abel to Zechariah will come upon that generation. That this pronouncement of judgment has the destruction of Jerusalem and the temple behind it becomes clear when Jesus (who, in the context of Matthew, is the Immanuel/"God with us," see 1:23) "laments" over Jerusalem in 23:37, claims that the temple will be left desolate in 23:38, and then embodies the departure of the Shekinah from "that house" by walking out of the temple in 24:1.[21] The import of this episode is immediately explained in Matthew 24:2—the temple, and by implication the city in which it sits, will be destroyed.

There are, then, three themes in this context that align remarkably well with Lamentations 4:13: the condemnation of the religious leadership of Jerusalem, the accusation that the religious authorities have shed righteous blood, and the connection between the shedding of that blood and the destruction of Jerusalem and the temple. This means Matthew 23:35 and Lamentations 4:13 share not only lexical and formal agreement but also thematic agreement.

Yet, beyond the striking thematic and lexical similarities, a third factor points to an allusion to Lamentations 4:13 at Matthew 23:35. Specifically,

---

21. So D. B. Howell, *Matthew's Inclusive Story: A Study in the Narrative Rhetoric of the First Gospel*, JSNTSup 42 (Sheffield: JSOT Press, 1990), 153.

Jewish interpretive traditions of Lamentations also link the story of the murder of Zechariah with the destruction of the temple and Jerusalem.

For example, Lamentations Rabbah makes this association at various places throughout the book of Lamentations. Intriguingly, one of the passages where Zechariah receives special mention is Lamentations 4:13. At one point (see Lam. Rab. 113.i.1–2) the comments on 4:13 center on where in the temple Zechariah was killed. It is important to point out that Lamentations Rabbah consistently identifies this Zechariah with Zechariah son of Jehoiada, whose stoning in the temple is related in 2 Chronicles 24:21. At first glance this would seem to be a different individual than the Zechariah mentioned in Matthew 23:35, since Matthew identifies him as the υἱοῦ Βαραχίου, "son of Barachiah" (an apparent reference to the postexilic prophet of the book of Zechariah, who is identified in Zechariah 1:1 LXX as τὸν τοῦ Βαραχίου υἱόν, "the son of Barakiah"). Additionally, while Lamentations Rabbah does at times mention the destruction of both the first and second temples (e.g., Lam. Rab. 39.i.2–4), the account of Zechariah's death is always associated with Nebuchadnezzar's destruction of the first temple. Thus, Lamentations Rabbah appears to refer to a different Zechariah than the one mentioned in Matthew.

Nevertheless, the confusion evident in Jewish traditions surrounding the identity of the Zechariah who was stoned in the temple is well known,[22] and other interpretations of Lamentations that mention Zechariah's death appear to make the same identification of Zechariah as the postexilic prophet that Matthew does. For instance, at one point in the Targum of Lamentations, the speaker challenges YHWH to consider whether it is right for him to bring such suffering on his people as has been brought upon them during the siege and sack of Jerusalem (see Tg. Lam. 2:20). YHWH's "Attribute of Justice" replies, "Is it right to kill priest and prophet in the Temple of YHWH, as you killed Zechariah son of Iddo (זכריה בר עדוא), the High Priest and faithful prophet, in the Temple of YHWH on the Day of Atonement, because he reproached you, that you refrain from evil before YHWH?"[23]

The name זכריה בר עדוא is clearly the Aramaic for the postexilic prophet named זכריה בן־עדו (Zech. 1:1). But Zechariah 1:1 describes this prophet as both the son of Berekiah and the son of Iddo. The Targum of Lamentations, then, apparently identifies Zechariah as the postexilic prophet just as Matthew does.

Based on the way the Targum conflates the first and second destructions of the Jerusalem temple (Tg. Lam. 1:19), it likely refers here to the destruction

---

22. Davies and Allison point out that Zechariah the priest (2 Chron. 24) and Zechariah the prophet (Zech. 1:1) tend to be conflated in Jewish tradition (*Gospel according to Saint Matthew*, 3:318–19).

23. E. Levine, *Aramaic Version of Lamentations*, 68.

of the second temple since Zechariah son of Iddo was a postexilic prophet. If this is the case, then both Matthew and the Targum on Lamentations connect the destruction of the Jerusalem temple in 70 CE with the death of the same Zechariah, the postexilic prophet.

Yet, regardless of whether the Targum has 586 BCE or 70 CE in mind, the main point of interest is that its interpretive tradition exemplifies the same connections between the death of a Zechariah, the destruction of Jerusalem and the temple, and the book of Lamentations that are also evident in Lamentations Rabbah. Although dating the traditions in this literature is difficult, it seems likely that these links go back at least to the first century CE, since the connection between the motifs of Zechariah's death and the destruction of the temple also finds attestation in the Gospel of Matthew. Moreover, it seems unlikely that the links made in the Targum of Lamentations and in Lamentations Rabbah stem from a dependence on the Gospel of Matthew. It is more probable that the Targum, Lamentations Rabbah, and Matthew give incidental witness to a tradition of Jewish exegetical commentary that linked Lamentations, the story of Zechariah's death, and the destruction of Jerusalem and the temple prior to and independently of all of them.

If this is the case, then the combination in Matthew 23:35–24:2 of the mention of Zechariah's death; the destruction of Jerusalem and the temple; and the lexical, formal, and thematic links with Lamentations make it virtually certain that Matthew is actually alluding to Lamentations 4:13 in Matthew 23:35.

This is significant, given that in the context of Matthew 23–24, the allusion to Lamentations serves to provide scriptural warrant and general justification for the predicted judgment—namely, the destruction of Jerusalem and the temple—that will come upon the religious authorities of Jerusalem whom Jesus addresses. Yet as Matthew's story develops (especially in Matt. 27), he clearly uses Lamentations 4:13 as an intertext to further this broader agenda. In Matthew 23:35 he employs the themes introduced by the Lamentations allusion to frame the crucifixion of Jesus so as to present this moment as the act of righteous bloodshed par excellence.

At three key points in Matthew 27, the author clearly uses language reminiscent of 23:35 and the allusion to Lamentations 4:13. In this way, Matthew employs the themes and warnings evoked by the Lamentations allusion to portray Jesus as a righteous individual whose death, by implication, will bring judgment upon Jerusalem and the temple.

The first of these points occurs in Matthew 27:19 when Pilate's wife urges him to have nothing to do with τῷ δικαίῳ ἐκείνῳ (that righteous man). Here Jesus is explicitly described with the same terms used to describe Abel and the blood that was shed in 23:35—δίκαιος (righteous). Through his account of Pilate's wife's dream, Matthew informs his readers that Pilate's wife saw more than those calling for Jesus's crucifixion—shedding the blood of this righteous man will have disastrous consequences.

The second point in Matthew 27 that echoes 23:35 occurs during Pilate's show of washing his hands in order to distance himself from the act of crucifying Jesus. Here Pilate claims, ἀθῷός εἰμι ἀπὸ τοῦ αἵματος τούτου (I am innocent of the blood of this man; Matt. 27:24). Again, the idea of Jesus's blood, particularly in a context where Jesus has been described as "righteous," effectively brings 23:35 back to the reader's mind.

The third point in Matthew 27 that looks back to 23:35 is found in the people's response to Pilate in 27:25. While Pilate claims no responsibility for Jesus's death, Matthew comments that all the people replied, τὸ αἷμα αὐτοῦ ἐφ' ἡμᾶς καὶ ἐπὶ τὰ τέκνα ἡμῶν (his blood be upon us and upon our children). The language of "blood" coming "upon" those who are in Jerusalem seems to echo plainly the language of 23:35. The reader who has already perceived the resonance of 23:35–24:2 earlier in chapter 27 cannot fail to see the point here—Jesus's death is the kind of act that Lamentations suggests brings God's judgment against Jerusalem and its temple. Thus, the statement of Matthew 27:25 brings to a climax a motif that has run right through this chapter[24]— Jesus's death is an act of shedding righteous blood. With the background of Lamentations in mind, it is clear that this act will result in the desolation of Jerusalem and the temple. The point is driven home when, in what in this context must prefigure the coming judgment, the temple veil is ripped in two when Jesus dies (Matt. 27:51).[25]

By portraying Jesus as a righteous man in Matthew 27, the author recalls the themes of 23:35–24:2. In this way he further employs his earlier allusion to Lamentations in 23:35 to suggest that the shedding of Jesus's blood at the crucifixion becomes the primary reason for the temple's destruction. It is within this framework that Matthew's account of the crucifixion occurs. With this in mind, I propose that Matthew introduces two more allusions to Lamentations during his passion account—one in 27:34 and another in 27:39.

24. Following D. Senior, D. E. Garland suggests that "innocent blood" is the theme of Matt. 27 (D. E. Garland, *The Intention of Matthew 23*, NovTSup 52 [Leiden: Brill, 1979], 185). The only point at which I would quibble with this assessment is the deference shown to the form of the text found in NA[27] by favoring ἀθῷος (innocent) over δίκαιος (righteous). It would be more accurate to speak of the chapter's theme as that of "righteous blood."

25. R. E. Brown also links the rending of the veil with the judgment pronounced in Matt. 23:37–38, though he does not draw attention to the Lamentations allusion in Matt. 23:35 (*The Death of the Messiah: From Gethsemane to the Grave; A Commentary on the Passion Narratives in the Four Gospels*, Anchor Bible Reference Library [New York: Doubleday, 1994], 2:1102).

The common understanding of Matthew 27:34 takes the comment that the soldiers offer Jesus gall to drink as an allusion to Psalm 69:21 (69:22 MT; 68:22 LXX). Joel Marcus provides a good example of the way the case is argued when he speaks of Matthew "embellishing" Mark's account.[26] Here, for instance, Matthew shows his awareness of the broader context of Psalm 69 by "doubling" the allusion to the psalm introduced in Mark's passion narrative at 15:36.[27] In other words, Matthew understands that Mark's comment that Jesus is offered vinegar to drink (Mark 15:36) alludes to Psalm 69:21. This leads him to flesh out Mark's reading by changing the Markan wine mixed with myrrh (Mark 15:23) to wine mixed with gall (Matt. 27:34). Matthew thereby adds yet another allusion to Psalm 69:21 to his passion narrative.

This is a compelling argument, particularly in light of the fact that Matthew makes similar embellishments of Mark's citations of Psalm 22. For example, the words of the onlookers in Matthew 27:43, "He trusts in God; let God deliver him now, if he desires him" (RSV), are not found in Mark and are clearly an additional Matthean citation from Psalm 22. Thus, Matthew undoubtedly does at times embellish Mark's account by adding additional scriptural citations from passages Mark cites.

Yet good reasons may be adduced for concluding that Matthew does not here primarily bring Mark's account more closely in line with Psalm 69, but rather further alludes to Lamentations. First, while Psalm 68:22 LXX does use the word χολή, or "gall," it is interesting that this same word occurs twice in Lamentations (3:15, 19). Second, it is perhaps noteworthy that the form of χολή in Lamentations 3:15 and 3:19 is the same as the form in Matthew (i.e., genitive singular). Psalm 68:22, on the other hand, uses the accusative singular form. Matthew may well have composed his text in such a way that, from a visual and auditory perspective, the very form of the word used in 27:34 would resonate with those who knew the Greek translation of Lamentations well. Third, although such arguments would do little by themselves to establish an allusion, the fact that Lamentations has played such a significant role in the context of Matthew just prior to his passion account suggests that this lexical and formal correspondence might indicate another allusion to Lamentations.[28]

26. J. Marcus, "The Old Testament and the Death of Jesus: The Role of Scripture in the Gospel Passion Narratives," in *The Death of Jesus in Early Christianity*, ed. J. T. Carroll and J. B. Green, with R. E. Van Voorst, J. Marcus, and D. Senior (Peabody, MA: Hendrickson, 1995), 226. Similarly, Davies and Allison, *Gospel according to Saint Matthew*, 3:612–13; R. H. Gundry, *Matthew: A Commentary on His Handbook for a Mixed Church under Persecution*, 2nd ed. (Grand Rapids: Eerdmans, 1994), 569.
27. Marcus, "Death of Jesus," 226–27.
28. Additionally, the fact that Matthew may have already alluded to Lam. 3 earlier in his Gospel should be considered. Lam. 3:30 reads: δώσει τῷ παίοντι αὐτὸν σιαγόνα χορτασθήσεται

Fourth, the case for this allusion grows stronger in light of the fact that there appears to be yet another allusion to Lamentations just four verses later, in 27:39.

In the introduction to this chapter I drew attention to the scholarly consensus that Matthew 27:39 alludes to Psalm 22:7. The general arguments in favor of this conclusion are (1) there are three other very clear references to Psalm 22 in Matthew's passion narrative (Matt. 27:35, 43, 46), and (2) Psalm 22:7 (21:8 LXX) contains the derisive idiom κινεῖν κεφαλήν (to wag the head). Several factors, however, suggest that Matthew alludes primarily to Lamentations 2:15 in verse 39, rather than to Psalm 22:7.

First, Matthew 27:39 has more verbal overlap with Lamentation 2:15 than with Psalm 22:7. In the following comparison, exact agreements between Matthew and Lamentations are underlined in both texts. Similarities between Matthew and Lamentations are italicized. Exact agreement between Lamentations and Psalm 21 LXX are italicized and underlined.

Matthew 27:39	Lamentations 2:15	Psalm 21:8
	Ἐκρότησαν ἐπὶ σὲ	
Οἱ δὲ	χεῖρας *πάντες οἱ*	*πάντες* οἱ θεωροῦντές
παραπορευόμενοι	*παραπορευόμενοι* ὁδόν,	με ἐξεμυκτήρισάν με,
ἐβλασφήμουν αὐτὸν	ἐσύρισαν καὶ	ἐλάλησαν ἐν χείλεσιν,
κινοῦντες τὰς κεφαλὰς	*ἐκίνησαν τὴν κεφαλὴν*	*ἐκίνησαν κεφαλήν*
αὐτῶν	αὐτῶν ἐπὶ τὴν θυγατέρα Ιερουσαλημ	
	Εἰ αὕτη ἡ πόλις,	
	ἣν ἐροῦσιν Στέφανος δόξης,	
	εὐφροσύνη πάσης τῆς γῆς;	

By placing these passages side by side one can see clearly that Matthew 27:39 has far more in common with Lamentations 2:15 lexically and formally than

ὀνειδισμῶν (he will give the cheek to the one who strikes him, he will be sated with insults). Matt. 5:39 presents a similar idea when Jesus exhorts: ὅστις σε ῥαπίζει εἰς τὴν δεξιὰν σιαγόνα [σου], στρέψον αὐτῷ καὶ τὴν ἄλλην ([if] anyone strikes you on your right cheek, turn to him also the other). Davies and Allison point out that the parallel between these two texts was noted at least as early as Origen (*Gospel according to Saint Matthew*, 1:543). If this is an allusion to Lam. 3:30, then it strengthens the case for an allusion to 3:30 at Matt. 27:34 in two ways. First, it shows that Matthew is aware of at least part of Lam. 3, and, particularly in light of his knowledge of Lam. 4:13, it is safe to conclude that he knows more of the chapter. Second, as with Lam. 4:13, Lam. 3:30 may be echoed again later in Matthew when Jesus stands before the Sanhedrin. Matthew's description of Jesus being hit, especially in the face (26:67–68), is highly evocative of Matt. 5:39 and thus also of Lam. 3:30 (interestingly, both Lam. 3:30 and Matt. 26:68 use a form of the verb παίω). If Lam. 3:30 is echoed here, then there is yet another instance of Lamentations playing a role in the context immediately prior to the passion account.

with Psalm 21:8 LXX. Specifically, both use the plural participle οἱ παραπο-
ρευόμενοι (those who pass by), as well as a form of the idiom κινεῖν κεφαλήν
(to wag the head), where κεφαλή (head) is modified by both the article and
the plural pronoun αὐτῶν (their).[29]

Second, beyond mere verbal agreement, the contexts of Matthew 27:39
and Lamentations 2:15 share a theme that is not found in Psalm 22—the
destruction of the temple. The book of Lamentations tends to speak generally about the destruction of Jerusalem. In a handful of places, however, it
specifically addresses the temple's desolation. Lamentations 2 contains two
such passages (see 2:7, 20). For example, 2:7 reads:

ἀπώσατο κύριος θυσιαστήριον αὐτοῦ, ἀπετίναξεν ἁγίασμα αὐτοῦ, συνέτριψεν ἐν
χειρὶ ἐχθροῦ τεῖχος βάρεων αὐτῆς· φωνὴν ἔδωκαν ἐν οἴκῳ κυρίου ὡς ἐν ἡμέρᾳ
ἑορτῆς.

The Lord rejected his altar, he cast off his sanctuary, he shattered the wall of
her palaces by the hand of an enemy, they made a sound in the house of the
Lord as on a festival day.

In short, while 2:15 speaks about the destruction of Jerusalem in general, the
temple's demise is, not surprisingly, clearly in the immediate context.

Additionally, the comments spoken in Matthew 27:40 by "those who pass
by" and "wag their heads" do not derive from Psalm 22. This is somewhat
strange since Psalm 22:7–8 appears to provide a ready-made unit that would
fit the context of Matthew 27:39–40 perfectly. That is, those who are mocking,
hurling insults, and "wagging their heads" in Psalm 22:7 are the very ones
who immediately go on in 22:8 to say, "He trusted in God, let God now rescue
him if he desires him." Matthew clearly does quote Psalm 22:8, but this citation comes three verses later in Matthew 27:43, where he places the words of
Psalm 22:8 in the mouths of the chief priest, scribes, and elders. If Matthew
alludes to Psalm 22 in Matthew 27:39, it is odd that he decouples this allusion from his obvious quotation of Psalm 22:8. It would seem more natural
to have those who "pass by" and "wag their heads" in Matthew 27:39 say in
verse 40 exactly what those who "wag their heads" in Psalm 22:7 say in 22:8.

On the other hand, what the "passersby" do say in Matthew 27:40 picks up
the very theme present in the context of Lamentations 2:15—the destruction
of the temple. Those who pass by and wag their heads at Jesus state:

29. The verbal agreement between Lam. 2:15 and Ps. 21:8 LXX (note ἐκίνησαν κεφαλήν)
may suggest that Lamentations alludes to Ps. 22 (the Hebrew is also nearly identical). Thus, if
there is any cross-pollination between Matt. 27:35 and Ps. 22:7, it may well be present via an
allusion to Ps. 22 on the part of Lam. 2:15.

ὁ καταλύων τὸν ναὸν καὶ ἐν τρισὶν ἡμέραις οἰκοδομῶν, σῶσον σεαυτόν, εἰ υἱὸς εἶ τοῦ θεοῦ, [καὶ] κατάβηθι ἀπὸ τοῦ σταυροῦ.

The one who destroys the temple and in three days rebuilds [it], save yourself, if you are the son of God, and come down from the cross.

This comment, which shares nothing with Psalm 22, coheres perfectly with the context of Lamentations 2:15.

Finally, one should consider that the theme of the temple's destruction fits together well both with the role the allusion to Lamentations 4:13 played in Matthew 23:35–24:2 and with the Matthean context immediately prior to the account of Jesus's crucifixion. Earlier I argued that Matthew uses the theme of righteous bloodshed, and especially the shedding of Jesus's blood, to link the destruction of Jerusalem and the temple with the crucifixion of Jesus. Here the allusion to Lamentations 2:15 reinforces the same point. Unbeknownst to "those who pass by" and "wag their heads" at Jesus, his death, from Matthew's point of view, will lead to the temple's destruction.

When the texts are taken together, the overlap of language between Matthew 27:39 and Lamentations 2:15, the shared theme of the temple's destruction in the contexts of these verses, and the role Lamentations plays in Matthew just prior to his passion narrative establish the presence of an allusion to Lamentations 2:15 in Matthew 27:39.

Reexamining Matthew 27:4 and 27:24

Thus far I have been laying out a case that Matthew anticipates (see 23:35–24:2) and frames his account of Jesus's passion (27:19, 34, and 39) with allusions to Lamentations in order to make the point that Jesus's death at the instigation of the religious establishment stands as the act of righteous bloodshed that becomes the cause of the disastrous events of 70 CE.

If this case is generally sound, then the presence of variants in the manuscript tradition that use language amenable to the overall argument Matthew has constructed is tantalizing. Indeed, a reference to αἷμα δίκαιον (righteous blood) at the very beginning of the passion account would serve Matthew's polemic perfectly, since it would effectively recall to his readers' minds the ominous predictions that were made in chapters 23–24, predictions mediated through the connection in Lamentations of righteous bloodshed by the religious leadership with God's judgment on Jerusalem and the temple.

I have previously highlighted the fact that δίκαιος language indisputably appears in this portion of Matthew's narrative (see 27:19). This observation, particularly when taken together with the presence of other allusions to Lamentations throughout Matthew's passion account and the echo of Matthew 23:35 present in 27:24–25, suggests that Matthew effectively reminds his readers of the earlier allusion to Lamentations and encourages them to connect that allusion with the death of Jesus. It would not, then, be surprising to find him explicitly again using more language that would connect the passion narrative with Matthew 23:35–24:2 and thus with Lamentations. In fact, the manuscript tradition contains two more instances in Matthew 27—verse 4 and verse 24—where language highly evocative of Matthew 23:35 occurs.

In Matthew 27:4 the NA[27] and UBS[4] texts have Judas state, ἥμαρτον παραδοὺς αἷμα ἀθῷον (I have sinned by handing over innocent blood). There is an interesting variant, however, in which Judas says, ἥμαρτον παραδοὺς αἷμα δίκαιον (I have sinned by handing over righteous blood). Explaining the choice of the UBS[4] committee to favor ἀθῷον over δίκαιον, Bruce Metzger comments, "The weight of the external evidence here is strongly in support of ἀθῷον."[30] He goes on to add that on transcriptional terms a scribe would be more likely to make a change in the direction of harmonizing Matthew 27:4 with 23:35 and thus change ἀθῷον to δίκαιον, rather than shift away from δίκαιον to ἀθῷον.[31]

Metzger is correct that the bulk of the external evidence supports the UBS[4] reading. In fact, the only majuscules that support the presence of δίκαιον are the first corrector of B, L, and Θ. These are joined by five of six quotations by Origen,[32] the Latin versions, several Latin fathers,[33] and a handful of other

---

30. B. M. Metzger, *A Textual Commentary on the Greek New Testament*, 2nd ed. (New York: United Bible Societies, 1994), 55.

31. Metzger, *Textual Commentary*; so also D. A. Hagner, *Matthew 14–28*, WBC 33b (Dallas: Word Books, 1995), 811.

32. I found six instances where Origen clearly quotes or alludes to Matt. 27:4. The verse is referred to twice in *Contra Celsum*, and the quotations support αἷμα δίκαιον both times (see M. Borret, *Origen: Contre Celse*, SC 132 [Paris: Latour-Maubourg, 1967], 312). The Latin version of Origen's commentary on Matthew contains four quotations of the verse. Three of these are attested only in Latin and read *iustum* (thereby supporting δίκαιον), while the fourth is found both in the Latin translation and in a Greek fragment. This last quotation is particularly interesting since the Latin translation reads *iustum*, while the corresponding Greek fragment reads αἷμα ἀθῷον (see E. Klostermann, *Origenes Matthäuserklärung, II: Die lateinische Übersetzung Der Commentariorum Series*, Origenes Werke 11, GCS 38 [Leipzig: J. C. Hinrichs, 1933], 247). Given that lemmata are frequently subject to scribal alteration, the discrepancy between the Latin and the Greek is almost certainly indicative of a shift toward a known and preferred reading of the scriptural text in the transmission history of Origen's commentary. It would be difficult to say with certainty whether the shift occurred in the Latin or the Greek version of the commentary. Yet given the total dominance of the δίκαιον variant (in the form of *iustum*) in the Latin tradition (see n. 33 below for more information), one would be justified in being more suspicious of the Latin translation here than of the Greek fragment.

33. The Latin fathers who clearly quote or allude to Matt. 27:4 (see Ambrose, Ambrosiaster, Novatian, Hilary of Poitiers, and Jerome) along with the Latin versions unanimously

versions all of whose renderings suggest that the Greek *Vorlage* upon which their translations were based read αἷμα δίκαιον. On the other hand, numerous majuscules (e.g., ℵ, A, B, C, W, Δ, E, F, G, H, and Σ), minuscules, versions, and Greek fathers[34] attest ἀθῷον. In short, while δίκαιον seems clearly to have prevailed in the Latin tradition, ἀθῷον has much broader and stronger support in terms of numbers of manuscripts and of geographic distribution.

Yet in spite of this external evidence, good reasons can be adduced in support of reading δίκαιον instead of ἀθῷον at Matthew 27:4. First, Origen's *Contra Celsum* provides the earliest external attestation, and it is clear that, in this text at least, Origen knows αἷμα δίκαιον in Matthew 27:4.[35] This places the reading in Palestine not later than the middle of the third century. When coupled with the attestation of the Latin witnesses, the reading is shown to carry some significant support in terms of both age and geographic distribution.

Second, Matthew uses δίκαιος with relative frequency.[36] Excluding 27:4, ἀθῷος only occurs once in Matthew (27:24). Matthew, then, is more likely to have used δίκαιος than ἀθῷος.

Third, when one stops to consider what a scribe might have been likely to do, it is surely significant that the collocation of a form of αἷμα and a form of ἀθῷος is more common biblical language than the collocation of αἷμα and δίκαιος. Both phrases occur in the Septuagint, but the former collocation outnumbers the latter by more than five to one.[37] Given the relatively low number of occurrences of αἷμα together with δίκαιος, it seems more likely that a scribe familiar with biblical language would gravitate toward the more common phrasing of αἷμα plus ἀθῷος.

The probability that this happened in Matthew 27:4 increases dramatically when one considers the attribution of the account of Judas's returning the

---

read *sanguinem iustum*. This suggests that the Latin tradition is based on a *Vorlage* that read δίκαιον rather than ἀθῷον.

34. The UBS[4] apparatus lists Origen 1/4, Eusebius, Cyril of Jerusalem, Epiphanius, Chrysostom, Hesychius, and Maximus. I was unable to find any reference to the verse in Hesychius, but I have personally confirmed the presence of ἀθῷος in the other fathers listed in the UBS apparatus (the four references in Origen, however, should be modified to six, because δίκαιος is attested twice in Greek and four times in Latin, with the corresponding Greek fragment of one of the Latin citations reading ἀθῷον—see n. 32 above).

35. See n. 32 above.

36. In addition to the verse in question, Matthew uses the adjective seventeen times: 1:19; 5:45; 9:13; 10:41 (3x); 13:17, 43, 49; 20:4; 23:28, 29, 35 (2x); 25:37, 46; 27:19.

37. The collocation of αἷμα and ἀθῷος shows up a total of twenty-one times in the following LXX texts: Deut. 27:25; 1 Kgdms. 19:5; 25:26, 31; 3 Kgdms. 2:5; 4 Kgdms. 21:16; 24:4 (2x); 2 Chron. 36:5 (2x); Esther 8:12; 1 Macc. 1:37; 2 Macc. 1:8; Pss. 93:21; 105:38; Jer. 2:34; 7:6; 19:4; 22:3, 17; 33:15. As previously noted, the collocation of αἷμα and δίκαιος occurs only four times in LXX: Prov. 6:17; Joel 4:19; Jon. 1:14; and Lam. 4:13.

money with its biblical citation to Jeremiah in Matthew 27:9–10. Davies and Allison point out that there are a number of points of contact in Matthew 27:3–10 with passages such as Zechariah 11:12–14 as well as Jeremiah 18, 19, and 32.[38] Interestingly, of the twenty-one instances of the collocation of αἷμα and ἀθῷος in the Septuagint, six of them occur in Jeremiah (cf. 2:34; 7:6; 19:4; 22:3, 17; 33:15). In view of the attribution of the biblical quotation in Matthew 27:9 to Jeremiah, it seems entirely possible that a scribe might attempt to harmonize the relatively rare αἷμα δίκαιον of Matthew 27:4 to the better known and more frequent language in Jeremiah. Since the entire story of Judas returning the money to the religious authorities is attributed by Matthew to Jeremiah, one can well understand why an early scribe might gravitate toward the more common phrasing in Jeremiah (i.e., αἷμα ἀθῷον) and effectively bring the account more closely in line with the language of the Matthean attribution.

Fourth, bearing all these points in mind, it is surely significant that the presence of δίκαιος language at exactly this place in Matthew's narrative makes excellent sense in light of the connections I have shown above between Lamentations, righteous bloodshed by the hands of the Jewish religious leadership, Jesus's crucifixion, and the temple's destruction.

In Matthew 27:1–9 Judas seeks to return the money he received from the religious leaders for betraying Jesus. The mention of blood in 27:4, the emphasis placed on the religious leadership, and the reference to Jeremiah in Matthew 27:9 all serve to bring the warnings of chapters 23–24, and especially the allusion to Lamentations in 23:35, back to mind. Given this apparent echo of 23:35, it seems on the whole more likely that the harmony evident between the variant reading αἷμα δίκαιον of Matthew 27:4 and the αἷμα δίκαιον of Matthew 23:35 was in fact what Matthew wrote and, contra Metzger, not the result of scribal ingenuity.[39]

---

38. Davies and Allison, *Gospel according to Saint Matthew*, 3:558–59.

39. This point is bolstered somewhat by the lack of evidence that the fathers were making connections between Matt. 23:35 and 27:4 or between Matt. 27 and Lamentations. I found no references to Lam. 4:13 in relation to Matt. 27 in the *Biblia Patristica*. Nor did any of my work in the fathers' quotations of Matthew suggest that they were making links to Lamentations. I found only one instance in which a father connects Matt. 23 and 27. Hilary of Poitiers— whose text is among the few that, like L, demonstrably attest the presence of δίκαιος/*iustus* in 27:4 and 27:24 (see also Ambrose and Jerome)—links 27:24 and 23:35 while commenting on Ps. 57. Hilary writes, "And these are people of blood, for the blood of all who were slain from Abel until Zechariah is demanded of them and, when washing his hands, they were declaring to Pilate the blood of the righteous one to be upon them and theirs" (my translation; Hilary's Latin: "Adeo autem hi uiri sanguinum sunt, ut omnium ab Abel usque ad Zachariam interfectorum ab his sanguis sit reposcendu et abluente manus suas Pilato super se suosque esse iusti sanguinem sint professi"; see A. Zingerle, *S. Hilarii Episcopi Pictauiensis: Tractatus Super Psalmos*, CSEL 22 [Leipzig: G. Freytag, 1891], 180). The mention of Pilate's handwashing

Additionally, it would make good sense in 27:4 for Matthew to have Judas use the language of 23:35. The presence of αἷμα δίκαιον in 27:4 would serve at least two functions. First, since this is toward the beginning of the passion narrative, it provides a clear point of contact between the warning given in chapters 23–24 and the act of killing Jesus. Since Matthew continues to reference Lamentations throughout his passion narrative, such a move prompts readers to begin thinking again of 23:35 and thus also of Lamentations. Second, Judas's comments would serve as an obvious warning to the religious leaders that the course they are embarking on will bring about the temple's destruction. In other words, this is a polemic. Such a warning, with its implicit appeal to the very themes from Lamentations that Matthew has previously stressed, leads the reader to view the leaders as being without excuse. Yet instead of taking this warning seriously, Matthew has them curtly respond to Judas, σὺ ὄψῃ (you see [to it]).

In sum, when viewed in light of the case I have laid out in support of Matthew's use of Lamentations as an intertext to portray Jesus's death as the shedding of righteous blood par excellence, the evidence from intrinsic probability strongly suggests that, in spite of the external evidence, good warrant exists for concluding that the variant attested by the corrector of B, L, Θ and by the Latin tradition is the original reading of Matthew 27:4. That is, given that (1) the effect of the variant is both to connect the death of Jesus with the prediction/warning of Matthew 23:35–24:2 and thus with the allusion to Lamentations and to implicate the Jewish leaders in Jerusalem in the shedding of this righteous blood and thus lay the blame for the temple's destruction at their feet, and that (2) these effects cohere perfectly with the broader argument Matthew is constructing both before (see 23:35) and during his passion narrative (see 27:19, 25, 34, and 39), it seems much more likely that this variant belonged to Matthew's original text than that a scribe modified the text in such a way that these connections were further emphasized.

Similar points may be made with respect to the variant found in Matthew 27:24. Here the NA[27] and UBS[4] texts have Pilate respond to the request that Jesus be crucified by stating, ἀθῷός εἰμι ἀπὸ τοῦ αἵματος τούτου· ὑμεῖς ὄψεσθε (I am innocent of the blood of this one, you see to it). There is, however, solid manuscript evidence in which Pilate replies, ἀθῷός εἰμι ἀπὸ τοῦ αἵματος τοῦ δικαίου τούτου· ὑμεῖς ὄψεσθε (I am innocent of the blood of this righteous one, you see to it).

---

as a testimony regarding Jesus's just blood (found only in Matt. 27:24) and the collocation of the just blood of Abel and Zechariah (found in Matt. 23:35) demonstrate that Hilary is reading these two texts together.

As with Matthew 27:4, the editors of the NA²⁷ and UBS⁴ chose not to include the variant for two main reasons. First, some early and strong external evidence excludes the phrase τοῦ δικαίου. For example, B, D, and Θ, as well as some of the Latin manuscripts and other versions, exemplify a text without this variant. Additionally, the earliest witnesses such as Eusebius and Novatian, as well as several later fathers like Ambrosiaster, Basil the Great, and Chrysostom, show no knowledge of the qualifier δίκαιος.⁴⁰ Metzger also points out that "the best representatives of the Alexandrian and Western texts" do not attest the variant.⁴¹ Second, at the transcriptional level, Metzger judges that the textual plus is probably "an accretion intended to accentuate Pilate's protestation of Jesus's innocence."⁴² Nevertheless, several points can be put forward that, especially when taken together, tip the balance in favor of the original status of τοῦ δικαίου in 27:24.

First, this longer variant is not without strong external support. The phrase τοῦ δικαίου τούτου is read in the majuscules ℵ, L (the only majuscule to have a form of δίκαιος in both v. 4 and v. 24), W, E, F, G, H, and Σ. Multiple minuscules including ƒ¹, ƒ¹³, 33, and a host of representatives from the majority text also support its presence. Additionally, several Greek and Latin Fathers such as Ambrose, Cyril of Jerusalem, Jerome, Maximus of Turin, and Hilary of Poitiers attest this variant.⁴³ Finally, a similar variant involving a simple transposition reads τούτου τοῦ δικαίου and is attested by A, Δ, and some Latin witnesses.⁴⁴

Second, the omission of τοῦ δικαίου in Matthew 27:24 can be easily accounted for as an instance of parablepsis occasioned either by homoioteleuton or homoioarcton. If the original text read ἀπὸ τοῦ αἵματος τοῦ δικαίου τούτου,

40. For Eusebius, see J. B. Pitra, *Analecta Sacra Spicilegio Solemensi Parata* (Venice: Mechitartistorum Sancti Lazari, 1883; repr., Farnborough: Gregg Press, 1966), 3:415; for Novatian, see G. F. Diercks, *Novatiani Opera*, CCL 4 (Turnhout: Brepols, 1972), 269; for Ambrosiaster, see H. J. Vogels, *Ambrosiastri Qui Dicitur Commentarius in Epistulas Paulinas: In Epistulas ad Corinthios*, CSEL 81.2 (Vienna: Hölder-Pichler-Tempsky Kg., 1968), 25; for Basil, see Y. Courtonne, *Saint Basile: Lettres* (Paris: Belles Lettres, 1966), 3:64; for Chrysostom, see PG 58:765.
41. Metzger, *Textual Commentary*, 56–57.
42. Metzger, *Textual Commentary*, 57.
43. For Ambrose, see M. Petschenig, *Sancti Ambrosii Opera: Explanatio Psalmorum XII*, CSEL 64 (Leipzig: G. Freytag, 1919), 393; for Cyril of Jerusalem, see *Cyrilli Hierosolymorum archiepiscopi Opera quae supersunt omnia*, ed. W. C. Reischl and J. Rupp, CPG 3585/2 (Hildesheim: Olms, 1967), 2:54; for Jerome, see D. Hurst and M. Adriaen, *S. Hieronumi Presbuteri Opera*, 1.7, CCL 77 (Turnhout: Brepols, 1969), 266; for Maximus of Turin, see A. Mutzenbecher, *Maxmi Episcopi Taurinensis*, CCL 23 (Turnhout: Brepols, 1962), 228; for Hilary of Poitiers, see Zingerle, *S. Hilarii Episcopi Pictauiensis*, 180.
44. The fuller list of witnesses found in the NA²⁷ apparatus shows the reading supported by ℵ L W ƒ¹,¹³ 33 𝔐 lat syᵖ·ʰ saᵐˢˢ mae bo. Additionally the reading τούτου τοῦ δικαίου occurs in A Δ *pc* aur f and h, while τοῦ δικαίου is read in 1010 *pc* and boᵐˢ.

one can see how the string of genitive endings in τοῦ δικαίου τούτου might have led to the accidental loss of τοῦ δικαίου by way of homoioteleuton. On the other hand, one can just as easily see how the presence of the initial τοῦ and the τούτου might have led a scribe to skip the phrase inadvertently by way of homoioarcton. In either case, the shorter reading adopted by NA[27] (i.e., ἀπὸ τοῦ αἵματος τούτου) is easily explained. Indeed, such a hypothesis would well explain the data one finds in the manuscript tradition. The longer reading found in ℵ and L more readily explains the existence of both the manuscripts that contain the elements τοῦ δικαίου and τούτου in inverted order, and those manuscripts that read only τοῦ δικαίου,[45] than does the hypothesis that the shorter reading is original.

Third, a few points as regards internal evidence stand in favor of the presence of τοῦ δικαίου in Matthew 27:24.[46] As previously noted, the term δίκαιος is not uncommon in Matthew.[47] Yet this point proves even more poignant here, since the term fits the immediate context so well. In Matthew 27:19 Pilate's wife has just described Jesus as "that righteous man." There is, then, good internal justification for Pilate to refer to Jesus in the same terms; that is, as τοῦ δικαίου τούτου, "this righteous man."

Fourth, intrinsic probability once again suggests this variant is not, contra Metzger, a scribal accretion heightening Jesus's cachet but rather an original part of Matthew's Gospel. In Matthew 27:24 Pilate washes his hands to indicate his innocence with regard to Jesus's death. He then lays the responsibility for crucifying Jesus squarely on the religious authorities by using the very words they spoke to Judas in 27:4 against them: ὑμεῖς ὄψεσθε (you see [to it]). Given the connection made in chapter 27 between verse 4 and verse 24 by having Pilate mimic the words of the Jewish religious authorities, and given the larger argument linking righteous bloodshed and the temple's destruction in Matthew, it would make perfect sense for Matthew to have Pilate describe Jesus as δίκαιος. If Matthew originally did have Pilate speak of Jesus as a "righteous" man, then, in light of Matthew's allusions to Lamentations, the implication of Pilate's comments is perfectly clear—Jesus's death will result in the temple's destruction. Again, such a warning serves to heighten the culpability of the Jewish leaders in Jerusalem in the eyes of the reader.

I would add that it is surely no accident that in the face of this second warning Matthew presents the response of the people in 27:25 not only in

---

45. See n. 44 above for a summary of the manuscript tradition for these readings.

46. Garland comments that the internal evidence is strong enough to conclude that the phrase is original, though he fails to mount an argument (*Intention of Matthew 23*, 185).

47. Gundry, who also thinks δίκαιος belongs in the text, sums all this up nicely when he states, "Matthew has a penchant for δίκαιος" (*Matthew*, 565).

terms reminiscent of 23:35 and the allusion to Lamentations found there but also in terms of full culpability in the death of Jesus.[48]

To summarize, if, as I have tried to show, Matthew employs Lamentations to construct an argument that (1) links the shedding of righteous blood on the part of the religious leaders with the destruction of the temple and (2) presents Jesus's crucifixion as the act of shedding righteous blood par excellence, then it would make perfect sense for him to use δίκαιος language precisely at points like 27:4 and 27:24, where one or more of these elements is being emphasized.

Conclusion

In this chapter I have argued that Matthew alludes to Lamentations three times in chapters 23 and 27 of his Gospel (23:35; 27:34; 27:39). The fact that these allusions come from Lamentations 2, 3, and 4, that the allusion to Lamentations 4:13 resonates throughout the scenes that immediately precede the crucifixion (cf. Matt. 27:19, 24–25), and that the allusion to Lamentations 2:15 is so closely related thematically to the way Matthew uses Lamentations 4:13, all suggest that Matthew has employed Lamentations as a significant intertext. The allusions to Lamentations function as scriptural warrant for interpreting certain historical events theologically and polemically—namely, for understanding Jesus's crucifixion as the act of righteous bloodshed par excellence that directly results in the destruction of Jerusalem and the temple.

If these arguments are basically sound, I suggest further that the variants in the textual tradition at Matthew 27:4 and 27:24 that contain δίκαιος should, mainly on the grounds of intrinsic probability, be considered original and thus restored to our eclectic text. The reading of L, while singular among the majuscules, attests the reading that both coheres well with Lamentations' role in Matthew's passion narrative and best explains the existence of the variants in 27:4 and 27:24.

---

48. One might object that Matthew has all Jews in view here, not only the religious leaders of Jerusalem. The link, though, between Matt. 27:24 and 27:4, coupled with the fact that Matthew explicitly blames the religious leaders for agitating the crowd (27:20), suggests that even here Matthew still has the religious leaders squarely in mind. On this point see especially A.-J. Levine, who argues persuasively that the key contrasts and tensions in Matthew's Gospel run along the social axis and not the ethnic axis. She points out, for example, that the common people are described as being like sheep without a shepherd (9:36). Part of the tension in the Gospel, then, turns on who will be the rightful shepherd of the people. Thus, one of the main points of conflict in Matthew is between the leaders, who are attempting to lead the people, and Jesus, who, as the Messiah, is the one appointed by prophecy (2:6) to shepherd the people (*Social and Ethnic Dimensions*, 94–104, 215–22, 261–71).

More significantly, though, it follows from my argument that Matthew's link between Jesus's crucifixion and the temple's destruction cannot simply be assumed to reflect anti-Judaism in Matthew. Too often Matthew has been read anachronistically such that later uses of this Gospel in anti-Jewish polemic are simply assumed to be in keeping with the original meaning of the text. Yet Matthew's allusion to Lamentations, especially because his appeal to this text both focuses the blame for shedding Jesus's righteous blood on the Jewish leaders in Jerusalem and provides a scriptural paradigm for interpreting and explaining the events of 70 CE, suggests that one cannot simply assume Matthew's claims are anti-Jewish. Matthew's appeal to Lamentations makes it far more likely that he envisions himself speaking a prophetic word. In chapters 23 and 27, Matthew engages in intra-Jewish conversation by polemically patterning his critique of the Jewish religious leadership in Jerusalem on the Jewish prophetic tradition—an interpretive move that bears remarkable resemblance to the one made in the Targum for Lamentations.

Matthew's claim that Jesus's death at the instigation of the religious leaders led to the temple's destruction is no more an invective against Judaism than is the similar accusation made in the Targum. Like the Targum, Matthew has creatively applied a theological paradigm for interpreting the destruction of the temple provided in Jewish prophetic Scriptures (specifically, that the sin and failure of Jewish religious leadership has catastrophic results for Jerusalem and the temple) to a contemporary situation he finds strikingly similar to the one in Lamentations. In this way, Matthew, albeit in light of his conviction that Jesus is the Messiah, is, like so many of the prophets before him, calling his kinfolk to repent if they would truly possess the kingdom.

13

The Sign of Jonah and the Prophet Motif in the Gospel of Matthew

Moving toward the Gentile Mission

Scholars have long recognized that the Gospel of Matthew uses the critical voice of the prophets as a model for portraying Jesus's ministry.[1] In particular, Matthew's appeal to the prophets anchors Jesus's critique of the Jewish religious leaders and their hostile response to Jesus and his followers (e.g., Matt. 5:12; 23:29–34). One of the more enigmatic prophetic references in the Gospel is that of "the sign of Jonah the prophet" (12:39; 16:4). A host of proposals have been advanced to explain the link between Jonah's stay in the belly of the fish for three days and three nights and the Son of Man's dwelling three days and nights in the heart of the earth. Interpreters often wonder how this response addresses the request of the scribes and Pharisees for a sign (12:38).

Explanations for what Matthew took to be the content of this sign range from the most prominent view, that the sign alludes primarily to Jesus's death and resurrection on the third day,[2] to less well-accepted conclusions that Jesus

---

1. Not only does Matthew repeatedly emphasize ways in which events related to Jesus fulfill statements from the prophets (e.g., 1:22; 2:15; 8:17; 12:17; 13:35; 21:4), he clearly patterns his presentation of Jesus on significant prophetic figures from the past, such as Moses (see D. C. Allison, *The New Moses: A Matthean Typology* [Minneapolis: Fortress, 1993]) and Jeremiah (see M. P. Knowles, *Jeremiah in Matthew's Gospel: The Rejected Prophet Motif in Matthean Redaction*, JSNTSup 68 [Sheffield: JSOT, 1993]).

2. S. Chow, *The Sign of Jonah Reconsidered: A Study of Its Meaning in the Gospel Traditions*, CBNTS 27 (Stockholm: Almqvist & Wiksell, 1995), 88–91; W. D. Davies and D. C. Allison,

points to John the Baptist,[3] to his death and/or suffering,[4] to his three days in the grave as confirming his prophetic credentials,[5] to his parousia,[6] to his presence and preaching of repentance,[7] to his descent into Hades and preaching to the souls there,[8] or to the conversion of gentiles.[9] In this chapter I approach the question of the sign of Jonah in Matthew from an intertextual perspective. In doing so, I suggest that Jesus's references to Jonah function metaleptically for Matthew.[10] The Matthean allusion to Jonah's sojourn in the belly of the fish, in other words, invokes the larger context of the Jonah story for the biblically literate reader.[11] Among the primary elements of the story of Jonah are the

---

The Gospel according to Saint Matthew, 3 vols., ICC (Edinburgh: T&T Clark, 1988–97), 2:352; R. A. Edwards, *The Sign of Jonah in the Theology of the Evangelists and Q*, Studies in Biblical Theology 2/18 (London: SCM, 1971), 98, 107; R. T. France, *The Gospel of Matthew*, NICNT (Grand Rapids: Eerdmans, 2007), 491; D. A. Hagner, *Matthew 1–13*, WBC 33a (Dallas: Word Books, 1993), 354; J. Jeremias, "Ionas," *TWNT* 3: 410–13, here 412; U. Luz, *Das Evangelium Nach Matthäus (Mt 8–17)*, EKKNT 1/2 (Zurich: Benziger Verlag, 1990), 277–78; E. H. Merrill, "The Sign of Jonah," *JETS* 23 (1980): 23–30; J. Swetnam, "No Sign of Jonah," *Biblica* 66 (1985): 126–30.

3. J. H. Michael, "The Sign of Jonah," *JTS* 21 (1920): 146–59.

4. E.g., J. Nolland, *The Gospel of Matthew: A Commentary on the Greek Text*, NIGTC (Grand Rapids: Eerdmans, 2005), 511–12.

5. A. Sand, *Das Evangelium nach Matthäus*, 6th ed. (Regensburg: Friedrich Pustet, 1986), 266–67.

6. A. Vögtle, "Der Spruch vom Jonaszeichen," in *Synoptische Studien: Alfred Wikenhauser zum 70. Geburtstag am 22. Februar 1953 dargebracht von Freunden, Kollegen und Schülern*, ed. A. Vögtle and J. Schmid (Munich: Zink, 1953), 230–77, esp. 276–77. Cf. the opinion of R. Bultmann that the saying originally meant the return of Jesus from afar—namely, his parousia, when he would come again as the eschatological judge (*Die Geschichte der synoptischen Tradition*, 2nd ed. [Göttingen: Vandenhoeck & Ruprecht, 1931], 124).

7. E.g., T. W. Manson, *The Sayings of Jesus* (London: SCM, 1950), 89–90.

8. G. M. Landes, "Matthew 12:40 as an Interpretation of 'The Sign of Jonah' against Its Biblical Background," in *The Word of the Lord Shall Go Forth*, ed. C. L. Meyers and M. O'Connor (Winona Lake, IN: Eisenbrauns, 1983), 665–84.

9. V. Mora, *Le Signe de Jonas* (Paris: Cerf, 1983), esp. 90–97, 130–34.

10. R. B. Hays explains metalepsis as a literary echo that links two texts such that "the figurative effect of the echo can lie in the unstated or suppressed points of resonance between the two texts." Readers rightly interpret such allusive echoes in a given text—say, text B—by understanding text B "in light of a broad interplay with text A [i.e., a different text], encompassing aspects of A beyond those explicitly echoed [in B]" (*Echoes of Scripture in the Letters of Paul* [New Haven: Yale University Press, 1989], 20).

11. Some scholars have argued that parts of the larger context of Jonah are in play (e.g., P. Seidelin, "Das Jonaszeichen," *Studia Theologica* 5 [1952]: 119–31, who argues for the importance of the prayer of Jonah in Jon. 2 for the Matthean context). I suggest in another essay that Matthew's allusions to the story of Jonah also contribute to his larger claims that Jesus *is* the God of Israel present with his people (see D. M. Moffitt, "God Attested by Men: Echoes of Jonah and the Identification of Jesus with Israel's God in the Storm-Stilling Stories of Matthew's Gospel," in *A Scribe Trained for the Kingdom of Heaven: Essays on Ethics and Christology in Honor of Richard B. Hays*, ed. D. M. Moffitt and I. A. Morales (Langham, MD: Lexington Books/Fortress Academic, 2021), 25–45.

power of Israel's God over the chaos of the sea, the account of the great fish swallowing and expelling Jonah, the role of the prophet of God, and the correlated themes of the penitent response of gentiles to the prophetic message of judgment and the extension of God's salvific mercy to gentiles.

Matthew, I argue, recontextualizes these larger themes within his portrayal of Jesus as a prophet of God. Thus, the content of the sign of Jonah moves well beyond a simple indicator of any one event or theme in Jesus's life and ministry. Not only does the "sign" point to Jesus's death and resurrection; it also points to the extension of God's mercy to those outside of the covenant community of Israel. An intertextual perspective suggests, largely against the grain of modern scholarship, that the sign of Jonah cannot be reduced to one referent,[12] nor does it merely provide Matthew with an easy proof text for Jesus's resurrection. It brims with significance. In particular, it fits within the larger Matthean emphasis on the mission of a true prophet. The sign even extends out to encompass the mission and message of Jesus's early followers to the gentiles.

Within this broader conception of the sign of Jonah in Matthew, the story of Jonah's disgorgement from the fish and subsequent mission to Nineveh clarifies that Jesus's resurrection marks the pivotal shift in Matthew's narrative *from* Jesus's ministry among the lost sheep of the house of Israel *to* the mission of his followers to the gentiles. In keeping with Matthew's emphasis on Jesus's prophetic role, then, the Jonah story allows him to recast the post-resurrection proclamation of the kingdom of heaven to the gentiles as both a prophetic sign of divine mercy for gentiles and a critique of Jewish religious leadership. Before examining these themes in Matthew's Gospel, I turn first to a brief summary of the main elements of the narrative of Jonah.

A Synopsis of Jonah's Story

Jonah's story begins with the word of the LORD coming to Jonah and telling him to go preach against Nineveh. Instead, Jonah chooses to catch the first boat for Tarshish. A huge storm arises. Jonah instructs the sailors to cast him into the sea, which immediately becomes calm. Jonah is promptly swallowed by a great fish. Upon seeing these wonders, the gentile sailors are amazed and make sacrifices and vows to the God of Israel. In the belly of the fish, Jonah prays for redemption from the grave and has faith in God's salvation. After three days, God commands the fish to spit Jonah out onto dry land. The

---

12. Chow, for example, dismisses the view that gentile conversion is an important element of the sign of Jonah in Matthew (*Sign of Jonah Reconsidered*, 88).

word of the LORD then comes to Jonah again. This time he chooses to go to Nineveh. Once there, Jonah proclaims God's coming judgment, and, to his dismay, the people repent. Jonah waits to see if his prophecy of God's coming judgment will still be fulfilled, but in response to the city's repentance God graciously relents from destroying the city. Jonah then expresses to God his own frustration at the extension of God's mercy to Nineveh.

From this précis at least three themes emerge with particular clarity: first, that the God of Israel controls creation, especially the sea and the weather; second, that this God allows for gentiles to repent, even to the extent of saving them from coming judgment; and, third, that this God's own people might begrudge the extension of such mercy to gentiles. In addition to these themes, it is noteworthy that the structure of the narrative moves from Jonah's call to his flight, his death-like and resurrection-like experiences with the fish, his proclamation to the gentiles, the repentance of those gentiles, and his grumbling about God's graciousness. Several of these themes and points of this narrative align well with elements in Matthew's Gospel, the most prominent being the extension of God's mercy to repentant gentiles. I turn, then, to consider the possibility that the story of Jonah informs the agenda of Matthew in more extensive ways than often supposed.

Allusions to Jonah in Matthew's Gospel

The two references to the "sign of Jonah" in Matthew constitute obvious allusions to Jonah. The Matthew 12 text and the possible nature of the sign will be discussed in greater length later in this essay. I note for now that Matthew's doubling of this saying suggests the importance of this prophet for Matthew's portrayal of Jesus.

Well before the explicit mention of Jonah in Matthew 12, though, it seems plausible to suggest that biblically literate readers of the Gospel would already have begun to suspect some connection with Jonah in the story of Jesus calming the storm (Matt. 8:23–27). To be sure, this account has not been included by Matthew because of his interest in Jonah. He finds it in Mark, one of his sources. Nevertheless, from an intertextual perspective, the original readers of Matthew and probably Matthew himself would have had good reason to be reminded of Jonah. As Davies and Allison point out, both the Jonah story and the stilling-of-the-storm story contain the following elements: (1) a departure by boat, (2) a violent storm at sea, (3) a sleeping main character, (4) terrified sailors, (5) a miraculous stilling of the storm in some way related to the main character, and (6) a marveling response by the sailors.[13] These similarities suggest a strong connection between this Synoptic pericope and the story of Jonah. Moreover, recognizing the allusion to the Jonah story here provides an implicit answer to the disciples' question, "What kind of man is this?" Those who reflect on the echo of the storm scene in Jonah will also readily recognize that Jesus plays the role of Israel's God in that story—the one who has control over creation and, in particular, the stormy sea.

Astute readers will also likely puzzle over another detail in the Jonah story. In that account the *gentile* sailors are amazed when the storm subsides and respond by submitting to the authority of Israel's God. They take it upon themselves to offer sacrifices and vows to this God who clearly holds power over the sea. Some later rabbis reflected on this portion of the text and even concluded that the sailors went to Jerusalem, got circumcised, and became Jewish proselytes.[14] In Matthew, however, Jesus's Jewish disciples apparently fail to make the connection. The pericope's echoes of the larger Jonah narrative prompt the reader to reflect on the question "Who then is this man" in light of the realization of the gentile sailors—this man has the power of Israel's God, the power to control the sea.[15] That the gentiles in the Jonah story get this point while the Jewish disciples in the Gospel narrative do not correlates with another theme that runs through Matthew's Gospel and is a prominent feature of the book of Jonah—the conversion of gentiles to Israel's God.

Throughout Matthew, hints of the extension of God's redemptive grace to the gentiles can be seen. In the genealogy at the beginning of the Gospel, the gentile women Rahab and Ruth (1:5) are conspicuous by their inclusion as mothers in a largely patrilineal genealogy.[16] Bathsheba is not mentioned, but Uriah the Hittite (who is not, strictly speaking, in the line of descent) is (1:6). The first visitors of the Christ child are gentiles—magi from the east who come to worship him (2:1–2). Later, when Jesus begins his ministry in Galilee, Matthew points his readers to Isaiah 9:1–2, where Galilee is dubbed "Galilee of the gentiles," a land where people live in darkness (4:15–16). As proof that the gentiles in Galilee have begun to see a great light, Jesus meets a centurion in Capernaum whose servant is ill. Jesus heals him from a distance and praises the centurion, commenting that he has not found anyone in Israel

---

13. Davies and Allison, *Gospel according to Saint Matthew*, 2:70.

14. So, e.g., Pirqe R. El. 10.

15. It may be significant that the second mention of the sign of Jonah involves a rebuke related to interpreting the weather correctly.

16. This is widely recognized (e.g., Davies and Allison, *Gospel according to Saint Matthew*, 2:74–75).

with faith as great as the centurion's (8:10). Then, driving home the point that gentiles will be redeemed, Jesus adds that many from the east and the west will come and recline at table with Abraham, Isaac, and Jacob in the kingdom of heaven while the sons of the kingdom shall be cast outside (8:11–12).

At other points the text indicates future blessings for the nations. In 12:18–21 Matthew cites Isaiah 42:1–4 and includes in Matthew 12:21 the comment that the nations (ἔθνη) will hope in the name of the figure spoken of by Isaiah—that is, for Matthew, in Jesus's name. Again in Matthew 15:21–28, Jesus heals a gentile, the daughter of a Canaanite woman. The notion in 21:43 that the Jewish religious leadership will be excluded from the kingdom, which will be given to a people (ἔθνει) worthy of it, further points to gentile conversion. In 24:14 Jesus prophesies that the gospel of the kingdom will be proclaimed to all the nations before the end comes. Finally, in 28:18–20, Jesus explicitly commands his disciples to go out and preach to all the nations (πάντα τὰ ἔθνη).

Thus, the motif of gentile conversion runs like a scarlet thread through this Gospel. One of the curious aspects of the presence of this motif in Matthew, however, is the dissonance it creates with explicit claims in the text and pointed directives by Jesus that his mission is only to the lost sheep of Israel. To turn again to the beginning of the Gospel, the angel that appears to Joseph and quiets his concerns about Mary's pregnancy also informs him that Mary's baby is to be named Jesus because he will save "his people" (τὸν λαὸν αὐτοῦ) from their sins (1:21). The apparent conflation in Matthew 2:6 of material from Micah 5:1–3 LXX with the report of God's word to David in 2 Samuel 5:2 (2 Kgdms. 5:2) // 1 Chronicles 11:2 LXX allows Matthew to craft a prophetic word that clarifies that the ruler who will come from Bethlehem (Mic. 5:1) is the Messiah, Jesus, who will not only save God's people but also be their shepherd.[17] Thus, Matthew 2:6 effectively identifies Micah 5:3's reference to the coming ruler from Bethlehem as one who "will shepherd his flock in the strength of the Lord" (ποιμανεῖ τὸ ποίμνιον αὐτοῦ ἐν ἰσχύι κυρίου) and the one who "will shepherd my people Israel" (ποιμανεῖ τὸν λαόν μου τὸν Ἰσραήλ; cf. 2 Kgdms. 5:2 // 1 Chron. 11:2 LXX). In keeping with this shepherd theme, Jesus sends out his twelve disciples in Matthew 10:5–6 with the command *not* to go to the gentiles or the Samaritans but rather to go to the lost sheep of the house of Israel. Moreover, even in the story of the healing of the Canaanite woman's daughter, Jesus coldly rebuffs her first few

---

17. Davies and Allison (*Gospel according to Saint Matthew*, 1:242–43) must be correct when they note that the prophetic word here constitutes more of an interpretation than a quotation of Mic. 5:2. As they point out, the use of the language from 2 Sam. 5:2 // 1 Chron. 11:2 allows Matthew to highlight not only Jesus's associations with David but also the key word λαός.

requests with the respective comments that he was sent only to the lost sheep of Israel and that it would not be appropriate to give the children's bread to the dogs (15:24, 26).

Inherent, then, to Matthew's Gospel is the palpable tension between the extension of God's mercy both to Jews *and* to gentiles. Jesus's mission is directed to the Jews, but gentiles are proleptically being included and promised more to come. This tension undoubtedly reflects something of the historical realities of Jesus's mission and the phenomenon of gentile conversion in Matthew's own time. In any case, the tension created by Matthew's hints at gentile inclusion and Jesus's own command to ignore gentiles does not find resolution until the end of the Gospel. Only as the Gospel comes to a close and the disciples are again in Galilee does Jesus explicitly command them to begin doing what he forbade them from doing in chapter 10—go out to preach to all the nations.

The question that this presents to the reader of Matthew is, What has changed? Why, at the end of the Gospel, does Jesus now command a mission to the gentiles? Two interrelated moments in the narrative suggest an answer: Jesus's death and resurrection. In Matthew 21:33–46 Jesus draws on God's comparison in Isaiah 5:1–7 of his people to a vineyard that produces bad grapes to tell a parable of tenants who are entrusted with their master's vineyard and who kill the messengers and eventually the master's own son when he comes to reclaim the vineyard. There can be little doubt that Matthew intends not only an allusion to Jerusalem's history of killing God's prophets but also to the role the leaders of the city played in crucifying Jesus. The punishment the master metes out to the tenants—taking away the vineyard and giving it to others—therefore represents a prediction that the crucifixion of Jesus will result in the kingdom being taken from the Jewish religious leaders and given to others.

The crucifixion, however, is not the only significant moment standing between Jesus's mission to the lost sheep of Israel and the so-called Great Commission of Matthew 28:18–20. The other element is the return of Jesus to Galilee, the place where those living in darkness see a great light, and the corresponding proclamation that all authority and power has been given to him. That is to say, the mission to the gentiles does not begin until *after* Jesus's resurrection.

One noteworthy point here is that the interrelated motifs of Jesus's death, his resurrection, and the mission to the gentiles are highly reminiscent of the larger story of Jonah. Not only do these motifs line up with some of the major themes in Jonah, but the narrative pattern of the extension of God's redemptive mercy to the gentiles after Jesus's death and resurrection also tracks with the basic narrative movement of Jonah's story. Specifically, the Ninevites receive God's mercy only *after* Jonah's death-like stay in the belly of the great fish—depicted as being in Sheol/Hades in Jonah 2:2—and after his resurrection-like expulsion onto dry land. Is this parallel simply an accident of these two texts, or did Matthew actively reflect on the story of Jonah as he worked out the tension of gentile conversion in his Gospel? An examination of the sign-of-Jonah pericope hints at the probability of the latter suggestion.

The Sign of Jonah the Prophet and Gentile Conversion

The first mention of Jonah in Matthew's Gospel directly follows Matthew's version of the Beelzebul controversy pericope (12:22–32). That encounter ends with a sharp critique of the Jewish leaders and a discussion of people being likened to trees that will be called to account for the fruit of their words and deeds on the day of judgment (12:33–37). The sign-of-Jonah pericope begins with the Pharisees and teachers of the law requesting a sign from Jesus. Jesus responds that a wicked and adulterous generation asks for a sign and that none will be given except for the sign of Jonah the prophet.

Among the differences between Matthew's and Luke's renditions of this pericope is the explicit identification in Matthew of Jonah as *a prophet*.[18] Given the importance of the prophets for Matthew, this comment is surely important. Throughout this Gospel the fate of the prophets plays an especially significant role. Prophets are typically persecuted figures (see, e.g., 5:11–12; 17:11–13). Matthew not only envisions Jesus as a "rejected prophet" like Jeremiah[19] but also puts the followers of Jesus who proclaim Jesus's message to their fellow Jews in the same category (see esp. Matt. 23:29–39). In Matthew prophets are generally God's messengers sent to God's people and persecuted or even killed by them.

On this point, however, Jonah presents an obvious contrast. Jonah the prophet was neither rejected nor persecuted. Instead, his message was received and resulted in repentance. The chief difference between Jonah and the other prophets was his audience. Jonah went to the gentile city of Nineveh. That Matthew has this distinction of audience and response in mind when

18. The test requested by some for Jesus to give a sign from heaven and Jesus's refusal to give such a sign is attested in the triple tradition (Matt. 16:1, 4 [cf. 12:38–39]//Mark 8:11–12// Luke 11:16, 29). The sign-of-Jonah saying and the related material, however, show up only in Matthew and Luke (Matt. 12:39–42; 16:4//Luke 11:29–32).

19. See M. P. Knowles's excellent study *Jeremiah in Matthew's Gospel: The Rejected Prophet Motif in Matthean Redaction*, JSNTSup 68 (Sheffield: JSOT Press, 1993). Notably, too, Jesus is explicitly called a prophet in Matt. 21:11.

referring to the sign-of-Jonah saying is evident by the fact that, immediately following Jesus's comment about Jonah's three-day sojourn in the belly of the fish (12:40), he adds that in the final judgment the people of Nineveh will testify against those who reject Jesus, because the Ninevites repented at Jonah's message (12:41).

This presentation of the sign-of-Jonah saying is remarkably different from the Lukan account, where the comment about the Queen of the South coming to hear Solomon bisects the Jonah material. The sign of Jonah in Luke is introduced, but the mention of Jonah's preaching and the gentiles' repenting is split off from the sign by the interjection of the Queen of the South material. Matthew's redaction appears to place special emphasis on the transition *from* the three-day sojourn of Jonah and the Son of Man *to* the mention of Jonah's preaching and the Ninevites' repentance. Thus, in Matthew, Jonah is a prophet but one whose example breaks the pattern of the other prophets highlighted in the Gospel. Significantly, the deviation occurs at the level of audience—Jonah preached to gentiles. The other prophets mentioned in Matthew preached to God's people.

With this in mind, the incident that stands between the gentile response to Jonah's message and his three days and nights in the fish's belly—his resurrection-like expulsion—can be recognized as important to anyone familiar with the contours of the story. Put differently, from the standpoint of intertextual hermeneutics, the absence of the reference to Jonah's being spit out of the fish is precisely what draws the biblically literate reader's attention and causes one to reflect on that part of the story. The mention of Jonah's sojourn in the fish prompts the biblically literate reader to reflect on the fact that Jonah did not stay in the fish. Something changed his situation so that he did indeed go to Nineveh and preach.

Many recognize that the references to Jonah's stay in the fish and the Son of Man's stay in the earth point beyond themselves to the redemption of Jonah and Jesus from their respective places of confinement. That is, the mentions of Jonah's dwelling for three days and nights in the belly of the fish and the Son of Man's dwelling in the heart of the earth ultimately point forward to the salvation of these prophetic figures from those realms. Just as Jonah was spit out of the fish after three days and nights, so also Jesus will emerge from death.

The argument of this essay, however, is that Matthew has more in mind than just the death and resurrection of Jesus when he speaks of the "sign of Jonah." In keeping with the pattern of the Jonah narrative, he finds Jonah's proclamation of God's word to the gentiles after Jonah's "resurrection" and their subsequent repentance important. This conclusion is suggested not only by the movement in Matthew 12:40–41 from the Son of Man's three days in the heart of the earth to the mention of the future resurrection of the Ninevites because of their repentance but also from the fact that this very pattern from Jonah helps resolve the tension in Matthew between gentile conversion and the Jewish mission. For it is only after Jesus's resurrection from dwelling in the heart of the earth that he then commands his disciples to proclaim his words and teaching to the nations so that they, too, can become disciples.

Whereas the Jewish religious leaders treat the prophet Jesus just as so many of God's prophets of old were treated, a number of gentiles in the Gospel, by way of contrast, are receptive to the word of this prophet, just like the people in Nineveh received Jonah's message. The way this observation coheres with the movement of Matthew's Gospel toward its climactic end, the commissioning of the gentile mission after Jesus's resurrection, suggests that the references to the sign of Jonah form part of a broader engagement in the Gospel with the larger story of Jonah.

The sign of Jonah, therefore, may well be understood by Matthew as something bigger than a simple proof text for Jesus's resurrection (or any other overly specific explanation). Rather, the sign of Jonah is part of a larger intertextual allusion to the story of Jonah—specifically, the movement in the Gospel from the Jewish mission to Jesus's death and resurrection, culminating in the commencement of the gentile mission.[20] In addition, this appeal to Jonah can be seen to function both as a legitimation of the gentile mission and as yet another appeal in Matthew to the tradition of the prophets criticizing their fellow Jews.

Conclusion

In closing I briefly note two points. First, the plausibility of the general thesis of this chapter finds some support in the fact that at least a few ancient interpreters of Matthew were led by the text to make links between Jesus and Jonah not unlike the ones I have outlined above. Augustine, for example, wrote that "as Jonas went from the ship into the belly of the whale, so Christ went from the tree into the tomb, or into the abyss of death; and as Jonas was sacrificed for those endangered by the storm, so Christ was offered for those who are drowning in the storm of this world; and as Jonas was first commanded to preach to the Ninevites, but his prophecy did not come to them until after the whale had vomited him out, so the prophecy made to the Gentiles did not

20. A similar collocation of motifs occurs in Matt. 15:1–20; 21:33–46.

come to them until after the resurrection of Christ."[21] Time does not permit a more detailed discussion of this quote, but the main lines of thought are clear. By way of analogy to the plotline in the Jonah narrative, Augustine sees the gentile mission flowing directly out of Jesus's resurrection.

Second, Matthew's recontextualization of the story of Jonah exemplifies one way in which early followers of Jesus appealed to Jewish Scripture, and the prophets in particular, to make arguments about Jesus and about the early communities that followed him. The story of Jonah provides Matthew with a biblical *pattern* that helps explain both Jesus's focus on the lost sheep of the house of Israel before the crucifixion and the expansion of the proclamation of the gospel to the gentiles by Jesus's early followers after his resurrection. But Matthew also uses Jonah to critique his fellow Jews. With the larger narrative of Jonah in view, Jesus's references to the sign of Jonah in Matthew indicate that those Jews who are watching gentiles becoming followers of Jesus are faced with a choice. They can recognize this as a sign of something akin to the extension of God's grace to the Ninevites, or they can become embittered like Jonah did. In Matthew's view the latter choice pits them against the expanded, redemptive work God is presently doing in Jesus, a prophet far greater than Jonah.

21. From Augustine's *Letter 102* in *Saint Augustine: Letters*, trans. W. Parsons, vol. 2, FC 18 (New York: Fathers of the Church, 1953), 173. Similarly, see Cyril of Jerusalem's *Lenten Lecture 14*, 17–20, in *The Works of Saint Cyril of Jerusalem*, trans. L. P. McCauley and A. A. Stephenson, vol. 2, FC 64 (Washington, DC: Catholic University of America Press, 1970), 43–45. Cyril does not clearly locate the proclamation of the gospel to the gentiles after the resurrection the way Augustine does, but he does note several points of correspondence between the traditions about Jesus, especially as given in Matthew, and the narrative sweep of Jonah. These include the stilling of the storm, the descent into the realm of death, the resurrection from that realm, and the proclamation of God's message, which Cyril identifies as the message of repentance (notably, though, Jonah is sent in the biblical account to proclaim only judgment against Nineveh, not repentance—so Jon. 1:2; 3:1, 4; cf. 3:9, where the king of Nineveh does not know if God's anger will relent even though the people are repenting).

14

Atonement at the Right Hand

The Sacrificial Significance of Jesus's Exaltation in Acts

Nowhere is Luke's presumed lack of interest in the sacrificial dimensions of the salvation Jesus accomplished more apparently obvious than in his largely nonsacrificial reflection on the crucifixion, either in his Gospel or in Acts. Luke's reluctance to explain how Jesus's death effected salvation, particularly in terms of sacrificial categories, seems especially obvious in his telling choice not to include Mark 10:45's ransom saying in his parallel rendering (cf. Luke 22:27). Luke does little to associate Jesus's death with concepts often correlated with Jewish sacrificial practice: forgiveness of sins, repentance, and purification.

The variety of explanations for and interpretations of Luke's soteriology in modern secondary literature illustrates the extent to which scholars have puzzled over this phenomenon in Luke's writings.[1] Several interpreters argue that Luke simply has little or no sense of the cross as a salvific event.[2]

I am especially grateful to Tobias Nicklas, Kai Akagi, and the anonymous reviewer for their critical feedback on earlier versions of this chapter.

1. See the excellent survey of views in F. Bovon, *Luke the Theologian: Fifty-Five Years of Research (1950–2005)*, 2nd ed. (Waco: Baylor University Press, 2006), 183–90.

2. J. M. Creed's claim that Luke has "no *theologia crucis* beyond the affirmation that the Christ must suffer, since so the prophetic scriptures had foretold" (*The Gospel according to St. Luke: The Greek Text with Introduction, Notes and Indices* [London: Macmillan, 1930], lxxii) is often cited. Similarly, see H. Conzelmann, *The Theology of St. Luke*, trans. G. Buswell (London: Faber and Faber, 1961), 201; C. H. Dodd, *The Apostolic Preaching and*

Others suggest that while the crucifixion is salvific for Luke, he does not conceive of either that salvation or the cross in sacrificial terms.[3] Some do detect hints in Luke-Acts of the sacrificial implications of Jesus's suffering but still recognize that Luke's portrayal of the sacrificial significance of these events is at best underdeveloped.[4] A few have challenged the view that Luke systematically downplays the sacrificial significance of the cross at all.[5] In general, however, Luke's relative silence on these matters has baffled modern

---

Its Development (London: Hodder & Stoughton, 1936), 25; M. C. Parsons and R. I. Pervo, *Rethinking the Unity of Luke and Acts* (Minneapolis: Fortress, 1993), 113; P. Vielhauer, "On the 'Paulinism' of Acts," in *Studies in Luke-Acts,* ed. L. E. Keck and J. L. Martyn (Nashville: Abingdon, 1966), 33–50, here 36–37, 42–43, 45 (originally published as "Zum 'Paulinismus' der Apostelgeschichte," *EvT* 10 [1950/1951]: 1–15).

3. R. J. Karris, for example, argues that Luke does not depict Jesus's death as an expiation for sins because he wants to show instead how Jesus's total faithfulness and obedience to God reveals God's faithful commitment not to abandon creation even in experiences such as the unjust killing of the innocent (*Luke: Artist and Theologian; Luke's Passion Account as Literature* [New York: Paulist Press, 1985], 80, 115). In Luke, in other words, Jesus shows that God does not separate himself from things that are polluted and unclean (as a sacrificial logic might imply) but determines instead to forgive and to remain with creation (esp. 121–22). In the context of Luke's larger narrative, the resurrection/exaltation of Jesus signifies the full extent to which God was with Jesus even through death, and to which God affirms and vindicates the outcasts and those who faithfully suffer injustice as Jesus did (98–99, 101, 108–9, 115).

Similarly, J. Neyrey argues that Jesus's death is shown to be salvific by being depicted as the primary act of Jesus's exemplary faith in and obedience to the God who saves. Thus, although Luke "does not favor sacrificial metaphors" when he reflects on Jesus's death (*The Passion according to Luke: A Redaction Study of Luke's Soteriology* [New York: Paulist Press, 1985], 158), by highlighting Jesus's exemplary faith in the God who can raise the dead, Luke portrays Jesus as the "Saved Savior" on the cross, who has become the example and source of salvation, even a new Adam, for others (129–92). Cf. R. Zehnle, "The Salvific Character of Jesus' Death in Lucan Soteriology," *TS* 30 (1969): 420–44.

4. The longer reading of both Luke 22:19–20 and Acts 20:28 appears to invoke sacrificial categories. The language of "blood" in these texts is usually assumed to be a metonymy for Jesus's death. Here, then, Luke at least hints at the sacrificial implications of Jesus's death. So, e.g., C. K. Barrett, who finds "the barest hint (Acts 20:28) of an atoning death" in Luke's theology (*Luke the Historian in Recent Study* [London: Epworth, 1961], 47; cf. 23, 59); R. H. Fuller, "Luke and the Theologia Crucis," in *Sin, Salvation, and the Spirit: Commemorating the Fiftieth Year of the Liturgical Press,* ed. D. Durken (Collegeville, MN: Liturgical Press, 1979), 214–20; J. Jervell, *The Theology of the Acts of the Apostles* (Cambridge: Cambridge University Press, 1996), 98; C. F. D. Moule, "The Christology of Acts," in *Studies in Luke-Acts,* ed. L. E. Keck and J. L. Martyn (Nashville: Abingdon, 1966), 159–85, here 171, 173). Some argue, however, that these two texts are so liturgical and even Pauline in flavor that they are unlikely to represent Luke's own perspective (e.g., J. Kodell, "Luke's Theology of the Death of Jesus," in Durken, *Sin, Salvation, and the Spirit,* 221–30, here 223; Zehnle, "Salvific Character of Jesus' Death," 439–40).

5. U. Mittman-Richert argues that the role of the "servant" in the so-called fourth servant song of Isa. 52–53 underlies the soteriological significance of Jesus's death and exaltation in Luke. This, she thinks, allows one to recognize the sacrificial dimensions of Jesus's death, particularly as this initiates a new covenant as stated in the Eucharist pericope of Luke 22:14–38 (*Der Sühnetod des Gottesknechts: Jesaja 53 im Lukasevangelium* [Tübingen: Mohr Siebeck, 2008], esp. 54–85).

interpreters. Vernon Robbins, noting that "there is no direct statement that Jesus died a sacrificial death to save humans from their sins," allows that Luke 22:20 may gesture toward Jesus's sacrificial death. But he adds, "The presence of this verse in Luke makes it all the more remarkable that there is no sacrificial language in the preaching in Acts."[6] Jacob Jervell summarizes the modern consensus well when he comments that Luke has thrust sacrificial ideas about Jesus's death "into the background for some inscrutable reason."[7]

In light of these observations, Luke's widely recognized tendency to emphasize the salvific importance of Jesus's exaltation over that of the crucifixion is all the more intriguing.[8] While this is clearest in Acts, even in his Gospel, Luke appears to direct the reader's gaze beyond the cross to Jesus's ascension. Thus, Jesus's conversation with Moses and Elijah during the transfiguration focuses on his "exodus" (τὴν ἔξοδον) or departure, which he is about to fulfill "in Jerusalem" (ἐν Ἰερουσαλήμ) (Luke 9:31). Jesus's pivotal decision in Luke 9:51 to set his face toward Jerusalem is described as a choice primarily oriented toward the days of his being "taken up" (ἀνάλημψις, cf. Acts 1:2), rather than one oriented toward either his crucifixion or his resurrection per se. Luke locates Jesus's suffering as a prerequisite for his entering his glory (Luke 24:26). Luke's account of Jesus's ascension into heaven at the end of the Gospel (24:51) and particularly at the beginning of Acts (1:9–10) also seems to confirm this focus.[9] One even wonders if his curiously cropped quotation

6. V. K. Robbins, "Priestly Discourse in Luke and Acts," in *Jesus and Mary Reimagined in Early Christian Literature*, ed. V. K. Robbins and J. M. Potter (Atlanta: SBL Press, 2015), 13–40, here 33; cf. 38–39.

7. Jervell, *Theology of the Acts*, 98. Similarly, I. H. Marshall explains that in Acts "the atoning significance of the death of Jesus is not altogether absent . . . , but it is not the aspect which Luke has chosen to stress. His presentation of the saving work of Jesus is consequently one-sided. But it is going too far to say that he has no rationale of salvation. He demonstrates quite clearly that salvation is bestowed by Jesus in virtue of His position as the Lord and Messiah. What is lacking is rather a full understanding of the significance of the cross as the means of salvation" (*Luke: Historian and Theologian* [Grand Rapids: Zondervan, 1971], 175). J. A. Fitzmyer argues that Luke does have a *theologia crucis* but that its logic can only be fully understood in light of Jesus's transferral to the glory of paradise, which is closely collocated with the crucifixion in the earliest traditions. According to Fitzmyer's understanding of Luke 24:43, Jesus's entry into paradise, or his glory—his exaltation—on the day of his death is what brings the soteriological benefits of the Christ event to humanity (*Luke the Theologian: Aspects of His Teaching* [New York: Paulist Press, 1989], 210–22).

8. So, e.g., Marshall, *Luke*, 169–75, esp. 174. J. B. Tyson, *The Death of Jesus in Luke-Acts* (Columbia: University of South Carolina Press, 1986), 170, writes that Luke "seems uninterested in piercing through to an understanding of the theological reason for the death [of Jesus] or in analysing what it was intended to accomplish. The benefits of forgiveness of sins and the Spirit are more closely connected with the resurrection than the death."

9. I assume the longer, "non-Western" form of these texts as printed in NA[28]. Obviously, Luke's emphasis on the ascension of Jesus is blunted if one adopts the shorter, "Western"

of Isaiah 53:8 in Acts 8:33 might allude to Jesus's ascension—the moment when "his life was lifted up [αἴρεται] from the earth."[10]

Given this (and other Lukan emphases), Ernst Käsemann argued that the peculiar account Luke develops of the location of the cross in the history of salvation indicates his attempt to shift the salvific emphasis away from Jesus's death to the outpouring of the Spirit and the creation of the church as an institution. Luke, Käsemann famously suggested, has replaced an earlier, apocalyptic *theologia crucis* with a more Hellenistic *theologia gloriae*.[11] Be that as it may, Luke plainly does connect the salvific benefits of repentance, the forgiveness of sins, and purification with Jesus's heavenly ascension and elevation to God's right hand more clearly and consistently than he ever does with the crucifixion.

This chapter explores a fresh rationale for Luke's emphasis on Jesus's exaltation and his apparently "inscrutable reasons" for not vesting Jesus's death with more overt sacrificial significance. Luke, I argue, probably knew that Jewish blood sacrifice did not directly connect the slaughter of the victim with the atoning benefits of the sacrifice. Sacrifice is a process, the culminating elements of which are the priest's approach to God and the corresponding conveyance of the material of the sacrifice into God's presence. These aspects within the process are most closely linked with securing the goals of forgiveness and purification.

Such an understanding of sacrifice allows the inference that Luke, were he interested in thinking about salvation from the standpoint of Jewish sacrifice, might have emphasized the salvific benefits of Jesus's heavenly exaltation over those of Jesus's death. Luke, that is, could have understood Jesus's exaltation in sacrificial terms: as the conveyance of the material of the sacrifice—Jesus himself—into God's heavenly presence.[12] That Luke does think this way is, I

---

readings, which are among the so-called Western non-interpolations. Even if, however, one accepts the shorter form of these passages in Luke-Acts, this would not greatly impact the larger claims of the argument advanced here.

10. Cf. the use of the cognate ἐπαίρω in Acts 1:9.

11. E. Käsemann, "Ministry and Community in the New Testament," in *Essays on New Testament Themes*, trans. W. J. Montague (Philadelphia: Fortress, 1982), 63–94, here 92–93.

12. It is possible that Luke did not recognize the sacrificial nuances present in the traditional conception of Jesus's exaltation that he had received. Thus he could be unwittingly passing on an account that suggests links between Jesus's heavenly position and sacrificial categories. This might explain why these categories are not more explicitly developed. M. Wolter's argument, however, that Luke has not highlighted sacrificial concepts because of his missional or outsider orientation seems more plausible ("Jesu Tod und Sündervergebung bei Lukas und Paulus," in *Reception of Paulinism in Acts*, ed. D. Marguerat [Leuven: Peeters, 2009], 15–35). Wolter's understanding of sacrifice differs from the one presented here, but the possibility that Luke knew that his gentile readers would not grasp the particulars of Jewish sacrificial rituals,

argue, suggested by his clear linking of Jesus's departure from the earth and elevation to God's right hand with the accomplishment of forgiveness and purification (i.e., key elements of sacrificial atonement) and the correlated outpouring of the Spirit. That Luke identifies Jesus's exaltation to God's right hand as the culmination of Jesus's salvific work implies a sacrificial logic—of which Luke himself was probably aware—underlying the larger story he tells about Jesus and Israel's redemption.

To make this case I first examine some key assumptions about Jewish sacrifice and atonement. This digression will provide a useful lens for reevaluating Luke's connections in Acts between Jesus's heavenly exaltation and the notions of repentance, forgiveness of sins, purification, and the outpouring of the Holy Spirit.

Sacrifice and Sacrificial Atonement

This section discusses two central points that provide necessary background for the subsequent exegesis of Acts: first, a brief exploration of the ways in which Jewish blood sacrifice seems to work, and second, some reflections on the relationship between purity and proximity to God.

The Process and Logic of Sacrifice

While Leviticus both speaks at length about what to do for particular sacrifices and offers assurance that these sacrifices are effective, the text provides little explicit reflection on why or how they work. A number of recent studies of Israelite and later Jewish blood sacrifice have nevertheless shed fresh light on the inner logic of these matters.[13]

Among the more important conclusions highlighted in some of these works is the recognition that Levitical sacrifice is an irreducible, hierarchically structured process.[14] That is to say, within the sequence of rituals that

---

especially insofar as these differed in significant ways from those of their own socio-religious context, still applies.

13. So, e.g., C. A. Eberhart, *Studien zur Bedeutung der Opfer im Alten Testament: Die Signifikanz von Blut- und Verbrennungsriten im kultischen Rahmen*, WMANT 94 (Neukirchen-Vluyn: Neukirchener, 2002); Eberhart, *The Sacrifice of Jesus: Understanding Atonement Biblically*, Facets (Minneapolis: Fortress, 2011); R. E. Gane, *Cult and Character: Purification Offerings, Day of Atonement, and Theodicy* (Winona Lake, IN: Eisenbrauns, 2005); J. Milgrom, *Leviticus 1–16: A New Translation with Introduction and Commentary*, AB 3 (New York: Doubleday, 1991), esp. 133–489.

14. See esp. Gane's detailed discussion and explanation of this larger point (*Cult and Character*, 3–24).

constitute the process of a particular sacrifice, the atoning benefits of forgiveness of sins and/or purification are more closely associated with the acts
of blood manipulation and the burning of parts or all of the body of the
victim than with any other elements of the process.[15] The culminating events
in this process—the ones with which the removal of sin and/or impurity are
most closely linked—are typically those activities that involve the priests
drawing nearer to God's presence by moving through the progressively more
sacred spaces of the temple complex and/or conveying the sacrificial elements into the divine presence.[16] This suggests that the use and conveyance
of the blood and parts of the body of the victim, actions performed only by
the priests at the various altars, stand at the center of the process of blood
sacrifice.

One of the central goals orienting this larger process was effecting "atonement" (כפר, MT; ἐξιλάσκομαι, LXX). Frequently this goal shows up in summarizing statements that speak of the purpose of a given sacrifice and/or of the
whole process of the sacrifice.[17] Throughout Leviticus, atonement is directly
linked with the activities of the priests at the altars, especially applying blood
to parts of them and burning various elements of the sacrifices on the outer
one.[18] These last points are worth emphasizing since the act of slaughtering
the victim was neither done exclusively by the priests[19] nor ever done on any of
the altars.[20] The close link between atonement and the priestly activities at the
altars, therefore, (1) indicates that the slaughter was not the central moment
in the sacrifice and (2) explains why the slaughter was not the element in the
process that effected the atoning goals of the sacrificial process.

A brief discussion of the central Yom Kippur sacrifices illustrates these matters well. In Leviticus 16:6 and 11a Aaron is instructed on how to offer a bull

15. E.g., Eberhart, *Sacrifice of Jesus*, 85; Gane, *Cult and Character*, esp. 67.
16. Gane defines "sacrifice" as "a religious ritual in which something of value is ritually
transferred to the sacred realm for utilization by the deity" (*Cult and Character*, 16).
17. See, e.g., Lev. 1:4; 5:6, 10, 16, 18; 6:7; 7:7; 9:7; 12:7–8; 14:18–20, 30–31; 15:15, 30; 16:6,
11, 24, 30–34; 19:22; 23:28. Cf. Milgrom (*Leviticus 1–16*, 925), who notes that the verb "to
offer" (עשׂה) refers at times to the entire process of sacrifice.
18. See, e.g., Lev. 4:20, 26, 31, 35; 5:13; 6:30; 8:15; 17:11.
19. See esp. the discussions in Gane, *Cult and Character*, 60; Milgrom, *Leviticus 1–16*, 154.
According to Josephus (*Ant.* 3.226), the practice of male worshipers slaughtering at least some
of their sacrifices was still in place in the late Second Temple period. See the discussion of this
practice and the opposing evidence in Philo in E. P. Sanders, *Judaism: Practice and Belief, 63
BCE–66 CE* (London: SCM, 1992) 106–7, 109.
20. The only animals slaughtered at the altar are birds. Even these, though, are not killed
on the altar. Their necks are wrung by the priest as he stands at the altar and, unlike the blood
of animals from the flock and herd, their blood is applied directly to the altar rather than
being first collected in a bowl and then manipulated and poured out by the priest (cf. Sanders,
Judaism, 110).

in order to atone for himself and his house. These are summary statements. The detailed process for performing this offering and thus for accomplishing atonement is then spelled out in 16:11b–14, 17. Similarly, in 16:7–10 the sin offering of the two goats is summarized. The performance of these rituals is then described in 16:15–22, where certain constitutive elements of the sacrificial process are specifically identified as effecting atonement for the high priest, for his house, and for the people. These are (1) applying the blood of the bull and one of the goats in the holy of holies (16:15–17; cf. 16:27), (2) sending the live goat away laden with sin (16:20–22),[21] and (3) burning the appropriate offerings on the outer altar (16:24–25). The sanctuary and the altar of incense also require atonement, which is done by applying blood to the mercy seat and then to that inner altar (16:16, 18–20). With the exception of the living goat (the so-called scapegoat), the details of Leviticus 16 largely fit the larger pattern noted above, in which the priestly activities at the various altars are identified as the elements within the sacrificial process that achieve atonement.

In sum, in the case of atoning sacrifice, a number of elements constitute a sacrifice, but the accomplishment of the atoning goals of the constitutive rituals is most closely linked with those elements performed by the priests at the altars—specifically, the application of blood and the burning of various parts of the victim. The fact that these elements of the process are linked with the various altars and performed only by the priests (and on Yom Kippur only by the high priest) suggests that the center of blood sacrifice is drawing near to God and conveying the material of the sacrifice into his presence. This is probably the reason why forms of the root קרב are so central in the biblical accounts of sacrifice.[22]

---

21. While the goat is not said here to make atonement, a comparison of the summary statement in Lev. 16:10 with the detailed description of the ritual in 16:20–22 suggests this conclusion (cf. N. Kiuchi, *The Purification Offering in the Priestly Literature: Its Meaning and Function*, JSOTSup 56 [Sheffield: JSOT Press, 1987], 149–51; B. J. Schwartz, "The Bearing of Sin in the Priestly Literature," in *Pomegranates and Golden Bells: Studies in Biblical, Jewish, and Near Eastern Ritual, Law, and Literature in Honor of Jacob Milgrom*, ed. D. P. Wright et al. [Winona Lake, IN: Eisenbrauns, 1995], 3–21; J. Sklar, *Sin, Impurity, Sacrifice, Atonement: The Priestly Conceptions*, HBM 2 [Sheffield: Sheffield Phoenix, 2005], 96–97).

22. R. E. Gane puts the point well, stating:

> In Hebrew, the idea of "sacrifice" in general is conveyed by the noun *qorban*. . . . The meaning of *qorban* is associated with that of the Hiphil verb from the same root *qrb* (lit., "cause to come near"), which can refer not only to preliminary conveyance of offering material to the ritual location (e.g., [Lev.] 1:3), but also to formal ritual presentation to the Lord (e.g., 1:5, 13). This formal presentation *transfers something to the holy God for his utilization*. So a *qorban* (sacrifice, sacrificial offering) *makes* something *holy* by giving it over to the holy domain of God. (*Leviticus, Numbers*, NIV Application Commentary [Grand Rapids: Zondervan, 2004], 78).

Sacrifice, Purity, and Proximity to God

The emphasis just noted on drawing near to God dovetails with another
important aspect of sacrifice and, in particular, atonement. Several modern
studies have shown that within the realm of Jewish ritual purity, one's state
of purity was a major factor when one was considering both how close one
could come to God's presence and God's willingness to dwell among his
people.[23]

Some of the work of Jonathan Klawans provides useful heuristic categories for thinking about the complex issues of Jewish purity. Klawans argues
that two different and parallel systems of purity exist in the Levitical system:
ritual purity and moral purity.[24] Ritual purity is primarily a matter of one's
external condition. This kind of defilement can be contagious and can be
spread by contact. At its core, ritual impurity appears to be about matters
of mortality.[25] Further, ritual impurity is a major obstacle when one tries to
come close to God's presence. God does not permit ritually impure persons
or items to come close to his presence. To bring impure mortality into God's
sacred space is to be guilty of sin. The need for people to be in a ritually pure
state therefore appears to be primarily about rendering mortal humanity fit to
draw near to God's presence. In cases of certain major ritual impurities (e.g.,
skin diseases, giving birth), sacrifice—especially the חטאת—is necessary to
remove the impurity (e.g., Lev. 12:6–8).[26]

Moral purity has to do with obeying God's commands. The violation of
divine directives results in moral defilement. A person's moral impurity is
not external or contagious. Nevertheless, while ritual and moral purity are
distinct, both problematize the relationship between God and his people in
similar ways. Ritual impurity prevents the people from approaching God.
Moral impurity threatens their ability to dwell in the land, which becomes defiled by some sins, and it threatens them with God's punitive response.[27] Both
kinds of impurity further stand in the way of God and his people dwelling
together because both convey defilement to the sanctuary.[28] The sanctuary
needs regular purification if God's presence is to remain there. The people

Cf. Eberhart, *Sacrifice of Jesus*, 71; J. Klawans, *Purity, Sacrifice, and the Temple: Symbolism and
Supersessionism in the Study of Ancient Judaism* (Oxford: Oxford University Press, 2006), 69.

23. E.g., H. Maccoby, *Ritual and Morality: The Ritual Purity System and Its Place in Judaism*
(Cambridge: Cambridge University Press, 1999), 1, 11, 27, 47, 170.

24. J. Klawans, *Impurity and Sin in Ancient Judaism* (Oxford: Oxford University Press,
2000); cf. Maccoby, *Ritual and Morality*.

25. See Maccoby's critique of Milgrom (*Ritual and Morality*, esp. 32, 49–50, 207–8).

26. Gane, *Cult and Character*, 112–23; Kiuchi, *Purification Offering*, 53–59.

27. Klawans, *Impurity and Sin*, 26–27; Sklar, *Sin, Impurity, Sacrifice, Atonement*, esp. 42–43.

28. See esp. Sklar, *Sin, Impurity, Sacrifice, Atonement*, 154–59.

need regular purification in order to dwell in relative safety near God's presence and to approach that presence.

It further appears to be the case that sacrificial atonement in the fullest sense—that is, the state that results from solving the problems of both moral and ritual impurity so that God and humanity can dwell together—requires the removal of the threat of divine punishment by way of redemption or ransom *and* the purification of the people, the land, and the sanctuary from the problems created by both mortality and sin.[29] Sacrificial atonement, in other words, is effected when the defilement from both moral and ritual impurities is purged by sacrificial offerings. All of this is essential to enable and maintain the dwelling of God's presence in the midst of his people and to enable God's people to be near to God's presence.[30]

Once again, Yom Kippur nicely illustrates this dual atoning action and its importance for enabling and maintaining God's presence among his people. As noted above, Leviticus 16:15–20 states that the sin offerings presented by the high priest on this day, in addition to atoning for him and for the people, also atone for the holy place, the tent of meeting, and the altars by way of blood application. Further, 16:16 identifies both the uncleanness (i.e., ritual impurity) and the sins of the people as the sources of defilement that make the annual purification necessary.[31] The clear implication is that both the people's ritual impurities and their moral failures/sins have defiled them and the sacred precincts, all of which consequently need atonement.[32] Sacrifice, because it atones for sin and impurity, is therefore an essential part of maintaining the covenant relationship.

Summary

The preceding discussion implies some important points for the arguments about Acts that follow. First, a reduction or conflation of blood sacrifice with the act of slaughtering the victim for the sake of dealing with sin is a conceptual mistake. Leviticus simply does not support either the inference that the act of slaughter achieved the atoning goals of the sacrifice or that atonement can be reduced merely to the forgiveness of sins. Rather, the process of sacrifice was an important element for achieving both ritual and moral purity. Second, the slaughter of the victim, while a necessary step in the sacrificial

29. Sklar, *Sin, Impurity, Sacrifice, Atonement*, 181–87.
30. Esp. Klawans, *Purity, Sacrifice, and the Temple*, 68–72. Cf. Exod. 29:37–46.
31. Schwartz, "Bearing of Sin," 6–7, 17.
32. This is not at all to diminish the importance of the people's need to rest from work and to afflict themselves (Lev. 16:31) as vital elements of the process. See esp. Schwartz, "Bearing of Sin," 20–21.

process (when such a sacrifice involved an animal victim),[33] never occurred on any of the Jewish altars and was never by itself sufficient to procure the atoning benefits that the entire process aimed to obtain.[34] Third, the hierarchical structure of the process suggests that the atoning benefits of sacrifice are primarily connected with the priestly activities that occurred at the altars as the priests drew near to God and conveyed the sacrificial materials into his presence.[35] Priestly acts at the altars achieved atonement. Fourth, sacrificial atonement, which resolves the problem of sin (moral impurity) or the problem of mortality (ritual impurity)—or, as on Yom Kippur, both of these problems—was essential for enabling God and his people to dwell together.

With these points in mind, I turn to examining a few key texts in Acts. Luke nowhere gives plain expression to the assumptions just outlined about sacrifice as a hierarchically structured ritual or about the logic of purity. Nevertheless, he does identify Jesus's elevation to God's right hand as the primary mechanism that accomplishes forgiveness of sins, purification, and the outpouring of the Holy Spirit, which suggests that a sacrificial logic informs his understanding of the significance of Jesus's exaltation.

Purification, Forgiveness, and the Outpouring of the Spirit in Acts

Space does not allow either a full assessment of forgiveness and purification in Luke-Acts or a thorough exegetical engagement with all the potentially relevant details. The next two sections of this chapter aim instead to show that Luke's emphasis on Jesus's exaltation and the atoning benefits it affords corresponds well with the conception of sacrifice and sacrificial atonement (i.e., forgiveness and purity) just discussed. To this end, three aspects of Acts are particularly noteworthy: (1) the logic used by Peter and others to make sense of Cornelius's purification, (2) the ways in which this logic parallels Luke's connection between Jesus's exaltation and the outpouring of the Spirit

33. That grain sacrifices could be used to effect purification and forgiveness in some cases further suggests that slaughter is not the definitive event in Jewish purification/sin sacrifices (cf. Eberhart, *Sacrifice of Jesus*, 99–101).

34. The same logic holds for all the other elements of the process as well—none of them can stand alone. To quote Gane again, "Like systems in general, rituals are structured hierarchically, with smaller systems constituting wholes embedded in larger systems. At each level, a 'whole possesses distinctive emergent properties—properties not possessed by the parts comprising the whole.' In the Israelite system of rituals, the whole is indeed greater than the sum of its parts. A ritual or ritual complex achieves its goal only if it is performed in its entirety, with its activities in the proper order" (*Cult and Character*, 19–20).

35. See in this regard the clear emphasis on the priests approaching God and offering him blood and fat in Ezek. 44:15–16.

on Pentecost, and (3) Luke's linking of forgiveness and purification with Jesus's exalted position at God's right hand. I turn first, then, to the Cornelius narrative.

The well-known story of the gentile Cornelius receiving the Holy Spirit and its connection with Peter's vision of God instructing him to kill and eat impure animals has been the object of substantial study from a variety of angles in the secondary literature.[36] What has, at least to my knowledge, garnered less attention is the way in which the logic of the account of Cornelius's purification correlates with the sacrificial understanding of atonement detailed above. Indeed, this recognition suggests that God's purifying work is not simply a matter of divine declaration but is, rather, the direct result of Jesus's exaltation.

In Acts 10 Luke provides the meaning of Peter's vision by way of Peter's own explanation of what God has shown him. In the vision God tells Peter to do something contrary to the purity laws given by Moses: to kill and eat animals declared impure by the Mosaic law. Peter declines the offer, highlighting his compliance with Mosaic legislation. The animals, he says, are common (κοινός) and impure (ἀκάθαρτος).[37] He has never violated the law of Moses on this point. God then tells him not to call common (κοινός) what God has purified (ἐκαθάρισεν, vv. 15–16). This happens three times.

Whatever the vision's meaning for the actual status of animals, Peter later concludes that its implications extend beyond the realm of *kashrut* regulations. Thus, in Acts 10:28 he states that whereas it is common knowledge that a Jew like himself was not to fraternize too closely with a gentile like Cornelius, God has shown him that he ought "to call no one common [κοινόν] or impure [ἀκάθαρτον]" (cf. Acts 11:3). The logic of Peter's self-realization appears to be that in his vision God was telling him that certain things that he once knew to be impure have now been made pure.

Precisely this implication is vividly and powerfully demonstrated to Peter and the other Jews with him when, as Peter is speaking at Cornelius's home

36. See, for a few examples, M. Dibelius, "The Conversion of Cornelius," in *Studies in the Acts of the Apostles*, ed. H. Greeven, trans. M. Ling and P. Schubert (New York: Scribner's Sons, 1956), 109–22; G. D. Nave, *The Role and Function of Repentance in Luke-Acts*, SBL Academia Biblica 4 (Atlanta: Society of Biblical Literature, 2002), 208–17; M. L. Soards, *The Speeches in Acts: Their Content, Context, and Concerns* (Louisville: Westminster John Knox, 1994), 70–79; S. G. Wilson, *The Gentiles and the Gentile Mission in Luke-Acts*, SNTSMS 23 (Cambridge: Cambridge University Press, 1973), 172–78, 191–94; R. D. Witherup, "Cornelius Over and Over and Over Again: 'Functional Redundancy' in the Acts of the Apostles," *JSNT* 49 (1993): 45–66.

37. To call something "common" is another way to speak of impurity. Thus there seems to be no real distinction between the terms here (e.g., C. S. Keener, *Acts: An Exegetical Commentary*, 4 vols. [Grand Rapids: Baker Academic, 2012–15], 2:1772).

about Jesus's death, resurrection, and the coming judgment, the gift of the Holy Spirit is poured out "even upon the gentiles" (Acts 10:45).

Luke does not in Acts 10 plainly affirm that the gentiles have been purified. Yet this conclusion follows not only from Peter's comment in 10:28 but ultimately, and more explicitly, from the fact that the gentiles have become receptacles fit for the Spirit. Gentiles are also among those *to whom the Holy Spirit can be given.* Some argue that the inclusion of gentiles without their first being required to become Jewish converts is essentially driven by divine fiat.[38] The visions of Cornelius and Peter, as well as the manifestation of the Spirit, force the early church to accept God's decision even though it cuts against their understanding of the law and purity. This does not, however, fully explain the logic of the account.

Without question, Luke uses the story to illustrate God's leading in the matter of gentile inclusion. Yet this inclusion, particularly insofar as the account of Cornelius's conversion echoes the events of Acts 2 (see below), points to the conclusion that the forgiveness and purification Jesus made available to Jews is also available to gentiles. To put the matter differently, the logic that drives the narrative works as follows: the outpouring of the gift of the Spirit upon gentiles implies that these gentiles have been purified and are therefore able to be recipients of this gift. Given this logic, one suspects that concepts of Jewish sacrifice, and in particular the importance of such sacrifices for making purification and forgiveness, are near to hand for Luke.

Two related lines of evidence substantiate this suspicion. First, the summary conclusions that Luke draws in Acts 11:16–18 and 15:8–9 regarding the outpouring of the Holy Spirit upon Cornelius and his house make the connections between repentance/forgiveness, purification, and the reception of the Spirit more explicit than does the Acts 10 account itself.

In Acts 11 Peter defends his actions at Cornelius's house to some who take offense at his associating with gentiles. He explains that as he was speaking to Cornelius, God sent the Holy Spirit to Cornelius and to his house. On the basis of the Spirit's presence Peter goes on to say in 11:17, "If God gave the same gift to them [i.e., gentiles] as also to us who believe upon the Lord Jesus Christ, who was I that I should be able to hinder God?" The ramifications of gentiles being recipients of the Spirit are immediately clear to those challenging Peter: God, they conclude, must have granted repentance unto life even to the gentiles (11:18). Importantly, this "Gentile Pentecost"[39] prompts them to

---

38. E.g., E. Haenchen, *The Acts of the Apostles: A Commentary* (Louisville: Westminster John Knox, 1971), 362–63. Cf. J. B. Tyson, "The Gentile Mission and the Authority of Scripture in Acts," *NTS* 33 (1987): 619–31, esp. 629–30.

39. Wilson, *Gentiles and the Gentile Mission*, 177.

reason retrospectively from the presence of the Spirit to the conclusion that the gentiles have been given repentance unto life—a conclusion that plainly implies that the gentiles' sins have been forgiven (cf. Luke 24:47; Acts 2:38; 5:31).

In Acts 15:8–9 Peter similarly declares that God, who knows the heart, affirmed for the gentiles that they could hear, believe, and be saved by the word about Jesus by "giving them the Holy Spirit just as [it was given] to us and making no distinction between us and them, purifying [καθαρίσας] their hearts by faith." Again, God's act of giving the Spirit is retrospective and irrefutable proof that those who receive the Spirit have been purified.

When viewed together, these summaries of the significance of the Cornelius account suggest two corresponding points: (1) the language of "the repentance unto life" and "the purification of the heart" are closely related ways of referring to the same reality—specifically, both phrases describe a state in which one is able to receive the Holy Spirit; and (2) the reception of the Spirit is the proof that allows one to deduce, retrospectively, that someone has been granted the necessary forgiveness and corresponding state of purification.

The relationship between the state of forgiveness and purification and the ability to receive the Spirit correlates remarkably well with the basic logic of the atonement effected by blood sacrifice and the corresponding presence of God with his people detailed under the heading "Sacrifice and Sacrificial Atonement" above. As was shown, one of the central concerns of the sacrificial system was to bring about and maintain the states of forgiveness and purity necessary for the presence of God to remain among the people by dwelling in the holy of holies. God's presence at the temple and the people's ability to draw near to God were predicated on the performance of the sacrificial rituals prescribed by the law. From this perspective, Luke's language of repentance and purification, and in particular the connection of these with the outpouring of God's Spirit, points toward the conclusion that sacrificial categories are in fact informing his argument.

A second line of evidence further confirms the suspicion that cultic categories underlie the logic of Luke's narrative. Some point out that one of the images invoked by the rushing wind and the tongues of fire that come to rest upon the apostles' heads on Pentecost when the Spirit is first poured out is the appearance of the glory of the LORD as described in Jewish Scripture.[40] Of particular note are the descriptions in Exodus 40:34–38 and Leviticus 9:23–24 (cf. Num. 9:15–23) of the glory of the LORD filling the tabernacle and resting

40. E.g., Keener, *Acts*, 2:801–4. Cf. J. B. Chance, *Jerusalem, the Temple, and the New Age in Luke-Acts* (Macon, GA: Mercer University Press, 1988), 42–43.

upon it as a cloud by day and a fire by night after Moses had consecrated the priests and completed setting up and purifying all the tabernacle's spaces and accoutrements (Exod. 40:1–15, 29–32; Lev. 8:10–9:21). Here, after the consecration and inauguration of the tabernacle, God's glory takes up residence in the sanctuary in the form of fire and cloud. In accord with the logic of sacrifice, a close relationship exists in these texts between the inaugurating sacrifices, the installation of the priests, and the fiery manifestation of God's presence in the sanctuary (cf. 2 Chron. 5:1–7:7).

Along these lines, it may be significant that one pre-Lukan text that uses the language of "tongues of fire" is 1 Enoch. In 1 Enoch 14, Enoch ascends into heaven and sees that portions of the heavenly temple, and perhaps most conspicuously the heavenly holy of holies, are made up of "tongues of fire." Glen Menzies insightfully comments that in 1 Enoch 14 the function of these "tongues of fire" in heaven appears to be "to delimit spheres of holiness as one approaches closer and closer to the presence of God."[41]

Thus, the likely allusion in Acts 2 to the fiery glory of God's presence filling the tabernacle and dwelling among the people in the holy of holies further implies an underlying logic of sacrificial atonement, since the glory of God did not take up residence in the tabernacle until everything had been purified by Moses. To put the point differently, these accounts imply that before one could come into such close proximity with the divine that the Spirit would actually be given and the sign of the divine presence would rest upon him or her, something would have had to happen that made that person pure. From the standpoint of Second Temple Judaism, one of the most natural contexts for that kind of purification would be the sacrificial system.

In light of this evidence, the narrative of Acts suggests that the experience of the gift of the Spirit's outpouring led Jesus's early followers to assume that he had done something to make them pure in some new and amazing way, and their logic worked the same way with respect to Cornelius. If this is right, then the inference seems to follow that Jesus actually made some kind of sacrifice that purified people to the point that they could be recipients of God's own Holy Spirit. Moreover, when the Spirit is given to Cornelius and his household, Peter and his fellow Jewish believers appear to infer that this sacrifice allowed even the gentiles to be purified. This further suggests that the logic of Acts 10 does not cut against the sacrificial logic of forgiveness and purification; rather, it extends the reach of Jesus's sacrifice and the forgiveness and purification he effects even to gentiles. The atoning effects of Jesus's work underlie the

---

41. G. Menzies, "Pre-Lucan Occurrences of the Phrase 'Tongues of Fire,'" *Pneuma* 22 (2000): 27–60, here 41.

extension of forgiveness and purification to Cornelius and his house. The question, however, remains: If this is the correct logic for understanding the narrative here, when and where did Jesus offer this sacrifice?

One might assume that the answer to the preceding question would have to be that Jesus made this offering when he gave himself up to death on the cross. As noted above, however, exactly this assumption has led scholars to puzzle over the problem of Luke's lack of overt interest in the sacrificial significance of Jesus's crucifixion and surprising emphasis on Jesus's ascension and exaltation instead. The logic of sacrifice and sacrificial atonement under the preceding section "Sacrifice and Sacrificial Atonement" suggests that this "problem" may be due more to a misunderstanding of how the process of Jewish blood sacrifice actually worked than to some inscrutable Lukan agenda. In the next section of this chapter, I argue that texts such as Acts 2:33 and 5:31 provide answers, albeit implicitly, to the questions of when, where, and how Jesus offered the sacrifice that resulted in forgiveness and purification.

Acts and the Sacrificial Significance of Jesus's Place at God's Right Hand

Joel Green notes that "perhaps the clearest affirmation in Acts of the soteriological meaning of Jesus's exaltation comes in 5:30–31."[42] Here, he continues, one finds "a straightforward affirmation that Jesus's confirmation as Savior, as the one who 'gives' repentance and forgiveness, is grounded in his resurrection and ascension."[43] This seems to me to be exactly right. In fact, the syntax of the verse virtually demands this conclusion.

The main clause of Acts 5:31 reads, τοῦτον ὁ θεὸς ἀρχηγὸν καὶ σωτῆρα ὕψωσεν τῇ δεξιᾷ αὐτοῦ (God exalted this one [i.e., Jesus] to his right hand as Prince and Savior). The infinitival phrase that modifies this main clause gives the purpose of this exaltation: δοῦναι μετάνοιαν τῷ Ἰσραὴλ καὶ ἄφεσιν ἁμαρτιῶν (*in order to give* repentance to Israel and forgiveness of sins). Taken at face value, the verse presents a clear rationale for Jesus's exaltation: so that Israel would be able to repent and have their sins forgiven. The sacrificial overtones of repentance and forgiveness of sins go almost without saying; indeed, these are two major themes of Yom Kippur. Here, though, the cross is not identified as the element in the larger narrative of the early Christian

---

42. J. B. Green, "'Salvation to the End of the Earth' (Acts 13:47): God as Saviour in the Acts of the Apostles," in *Witness to the Gospel: The Theology of Acts*, ed. I. H. Marshall and D. Peterson (Grand Rapids: Eerdmans, 1998), 83–106, here 97.

43. Green, "'Salvation to the End of the Earth,'" 97.

confession about Jesus that produces these atoning results. Rather, it is the exaltation of Jesus to God's right hand that provides these benefits.

That Luke really means to identify the exaltation of Jesus as the event that effects atonement can also be inferred from Acts 2:33. Peter states in this verse that Jesus's pouring out of the Holy Spirit upon his followers comes as the result of his being exalted to the Father's right hand and receiving the gift of the Spirit (cf. John 16:7). Moreover, the outpouring of the Holy Spirit in Acts 2 is taken to be a sign that now, after Jesus's ascension, the day of salvation has arrived (cf. 2:21, 38).[44] If, as argued earlier, the implication here is that purification and forgiveness precede the reception of the Spirit, then the logical and temporal sequence in this passage correlates well with the statement in 5:31 that Jesus's exaltation occurred for the very purpose of achieving the forgiveness of Israel's sins. More simply put, both 2:33 and 5:31 suggest that Jesus's exaltation to God's right hand accomplished the kind of atoning benefits that the sacrificial system was designed to achieve and maintain. If this is correct, then it is plausible to conclude that Jesus's presence at God's right hand is a constitutive element of his atoning sacrifice. That is to say, Luke predicates the benefits of forgiveness and purification upon Jesus's exaltation, which coheres well with the process of Jewish sacrifice and the conception of atonement described under the heading "Sacrifice and Sacrificial Atonement" above.

One additional piece of evidence lends support to this conclusion. A number of biblical, Second Temple, and early Christian texts correlate the holy of holies with the divine throne room and the divine throne with the mercy seat, or cover, on the ark of the covenant.[45] If Luke is aware of such conceptions, then Jesus's location at the right hand of God in heaven would also imply his presence at the heavenly mercy seat, which corresponds with the place on earth where the high priest ministered by presenting blood once a year on Yom Kippur to obtain forgiveness and purification.

Hints in the account of Stephen's heavenly vision in Acts 7 suggest that Luke is aware of this conception. As Stephen looks into the heavens, which he has just referred to in juxtaposition with the temple in Jerusalem (7:47–50), he sees God's glory and Jesus as the Son of Man standing at God's right hand (7:55–56). That Stephen looks into the heavenly holy of holies may be inferred from his seeing the glory of God, which is often associated with God's presence in the holy of holies in Jewish Scripture.[46] Moreover, Stephen

44. Cf. Marshall, *Luke*, 178.
45. See, e.g., Lev. 16:2; 2 Kings 19:15; Pss. 80:1; 99:1; Isa. 6:1–4; 37:16; Ezek. 10:1–5; 43:6–7; Heb. 8:1–2 (cf. 4:16; 10:19–22); 1 En. 14:8–20; T. Levi 3:4–5; 5:1.
46. E.g., Exod. 40:34–35; 1 Kings 8:11; 2 Chron. 5:14; 7:1–2; Ezek. 10:4.

closely links heaven with God's true sanctuary (cf. 7:44, 48–49). But why does Jesus stand?[47] If Stephen is viewing the heavenly sanctuary, then Jesus's posture is remarkably similar to that of a high priest in the holy of holies who stood before the mercy seat to offer the blood on Yom Kippur.[48] The fact that Stephen has this vision while on trial before the Jewish high priest (7:1) for speaking against the temple in Jerusalem (6:13–14) further implies an intentional contrast between the heavenly temple and its high priest, who serves at God's heavenly throne/altar, and their earthly counterparts.[49] Luke, in other words, here associates God's heavenly throne with the heavenly sanctuary where Jesus ministers. These observations lend support to the view that the links in Luke-Acts between forgiveness, purification, and Jesus's exaltation are conceptualized in terms of the conveyance and presentation of an atoning sacrificial offering into God's presence.

In sum, Luke's predication of the new manifestation of the Spirit at Pentecost upon Jesus's exaltation to God's right hand (Acts 2:33) as well as the links he makes between Jesus's present location, repentance, forgiveness of sins, purification, and the ability to receive the Spirit (2:38; 5:31; 10:15, 28, 43; 11:18; 15:7–9) imply the influence of a sacrificial concept of atonement below the surface of his narrative. Once one grasps that Jewish sacrifice is a process whose central atoning elements consist of the priests' activities at the altars as they draw near to God and convey the sacrifice into God's presence, it becomes clear that the underlying logic of Luke's general emphasis throughout Acts on the salvific effects of Jesus's exalted position is consistent with these aspects of Jewish sacrificial practice.[50]

47. L. T. Johnson is one of the few to include the suggestion that Jesus adopts a cultic posture, though he does not definitively endorse this view or develop it (*The Acts of the Apostles*, Sacra Pagina 5 [Collegeville, MN: Liturgical Press, 1992], 139). C. P. M. Jones is more confident ("The Epistle to the Hebrews and the Lucan Writings," in *Studies in the Gospels: Essays in Memory of R. H. Lightfoot*, ed. D. E. Nineham [Oxford: Blackwell, 1955], 113–43, esp. 128). The argument of this chapter suggests one more member among the "family resemblances" between Luke-Acts and Hebrews that Jones attempts to identify. For discussions of other possible explanations, see, e.g., D. L. Bock, *Acts*, BECNT (Grand Rapids: Baker Academic, 2007), 311–12; F. F. Bruce, *The Book of the Acts*, rev. ed., NICNT (Grand Rapids: Eerdmans, 1988), 155–56.

48. Other early Christians conceptualized Jesus's presence at God's right hand in high-priestly terms. This is suggested by the allusions to Ps. 110:1 in Rom. 8:34 and Hebrews, esp. Heb. 1:3; 7:25; 8:1–2; 9:11–12, 24; 10:12–13 (cf. also 1 John 1:8–2:2; Rev. 1:12–13; 5:6–7).

49. Keener also notes the possibility that this imagery might imply Jesus's status as the heavenly high priest but deems the idea "more conspicuous in Luke-Acts by its absence" (*Acts*, 2:1441n1408). The larger argument advanced here, however, greatly increases the plausibility of such an interpretation.

50. It may be objected that Luke also links these benefits with the resurrection of Jesus (e.g., Luke 24:46–49; Acts 13:26–39). Limitations of space preclude a full discussion of these

The Cross and Early Christians, in Retrospect

If the preceding analysis is more or less correct, it follows that Luke is not likely to have thought that Jesus's death by itself could bear the full weight of procuring purification and forgiveness. Moreover, if he understood the culmination of sacrifice in terms of a priest (perhaps especially the high priest) approaching God and conveying offerings into the divine presence, then a new interpretive option for understanding his emphasis on the salvific significance of Jesus's exaltation becomes clear: Jesus's ascension and exaltation to God's right hand are the culmination of his sacrificial and atoning work. That is why Luke highlights these elements of the incarnation as achieving forgiveness and purification.

Such a conclusion invites further reflection. Luke clearly describes the outpouring of the Spirit as an event that occurred *after* Jesus's ascension to the Father. Historical-temporal realities are likely to underlie Luke's claim here: the earliest followers of Jesus did not experience the ecstatic presence of the Spirit until some time had passed after Jesus's crucifixion.[51] In historical terms, Luke's account coheres with the fact that Jesus's crucifixion did not directly produce the experience of the outpouring of the Spirit. If the earliest Christians thought that Jesus's crucifixion alone was a sacrifice fully sufficient for obtaining their forgiveness and purification, this temporal gap would be difficult to explain.

The thesis outlined above suggests, however, that early Christians who reflected on this historical sequence might have recognized more fully something profound about the crucifixion and ascension elements of the incarnation. Specifically, I propose that the fact of their experience of the outpouring of the Spirit at some point after the crucifixion probably enabled them to see in retrospect that Jesus's death was an essential *part* of the larger process of his atoning sacrifice. In light of their conviction that they had received the Spirit, which is presented in Acts as the proof that they had been purified and forgiven, early Christians could have understood Jesus's death as one element in the process of his sacrifice. On this account, it is unlikely that they would confuse or conflate the idea of Jesus's sacrificial death with the notion that his death was the sum total of his sacrifice.[52]

---

texts. Nevertheless, it is worth noting that while Luke distinguishes between Jesus's resurrection and exaltation, they are closely linked (esp. Chance, *Jerusalem, the Temple*, 64–65).

51. A similar pattern occurs in John's Gospel (cf. John 16:7 and 20:17–23). Here, too, Jesus's resurrection and ascension precede the disciples' reception of the Spirit.

52. To speak about a sacrificial death is not necessarily the same thing as to speak about death *as* a sacrifice. When an animal is slaughtered as a sin offering, that death is clearly sacrificial (unlike, say, slaughtering an animal in an agricultural setting). As demonstrated in the discussion of sacrifice given above, however, the slaughter/death of the animal is not the definition or sum

The experience of the Spirit, as well as the temporal space between the crucifixion and that experience, might be partly rendered intelligible as a salvific event by way of appeal to Jewish sacrificial practice. If, as I have argued that Acts implies, the experience of the Spirit's presence among Jesus's followers led them to infer that Jesus had somehow purified them and forgiven their sins, it is plausible to imagine that they would conclude that Jesus must have done something that effected sacrificial atonement on their behalf. In view of the process of sacrifice described above, it hardly seems a stretch to imagine that they would particularly link this atonement with Jesus's present location at God's right hand in heaven.[53] The entire *process* of Jewish blood sacrifice, in other words, may have provided them with critical elements for filling out the script or narrative to explain how the death, resurrection, and ascension of Jesus resulted in purification and the outpouring of the Spirit.

To press the point a bit further, if they conceived of sacrifice as a process, early Christians could plausibly be imagined as having needed something more than Jesus's death to understand how Jesus had made their experience of purification and forgiveness possible. It seems highly unlikely that a first-century Jew would link the bare fact of Jesus's death with the atoning results of the sacrificial system. Historically, one suspects that something more was necessary. That "something more," I suggest, was the connection between Jesus's absence and the experience of the presence of the Spirit.[54]

Conclusion

As noted at the beginning of this chapter, many scholars have rightly highlighted Luke's "failure" to unpack the sacrificial meaning of the crucifixion. The preceding argument suggests that they have wrongly, however, assumed that Luke has therefore thrust a sacrificial model of Jesus's atoning work into the background of his narrative. Texts such as Acts 2:33 and 5:31, especially when viewed together with the other aspects of Acts that connect forgiveness and purification with Jesus's heavenly exaltation, imply instead that Luke's

---

total of sacrifice. Indeed, what is actually offered as the sacrifice is not the death of the animal but its blood/life and bodily material.

53. That Ps. 110:4 already informed their understanding and application of Ps. 110:1 to Jesus also seems highly likely.

54. This explanation does not intend to reduce early Christian thinking about Jesus's death only to retrospective reflection. A confluence of other factors must also be considered (Jesus's ransom saying, martyr traditions, etc.). Rather, I am here suggesting that the fact of Jesus's absence and the correlated experience of the Spirit were crucial for helping to develop and clarify sacrificial conceptions of Jesus's work precisely because they allow for a strong analogy between key elements in the Christ event and the larger logic and practice of sacrifice.

linking of repentance, purification, forgiveness of sins, Jesus's elevation to God's right hand, and the pouring out of the Holy Spirit owes much to an underlying Jewish sacrificial model of atonement.

That the sacrificial logic inherent within these connections has so often gone unrecognized in modern scholarship appears to stem from an overly reductive conception of sacrifice and how it works. Sacrificial slaughter, rather than being the focal point of the ritual, is one among a number of constitutive elements. Given the hierarchical structure of the process of sacrifice, approaching the divine presence and conveying or presenting the sacrifice to God are the foci of the ritual, the elements most closely linked with the accomplishment of sacrificial atonement. That Luke does not identify Jesus's death per se with the atoning results of forgiveness and purification can be partly explained, then, by appeal to this kind of Jewish sacrificial logic. Thus, a sacrificial logic probably does inform Luke's understanding of Jesus's saving work. This explanation provides a plausible rationale for why he directly connects the risen Jesus's exaltation to God's right hand with the atoning benefits that Jesus has achieved.

In conclusion, a few thoughts about the possible significance of this thesis for larger approaches to the study of Luke-Acts are in order. First, the argument pursued here goes some way toward explaining why Acts, more than the Gospel of Luke, emphasizes the proclamation of the resurrected and reigning Christ as enabling the new reality of the offer of the forgiveness of sins, purification, and the outpouring of the Spirit. The sacrificially atoning effects of Jesus's salvific work (forgiveness of sins and purification) probably do not follow for Luke from a nonsacrificial logic that connects these directly with or deduces them exclusively from the event of Jesus's death. More important for achieving these sacrificial benefits is his exaltation to God's right hand. This is the time and place at which he presented and offered his sacrifice to God. Second, while there is no doubt that a great deal can be and has been learned about Luke-Acts by locating the text in a variety of Greco-Roman contexts, the findings of this essay suggest in fresh ways the essential importance of the larger Jewish religious context for interpreting Luke's work, as well as ways in which his understanding of who Jesus is and what Jesus has done respect and cohere with that context.

15

Affirming the "Creed"

The Extent of Paul's Citation of an Early Christian Formula in 1 Corinthians 15:3b-7

In 1922 Adolf von Harnack published an essay in which he suggested that the accounts of Jesus's post-resurrection appearances to Peter and James mentioned in 1 Corinthians 15:5 and 7 indicated that these individuals were leaders of competing factions in the early church.[1] He argued, on the one hand, that within the pre-Pauline formula quoted in verses 3b–5 the appearance motif served as evidence for the reality of Christ's resurrection. On the other hand,

I first proposed the thesis of this chapter in a seminar at Duke University led by Joel Marcus. I am especially grateful to him both for his critical comments and for encouraging me to pursue the idea further. I have subsequently presented versions of this chapter to the Christianity in Antiquity Colloquium of the Department of Religious Studies, the University of North Carolina at Chapel Hill; the New Testament Section of the 2006 Regional Society of Biblical Literature conference (SECSOR), Atlanta, GA; and the German-English New Testament Colloquium of the Evangelisch-Theologisches Seminar, Eberhard Karls Universität Tübingen. I benefited greatly from these conversations, but the critiques and comments of Bart Ehrman, Hermann Lichtenberger, and David deSilva were particularly helpful. I am also grateful to Hans Arneson, Leroy Huizenga, Timothy Sailors, and Rodrigo Morales for reading and commenting on versions of this chapter. Finally, I wish to thank the Deutsch-Amerikanische Fulbright Kommission and the Institute of International Education as well as Hermann Lichtenberger and the Institut für antikes Judentum und hellenistische Religionsgeschichte.

1. A. von Harnack, *Die Verklärungsgeschichte Jesu: Der Bericht des Paulus (I. Kor. 15, 3 ff.) und die beiden Christusvisionen des Petrus* (Berlin: Verlag der Akademie der Wissenschaften, 1922), 62–80.

he claimed that the appearances to Peter and the Twelve (v. 5) and to James and the apostles (v. 7) could be isolated from the pre-Pauline formula. He thought these traditions originally circulated independently and served to legitimate the authority of Peter and James as leaders in their respective communities.

Harnack's larger thesis has not been broadly endorsed, but his conclusion that only verses 3b–5 belong to the pre-Pauline formula cited in 1 Corinthians 15 helped shape an enduring consensus that Paul himself extended the appearance motif of the formula (i.e., vv. 6–7). Harnack was not the first to draw this conclusion,[2] but the kinds of arguments he made are seldom questioned and often repeated. For the past century the consensus position has been that only verses 3b–5 are part of a discrete pre-Pauline formula.

Against this view I argue that the extent of the so-called creed[3] reaches from verse 3b to verse 6a and also includes verse 7. To make this case I first review and then critique Harnack's arguments. In the course of my critique I point out overlooked phenomena in the text. I then turn to examine some of the explanations offered for why Paul would have enlarged the list of appearances—as he must have done if verses 6–7 are not part of the formula. I contend that the reasons usually given for why Paul added more witnesses fail to explain adequately both the form of the text and the progression of the argumentation in 1 Corinthians 15. There are better reasons to think that only verses 6b and 8 represent Paul's additions to the preformulated "creed" than to suppose that he is responsible for redacting and/or adding all of the material in verses 6–7. Yet if this thesis can be sustained, it further suggests that while Harnack may have mistakenly assumed that within the formula the witnesses function as proof for Jesus's resurrection, he rightly saw that the appearance motif most likely served to legitimate early Christian leaders.

The Majority's Text: The Case for Limiting the Citation of the Formula to Verses 3b–5

Harnack gives four arguments for why Paul's citation of a preformed unit of traditional material in 1 Corinthians 15 ought to be limited to verses 3b–5. He notes first the shift from the four ὅτι's in verses 3b–5 to the ἔπειτα in verse 6. In his view this change marks a new construction that signals a transition from

---

2. See, e.g., G. Heinrici, *Erster Brief an die Korinther*, KEK 5 (Göttingen: Vandenhoeck & Ruprecht, 1888), 434; A. Seeberg, *Der Katechismus der Urchristenheit* (Leipzig: Georg Böhme, 1903), 50–54.

3. Throughout this chapter, the term "creed" will be placed in quotes and only indicates a unit of formulaic material. The term is not intended to denote the more fully developed formulas one finds in the third and fourth centuries.

Paul's recitation of the formula to his own reporting of additional encounters with the risen Jesus. Harnack argues, "After the words εἶτα τοῖς δώδεκα another construction occurs: up to this point it has been ὅτι . . . καὶ ὅτι . . . καὶ ὅτι . . . καὶ ὅτι. Now, however, he no longer reports but directly narrates: ἔπειτα ὤφθη κτλ."[4] He comments further, "This is already a strong argument but it is not yet decisive."[5] Thus he provides a second argument. "The words ἐξ ὧν οἱ πλείονες μένουσιν ἕως ἄρτι, τινὲς δὲ ἐκοιμήθησαν [v. 6b]," he writes, "certainly do not belong to the tradition [i.e., creed]; Paul indisputably added them himself. Yet this makes it much easier to suppose that here he does not continue reporting but offers his own account."[6] His third argument relates closely to the second one. If the new construction begun in verse 6 ends with Paul's own commentary in verse 8, it follows that verses 6–7 must also have been added by Paul. To quote Harnack again: "The three final clauses (ἔπειτα . . . ἔπειτα . . . ἔσχατον) are formally constructed in a similar way, as are the four preceding clauses that begin with ὅτι. The third of these final clauses, however, is clearly not part of the tradition but is the Apostle's own narration. Therefore, the first two of the final three clauses should also not be considered part of the tradition."[7]

Harnack's fourth point focuses on the supposed internal structure of 1 Corinthians 15:3b–5. Significantly, this is also the argument Harnack considered "to be the most important."[8] In his words: "When one looks particularly at the material reported with the ὅτι's, one sees at the start that the reported material does not consist of five parts but only of four."[9] He goes on to add, "Actually, not four but really only two; namely, *two main clauses and two associated clauses that validate them.*"[10]

---

4. Translations of Harnack throughout this chapter are mine. Harnack's original German is preserved in the notes. "Nach den Worten εἶτα τοῖς δώδεκα tritt eine andere Konstruktion ein: bisher hieß es ὅτι . . . καὶ ὅτι . . . καὶ ὅτι . . . καὶ ὅτι, nun aber wird nicht mehr referiert, sondern direkt erzählt: ἔπειτα ὤφθη κτλ" (Harnack, *Die Verklärungsgeschichte Jesu,* 63).

5. "Schon dieses Argument ist sehr stark, aber es entscheidet noch nicht" (Harnack, *Die Verklärungsgeschichte Jesu,* 63).

6. "Die Worte ἐξ ὧν οἱ πλείονες μένουσιν ἕως ἄρτι, τινὲς δὲ ἐκοιμήθησαν [v. 6b] gehören sicher nicht zur Überlieferung; Paulus hat sie unstreitig von sich aus dieser hinzugefügt. Aber dann ist doch die Annahme viel einfacher, daß er hier überhaupt nicht mehr referiert, sondern selbst erzählt" (Harnack, *Die Verklärungsgeschichte Jesu,* 63).

7. "Die drei Schlußsätze (ἔπειτα . . . ἔπειτα . . . ἔσχατον) sind formell ebenso gleichartig gebaut wie die vier mit ὅτι eingeführten voranstehenden Sätze; der dritte von ihnen ist aber sicher nicht mehr ein Teil der Überlieferung, sondern Erzählung des Apostels selbst; also werden auch die beiden ersten nicht zur Überlieferung zu rechnen sein" (Harnack, *Die Verklärungsgeschichte Jesu,* 63).

8. ". . . als das wichtigste" (Harnack, *Die Verklärungsgeschichte Jesu,* 63).

9. "Betrachtet man das mit ὅτι gegebene Referat genauer, so ist zunächst festzustellen, daß es nicht fünf Mitteilungen enthält, sondern nur vier" (Harnack, *Die Verklärungsgeschichte Jesu,* 63).

10. "Aber auch nicht vier, sondern nur zwei, nämlich *zwei Hauptsätze und zwei sie sicherstellende Begleitsätze*" (Harnack, *Die Verklärungsgeschichte Jesu,* 63).

The "creed" therefore contains a double focus and a corresponding 2 × 2 structure. There are two main clauses, each containing a fundamental assertion, and both of these are further supported by an accompanying clause that provides evidence to substantiate their assertions. As Harnack put it, the two main clauses "attest to the two decisive facts upon which all Christian belief is founded: *the salvific death and the resurrection*,"[11] while the two accompanying clauses serve to shore up the certainty of these foundational affirmations. "The burial," he comments, "confirms the reality of the death and the appearance secures the reality of the resurrection."[12] Moreover, he finds this logic and structure so compelling that the notion that such a structure "would have been weighed down by the added visions of the five hundred brothers, and of James, and of all the Apostles, is an unbelievable assumption, since these additions no longer conform to the formulaic character of the tradition."[13] Therefore, with respect to 1 Corinthians 15:6–7, "one can say with confidence that Paul himself crafted them so as to distinguish between the reported material and the narrated material."[14]

In sum, given that the list of witnesses mentioned in 1 Corinthians 15:6–7 are introduced with the adverb ἔπειτα (i.e., the series of καὶ ὅτι's does not continue) and given that verses 6b and 8 speak of matters that Paul relates from his own time, Harnack concludes that this list overextends the formula's element of verification for the resurrection and in so doing weighs down or disrupts the self-evident 2 × 2 structure of the material in verses 3b–5. Since this overextension also includes commentary from Paul, it follows that Paul added all of it. In addition, since the 2 × 2 structure in verses 3b–5 correlates with the two essential affirmations of early Christian proclamation (Jesus's salvific death and Jesus's resurrection), only that material "is really the gospel (in nuce), which was designated as such by Paul in his introduction (v. 1)."[15] The pre-Pauline formula, therefore, encompasses only verses 3b–5.

Harnack's case, especially his argument regarding the break in the ὅτι construction and his claim about the balanced 2 × 2 structure of 1 Corinthians 15:3b–5, has contributed to a near universal consensus. Indeed, with

11. ". . . bezeugen die beiden entscheidenden Tatsachen, auf die sich aller Christenglaube gründet, *den Heilstod* und *die Auferstehung*" (Harnack, *Die Verklärungsgeschichte Jesu*, 63–64).

12. "Das Begräbnis stellt den wirklich erfolgten Tod und die Visio stellt die wirklich erfolgte Auferstehung sicher" (Harnack, *Die Verklärungsgeschichte Jesu*, 64).

13. ". . . noch durch die Anhängsel der Visionen der 500 Brüder, des Jakobus und aller Apostel beschwert gewesen ist, ist eine unglaubliche Annahme, da diese Anhänge dem formelhaften Charakter der Überlieferung nicht mehr entsprechen" (Harnack, *Die Verklärungsgeschichte Jesu*, 65).

14. ". . . darf man zuversichtlich sagen, daß Paulus selbst alles getan hat, um Referat und Erzählung . . . zu unterscheiden" (Harnack, *Die Verklärungsgeschichte Jesu*, 65).

15. ". . . ist wirklich das Evangelium (in nuce), wie sie als solches in der Einleitung (v. 1) von Paulus bezeichnet worden ist" (Harnack, *Die Verklärungsgeschichte Jesu*, 64–65).

the exception of a few scholars who have argued for an even shorter original "creed,"[16] and a few who caution against the conclusion that this is a pre-Pauline formula at all,[17] the majority position for the last century has been that represented by Harnack.[18] Arguments defending the presence and extent of the "creed," when offered at all, often do little more than add supplemental comments to the 2 × 2 structure Harnack highlighted.[19]

16. E.g., J. Héring, *La Première Épître de Saint Paul aux Corinthiens* (Paris: Delachaux & Niestlé, 1959), 134. A few scholars have taken up Harnack's theory that Paul redacted two competing appearance traditions and have used it to argue that the original formula ends either with v. 4 or with v. 5a. See, for instance, E. Bammel, "Herkunft und Funktion der Traditionselemente in 1. Kor. 15,1–11," *Theologische Zeitschrift* 11 (1955): 401–19; H.-W. Bartsch, "Die Argumentation des Paulus in 1 Cor 15,3–11," *ZNW* 55 (1964): 261–74; and, with reservations, P. Winter, "1 Corinthians XV 3b–7," *NovT* 2 (1957): 142–50. As will be discussed below, however, attempts to argue that the list of appearances represents material originally distinct from the older formula and then added by Paul stand and fall with the strength of the case for why Paul would have extended the appearance element of the "creed" in the first place.

17. E.g., A. Robertson and A. Plummer, *A Critical and Exegetical Commentary on the First Epistle of St. Paul to the Corinthians*, ICC (Edinburgh: T&T Clark, 1929), 333, describe this text as "almost a creed; but we need not suppose it had already been formulated." See also P. Bachmann, *Der erste Brief des Paulus an die Korinther*, Kommentar zum Neuen Testament 7 (Leipzig: Deichertsche, 1936), 428–29; and, more recently, D. E. Garland, *1 Corinthians*, BECNT (Grand Rapids: Baker Academic, 2003), 684. The stylistic alternation that I discuss below, however, points in the direction of pre-Pauline formulation.

18. Notably, the shift from ὅτι to ἔπειτα led J. Weiss—one of the few who held the view that the appearances in vv. 6–7 probably belonged to the "creed"—to suggest that Paul himself reformulated the list of appearances for the purposes of stylistic variation. See *Der erste Korintherbrief* (Göttingen: Vandenhoeck & Ruprecht, 1910), 351.

19. For instance, in his well-known suggestion that 1 Cor. 15 contains a Greek translation of an earlier Aramaic confession, J. Jeremias credits Harnack with demonstrating that "[the creed] consists of the verses 1 Cor. 15:3b from Χριστός to 1 Cor. 15:5 δώδεκα, as indicated by the break in the construction between v. 5 and v. 6" (my translation; Jeremias's original: "es umfaßt die Verse 1.Kor. 15,3b von Χριστός bis 1.Kor. 15,5 δώδεκα, wie u.a. der Bruch der Konstruktion zwischen V.5 und 6 beweist"; see J. Jeremias, *Die Abendmahlsworte Jesu* [Göttingen: Vandenhoeck & Ruprecht, 1960], 95). Additionally, some of the key monographs of the last century on the forms and development of early Christian liturgical and confessional material consider the question of the "creed's" extent a settled matter and move on from that assumption for the purposes of their own comparative work (e.g., V. H. Neufeld, *The Earliest Christian Confessions* [Leiden: Brill, 1963]; R. Deichgräber, *Gotteshymnus und Christushymnus in der frühen Christentheit: Untersuchungen zu Form, Sprache und Stil der frühchristlichen Hymnen*, SUNT 5 [Göttingen: Vandenhoeck & Ruprecht, 1967]). Deichgräber actually comments, "1 Cor 15:3–5 can serve as a paradigmatic example of a 'Christian creed'" (my translation; Deichgräber's German: "Als ein Musterbeispiel [eines "Christusbekenntnisses"] mag 1 K 15,3–5 dienen"; *Gotteshymnus und Christushymnus*, 108). He adds, "It is unnecessary here to delve into all the particular problems and the nearly endless literature. A broad consensus holds today regarding the extent of the creedal formula: the old text extends only to v. 5" ("Es ist nicht notwendig, hier auf alle Einzelprobleme und auf die nahezu uferlose Literatur einzugehen. Über die Abgrenzung der Formel herrscht heute weitgehen Einigkeit: Der alte Text reicht nur bis V.5"). In his opinion, the a–b, a′–b′ (i.e., 2 × 2) structure of vv. 3b–5 "is completely clear" ("ist völlig klar"). See also K. Wengst, *Christologische Formeln und Lieder des Urchristentums*, Studien zum Neuen

Structural Limitations: Assessing the Case for Limiting the Creed

In assessing Harnack's claim, I begin by noting that it simply does not follow that the presence of material that clearly comes from Paul in the immediate context of 1 Corinthians 15:3b–5—namely, 6b and 8—makes it easier to conclude that verses 6a and 7 also do not belong to the original formula. This is not the linchpin of Harnack's argument, but it is nevertheless important to recognize that the status of verses 6a and 7 relative to verses 3b–5 cannot be determined by the fact that verses 6b and 8 are obviously Pauline. It no more follows from the presence of verses 6b and 8 that verses 6a and 7 come from Paul than that verses 3b–5 are Pauline, since he obviously wrote verses 1–3a and verses 8–58. The relationship of verses 6a and 7 to verses 3b–5 must be decided on different grounds.

A more significant element in Harnack's case concerns the shift between 1 Corinthians 15:5 and 6 from καὶ ὅτι to ἔπειτα. Harnack and others[20] suggest that this shift signals an obvious break in the formula. It is unclear, however, that this change in construction necessitates the conclusion that Paul has ceased citing the tradition and begun adding his own commentary. In fact, two features of verses 6–7 indicate that the break in the ὅτι pattern does not necessarily need to be interpreted as a transition from the traditional formula.

First, in contrast to the material in 1 Corinthians 15:3b–5, the ἔπειτα clauses in verses 6–7 continue to recount an element of the formula already presented—the listing of appearances of the risen Christ. Yet this is significant since prior to this point one sees a clear pattern in the traditional material— each instance of ὅτι introduces a new motif. This pattern continues until verse 5b, where, for the first time, the repetition of a creedal motif occurs. Intriguingly, this repetition is effected by the use of εἶτα and not another ὅτι (as one might have expected given the previous pattern).[21] At the very least this

---

Testament 7 (Gütersloh: Gütersloher Verlagshaus, 1972), 92–101. Of these three, only Wengst mounts a significant defense for limiting the formula.

20. E.g., P. Feine, *Die Gestalt des apostolischen Glaubensbekenntnisses in der Zeit des Neuen Testaments* (Leipzig: Dörffling & Franke, 1925), 48; and, more recently, Bartsch, *Die Argumentation des Paulus*, 263; H. Conzelmann, *1 Corinthians*, Hermeneia (Philadelphia: Fortress, 1975), 257; J. Kloppenborg, "An Analysis of the Pre-Pauline Formula in 1 Cor 15:3b–5 in Light of Some Recent Literature," *CBQ* 40 (1978): 351–67, esp. 351–52; W. Schrage, *Der erste Brief an die Korinther, IV, 1 Kor 15,1–16,24*, EKKNT 7/4 (Düsseldorf: Benziger, 2001), 19–21. See also n. 16 in the present chapter.

21. One might object that the εἶτα of 1 Cor. 15:5 ought not to be considered on equal terms with the other ὅτι clauses since it does more than the paratactic string of ὅτι's by introducing a relatively clear chronological marker. I would point out, however, that the use of εἶτα here is no less paratactic than the ὅτι sequence. One should also note that the formula already shows a chronological progression. The enumeration of died, buried, rose, and appeared is by its very nature chronological. It hardly seems problematic to suppose that adding the appearance to

suggests that the shift away from the ὅτι construction actually begins in verse 5b, before the ἔπειτα sequence starts in verses 6–7. Also, while the paucity of undisputed formulaic material makes it difficult to reach a firm conclusion, it is interesting to note that precisely where the ὅτι sequence ends, another pattern appears—the repetition of a creedal motif (ὤφθη).

Second, there are neglected structural phenomena in 1 Corinthians 15:6–7 that need to be considered. If one considers verses 6–7 together with verse 5b, a striking εἶτα . . . ἔπειτα . . . ἔπειτα . . . εἶτα pattern of coordinating terms emerges. To illustrate this I have included the text of 15:3–8 below.

3 παρέδωκα γὰρ ὑμῖν ἐν πρώτοις, ὃ καὶ παρέλαβον,
   ὅτι Χριστὸς ἀπέθανεν ὑπὲρ τῶν ἁμαρτιῶν ἡμῶν κατὰ τὰς γραφὰς
4 καὶ ὅτι ἐτάφη
   καὶ ὅτι ἐγήγερται τῇ ἡμέρᾳ τῇ τρίτῃ κατὰ τὰς γραφὰς
5 καὶ ὅτι ὤφθη Κηφᾷ
   εἶτα τοῖς δώδεκα·
6 ἔπειτα ὤφθη ἐπάνω πεντακοσίοις ἀδελφοῖς ἐφάπαξ,
   ἐξ ὧν οἱ πλείονες μένουσιν ἕως ἄρτι,
   τινὲς δὲ ἐκοιμήθησαν·
7 ἔπειτα ὤφθη Ἰακώβῳ
   εἶτα τοῖς ἀποστόλοις πᾶσιν·
8 ἔσχατον δὲ πάντων ὡσπερεὶ τῷ ἐκτρώματι ὤφθη κἀμοί.

The remarkable parallels here between 1 Corinthians 15:5b–6a and 7 are obvious. Indeed, if for the sake of argument one momentarily excludes the material indisputably added by Paul (i.e., vv. 3a, 6b, and 8),[22] the following text results:

3b ὅτι Χριστὸς ἀπέθανεν ὑπὲρ τῶν ἁμαρτιῶν ἡμῶν κατὰ τὰς γραφὰς
4 καὶ ὅτι ἐτάφη
   καὶ ὅτι ἐγήγερται τῇ ἡμέρᾳ τῇ τρίτῃ κατὰ τὰς γραφὰς
5 καὶ ὅτι ὤφθη Κηφᾷ
   εἶτα τοῖς δώδεκα·
6 ἔπειτα ὤφθη ἐπάνω πεντακοσίοις ἀδελφοῖς ἐφάπαξ, . . .
7 ἔπειτα ὤφθη Ἰακώβῳ
   εἶτα τοῖς ἀποστόλοις πᾶσιν·

---

the Twelve with another καὶ ὅτι would in any way fail to communicate a continuation of the chronological recounting of the events listed. Thus it appears that the ὅτι construction actually breaks before v. 6. From the evidence, one can at least say that that break in the ὅτι construction correlates with a remarkable change in the undisputed traditional material—the shift from introducing a new motif to that of repeating a motif already introduced.

22. See my discussion below as well as sections "The Legitimation Position" and "The More Than Five Hundred" below for my argumentation for excluding this material.

Even with verse 6b present, the εἶτα . . . ἔπειτα . . . ἔπειτα . . . εἶτα sequence is unmistakable, but in this modified version the pattern shows up with particular clarity. Obviously, the two ἔπειτα's are not grammatically dependent upon the ὅτι construction. To my knowledge, however, scholars have not recognized the significance of the fact that while the ἔπειτα's do not depend grammatically on the ὅτι sequence, they are logically dependent on the last instance of ὅτι—that is, like verse 5b, they simply repeat the motif already introduced by the final ὅτι clause.

Perhaps more importantly, however, the sequence of εἶτα . . . ἔπειτα . . . ἔπειτα . . . εἶτα creates a remarkably rhythmic pattern enhanced by the fact that the two εἶτα phrases share the distinction of eliding their verbs, while the two ἔπειτα clauses both have their verbs present. Thus, although there is no grammatical subordination of the ἔπειτα . . . ἔπειτα . . . εἶτα sequence in 1 Corinthians 15:6–7 to the material in verses 3b–5 (as with the preceding material, the syntax remains strictly paratactic), there is nonetheless a clear chiastic pattern.[23] When read aloud, the sequence likely to catch the auditors' ears can be visually depicted as follows:

```
5    καὶ ὅτι ὤφθη Κηφᾷ
           εἶτα τοῖς δώδεκα
6a             ἔπειτα ὤφθη ἐπάνω πεντακοσίοις ἀδελφοῖς ἐφάπαξ,
7              ἔπειτα ὤφθη Ἰακώβῳ
           εἶτα τοῖς ἀποστόλοις πᾶσιν·
```

Intriguingly too, the last ὅτι clause and the last ἔπειτα clause show some obvious structural similarities. I have supplied the text below.

```
5    καὶ ὅτι ὤφθη Κηφᾷ
           εἶτα τοῖς δώδεκα
7    ἔπειτα ὤφθη Ἰακώβῳ
           εἶτα τοῖς ἀποστόλοις πᾶσιν.
```

Both verses 5 and 7 introduce a single figure (Κηφᾶς and Ἰάκωβος, respectively), and both then go on to add a larger group by means of a phrase con-

---

23. Surprisingly, this pattern receives very little attention in the secondary literature. Two notable exceptions are W. Schenk, "Textlinguistische Aspekte der Strukturanalyse: Dargestellt am Beispiel von 1Kor XV.1–11," *NTS* 23 (1977): 469–77, esp. 472–74; and, more recently, A. Eriksson, *Traditions as Rhetorical Proof: Pauline Argumentation in 1 Corinthians*, Coniectanea Biblica: New Testament Series 29 (Stockholm: Almqvist & Wiksell, 1998), 86–89.

joined by εἶτα in which the verb is implicit. There is, then, yet another level of parallelism that holds between verse 5 and verse 7.[24]

This last parallel is particularly striking since the use of ἔπειτα here in 1 Corinthians 15:7 is not only consistent with the repetition of the ὤφθη motif in verse 5b already discussed but, more interestingly, participates at the same time in the clear pattern created by the εἶτα . . . ἔπειτα . . . ἔπειτα . . . εἶτα sequence. In this way the presentation of the post-resurrection encounters mentioned in verse 7 not only mirrors the structure of those found of verse 5; it both continues the paratactic syntax of verses 3b–5 and repeats the motif introduced in verse 5 while also contributing to the staccato-like rhythm of the εἶτα . . . ἔπειτα . . . ἔπειτα . . . εἶτα sequence. Thus there are a number of remarkable structural and syntactical relationships between verses 3b–5, on the one hand, and 6a and 7, on the other.

Given that I have relied on excluding 1 Corinthians 15:6b and 8 from the analysis thus far, it is fitting that I briefly comment on this material. I say more about these portions of the text below, but in light of the discussion above, some stylistic observations are in order. I highlight two significant phenomena. First, Paul's style before and after the creedal citation corresponds perfectly with the style of the material in verses 6b and 8. Second, the style of the material of verses 3b–5 coheres well with that of verses 6a and 7. That is, there is a precise alternation between Paul's style and the style of the formula that exactly correlates with the presence of material known to have come from Paul.

First Corinthians 15:1 marks a natural transition in the epistle. The new section begins with the postpositive conjunction δέ and then continues in verses 1–2 with a series of relative clauses. In verse 3a one finds the postpositive γάρ and another relative clause. Thus in Paul's introduction to the creedal citation there is a clear pattern of postpositives and grammatical subordination by way of relative clauses. In verses 3b–6a not a single postpositive or relative clause occurs. Additionally, however, the clauses in verses 3b–6a also manifest a distinct pattern. Syntactically, this material is characterized by simple parataxis facilitated by a coordinating term followed immediately by a verb (excepting the first clause, where the subject occurs between the conjunction and the verb).

In light of these observations about the stylistic character of 1 Corinthians 15:1–3a and 3b–6a, it is curious that at the very point where one arrives at

---

24. While Harnack does not discuss the εἶτα . . . ἔπειτα . . . ἔπειτα . . . εἶτα sequence, he is aware of the parallels between vv. 5 and 7. In fact, these parallels are part of the evidence he adduces to argue that Paul has appended an earlier, preformulated appearance tradition about James and the apostles that circulated independently of the tradition about Peter and the Twelve (Harnack, *Die Verklärungsgeschichte Jesu*, 67–68).

material that is certain to have come from Paul (i.e., v. 6b), one finds a shift in syntax that matches the style of verses 1–3a. That is, verse 6b consists of a relative clause and contains the postpositive δέ. Then in verse 7 the same conjunction-verb parataxis characteristic of verses 3b–6a recurs. The style shifts again, however, in verse 8, where one finds both another instance of δέ and a break in the word-order pattern of coordinating term followed by a verb. In the clause of verse 8 the verb has been shifted all the way to the end. Moreover, one should note that verses 9–11 contain four more postpositives and a number of relative clauses.

Put differently, the material prior to 1 Corinthians 15:3b–6a, the material of verse 6b, and the material of verses 8–11—that is, precisely the material known to come from Paul—shows stylistic coherence.[25] Of particular note here is the penchant in this material for postpositives and relative clauses. By way of contrast, the material of verses 3b–6a and 7 is characterized by a consistent word order and a simple paratactic style that completely lacks postpositives and relative clauses. This is a remarkable coincidence, particularly in view of the earlier discussion regarding the relationships between verses 3b–5 and 6a and 7. Thus not only are there several fascinating structural parallels and patterns within the material of verses 3b–6a and 7; there is also an exact correlation between the stylistic and grammatical breaks in that material and the presence of material that coheres with Paul's style in the larger context.[26]

25. Here too one finds a phenomenon largely ignored in the secondary literature. One exception is the discussion in P. Stuhlmacher, *Das paulinische Evangelium, I, Vorgeschichte*, FRLANT 95 (Göttingen: Vandenhoeck & Ruprecht, 1968), 267–76. Stuhlmacher recognizes the difference between the style of vv. 6a and 7, on the one hand, and Paul's style in vv. 6b and 8, on the other. He thinks, however, that there is still a shift in style from v. 5 to v. 6a. Thus he is of the opinion that Paul has enlarged the tradition with other preformulated material to create his own expanded "credo" (see esp. 275–76).

26. Eriksson, *Traditions as Rhetorical Proof*, 86–89, argues that the break in the ὅτι construction suggests Paul redacted independent appearance accounts and then appended them to the original formula. In contrast with Harnack's view, though, Eriksson rightly highlights the chiastic εἶτα . . . ἔπειτα . . . ἔπειτα . . . εἶτα pattern. Given this sequence, he concludes that the original formula must have ended at v. 5a. Paul then devised the chiasm of vv. 5b–7 when he added the other appearances. Eriksson further suggests that Paul placed his own commentary in the middle of the chiasm in order to draw attention to the fact that some of those to whom Jesus appeared had died (see esp. his discussion on p. 254). As will become clear, I also think Paul inserted v. 6b to emphasize the death of some of the five hundred (see under the heading "The More Than Five Hundred" below). The problem with Eriksson's analysis, however, is twofold. First, if Paul is responsible for adding the "witnesses," it is curious that he did not formulate vv. 6–7 in such a way as to include himself in the chiastic structure (for more on this point see under the heading "The Legitimation Position" below). Second, and more importantly, Eriksson fails to account for the alternating style that occurs here. It seems on the whole simpler to suppose that Paul inserted v. 6b into the preformed structure of vv. 6a and 7 than to suppose that he copied the "creed's" style (v. 6a), used his own style

I would suggest that the alternating style here provides strong evidence that verses 3b–6a and 7 belong together as part of the formula.

In sum, six important points suggest the prudence of not placing too much weight on the shift from the ὅτι constructions to the εἶτα . . . ἔπειτα . . . ἔπειτα . . . εἶτα sequence when assessing the extent of the creedal citation. These points are as follows: (1) The ὅτι construction actually appears to break with the εἶτα of 1 Corinthians 15:5b. (2) The break in verse 5b correlates with the repetition of the appearance motif rather than the introduction of a new motif. (3) The shift that begins with the repetition of the appearance motif in verse 5b coheres well with the following ἔπειτα . . . ἔπειτα . . . εἶτα sequence in verses 6–7. (4) The εἶτα . . . ἔπειτα . . . ἔπειτα . . . εἶτα pattern shows many remarkable parallels and relationships both between verse 5 and verses 6–7 and within verses 6–7. (5) The ἔπειτα clauses continue the word order and paratactic syntax of verses 3b–5. (6) The breaks in the style of verses 3b–6a and 7 (i.e., v. 6b–c and vv. 8–11) correspond with the syntax and style of Paul. In other words, the real outlier in verses 3–7 is not all the material of verses 6–7 but only that of verse 6b (ἐξ ὧν οἱ πλείονες μένουσιν ἕως ἄρτι, τινὲς δὲ ἐκοιμήθησαν).

It should be noted that several significant textual witnesses do not support NA[27]'s εἶτα . . . ἔπειτα . . . ἔπειτα . . . εἶτα.[27] The general lack of attention the secondary literature pays to the variations in this sequence likely follows from the fact that the semantic distinction between εἶτα and ἔπειτα is minimal.[28] My observations, however, suggest that even if the semantic distinctions may not be very sharp, the pattern created by the sequence is highly significant. I must therefore briefly defend the sequence as it stands in NA[27].

According to the apparatus of NA[27], the manuscript tradition attests six different permutations of the εἶτα . . . ἔπειτα . . . ἔπειτα . . . εἶτα pattern. These sequences and the witnesses that attest them (where this can be ascertained from the apparatus of NA[27] and my own additional research) are as follows:

1. εἶτα . . . ἔπειτα . . . ἔπειτα . . . εἶτα. This is the sequence in NA[27] and is attested by B, D[2], Ψ, 𝔐, Ambst.
2. εἶτα . . . ἔπειτα . . . ἔπειτα . . . ἔπειτα: 𝔓[46] 0243 1739 1881.

(v. 6b), imitated the formula again (v. 7), and then returned to his style when describing his encounter (v. 8).

27. The text of 1 Cor. 15:3–8 that Harnack relied on was, though, the same as that of NA[27].

28. See, for instance, the brief note on the text-critical issue in v. 7 in A. C. Thiselton, *The First Epistle to the Corinthians*, NIGTC (Grand Rapids: Eerdmans, 2000), 1207. Thiselton comments that the presence of εἶτα or ἔπειτα here "makes little or no difference to the sense of the second *then*."

3. ἔπειτα . . . ἔπειτα . . . ἔπειτα . . . ἔπειτα: ℵ* A 33 81 614 1175.

4. ἔπειτα . . . ἔπειτα . . . ἔπειτα . . . εἶτα: ℵ².

5. καὶ μετὰ ταῦτα . . . ἔπειτα . . . ἔπειτα . . . εἶτα: D*.

6. καὶ μετὰ ταῦτα . . . ἔπειτα . . . ἔπειτα . . . ἔπειτα: F, G.

Thus there are three variants for the first member of the sequence (εἶτα, ἔπειτα, or καὶ μετὰ ταῦτα) and two for the last member (εἶτα or ἔπειτα). Naturally, each variant must be assessed on its own merits.

The reading καὶ μετὰ ταῦτα in 1 Corinthians 15:5b has little to commend it.[29] Deciding between ἔπειτα and εἶτα, however, is more difficult. According to NA[27], the reading ἔπειτα is attested by ℵ A 33 81 614 1175 and *pc*, though one also finds support in Cyril of Jerusalem[30] and Eusebius.[31] The evidence listed in NA[27] for εἶτα is as follows: 𝔓[46] B D² Ψ 0243 1739 1881 𝔐 Or.[32] Ambrosiaster also provides support.[33] Both readings are therefore attested by

29. The variant is only attested in the original hand of D, the later majuscules F and G, and the old Latin and Vulgate. Notably, all of the majuscules containing this reading belong to the Western text family. The variant is therefore late and limited to one text type. At the level of internal evidence the secondary character of the variant is suggested by the fact that the chronological clarity of the phrase καὶ μετὰ ταῦτα makes it easier to suppose that a scribe provided a gloss for either εἶτα or ἔπειτα than to suppose that the slightly more temporally ambiguous adverbs εἶτα or ἔπειτα would have independently arisen in the MSS tradition had καὶ μετὰ ταῦτα stood in the original. Moreover, G. Fee, *The First Epistle to the Corinthians*, NICNT (Grand Rapids: Eerdmans, 1987), 717n17, points out that in keeping with the theological tendency of the Western tradition, this reading heightens Peter's importance.

30. See *S. patris nostri Cyrilli Hierosolymorum archiepiscopi Opera quae supersunt omnia*, ed. W. C. Reischl and J. Rupp, CPG 3585/2 (Hildesheim: Olms, 1967), 2:136, where Cyril, within a loose citation, comments, καὶ ὤφθη Κηφᾷ ἔπειτα τοῖς δώδεκα.

31. See his somewhat paraphrastic quotation in E. Schwartz, ed., *Eusebius Werke*, vol. 2, *Die Kirchengeschichte*, GCS 9/1 (Leipzig: Hinrichs, 1903), 82. In the text known as *Quaestiones Euangelicae* (questionably attributed to Eusebius) the evidence is mixed, with support for both ἔπειτα (see PG 22:1013a5) and εἶτα (see PG 22:989d5).

32. See M. Borret, *Origen: Contre Celse*, SC 132 (Paris: Cerf, 1967), 432. See also E. Klostermann, *Origenes Werke*, vol. 11, *Origenes Matthäuserklärung*, GCS 38 (Leipzig: Hinrichs, 1933), 266, where the Latin version of Origen's Matthew commentary cites 1 Cor. 15:5–6a as follows: "Visus est . . . Cephae, postea illis undecim, deinde apparuit aplius quam quingentis fratribus simul" (He appeared . . . to Cephas, after that to the Eleven, then he appeared to more than five hundred brothers at the same time). Given that there is no evidence in the MSS tradition to doubt the certainty of ἔπειτα in v. 6, the variation here between "postea" (after that) and "deinde" (then) suggests that the Greek *Vorlage* was εἶτα . . . ἔπειτα.

33. See H. J. Vogels, ed., *Ambrosiastri Qui Dicitur Commentarius in Epistulas Paulinas*, vol. 2, *In Epistulas ad Corinthios*, CSEL 81/2 (Vienna: Hoelder-Pichler-Tempsky, 1968), 166, where Ambrosiaster presents lemmeta from 1 Cor. 15:5–7 and then comments on them. The relevant lemmata read, "Et quia visus est Cephae . . . Postea illis undecim . . . Deinde apparuit plus quam quingentis fratribus simul . . . Deinde apparuit Iacobo . . . Postea apostolis omnibus" (And that he appeared to Cephas . . . after that to the Eleven. . . . Then he appeared to more than five hundred brothers at the same time. . . . Then he appeared to James. . . . After that

witnesses within the Alexandrian text family and, particularly in view of the additional patristic evidence, can boast some geographic distribution. The presence of εἶτα in 𝔓⁴⁶ and Origen, however, makes it the earliest attested reading. Thus the external evidence slightly favors εἶτα.

The internal evidence, though, tends a bit more decisively toward εἶτα. On the one hand, εἶτα could more easily be the result of parablepsis than ἔπειτα. On the other hand, excluding 1 Corinthians 15:5–7, the literature associated with Paul in the early centuries of Christianity attests the use of ἔπειτα ten times,[34] while εἶτα occurs only four times.[35] Given the high degree of semantic overlap shared by these two terms, it seems more likely that a scribe familiar with other Pauline texts would change εἶτα to the more common ἔπειτα than vice versa. It is also worth noting that within the undisputed Pauline letters εἶτα is never attested outside of 1 Corinthians 15. Thus at the level of probability, the occurrence of εἶτα proves the more difficult and so more likely reading. Furthermore, all of the major manuscripts that attest ἔπειτα in verse 5 also attest ἔπειτα in verse 7 and thus read ἔπειτα for all four members of the sequence.[36] It seems easier to explain this phenomenon as a tendency toward the creation of uniformity in the sequence (notably along the lines of the statistically more common Pauline term) than it is to assume that an originally uniform sequence was later altered by a change from ἔπειτα in verse 5 to εἶτα. Thus it may be concluded that εἶτα is the most probable reading of the original text. Therefore, the first three terms in the sequence may with relative certainty be taken to be εἶτα . . . ἔπειτα . . . ἔπειτα.

The final adverb in the sequence is the most uncertain one. In terms of external evidence the case for ἔπειτα is strong. The NA²⁷ cites the following evidence: 𝔓⁴⁶ ℵ* A F G K 048 0243 33 81 614 630 1175 1739 1881 and *al.* In addition, one can find support in Origen[37] and Eusebius.[38] The attestation for εἶτα, however, is hardly insignificant and consists of ℵ² B D Ψ 𝔐 and

---

to all the Apostles). The *postea . . . deinde . . . deinde . . . postea* sequence here suggests the sequence in the Greek *Vorlage* of Ambrosiaster's version was εἶτα . . . ἔπειτα . . . ἔπειτα . . . εἶτα.

34. See 1 Cor. 12:28 (2x); 15:23, 46; Gal. 1:18, 21; 2:1; 1 Thess. 4:17; Heb. 7:2, 27.

35. See 1 Cor. 15:24; 1 Tim. 2:13; 3:10; Heb. 12:9.

36. The manuscripts are as follows: the original hand of ℵ, A, 33, 81, 612, and 1175. Thiselton, *First Epistle to the Corinthians*, 1186, rightly notes that the presence of ἔπειτα in ℵ, A, 33 is "drawn from v. 7."

37. This reading occurs twice in his *Contra Celsum*; see Borret, *Origen: Contre Celse*, 432, 438. See also the Latin translation of Origen's homily on Numbers in W. A. Baehrens, ed., *Origenes Werke*, vol. 7, *Homilien zum Hexateuch in Rufins Übersetzung*, GCS 30 (Leipzig: Hinrichs, 1921), 271, which reads, "Deinde apparuit et omnibus Apostolis" (then he also appeared to all the Apostles) and thus also likely supports ἔπειτα.

38. See Schwartz, *Die Kirchengeschichte*, 82, and Eusebius's commentary on the Psalms (see PG 23:696c13), which both read ἔπειτα ὤφθη τοῖς ἀποστόλοις πᾶσιν.

Ambrosiaster.[39] As was the case above, both of these readings can claim geographical distribution and distribution among text types. The ἔπειτα variant finds support among some of the Alexandrian witnesses, in Eusebius of Caesarea, and in some later Western family texts. The εἶτα reading has support from the Alexandrian B and the remarkable correction of ℵ, the Western D, and Ambrosiaster. Nevertheless, the presence of ἔπειτα in 𝔓[46] and Origen makes it the earliest attested reading and tips the external evidence slightly in the favor of ἔπειτα.

The internal evidence, however, points toward εἶτα for essentially the same reasons as were argued earlier. Given the preference for ἔπειτα in Pauline literature and, even more, given that this final member of the sequence in question is preceded by two instances of ἔπειτα, it seems more probable that a scribe would gravitate toward ἔπειτα here than toward εἶτα. Thus, as with verse 5b, it is easier to explain how ἔπειτα would have arisen within the transmission of the text than to explain how εἶτα would have arisen had ἔπειτα been the original reading. The occurrence of εἶτα is therefore more likely to represent the original text.

I turn, then, to examine Harnack's structural argument. For Harnack, the decisive argument concerns the internal relationships among the ὅτι clauses. As was discussed above, he sees a 2 × 2 structure in which the two foundational assertions of Christian belief (Christ's death for sins and his resurrection) are presented in clauses 1 and 3 and then verified by evidence (Christ's burial and his post-resurrection appearances) in clauses 2 and 4.

That there are four ὅτι clauses is clear enough. It is less certain, however, that the second and fourth clauses are provided for the purposes of verifying the claims of the first and the third clauses. That is to say, Harnack's 2 × 2 structure is hardly self-evident. In fact, it rests on a critical interpretive assumption—that the second and fourth clauses are primarily evidentiary in nature.

Yet this assumption is open to question. The syntax of 1 Corinthians 15:3b–5, it should be noted, does not immediately suggest this conclusion. As has been observed, the four clauses are strung along by way of straightforward parataxis. There is no grammatical subordination of clauses 2 and 4 to clauses 1 and 3. Indeed, the more obvious logical relationship among the four clauses is simple chronology. What can be claimed for certain about verses 3b–5 is that the ὅτι clauses present a sequential list of events. It may also be significant that both the paratactic syntax and the chronological sequence[40]

---

39. See n. 33.

40. It may be objected that the adverbs εἶτα and ἔπειτα do not necessarily carry a chronological sense. While this is true, the context here strongly suggests a chronological meaning for the εἶτα . . . ἔπειτα . . . ἔπειτα . . . εἶτα sequence. The first εἶτα clearly locates the appearance to the

continue on in verses 6a and 7.[41] Moreover, as more formal Christian creeds do develop, they show a distinct tendency in the christological portions toward a chronological enumeration of events in Jesus's life. One already sees this in the development of the *regula fidei* in the second and third centuries. In Ignatius, Justin, Irenaeus, Tertullian, and Origen one finds numerous examples of litanies in which Jesus is declared to have been born of a virgin, suffered, died, risen again, and ascended into heaven.[42]

By the time one comes to the full-blown creeds of the third and fourth centuries, this pattern has crystallized into an essential element in the christological confession. The slightly expanded list in this later material enumerates Jesus's conception by the Holy Spirit, his birth of the virgin Mary, his suffering under Pontius Pilate, his death on a cross, his burial, his resurrection, his ascension into heaven, and his session at God's right hand. All these points are obviously thought to be of significance, but it is not clear that the components of the litany are structured as supporting points intended to supply evidence for earlier, more significant or essential assertions. Neither is it clear that the members of the litany somehow demonstrate the truth of the primary assertion that they actually do follow (i.e., belief in Jesus as the only son of God and Lord). They appear, rather, to be little more than a chronological series of declarations that trace key events in the life of Jesus.

Strictly speaking, none of this disproves Harnack's interpretive assumption. The data do, however, suggest a fairly consistent interest in the chronological recounting of certain key moments in the incarnation. There is little to support the notion that later chronological litanies were constructed in terms of

---

Twelve after Peter's. The first ἔπειτα most naturally continues this chronological progression. Additionally, Paul's ἔσχατον . . . πάντων tips the scales a bit more decisively in the direction of chronological progression. Paul, at least, interprets the sequence of appearances in chronological terms, with his own experience coming "last of all." Given the surrounding material, it seems highly unlikely that the second ἔπειτα and the second εἶτα deviate from this chronological pattern. Notably, the rhetorical analysis of I. Saw, *Paul's Rhetoric in 1 Corinthians 15: An Analysis Utilizing the Theories of Classical Rhetoric* (Lewiston, NY: Mellen, 1995), 230, also supports this understanding of the sequence.

41. Eriksson, *Traditions as Rhetorical Proof*, 88, has slightly updated Harnack's claim by suggesting that clauses 2 and 4 serve as "amplifications" for clauses 1 and 3. Eriksson thinks this follows from the structure of the text since clauses 1 and 3 contain the addition of an adverbial phrase and the testimony of Scripture. He asserts that the burial reference therefore "shows the reality of the death and the appearance the reality of the resurrection." Yet, as with Harnack, Eriksson's assessment of the structure looks more like an interpretive assumption than a conclusion that must follow given the paratactic syntax of the text. To reiterate, the conclusion that the ὅτι clauses are more than a chronological enumeration of events does not self-evidently follow from the structure of the formula.

42. For the relevant texts see A. Hahn and G. L. Hahn, *Bibliothek der Symbole und Glaubensregeln der Alten Kirche* (Breslau: E. Morgenstern, 1897), 1–11.

main points then proven by subordinate points. The function appears rather to be the simple enumeration of certain pertinent events. Thus, if the formula in 1 Corinthians 15 belongs somewhere in the developmental trajectory of early Christian creeds, then the structure of main assertion substantiated by evidence that Harnack finds here is remarkably singular.[43] Indeed, one might well wonder why, as Christianity spread and its confessional forms solidified, the element of verification that is so crucial to the structure Harnack identifies disappeared from confessional formulas in favor of substantial sections privileging a straightforward chronological litany of events. One might have expected exactly the opposite *Tendenz*. That the *regula fidei* and the later creeds show a high commitment to chronological enumeration, however, may itself point toward the centrality of this mode of presentation at the earliest stages of confessional formulation.

Thus far in my argument I have sought to call into question Harnack's conclusion about the extent of the "creed" in 1 Corinthians 15. There are sound reasons to doubt that the break in the ὅτι structure signals the end of the formula, and there are sound reasons to doubt that the formula follows a 2 × 2 structure where a fundamental assertion is then further proven by evidence in a supporting point. What is certain is the chronological character of the events listed. This does not rule out other logical relationships, but notably the evidence from later Christian formulas suggests that within the chronological enumeration the relationships among the clauses do not appear to be evidentiary in nature.

Yet all of these reasons for doubt may be countered. One might suggest that the structural phenomena I pointed to in 1 Corinthians 15:6–7 come from Paul himself. Perhaps he wanted to imitate the structure of the formula. Following Harnack, a few scholars have suggested that Paul here combines competing appearance formulas that were already in circulation with the older "creed."[44] In addition, Paul obviously appeals to the formula in order to use it in his argument regarding the resurrection in chapter 15. Thus he may have had good apologetic reasons for adding the appearances mentioned in verses 6–7 to his citation of the formula.

All of these points raise important issues that will guide the analysis in the next section of this chapter. If Paul did add the material in 1 Corinthians

43. The chronological and enumerative character of the formula and its possible relationship to later creeds is yet another of the characteristics of this passage that have been largely overlooked in the secondary literature. A notable exception is J. Schmitt, "Le 'Milieu' littéraire de la 'Tradition' citée dans 1 Cor., XV, 3b–5," in *Resurrexit: Actes du Symposium International sur la Résurrection de Jésus*, ed. É. Dahnis (Rome: Libreria Editrice Vaticana, 1974), 169–80.
44. See n. 16.

15:6–7, and if he did so in a way that carefully imitates the grammar and style of the formula, then presumably this additional material holds some significance for his argument. I turn then to a brief exegetical study of chapter 15. In particular, I want to focus attention on the role of the material in verses 6–7 in relation to the broader argumentation of the chapter. If good reasons can be adduced for why Paul would have added the witnesses, then perhaps the consensus position may be allowed to stand in spite of my quibbles. If, however, verses 6–7 cannot be adequately explained by the shape of the argument in chapter 15, then perhaps the doubts I have attempted to raise, and in particular the peculiar correlation between the alternation of Pauline style and the formula's style, may tip the balance of probability in favor of a longer "creed" than is usually supposed.

Is 1 Corinthians 15:1-11 Apologetic or Legitimation? The State of the Dichotomy

Given the assumption that Paul has added the material in 1 Corinthians 15:6–7 to the formula of verses 3b–5, commentators have set themselves to the task of explaining how this list of appearances contributes to the broader argument Paul makes in the chapter. Two basic explanations show up repeatedly in the literature. On the one hand, some think that Paul added the witnesses for primarily apologetic reasons. Taking his cue from the evidential nature of the appearances in verse 5, Paul expanded the list in order to provide more evidence for the reality of Jesus's resurrection.[45] On the other hand, many recognize the difficulty of squaring the apologetic explanation with the larger argument Paul makes in this chapter and suggest instead that he appended the extra witnesses mainly in order to segue into yet another defense of the

45. E.g., Fee, *First Epistle to the Corinthians*, 718–19, 729–31; H. Grass, *Ostergeschehen und Osterberichte* (Göttingen: Vandenhoeck & Ruprecht, 1970), 148; R. B. Hays, *First Corinthians*, Interpretation (Louisville: John Knox, 1997), 260; Kloppenborg, "Analysis of the Pre-Pauline Formula," 351–67; J. Lambrecht, "Line of Thought in 1 Cor 15,1–11," *Greg* 72 (1991): 655–70, esp. 664–70; J. Murphy-O'Connor, "Tradition and Redaction in 1 Cor 15:3–7," *CBQ* 43 (1981): 582–89 (though Murphy-O'Connor has rightly noted in response to me that he thinks v. 7 also serves a legitimating function; see esp. his *Keys to First Corinthians: Revisiting the Major Issues* [Oxford: Oxford University Press, 2009], 240n58); J. Plevnik, "Paul's Appeals to His Damascus Experience and 1 Cor. 15:5–7: Are They Legitimations?," *Toronto Journal of Theology* 4 (1988) 101–11; Schrage, *Der erste Brief an die Korinther*, 54–55; R. Sider, "St. Paul's Understanding of the Nature and Significance of the Resurrection in 1 Corinthians XV 1–19," *NovT* 19 (1977): 124–41; Thiselton, *First Epistle to the Corinthians*, 1205–8; D. Watson, "Paul's Rhetorical Strategy in 1 Corinthians 15," in *Rhetoric and the New Testament: Essays from the 1992 Heidelberg Conference*, ed. S. E. Porter and T. H. Olbricht, JSNTSup 90 (Sheffield: JSOT Press, 1993), 231–49, here 237.

legitimacy of his apostolic status.[46] I will briefly discuss these positions and then scrutinize them in light of the text.

In 1 Corinthians 15:1–2 Paul says that he preached his gospel to the Corinthians, they accepted it, they are standing in it, and they are being saved by it. Yet curiously he also feels the need to "remind" (γνωρίζω) them of this very gospel. In addition, he qualifies his statement about them being saved with the conditional clause "if you hold firmly to the message proclaimed to you" and adds the suggestion that they might have believed "in vain" (εἰκῇ). Why does he include such apparently disturbing warnings? Perhaps more significantly, can one reconcile the tension between Paul's statements? Does he think the Corinthians are being saved and standing in the gospel, or does he fear they have believed in vain?

On the basis of these tensions, a number of scholars conclude that Paul thinks some of the Corinthians have failed to remain committed to his gospel. The presence of the additional appearances of the resurrected Jesus in 1 Corinthians 15:6–7, coupled with the fact that the topic of resurrection forms the bulk of the subject matter in the chapter, has led many to posit that Paul genuinely worries that some of the Corinthians are denying something essential about Jesus's resurrection. The tendency among these interpreters is to focus on the way the Corinthians have strayed doctrinally from Paul's original proclamation to them by redefining Jesus's resurrection in terms of a spiritual/noncorporeal event. Thus he adds the list of witnesses found in verses 6–7 as further evidence to substantiate the reality of Jesus's resurrection.[47] One frequently finds in the literature the comment that Paul adds the "witnesses" so that anyone who doubts Jesus's resurrection will see that there are a great

46. For a few versions of this opinion see K. Barth, *Die Auferstehung der Toten: Eine akademische Vorlesung über 1. Kor 15* (Zürich: Evangelischer Verlag, 1953), esp. 75–86; C. Bussmann, *Themen der paulinischen Missionspredigt auf dem Hintergrund der spätjüdisch-hellenistischen Missionsliteratur*, Europäische Hochschulschriften: Reihe 23, Theologie 3 (Bern: Lang, 1971), 101–3; G. Claudel, *La Confession de Pierre: Trajectoire d'une Péricope Évangélique*, Études Bibliques (Paris: Gabalda, 1988), esp. 146–53; R. F. Collins, *First Corinthians*, Sacra Pagina 7 (Collegeville, MN: Liturgical Press, 1999), 531; H. Conzelmann, "Zur Analyse der Bekenntnisformel 1. Kor. 15,3–5," *EvT* 25 (1965): 1–11; E. Lohse, "St. Peter's Apostleship in the Judgment of St. Paul, the Apostle to the Gentiles," *Greg* 72 (1991): 419–35; W. Marxsen, *Die Auferstehung Jesu von Nazareth* (Gütersloh: Gütersloher Verlagshaus, 1968), esp. 97–98; R. Pesch, "Zur Entstehung des Glaubens an die Auferstehung Jesu," *Theologische Quartalschrift* 153 (1973): 201–28, esp. 212–18; P. von der Osten-Sacken, "Die Apologie des paulinischen Apostolats in 1Kor 15 1–11," *ZNW* 64 (1973): 245–62, esp., 254–60; U. Wilckens, "Der Ursprung der Überlieferung der Erscheinungen des Auferstandenen: Zur traditionsgeschichtlichen Analyse von 1.Kor. 15,1–11," in *Dogma und Denkstrukturen*, ed. W. Joest and W. Pannenberg (Göttingen: Vandenhoeck & Ruprecht, 1963), 56–95.

47. See n. 45. For a succinct presentation of this view see Sider, "St. Paul's Understanding," 124–41.

many people who, if questioned, can confirm the fact.[48] As will be discussed below, the major difficulty with this interpretation is that it fails to explain the actual logic of Paul's argument. If this position is correct, it is remarkable that Paul never appeals back to his "witnesses" or suggests someone go question them. Nor does he actually proceed to argue for either the reality or nature of Jesus's resurrection. Rather, his argument consistently assumes that the Corinthians agree with him about Jesus's resurrection.[49]

The other widely embraced position holds that Paul has added the witness material primarily to allow himself to take one more opportunity to justify his own apostolic authority. In this chapter I cannot do justice to the many nuances and permutations within this position. Rather, I will speak broadly about its general claims. This interpretation tends to emphasize that the list of appearances reaches its apex with Paul's own account of his encounter with the risen Christ (1 Cor. 15:8). Its adherents sometimes claim that neither Paul nor the "creed" is overly concerned with proving Jesus's resurrection. Instead, Paul enlarges the list of witnesses in order to link his own encounter with Christ to those of the other apostles. He thereby establishes the parity of his apostolic call and the content of his gospel proclamation with that of the others. It follows that one of his main goals in verses 1–11 is to reassert the legitimacy of his apostolic status and authority, not necessarily to demonstrate the historical reality of Jesus's resurrection. As I will show, this reading does not provide the best explanation for the actual form of the text.

While the approaches sketched above differ substantially in their assessment of the role of 1 Corinthians 15:1–11 in relation to the broader argument of the chapter, both tend to share two important points. Proponents of both views generally assume that the warnings of verse 2 are real. Paul genuinely suspects that the salvation of some in Corinth is in danger and that they have believed his gospel in vain. Yet, more importantly, both interpretations tend to agree that since Paul has added verses 6–7 to the "creed," grasping

---

48. E.g., Garland, *1 Corinthians*, 689; Hays, *First Corinthians*, 257; Schrage, *Der erste Brief an die Korinther*, 58; Sider, "St. Paul's Understanding," 128; Thiselton, *First Epistle to the Corinthians*, 1205; C. Wolff, *Der erste Brief des Paulus an die Korinther*, Theologischer Handkommentar zum Neuen Testament 7 (Leipzig: Evangelische-Anstalt, 1996), 371.

49. Several of those who hold this basic position rightly understand that Paul's argument works from Jesus's resurrection as the assumed ground. They nevertheless remain committed to the view that Paul added the material of vv. 6–7 for apologetic reasons. For a few examples see Fee, *First Epistle to the Corinthians*, 718–19; Thiselton, *First Epistle to the Corinthians*, 1177, 1182–208. For a similar tension, though from a different perspective on the debate, see R. Bultmann and K. Barth, "Die Auferstehung der Toten," in *Glauben und Verstehen: Gesammelte Aufsätze*, ed. R. Bultmann and M. Lattke, 4 vols. (Tübingen: Mohr, 1933–67), 1:38–64, esp. 54–55.

the function of these verses proves crucial for interpreting 1 Corinthians 15. I turn now to putting these interpretations to the test. In particular, it will be important to see how these interpretations align with Paul's argumentation and how well they explain the actual contours of the text.

The Logic of 1 Corinthians 15: Assuming the Resurrection

Paul claims in 1 Corinthians 15:12 that some of the Corinthians say, "There is no resurrection of the dead." In verses 13–19 he reasons that if there is no resurrection of the dead, then Jesus cannot have been raised from the dead (cf. vv. 13, 16). But, he continues, if Jesus was not raised, then faith in the gospel proclamation about Jesus's resurrection is "empty" (κενή) and hope in the promised results of that proclamation—especially redemption from sins—is useless (cf. vv. 14–17).

If this argument actually addresses the problem in Corinth, it is surely significant to note that not one time in 1 Corinthians 15:12–19 does Paul present a positive argument to demonstrate the reality of Jesus's resurrection. Quite the contrary: on the hypothetical premise that there is not a resurrection of the dead, he first constructs an argument that *demonstrates* that Jesus cannot have been raised from the dead, and then he shows the obvious futility of proclaiming this event and of believing in the redemptive significance of that proclamation. Thus the two conclusions he draws here—(1) that Christ has not been raised (cf. vv. 13b, 16b) and (2) that faith in the proclamation and promised results of his resurrection is empty (cf. vv. 14b–c, 17b–c)—are ones he presumes that his addressees would not want to endorse. A significant scholarly consensus recognizes that the logic of the passage unfolds in this way and further posits that Paul designed his argument to push the Corinthians toward the affirmation of a general resurrection of the dead by suggesting that their denial of such a resurrection *logically* leads to these undesirable conclusions.[50]

Yet if this understanding of Paul's logic is correct, it follows that the people with whom he is arguing do not disagree with him about the reality or nature

50. For a sampling of some of the more recent examples of this basic position see Fee, *First Epistle to the Corinthians*, 738–47; Garland, *1 Corinthians*, 696–703; J. Holleman, *Resurrection and Parousia: A Traditio-Historical Study of Paul's Eschatology in 1 Corinthians 15*, NovTSup 84 (Leiden: Brill, 1996), esp. 40–46; M. M. Mitchell, *Paul and the Rhetoric of Reconciliation: An Exegetical Investigation of the Language and Composition of 1 Corinthians*, Hermeneutische Untersuchungen zur Theologie 28 (Tübingen: Mohr Siebeck, 1991), 286–89; Saw, *Paul's Rhetoric in 1 Corinthians 15*, 223–32; Schrage, *Der erste Brief an die Korinther*, 108–37; J. S. Vos, "Die Logik des Paulus in 1 Kor 15,12–20," ZNW 90 (1999): 78–97, esp. 89–90; Wolff, *Der Erste Brief des Paulus an die Korinther*, 376–81.

of Jesus's resurrection. That is, if one assumes that Paul actually thought this argument might prove persuasive to those with whom he is disputing, then an important observation may be made—the force of the argumentation of 1 Corinthians 15:12–19 depends on their agreeing with him that Jesus actually rose from the dead. If they question or deny this point, then Paul's argument loses its force. In that case the first element of his argument—if there is no resurrection, then Jesus did not rise from the dead—simply concedes the point.

If, however, Paul thinks his argument is likely to be persuasive, then it follows that instead of constructing an argument intended to persuade some of the Corinthians to renew their flagging belief in the reality or nature of Jesus's resurrection, he actually uses that very commitment as leverage to persuade them to abandon their denial of the "resurrection of the dead." Paul's argument in 1 Corinthians 15:20–28, 29–34, and 35–58 supports this interpretation.

In 1 Corinthians 15:20–28, Paul turns immediately to argue for the positive implications of Jesus's resurrection: since Jesus has been raised (v. 20), it follows that there will be a resurrection of all those in Christ (vv. 22–23; see also 6:14). Just as in 15:12–19, the argument is not designed to prove or bolster belief in Jesus's resurrection. Rather it begins with the affirmation of Jesus's resurrection and then goes on to posit a broader, future resurrection of all those who belong to Christ as a result of that event (v. 23).[51] The function of verses 20–28, then, is to show that Jesus's resurrection renders false all of the negative conclusions drawn in verses 12–19. It therefore follows that the premise with which that argument began in verse 12—the view held by some in Corinth that there is no resurrection of the dead—is also false. Thus, in Paul's assessment at least, the problem at Corinth concerned not a denial of Jesus's resurrection but a denial of a general, future resurrection of the dead.[52]

The same can be said of his argument in 1 Corinthians 15:29–34 and 35–58. The baptism for the dead seems to be something done not on behalf of Jesus but on behalf of some other group of people (note the plural of νεκρός and αὐτός in v. 29). This also suggests that the point at issue continues to relate to the future resurrection.[53] Moreover, the problem Paul addresses in verses 35–58 has to do with the nature of resurrection bodies, and once again he

51. On this point, see especially Holleman, *Resurrection and Parousia*, 49–57.

52. For an excellent discussion of the various views that have been proposed regarding the exact nature of the problem Paul addresses, see Thiselton, *First Epistle to the Corinthians*, 1172–76.

53. Thiselton, to cite only one example, notes that the activity of "baptism for the sake of (or for) the dead would be senseless if resurrection is denied." See Thiselton, *First Epistle to the Corinthians*, 1240.

uses Jesus's resurrection as the ground from which he argues. The nature of the future resurrection is modeled on the resurrection of Jesus (see esp. vv. 39–49). Thus here too one finds not an argument for Jesus's resurrection but an argument from Jesus's resurrection. The resurrection bodies will be like that of Jesus, the heavenly human (vv. 48–49).[54]

All these observations suggest that if the "warnings" in verse 2 indicate genuine suspicion by Paul about the Corinthians' affirmation of Jesus's resurrection, he has built a remarkably poor case demonstrating why they are wrong. If, however, they affirm Jesus's resurrection but deny a general resurrection, his arguments, if granted, appear highly effective. It seems therefore more probable that rather than being real warnings or expressions of doubt, the comments in verse 2 that appear to call the Corinthians' faith into question merely anticipate the logical conclusions of the negative argument of verses 12–19.[55]

Paul, then, begins his entire argument by "reminding" the Corinthians of the gospel he preached because he wants to lay out the common ground they share with him.[56] He then appeals to an element of that common foundation (Jesus's resurrection) to argue for a general future resurrection. Put differently, Paul uses negative arguments in 1 Corinthians 15:12–19 to convince the Corinthians that if they really want to remain true to the gospel, they cannot deny the reality of a future resurrection of the dead. To persist in such a denial is logically tantamount to obviating their belief in the gospel, and this would, in effect, render the gospel message empty and call their hope of salvation into question (i.e., produce the very result Paul hinted at in v. 2). Paul then turns to make the positive arguments that Jesus's resurrection entails a future resurrection (vv. 20–28) and that this resurrection will be of the same kind as that of Christ (vv. 35–58). Therefore, one's labor in the Lord will not prove to be an empty endeavor. Thus, at no point does Paul build a case for the reality or nature of Jesus's resurrection. Yet, given this understanding of Paul's argument, there appears to be no apologetic reason for him to need or want to add the material of verses 6–7.

The Legitimation Position

While 1 Corinthians 15:1–7 and 11 clearly relate to Paul's broader agenda of laying out the common ground he and the Corinthians share, verses 8–10

54. So, for instance, Fee, *First Epistle to the Corinthians*, 793–95; Schrage, *Der erste Brief an die Korinther*, 310–14.
55. As noted by Fee, *First Epistle to the Corinthians*, 721.
56. In Thiselton's words, there is "virtually universal agreement" regarding this point. See Thiselton, *First Epistle to the Corinthians*, 1177. For some of the more recent expressions of this view see n. 49.

appear to have little to do with the larger argument. On the surface of it, this looks like a digression from the main argument.[57] Paul is heading toward his discussion of resurrection but takes one last chance to bolster his own authority along the way. Yet several scholars suggest that there is more going on here. They argue that, far from being a digression, appearances in verses 6–7 have been added by Paul as a segue into a discussion of his own apostolic legitimacy.[58] The assumption, however, that Paul added the material in verses 6–7 in order to legitimate his apostolic status contains some problems.

For instance, it is curious that Paul has described the additional appearances in 1 Corinthians 15:6–7 in language that coheres so well in terms of syntax and style with verses 3b–5, while not also describing his own experience in the same way. If he added the traditions found in verses 6–7 to the "creed" and crafted them such that they even cohere with the style of the "creed," why did he revert to his own style when describing his encounter? Why would he further distance himself from these traditions when he could easily have continued to imitate the style of the formula?

If, though, one supposes for the moment that the appearances already stand in the formula he cites, then an explanation for the form that this part of chapter 15 actually takes comes immediately to mind. Since the "creed" predates him, he cannot simply alter the style and grammar and write himself into the material relayed in verses 6–7. Moreover, if the Corinthians already know the formula[59]—as both Paul's introduction in verses 1–3a and his appeal to the formula as common ground suggest that they do—they would be well aware of the fact that Paul does not have a place in it. Furthermore, if the phrase "all the apostles" is part of the "creed," then his "digression" into a brief discussion of his apostolic authority makes perfect sense. That is, given his defensive stance throughout the letter, the mention of Jesus's appearance to the "apostles" in an authoritative tradition would naturally provide him an opportunity to return to the issue of his apostolic status. Thus, if the hypothesis of this chapter is correct, one can well understand why he would comment on his own apostolic status after citing an authoritative tradition that delineates the group of apostles but does not include him. It is easier, therefore, to explain the presence of verses 8–10 on the view that the appearances in verses 6–7 stood in the formula and so prompted his discussion of

57. So, for example, Fee, *First Epistle to the Corinthians*, 733; F. W. Grosheide, *Commentary on the First Epistle to the Corinthians*, NICNT (Grand Rapids: Eerdmans, 1953), 354; Hays, *First Corinthians*, 257–58.

58. See n. 46.

59. The "creed" is, after all, at least part of the traditional material that Paul originally "received and passed on" (cf. 15:3a) to the Corinthians.

apostolic authority than to assume that Paul went to the trouble of carefully
formulating the list of appearances with the goal of inserting one more defense
of his authority in the midst of his argument for the general resurrection.

The More Than Five Hundred

What then of 1 Corinthians 15:6b? Why does the apparently random comment "most of whom remain, though some have fallen asleep" occur? I have
pointed out above the stylistic shift present here. The way that this shift
both coheres with Paul's style and breaks the style of the material in verses
3b–6a and 7 already suggests that this is a Pauline interjection. I would add,
however, that while Paul never directly appeals to verses 6a and 7 in his argument, he does use the material in verse 6b to further his case. That is, unlike
verses 6a and 7, a potential rationale for the presence of verse 6b that coheres
with Paul's larger argument can be identified. He has added the remark in
anticipation of his claim that the denial of the general resurrection renders
the proclamation and salvific significance of Jesus's resurrection "empty."
Specifically, when Paul comments in verse 18 that those in Christ who have
"fallen asleep" are completely lost, his language recalls those of the five hundred who have "fallen asleep." Thus, in Paul's view, those to whom Christ
appeared but who have subsequently died have suffered the ultimate loss if
there is no resurrection from the dead. Of all people, they are truly among
those most to be pitied.

In defense of this reading I would note that in 1 Corinthians 15:11–19
Paul, by means of first- and second-person plural forms, consistently makes
a distinction between the Corinthians and those who have experienced an
appearance of the risen Christ. The distinction is clear in verse 11.[60] Here he
places on one side himself and those he just listed in verses 5–8[61] as having seen
the risen Christ by lumping them together as the "we" who preach. On the
other side stand the Corinthians, the "you" who believed. The ὑμῖν of verse
12 continues this reference to the Corinthians, as does the ὑμῶν of verse 14c.
The ἡμῶν of verse 14b along with the plural first-person verbs εὑρισκόμεθα

60. As Saw notes, this distinction actually begins in v. 1, where Paul makes a clear division
between himself as speaker and the Corinthians as audience. See Saw, *Paul's Rhetoric in 1 Corinthians 15*, 223. Saw also tracks the shift between "I"/"We" and "you" throughout vv. 11–19
but, in keeping with the consensus, appears to assume the final "we" in v. 19 refers generally to
all Christians (see esp. 224, 232–33).
61. As Conzelmann, *1 Corinthians*, 260–61, points out, ἐκεῖνος looks back to more than
just the apostles mentioned in vv. 7–10. The fact that Paul uses the remote form of the demon-
strative pronoun here seems to suggest that he has all of the witnesses mentioned here in view.

and ἐμαρτυρήσαμεν in verse 15 shift the focus back to Paul and the others who preach. The series of ὑμῶν's in verse 17 again addresses the Corinthians.

In 1 Corinthians 15:18 Paul mentions the loss of those who have fallen asleep. He then uses the first-person plural periphrastic ἠλπικότες ἐσμέν and the first-person plural copulative ἐσμέν in verse 19 to describe the pitiable state of some group if there is no future resurrection. In general, commentators assume that these plural forms refer either broadly to all Christians or to those in Corinth.[62] This assumption is reinforced by another—that those who have fallen asleep and are lost in verse 18 are either Christians in general or the Corinthian dead in particular. Yet the fact that Paul has so consistently delineated between "we" and "you" in the immediate context strongly suggests that the "we" in verse 19 continues this distinction. The "we" of verse 19 is the same "we" of verses 11–17. As previously noted, the "we" group in verse 11 consists of those mentioned in verses 5–8—those to whom Jesus appeared and who now preach Jesus's resurrection. This suggests that, rather than being a general statement about Christians, verse 19 points primarily to those to whom Jesus appeared and who proclaim the gospel message. These are the ones most to be pitied.[63]

---

62. For a few examples, see C. K. Barrett, *A Commentary on the First Epistle to the Corinthians*, BNTC (London: Adam & Charles Black, 1968), 349–50; Hays, *First Corinthians*, 261; J. Moffatt, *The First Epistle of Paul to the Corinthians*, Moffatt New Testament Commentary (London: Hodder & Stoughton, 1938), 242.

63. One might object that Paul's broader use of κοιμάω in vv. 20 and 51 suggests the validity of the interpretation usually assumed for vv. 18–19 (i.e., that Paul refers more generally to Christians who have died). Yet limiting the reference here primarily to those of the five hundred mentioned in v. 6b remains the most natural reading for the following reasons. First, the fact that κοιμάω has a broader referent in v. 20 is not by itself determinative of its possible referents in earlier occurrences. Paul clearly transitions in v. 20 from his negative argument to his positive argument for a future resurrection. In light of his new line of argumentation, a shift to a broader referent for κοιμάω in v. 20 would make good sense. Second, in the actual progression of the text, the only other place where anyone has been identified as having "fallen asleep" to this point is in v. 6b, where the term indisputably refers to some of the five hundred. Third, since Paul's consistent delineation between "we" and "you" in vv. 12–19 has kept the five hundred (who are part of the "we") in the immediate context, it is justifiable to think that his auditors would naturally link v. 18 with v. 6b. Fourth, if my larger hypothesis is correct and vv. 6a and 7 are creedal, then the original audience could have been expected to recognize a later reference in v. 18 to the earlier parenthetical comment that some of the five hundred "have fallen asleep." That is, the addition of v. 6b to the pre-Pauline formula would readily jump out to anyone already familiar with the "creed" (one thinks, for example, of how obvious it would be if someone publicly altered a recitation of a national anthem or pledge). Such an addition would have drawn their attention and caused them to wonder why Paul would have inserted it and identified some of the five hundred as having "fallen asleep." His further use of κοιμάω in v. 18 is therefore all the more likely to recall to their minds the strange interjection of v. 6b, particularly since it offers an explanation for the presence of the earlier comment—Paul highlighted the deaths of some of the five hundred in

Moreover, Paul's use of "fallen asleep" language in both verse 6 and verse 18 fits well with this reading. That is, in light of the fact that the "we" group of verses 11–19 includes the five hundred, the most natural content of the group of "those who have fallen asleep" in verse 18 is those of the five hundred whom Paul explicitly described as having "fallen asleep." Thus Paul concludes that if there is no general resurrection of the dead, the whole enterprise of gospel proclamation is empty and those engaged in it, those to whom Jesus appeared, are completely lost and deserve pity, not praise.

All of this is in keeping with Paul's negative argument in verses 12–19. He is here seeking to demonstrate the total futility of the gospel proclamation at every level if there is no resurrection of the dead. He wants to show that not only is the message of Jesus's resurrection—which he has reminded the Corinthians they affirm—rendered empty, but those who were commissioned to proclaim that message have themselves hoped in a lie. Their labor is empty, and those among them who have already died have perished completely.

Given the observations made earlier about the shift in style and grammar precisely here, in material known to have come from Paul, and given that the content of 1 Corinthians 15:6b so nicely anticipates Paul's argument regarding the utter emptiness of the gospel proclamation "if there is no resurrection of the dead," there are good grounds to explain verse 6b as Paul's addition to the formula. Never does Paul appeal to the appearances as proof establishing the certainty of Jesus's resurrection, nor does the logic of his argument require that he do so. What he does do, however, is appeal to the fact that some of those commissioned to preach the gospel, some of those to whom Jesus appeared, have died and thus are lost.

Conclusion

Earlier in this chapter I pointed out a number of remarkable relationships both between 1 Corinthians 15:3b–5 and 6a and 7 and within 6a and 7. I especially highlighted the stylistic coherence between the creedal material and verses 6a and 7, as well as the presence of Pauline style precisely in the material known to have come from Paul (vv. 1–3a, 6b, 8–11). Further evidence for this thesis, though, emerged when the larger question of why Paul would have added the appearances in verses 6–7 was addressed. Not only did the standard explanations not adequately answer that question, but the view that the "creed" includes verses 6a and 7 and that Paul added comments in verses 6b and 8

---

order to later use that to further his case for the futility of the gospel proclamation, if there is no resurrection of the dead.

offered a more satisfying account of the progression of the argument and the actual form of the text. The simplest explanation for the presence of verses 6a and 7 is that they belong to the "creed." Indeed, any suggestion that Paul added verses 6–7 as evidence to strengthen the case for the reality of Jesus's resurrection founders because it is not clear that this is how the appearances actually function in the formula and because he does not use them to this end in his argument. Moreover, unlike verses 6a and 7, verse 6b fits nicely with the larger argument Paul actually makes in chapter 15. Finally, his defense of his apostolic status in verses 8–10 can readily be explained as being prompted by the material present in the formula.

This last point also suggests another, more tentative conclusion. While the assumptions present in Harnack's 2 × 2 structure are less than self-evident, his recognition that Paul's comments in 1 Corinthians 15:8–10 serve as one more attempt to highlight the legitimacy of his apostolic status may prove valid—the appearance motif in the formula may actually function in the first instance as a means of marking out those who have the special responsibility of proclaiming the gospel message.[64] Paul's so-called digression suggests, at the very least, that he employed the list of appearances in this way. That is to say, while he never appeals to the appearances as evidence for Jesus's resurrection, he does use them to defend his own apostolic authority. Moreover, the sense of commission to proclaim the gospel fits perfectly with the argument he makes in verses 12–19. As I have sought to show above, the entire group of those to whom Jesus appeared is carried through the context by the "we"/"you" dichotomy. Yet it is exactly those commissioned to proclaim the gospel message, those to whom Jesus appeared, who have become false witnesses against God and are completely lost if there is no resurrection.

This observation may bring some of the nuance of Paul's argument here into sharper focus. If the appearances are primarily being used to make a point about commissioning, then there is a double-edged nature to the polemic in 1 Corinthians 15:12–19: the argument seems designed to drive the Corinthians to the conclusion that their denial of the general resurrection leaves them with both an empty faith and no other apostles they might want to pit against him. Paul's defense of his own status is therefore not a real digression.[65] He links his status and his message with that of the other apostles in verses 8–11.

---

64. Interestingly, the narration of at least some of the post-resurrection encounters in early Christian sources indicates that the commissioning element was closely correlated with the appearance traditions (see Matt. 28:16–20; Luke 24:44–49; John 21:15–19; Acts 1:6–9; 9:3–16).

65. Eriksson, *Traditions as Rhetorical Proof*, 233, rightly points to the importance of the motif of "emptiness" for the chapter when he notes that it functions as an inclusio (cf. vv. 2 and 58). The presence of this motif in v. 10 further suggests the extent to which vv. 8–10 are integrated into the larger argument.

His authority is predicated on the same condition as that of the others—the risen Christ appeared to him too (cf. 9:1–2).[66] None of this proves beyond doubt that the appearances in the formula must also function in this way. It seems likely, though, that Paul's appeal to the formula takes the form that it does here—that is, a discussion of legitimacy—because this is how he and the Corinthians interpreted the appearances.

In any case, the factors I have noted above point toward the conclusion that the actual length of the "creed" is longer than has generally been granted. The collocation of the structural and stylistic phenomena and the way this hypothesis so nicely explains the actual form of the text and progression of Paul's argument suggest that his citation of an early Christian "creed" here consists of 1 Corinthians 15:3b–6a and 7.

---

66. Paul's distinction between the language of "seeing" in 1 Cor. 9:1–2 (ἑόρακα) and that of "appearing" in 15:8 (ὤφθη) is almost certainly driven by little more than the presence of "appearance" language in the formula. Again, if my hypothesis is correct, Paul's atypical use of ὤφθη here shows how eager he is to connect his own appearance with that of the other apostles. His use of ὤφθη here clearly serves to describe his encounter as qualitatively on par with those mentioned in the formula, even if he was commissioned after all the others.

Author Index

Scripture and Ancient Writings Index